THE
Notorious
GUIDE TO
BRITAIN

THE

GUIDE TO
BRITAIN

By
PAUL DONNELLEY
The Sunday Times Top 10 Bestselling Author

MARDLE

First published in 2022 by Mardle Books
15 Church Road
London, SW13 9HE
www.mardlebooks.com

Hardback ISBN 9781914451072
eBook ISBN 9781914451126

A CIP catalogue record for this book is available from the British Library.

Every reasonable effort has been made to trace copyright-holders of material
reproduced in this book, but if any have been inadvertently overlooked the
publishers would be glad to hear from them.

Design and typesetting by Danny Lyle

Printed in the UK

10 9 8 7 6 5 4 3 2 1

Cover and book illustrations: Tom Woolley

Warning: contains graphic descriptions of violence.

Pour la fille sérieuse

Contents

Introduction

This book is intended to be a fun and informative trip around the highways (not forgetting the low ways) and byways of Great Britain. Within its pages you will find love and romance, murder and mayhem, royalty, aristocrats and commoners, politics and politicians, sex and scandal, sporting triumphs and disasters, millionaires and paupers, boffins and eccentrics, film stars and reality TV personalities and much more besides.

A note at first about what this book is not. It is not (mostly) a guide to where famous or notorious people were born or where they lived – several excellent guides on these subjects have already been published. (An exception to this is if something happened in that home: e.g. Enid Blyton's home, Green Hedges, is included because she became the world's most successful children's author there.) It is a guide to (where possible) the exact locations where events actually happened and when they occurred. This is often more difficult than it sounds...

All the locations in the book are in mainland Great Britain (apart from two) because I wanted to be able to drive (or get a train or cycle or walk) to them all.

This has turned out to be one of the most enjoyable books I have ever written – and I hope that it shows. If it causes you to discover something about the area in which you live or grew up, or persuades you to go sightseeing, then I feel my work will have been worthwhile.

The book contains thousands of facts and I have done my best to ensure its accuracy. If you come across a hopefully rare error, please contact the author via the publisher or via email paul@pauldonnelley. com, and it will be corrected in subsequent editions.

Chapter I

Great Britain:
Weird and Wonderful

ASDA
Wilson Street, Castleford, West Yorkshire WF10

The story of Asda began in the 1920s when the Asquith family ran a butcher's shop in Knottingley, West Yorkshire which expanded to seven stores. A group of dairy farmers, meanwhile, formed J.W. Hindell Dairy Farmers Ltd, becoming Associated Dairies and Farm Stores Ltd in 1949, with Arthur Stockdale as the managing director. In 1963, Peter and Fred Asquith took over Queens, an old cinema building in Castleford, and turned it into a supermarket. Two years later, on Monday 3 May 1965, the Asquiths asked Associated Dairies to run the butchers in store. A merger resulted in a new company, Asda (Asquith + Dairies). The Asquith brothers sold their stake in 1969. The ending of the retail price maintenance allowed Asda to offer customers products at prices it decided on rather than the Government. It bought three GEM (Government Exchange Mart) shops in Preston, Lancashire, Cross Gates, Leeds and West Bridgford, Nottingham and changed the shops' name to Asda in September 1965. The company began opening shops in the south in the 1970s, and in 1978 bought Allied Carpets. Asda Price first appeared in TV advertising in 1977, introducing the "Pocket Tap" – now the official sign language designation for the supermarket. The 100th Asda opened in 1981; the following year, the first shop in London saw the light of day. In May 1985, Asda merged with MFI (Mullard Furniture Industries) and the company became Asda-MFI Group plc. In 1986, Asda began selling its own branded products, and in 1987 sold off MFI. In 1989, designer George Davies was hired to launch his George at Asda fashion line. On Monday 26 July 1999, American corporate giant Walmart's £6.7 billion takeover made Asda a subsidiary of the US firm. The following year, the company launched Smart Price, its no-frills brand including cheese, fresh pies, frozen food, ready meals and detergents. In April 2018, a merger was proposed between Asda and Sainsbury's, but the deal was blocked on Thursday 25 April 2019 by the Competition and Markets Authority. On Friday 2 October 2020, Asda was bought by brothers Zubar and Mohsin Issa for £6.8 billion.

BOOTS THE CHEMIST
6 Goose Gate, Hockley, Nottingham NG11FF
The first store – the British and American Botanic Establishment – was opened by the devoutly religious John Boot in 1849. Formerly an agricultural worker, Boot moved to Nottingham to start a new business selling herbal remedies; very quickly became popular with the working classes, who could not afford to pay for a doctor. The system – the Thomsonian – allowed the poor in society to help themselves when it came to their healthcare. Boot died in 1860, aged 45, and his widow Mary and son Jesse, took over the shop. In 1871, the business was renamed M. & J. Boot. In 1877, Jesse Boot (b. at Nottingham Sunday 2 June 1850 d. at Vallée, Jersey CI Saturday 13 June 1931) took over the business and began a publicity blitz using the legend "Health for a shilling", which allowed the company to offer traditional medicines at much reduced prices. In 1883, the firm became Boots & Company Ltd. The next year, Jesse opened the first Boots pharmacy in Nottingham, appointing his first qualified pharmacist, Edwin Waring. In 1885, he opened manufacturing facilities in Island Street. In 1888, the firm was renamed once more, becoming Boots Pure Drug Company Ltd. The first flagship store opened in Pelham Street in 1892, selling a variety of goods, not necessarily linked to medicine. In 1898, the company started the Boots Booklovers' Library which allowed customers to borrow books at a reasonable price: in just a few years, almost half of Boots shops had libraries and by 1938, thirty-five million books a year were being borrowed. In July 1920, the company was sold to the United Drug Company of America. In 1924, Boots began offering a service fitting trusses for gentlemen.

The following year, Boots opened a twenty-four-hour pharmacy at its Piccadilly Circus branch. By 1933 – two years after Jessie died – Boots had 1,000 shops in the UK (the 1000th was in Galashiels). In 1934, the company launched its Number 7 brand of cosmetics. In 1951, Boots opened its first self-service shop at Burnt Oak, Edgware, north London. In August 1968, the firm bought the 614-shop chain Timothy Whites & Taylors Ltd: Timothy Whites vanished from the high street in 1985. In 2006, Boots Healthcare International was sold to Reckitt Benckiser and the Boots Group merged with Alliance Unichem to form Alliance Boots.

> **DID YOU KNOW?**
> The first pharmaceutical patent registered by Boots was in 1921, for a drug called Stabilarsan which was used to treat syphilis.

BIBA
87 Abingdon Road, Kensington, London W8 6AW

After running a successful mail order business, Stephen Fitz-Simon and his wife, fashion illustrator Barbara Hulanicki, opened their iconic store at this location, a former chemist, at 10am on Saturday 5 September 1964. Biba was the nickname of Hulanicki's younger sister, Biruta. Hulanicki (b. at Warsaw 8 December 1936) had copied fashions from Paris to make ready-to-wear clothes available to the under-thirties. Her first day was a great success as she remembered: "The shop was packed with girls trying on the same brown pinstripe dress in concentrated silence. Not one asked if there were any other styles or sizes. The louder the music played the faster the girls moved and more people appeared in the shop... I had sold every dress by 11." A second Biba opened in February 1966 on **Queen's Road, Brighton BN1**, but closed before the end of the year. In March of the same year, the shop moved to **19-21 Kensington Church Street, London W8 4LF** and then, on Monday 15 September 1969, to a former carpet shop at **120 Kensington High Street, London W8 7RL**, where the premises were nine times bigger than Abingdon Road, more than 80,000 square feet. The move was a qualified success – in the first year they made a profit of £400,000, but the finances were too much for Hulanicki and her husband, and they sold 75 per cent of Biba to Dorothy Perkins and

Dennis Day in December 1969. Nearly four years later, in August 1973, Dorothy Perkins was bought out by property group British Land. On Monday 10 September 1973, the company, now Big Biba, moved into the seven-storey former Derry and Toms department store at **99-117 Kensington High Street, London W8 5SA** and further expanded with more stores, children's clothes, a food hall and a private members' club, The Rainbow Room, in the roof gardens. It was said that a million people visited every week – David Bowie (see page 235) and Marc Bolan (see page 164) were regulars. Fashions changed but Biba did not or could not keep up with the times and British Land closed the store in September 1975. In 2009, House of Fraser successfully relaunched the Biba brand, but Barbara Hulanicki denounced the line as "too expensive" and for "failing to reflect the original Biba style". On Saturday 31 December 2011, she was awarded the OBE "for services to the Fashion Industry". In 2014, she agreed to serve as a consultant for Biba, her first involvement with the brand since 1975.

BORLEY RECTORY
Hall Road, Borley, Essex CO10 7AE

"The most haunted house in England" was built in 1863, on the site of an old Benedictine monastery (built in 1362) near the River Stour, on the instructions of the Reverend Henry Dawson Ellis Bull (b. at Essex Friday 23 November 1832, d. Blue Room, Borley Rectory, Monday 2 May 1892) who had been appointed pastor of the area the previous year. Borley Rectory was eventually three storeys high and had twenty rooms. The Reverend Mr Bull and his family of fourteen children lived there for many years until his death in 1892. It was in 1885 that P. Shaw Jeffrey (1862-1952), a university friend of Harry Foyster Bull, first claimed sightings of a ghostly nun in the rectory grounds. According to local lore, the apparition was the spirit of a fourteenth-century nun from Bures convent seven miles southeast of Borley, who had fallen in love with a monk from the monastery. Apparently they fled in a coach and horses but were captured. The coachman was beheaded, the monk hanged and the nun walled up inside the convent. (Unfortunately for the legend, there never was a convent at Bures, nor a monastery at Borley.) In 1886, a nurse staying at the rectory left because she said she heard phantom footsteps.

Harry Bull inherited the house and the pastorship. On Tuesday 12 September 1911, Bull married and moved to Borley Place, leaving his sisters at the rectory. Nine years later, he returned to live at Borley Rectory, and stayed there until his own death on Thursday 9 June 1927. Coincidentally, he also died in the Blue Room, which quickly gained a reputation for being haunted. On Saturday 28 July 1900, three of Harry Bull's sisters saw what they claimed was a ghostly nun in the garden: the area became known as "The Nun's Walk". After the rectory had been empty for a year, the Reverend Guy Eric Smith and his wife Mabel moved in on Tuesday 2 October 1928. During their tenure they complained of mysterious footsteps, doorbells ringing of their own accord and phantom stone throwing. The Smiths rang the *Daily Mirror* in June 1929 and, on Wednesday 12 June, the "ghost hunter" Harry Price of the Society for Psychical Research arrived at the house with his secretary and stayed for three days. Price returned for a second visit on Thursday 27 June 1929. On Sunday 14 July 1929, the Smiths moved out to Long Melford where they stayed for a few months. On Thursday 16 October 1930, the Reverend Lionel Algernon Foyster, his wife Marianne and their adopted daughter Adelaide moved in and stayed for five years. They moved out in October 1935 due to Foyster's ill health, not because of the apparent ghostly goings-on. The Foysters claimed to have witnessed more than 2,000 poltergeist phenomena, ranging from smashed glasses and stone throwing to mysterious writing on the walls. A strange force even apparently threw Marianne Foyster out of bed one night. Price called that period "the most extraordinary and best documented case of haunting in the annals of psychical research". Price leased Borley Rectory from June 1937 until 1938 and hired forty-eight assistants to assist with his investigation, the results of which were printed in his book *The Most Haunted House in England* (published on Saturday 3 August 1940, incidentally the same day that Reverend Guy Eric Smith died). Captain William Hart Gregson bought the property in December 1938; it was gutted by fire on Monday 27 February 1939 after he accidentally knocked over an oil lamp. The fire caught hold quickly and the rectory was destroyed beyond repair, being finally demolished in 1944. Harry Price died at Pulborough, Sussex on Monday 29 March 1948 and subsequently, authors have claimed that all the happenings at Borley Rectory were the result of misinterpreted natural occurrences, hoaxing, hearsay and damp and shoddy workmanship when the house was originally built: not ghosts.

BOY SCOUTS
Brownsea Island, Poole Harbour, Dorset BH13 7EE

Robert Baden-Powell held the first Boy Scout camp on Thursday 1 August 1907 here, 560 acres of woodland and open areas with two lakes. Baden-Powell, the hero of the Siege of Mafeking, was concerned about the moral rectitude and health of Britain's boys. He worried they were "drifting into hooliganism for want of guiding hands to set them on the right road". Therefore he set up what he called a "scheme", and twenty-two boys from different backgrounds ranging in age from 9 to 17 attended; the inaugural camp lasted until Thursday 8 August. Baden-Powell had visited Brownsea Island as a boy with his brothers. Of the twenty-two original scouts, the public schoolboys, or their parents, paid £1 while the working-class boys were all charged 3/6d each. They were arranged into four patrols and each had a different colour to identify them: Wolves (blue), Ravens (red), Bulls (green) and Curlews (yellow); they were kept busy from 6am until 9pm, learning about wildlife, tracking, personal responsibility, how to tie knots, first aid, history and the British Empire. The camp cost £55 2s 8d (£6,870 at 2022 values), making a loss of just over £24 (£2,900, 2022), but nonetheless Baden-Powell considered it a success. Six of the Brownsea boys later died on the Western Front. A reunion of the survivors from the first camp was held in 1928 at Baden-Powell's home, **Pax Hill, Bentley, Farnham, Hampshire GU10 5NG**.

BRITISH HOME STORES
452-456 Brixton Road, Brixton, London SW9 8EA

It was here in April 1928 that British Home Stores, a private company, opened its doors for the first time. The American owners wanted to compete with Woolworths (see page 32), so the most expensive item was on sale for one shilling, increased to five shillings the following year. After Brixton, the company opened branches in Church Street, Croydon, Harlesden, London and Ilford, Essex, boasting that 96 percent of its merchandise was made in Britain. From the start, the shops sold lighting and had self-service cafés and food departments. British Home Stores had seven branches by 1929 and became a public company on Thursday 15 December 1932, with £400,000 (£27,850,000 at 2022 values) issued capital. In 1960, despite its name, British Home Stores began to import stock. A columnist on *The Times* commented that "British Home Stores... has done more for the garment trade in Hong Kong than any other single buyer". All stores had shut by Sunday 28 August 2016, bringing a close to trading after eighty-eight years. On Thursday 29 September 2016, BHS re-branded online as The British Home Store and opened a website; they now trade online only.

BUTLIN'S HOLIDAY CAMP
Ingoldmells, near Skegness, Lincolnshire PE25 1NJ
Sir Billy Butlin opened his first holiday camp here on Easter Saturday, 11 April, 1936. Butlin himself had designed the camp, and proclaimed, "My plans were for 1,000 people in 600 chalets with electricity, running water, 250 bathrooms, dining and recreational halls, a theatre, a gymnasium, a rhododendron-bordered swimming pool with cascades at both ends and a boating lake." Work had begun on Wednesday 4 September 1935, cost £100,000 (£7,600,000 at 2022 values) to complete and was officially opened by aviatrix Amy Johnson. Butlin placed an advert in the *Daily Express* announcing the opening, inviting the public to book for a week's holiday. Butlin offered weekly holidays with full board and free entertainment, costing between 35 shillings (£113, 2022) and £3 (£227, 2022) according to the time of year. When the first guests failed to mingle, Butlin asked Norman Bradford, a camp engineer, to entertain them with jokes and merry quips – thus began the Butlin's Redcoat. In 1937, the number of beds was doubled and wireless and music hall stars began entertaining the campers on Sunday nights. A beauty contest was introduced in 1938, with the final at the Skegness carnival. The same year, a second camp opened at Clacton-on-Sea, Essex, but plans to open a third (at Filey) were curtailed by the start of the Second World War, when the Royal Navy took over Skegness and renamed the camp HMS *Royal Arthur* (Lord Haw-Haw later claimed it had been sunk with all hands). The wily Butlin offered to complete the camp at Filey for the RAF and

build two more (at Ayr and Pwllheli – HMS *Glendower*) for the Navy, with a deal to buy them back when the war ended, at three-fifths of their construction costs. He reopened Skegness on Saturday 11 May 1946. By 1947, Butlin was a millionaire. He bought hotels in Blackpool, Saltdean and Cliftonville and opened three more camps: at Bognor Regis on Saturday 2 July 1960 costing £2½million (£59½million, 2022); Minehead on Saturday 26 May 1962 at a cost of £2million (£47½million, 2022); and Barry Island on Saturday 18 June 1966 (it closed on Wednesday 31 December 1986). On Friday 9 August 1963, the Queen and the Duke of Edinburgh visited Pwllheli; Butlin was knighted the following year. A cashflow crisis in 1968 forced him to hand over control to his adopted son, Bobby. In 1972, the company was sold to the Rank Organisation for £43million (£623million, 2022). Sir Billy Butlin died of stomach cancer at his home on Jersey. He was 80.

CAMILLAGATE TAPE
Charles: Eaton Hall, Eaton Park, Eaton, Chester CH4 9ET
Camilla: Bolehyde Manor, Allington, Chippenham, Wiltshire SN14 6LW

On Sunday 17 December 1989, the Prince of Wales was staying at the Cheshire home of Anne, Dowager Duchess of Westminster, when he rang his long-term mistress Camilla Parker-Bowles at her home, Bolehyde Manor in Wiltshire. Unbeknown to either of them, their very private eight-minute conversation was being recorded. In it, Charles said, "Oh, God, I'll just live inside your trousers or something. It'd be much easier"; to which his lover replied, "What are you going to turn into? A pair of knickers? Oh, you're going to come back as a pair of knickers!" The heir to the throne then remarked, "Oh, God forbid; a Tampax, just my luck… My luck to be chucked down the lavatory and go on and on forever swirling around on the top, never going down!" The radio ham who recorded the Camillagate tape has never been publicly identified.

CAMPAIGN FOR NUCLEAR DISARMAMENT, THE
Falcon Fields, Aldermaston, Tadley, Berkshire RG7 4PR

The Campaign for Nuclear Disarmament held its first meeting on Monday 17 February 1958 at **Westminster Central Hall, Storey's Gate,**

London SW1H 9NH; it was attended by more than 5,000 people. It received support from intellectual left-wingers including the philosopher Bertrand Russell (1872-1970), playwright J.B. Priestley (1894-1984), historian A.J.P. Taylor (1906-1990) and Canon John Collins (1905-1982). It demanded that Britain give up its nuclear weapons. After the meeting, around 1,000 people marched on Downing Street and stood outside shouting, "Ban the bomb" and "Murderer" at Prime Minister Harold Macmillan, until police with dogs moved them away. By 1959, it had 270 branches throughout Britain. On 4 April 1958 (the coldest Good Friday in forty-one years), 4,000 protestors set out from Trafalgar Square to the Atomic Weapons Research Establishment at Aldermaston, fifty miles away, arriving on Monday 7 April. The people on the march were mainly Labour supporters, middle class and well educated. Two thirds were men and a half were Christians.

CASHPOINT
20 The Town, Enfield Town, Enfield, Middlesex EN2 6LS

The first cashpoint, or ATM, opened at Barclays Bank in Enfield on Tuesday 27 June 1967; the first person in Britain to use the machine was the actor Reg Varney. The cashpoint was not like those we use today – customers had to buy a punched card in advance for £10, which was then inserted into the machine. John Shepherd-Barron (1925-2010) invented the cashpoint, the idea coming to him while he was in the bath. The Enfield machine was the first of six pilot machines – the others being in Hove, Ipswich, Luton, Peterborough and Southend-on-Sea.

CHUNG LING SOO
Wood Green Empire, Theatre of Varieties, 14 High Road, Wood Green, London N22 6HH

Chung Ling Soo was a great oriental magician whose most celebrated trick was to catch two bullets fired at him from separate guns by assistants dressed as Boxers. Like Ray Teller of the American magic act Penn & Teller, Chung never spoke in public and used an interpreter when he spoke to journalists offstage. It was all an illusion: Chung Ling Soo was no more oriental than Paul Daniel or David

Copperfield. His real name was William Ellsworth Robinson, and he was born in Westchester County, New York on Tuesday 2 April 1861; he travelled worldwide, amazing people with his incredible trickery. His assistants would ask members of the audience to come on stage and mark the bullets to be fired at him. He would discreetly palm the bullets, and the guns would be fitted with substitute bullets that made a lot of noise and smoke but stayed safely in the barrel. On Saturday 23 March 1918 at the Wood Green Empire, London, one of the guns suffered a mechanical failure and the bullet was really fired, hitting Chung in the chest. He collapsed to the floor, managing to utter the words, "Oh my God. Something's happened. Lower the curtain." It was the only time that he spoke English in public. Taken to **Passmore Edwards Cottage Hospital, 48 Gunnersbury Lane, London W3 8EF**, he died the following morning aged 56. He is buried in **East Sheen Cemetery, Kings Ride Gate, East Sheen TW10 5BJ**.

COLONY ROOM CLUB, THE
41a Dean Street, London W1D 4PY

The Colony Room was a Soho drinking club that became notorious. It was opened by a foul-mouthed lesbian of Portuguese and Jewish heritage, Muriel Amelia Belcher, (b. at Edgbaston Friday 26 June 1908, the daughter of a moneylender she hated) on Wednesday 15 December 1948 at a time when pubs could not serve alcohol between 2.40pm and 6.30pm but private drinking clubs could. The Colony Room Club's most famous member was the artist Francis Bacon; Muriel called him "Daughter" and he called her "Mother". He was introduced by Brian Howard (on whom Anthony Blanche was based in Evelyn Waugh's May 1945 novel *Brideshead Revisited*, see page 255) after Bacon's father had thrown him out for wearing his mother's underwear. She gave him free drinks and £10 each week to bring in his rich and famous friends. The drinks there were said to be the most expensive in London; the first floor club was described as being like a small living room, with a bar at one end and just one lavatory. Westminster Council once wrote to the club saying that it was a health hazard, because its carpet was the most disgusting their inspector had ever seen. The club invested in a new green carpet, but Francis Bacon immediately ordered six bottles of champagne and poured them over it before declaring himself satisfied. Mercurial Muriel Belcher would sit at the bar during opening hours, dispensing her wisdom and insults: "Shut up cunty, order some more champagne" was a favourite phrase. Other famous members included George Melly (who said of her, "Muriel was a benevolent witch, who managed to draw in all London's talent up those filthy stairs. She was like a great cook, working with the ingredients of people and drink. And she loved money"), Daniel Farson, Tom Baker, Peter Blake, Jeffrey Bernard, Barry Humphries, Christine Keeler, Molly Parkin, Colin MacInnes (who used to enjoy sitting in there on sunny days with the curtains closed) and Liverpool poet Brian Patten, who described the Colony Room Club as "a small urinal full of fractious old geezers bitching about each other". Belcher died on Wednesday 31 October 1979 and the club was taken over by her faithful barman Ian "Ida" Board (b. at Exeter Monday 16 December 1929) who ran it until his own death from cirrhosis on Sunday 26 June 1994. Board's barman Michael Wojas (b. at London Thursday 9 August 1956 d. Sunday 6 June 2010 of cancer) succeeded him until 2008, when running the club had became financially unfeasible. When he auctioned some works of art and raised £40,000, some club members took him to court, saying he did not have the right to sell the art. An attempt to keep the club open failed and it closed for good in 2008. The Colony Room Club was part of the "Bermuda Triangle of Soho" along with **The French House, 49 Dean Street, London W1D 5BG** and **The Coach & Horses, 29 Greek Street, London W1D 5DH**. The Colony Room Club premises were converted into a two-bedroom flat.

DARWIN, JOHN AND ANNE
3 and 4 The Cliff, Seaton Carew, Hartlepool, Cleveland TS25 7AB
In the history of scams and cons, that perpetrated by the Darwins must rank near the very top for audacity. This seemingly ordinary couple embarked on a new life in Panama after John Ronald Darwin (b. Hartlepool Monday 14 August 1950), a former teacher, bank worker and prison warder, faked his death on Thursday 21 March 2002 by vanishing off the coast near North Gare, Seaton Carew in a canoeing accident. On Saturday 22 December 1973, Darwin had married Anne Stephenson in Blackhall. In December 2000, John and

his wife Anne bought numbers three and four The Cliff. Anne Carew made fraudulent insurance and pension claims. The plan was hatched when they faced losing their imposing seafront home: they had a property portfolio of twelve and were struggling to make mortgage repayments. John paddled into the sea in his home-made canoe and then apparently vanished. Mrs Carew, a doctor's receptionist, drove to a Durham police station to report her husband missing and then began the process of declaring him dead, conning insurers and pension funds out of £250,000. John was, in fact, living in Panama until a change in the law saw him return to England and fake amnesia in 2003. He lived in secret in a room in a bedsit the couple owned next door to the family home. In October 2007, Anne Darwin sold 3 The Cliff and moved to Panama permanently, while on Saturday 1 December, John surrendered at a central London police station saying he could remember nothing after 2000. Mrs Carew professed ignorance of his behaviour until a 2006 picture of the couple smiling in a Panama estate agents appeared online and was published in the *Daily Mirror* on Wednesday 5 December . The couple went on trial at Teesside Crown Court; found guilty in July 2008, John Carew was jailed for six years and three months after admitting seven charges of deception. He was released in January 2011. Anne was sentenced to six-and-a-half years in prison after a jury found her guilty of six counts of fraud and nine of money laundering. She was released from Askham Grange Prison near York in March 2011. On St Valentine's Day 2012, the Crown Prosecution Service said that £501,641.39 in life insurance and pension payouts given to Anne Darwin had been recovered. The Darwins are now divorced. A drama about the events, *The Thief, His Wife And The Canoe*, was broadcast in April 2022 starring Eddie Marsan as John Darwin and Monica Dolan as his wife.

ELEPHANT MAN
Liverpool Street Station, London EC2M 7QH

On Thursday 24 June 1886, Joseph Carey Merrick, the so-called Elephant Man because of the hideous disfiguring disease neurofibro-matosis that caused fleshy growths to appear on his body, arrived at Liverpool Street suffering from a severe bronchial infection, having been robbed and abandoned by an Austrian showman while working in Belgium. Thanks to the Victorian doctor Frederick Treves, Merrick moved to **The Royal London Hospital, Whitechapel Road, London E1 1FR,** where he stayed for the rest of his life in two rooms on Bedstead Square. Merrick died from asphyxiation there on Friday 11 April 1890 aged 27. Merrick's large head meant that he was unable to sleep in a supine position – it seemed that on his last night he tried to sleep lying down like "normal" people. His skeleton is on permanent private display at The Royal London Hospital. Dr Wynne Edwin Baxter led the judicial inquiry into Merrick's death and had also overseen the inquiries into Polly Nichols, Annie Chapman and Elizabeth Stride: the victims of Jack the Ripper. At the time of his death, at **170 Stoke Newington Church Street, London N16 0JL** on Friday 1 October 1920, Baxter had been Coroner for London for thirty-three years and was known as the "father of the London coroners", using the telegram address "Inquest, London".

GHOST VILLAGE
Imber, Salisbury Plain, Wiltshire SN10

Four years into the Second World War, the residents of this remote Wiltshire village were given days to evacuate their homes so it could be used by American troops practising for the D-Day invasion of Normandy in June 1944. In the late nineteenth century, the War Office began buying land on Salisbury Plain for military use, and by the outbreak of the Second World War, almost all of the land in and around Imber, with the exception of the church (St Giles, dating from the thirteenth century), the vicarage, a Baptist chapel, the schoolroom and The Bell Inn belonged to the Ministry of War. On Monday 1 November 1943, the people of Imber were called to a meeting in the village schoolroom and given just forty-seven days' notice to leave their homes. Compensation for the upheaval was limited, and the occupants of one farm had to be forcibly evicted by the Army. Albert Nash, who had been the village's blacksmith for more than forty years, was found sobbing over his anvil and later became the first resident to die and be brought back to Imber for burial. The inhabitants were told that they could return after the war, but the promise was broken and a rally attended by about 2,000 people on Sunday 22 January 1961 demanding the village be returned to its rightful owners

achieved little. An agreement was reached that the village would be
opened three days a year for people to visit their abandoned homes,
and the church would be maintained and opened for worship on the
Sunday closest to the feast of St Giles. The village is open to visitors
on other occasions: certain Bank Holidays and around Christmas.

HABITAT
77 Fulham Road, Chelsea, London SW3 6RE
Terence Conran (b. at Kingston upon Thames Sunday 4 October 1931
d. at Kintbury, Berkshire Saturday 12 September 2020) and his third
wife Caroline Herbert opened the first Habitat store in "rather dreary
premises" in Chelsea on Monday 11 May 1964. Its staff had uniforms
by Mary Quant and hairstyles by Vidal Sassoon. Conran wanted to
introduce a European way of shopping to London and put Habitat's
success down to selling cheap pasta storage jars just as London took
dried pasta to its heart. The shop sold paper pendant lamp shades and
continental quilts – later to become known as duvets. In 1966, Habitat
printed its first catalogue with illustrations by Juliet Glynn Smith.
That same year, the company began a mail order business. In 1971, it
began selling its first flat pack furniture and was floated on the Stock
Exchange in 1981. The following year it merged with Mothercare to
create Habitat Mothercare Group plc; another merger in 1986 saw
it become Storehouse plc, along with British Home Stores. Conran
left the company in 1989. On Friday 2 September 2016, Habitat was
bought by the Sainsbury's Group for £1.4 billion.

HARRODS
228 Borough High Street, Southwark, London SE1 1JX
"The top people's store" began in very humble circumstances
south of the river in Southwark. In 1824, Charles Henry Harrod
(b. at Lexden, Essex Tuesday 16 April 1799 d. at 2 Oxford Terrace,
Wellesley Road, Chiswick, Middlesex Tuesday 3 March 1885)
opened a shop in Borough High Street that was at various times a
draper, a mercer and a haberdasher. In 1832, he was running Harrod
and Wicking, Linen Drapers, Retail but the business lasted barely
twelve months; that same year he opened **Harrod & Co Grocers, 163
Upper Whitecross Street, Clerkenwell, London EC1**. Harrod began

supplying tea from premises at **4 Cable Street, Whitechapel, London E1 8JG** and opened new wholesale premises at **38 Eastcheap, London EC3M 1HD** in 1849. Harrod met and became friends with Philip Henry Burden, who ran a small grocers at **8 Middle Queen's Buildings, Knightsbridge, London SW3**. Burden lacked business acumen and Harrod took control of the shop in 1849. In 1853, Harrod moved his family above the shop, which was open from 8am to 11pm. He announced his retirement in 1861, but rather than passing the shop on to his son, Charles Digby Harrod (b. Monday 25 January 1841 d. Tuesday 15 August 1905), the old man sold it to him instead, the last payment being made in 1864. Charles junior worked hard and by 1868 the business, now at **105 Brompton Road, Knightsbridge, London SW3 1ES**, was taking £1,000 a week (£120,490 at 2022 values). Harrods began to stock perfumes, stationery and patent medicines on its way to creating the modern department store. In June 1870, the shop started offering a delivery service for local customers. It also only accepted cash; the invoices bore the legend: "MR HARROD begs to mention that he sells EXCLUSIVELY FOR CASH. All Country Orders MUST BE PAID FOR previous to their being dispatched." He had sixteen employees accounting for a £15 weekly wage bill, and two delivery boys who were each paid 10s. In 1874, the shop was enlarged with the purchase of leases at 101 and 103 Brompton Road, and Harrod's Stores appeared on the window for the first time. Harrod was a tough but fair employer – by 1880 he had 100 staff who received overtime pay (unusual for the time) and a sovereign on their annual holiday. He would sack staff at a moment's notice and fined them a penny-ha'penny for every fifteen minutes they were late. Disaster struck on Thursday 6 December 1883 when the store burnt down. The next day, Harrod wrote to all his customers promising their Christmas orders would be fulfilled but "will be delayed in the execution a day or two". With the help of businessman Edgar Cohen (b. at Whitechapel, London 1853 d. at London Sunday 29 January 1933), whom he had met on a bus when he had forgotten the money to pay for his fare, he found new premises to carry on trading. A new Harrods opened on the site of the old one in September 1884 and was soon taking £2,000 a week (£265,000, 2022). Exhausted, Charles Digby Harrod retired in 1889 and the shop became a limited liability company known as Harrod's Stores Limited. Sir Alfred Newton (b. at Hull Friday 19 October 1849 d. Monday 20 June 1921) became chairman and Harrod retired to Somerset and then Sussex. However, he returned when the new company struggled, even though he owned no shares in the business. In 1891 he appointed (Sir) Richard Burbidge (b. at Manor Farm, South Wraxhall, Wiltshire Tuesday 2 March 1847 d. at 51 Hans Mansions, Knightsbridge, London SW1X Thursday 31 May 1917) as general manager, becoming managing director two years later. It was Burbidge who made Harrods the success story that it is today. He reduced the opening hours by sixty minutes, introduced subsidised meals for staff and abolished the fines for tardiness. In 1894, work began on the frontage that is seen today; the work was completed in 1905. Nine years later Harrods bought the department store Dickins & Jones. His son, Sir (Richard) Woodman Burbidge took over in 1917 and grandson Sir Richard Grant Woodman Burbidge (b. at 35 Upper George Street, Marylebone, London W1 Saturday 7 December 1872 d. at Cisswood, Sandygate Lane, Lower Beeding, Horsham RH13 6NF Sunday 3 June 1945) took over in 1917 and his son, Sir Richard Grant Woodman Burbidge (b. at 53 Stanhope Gardens, Kensington, London SW7 5RF Wednesday 23 June 1897 d. at Walnut Tree Cottage, Ashampstead, Berkshire RG8 9RJ Wednesday 2 February 1966) took the reins in 1935. In 1920, Harrods snapped up another department store, Swan & Edgar, and, eight years later, bought DH Evans. In 1959, House of Fraser bought Harrods, before itself being sold to the Fayed brothers in 1985 for £615million.

DID YOU KNOW?

London's first escalator was unveiled at Harrods on Wednesday 16 November 1898, introduced by Richard Burbidge who believed customers would not want to climb so many steps. He also had a personal hatred of lifts. The first escalator rose forty feet into the air from the ground floor to the first, and was more like a conveyor belt with handrails. For customers who were discombobulated by their experience, an attendant offered free cognac or sal volatile (smelling salts) at the top. A lift replaced the escalator in 1909.

HITLER, ADOLF
102 Upper Stanhope Street, Toxteth, Liverpool L8 1UN

This eight-room, three-bedroom flat is supposedly where Adolf Hitler stayed when he arrived in 1912 to escape service in the Austrian army. It was the home of his half-brother Alois (1882-1956) and his Irish wife Bridget Elizabeth Dowling (b. at Dublin Friday 3 July 1891 d. at Long Island, New York Tuesday 18 November 1969). They had married in London in June 1910 and their only child, William Patrick Hitler, was born here on Sunday 12 March 1911, dying in New York on Friday 14 July 1987. Adolf stayed in England until April 1913 when Alois bought him a ticket back to Germany. There are lots of stories but no actual proof Hitler ever did visit England. Some claimed he worked as a waiter at the **Adelphi Hotel, Ranelagh Street, Liverpool L3 5UL** (this seems unlikely since it did not open until Monday 9 March 1914), while one man claimed he stood next to him at Goodison Park to watch Everton. Scousers joke that Hitler was there to scope out where to drop bombs on the city in thirty years' time. In 1978, Beryl Bainbridge published a novel, *Young Adolf*, about the visit to Liverpool. The house no longer exists.

KENTUCKY FRIED CHICKEN
92 Fishergate, Preston, Lancashire PR1 2NJ

The first Kentucky Fried Chicken in Britain appeared here in May 1965, with a cardboard cut-out of Colonel Sanders welcoming customers. The shop was set up by Bristolian Harry Latham (d. Thursday 23 May 2019) and his partner Raymond Allen. Working with the colonel, they soon expanded the franchise nationwide, with the first Kentucky Fried Chicken in London opening in North Finchley in November 1968. In 1991, the company changed its name to KFC.

LAVATORY
Fleet Street, London EC4

The Society of Arts opened the first public flushing lavatory on Monday 2 February 1852 in Fleet Street opposite the Royal Courts of Justice in a bid to stop disease spreading through "public fouling". It was for gentlemen only and the ladies had to wait nine more days for relief (that one opened in Bedford Street, London). The facilities were called "Public Waiting Rooms" and a staff of three ensured all was as it should be. The Society of Arts placed advertisements in *The Times* announcing the new public conveniences and 50,000 leaflets were distributed. The first loos were not a success – by the end of the first month just 58 men and two dozen women had used them. The cause of the failure may have been financial – the society charged tuppence for spending a penny. When the idea finally took off, Victorian loos were often ornate affairs: tiled underground chambers encircled by iron fences and crowned with arches or pergolas. Sadly, many are now closed due to vandalism, lack of local council investment or because they were used for other matters.

LYONS CORNER HOUSE
7-14 Coventry Street, London W1
In 1887, the first J. Lyons & Company was founded by the professional artist (Sir) Joseph Lyons (b. at Lant Street, Southwark, London SE1 1RB Wednesday 29 December 1847 d. at Hyde Park Hotel, 66 Knightsbridge, London SW1X 7LA Friday 22 June 1917), tobacconist Barnett Salmon (b. Sunday 24 May 1829 d. Thursday 11 February 1897) and his brothers-in-law, Isidore (b. Wednesday 13 August 1851 d. Friday 10 December 1920) and Montague Gluckstein (b. Tuesday 18 July 1854 d. Saturday 7 October 1922) at **34 Whitechapel Road, London E1 1DQ**. It received its first catering contract at the Newcastle Jubilee Exhibition that year. On Saturday 16 March 1889, a second firm was registered – J. Lyons & Company Ltd – which took over the contracts of J. Lyons & Company. The third iteration of J. Lyons & Company Ltd was registered on Tuesday 10 April 1894 and Joseph Lyons was appointed the managing director. On Thursday 20 September that year, it opened its first teashop at **213 Piccadilly, London W1J 9HF**: this was to be the beginning of a chain. The firm believed that the public wanted good quality fare, served in attractive surroundings by polite staff – and no alcohol. In other cafés of the time, tea was brewed in the morning and kept hot in large urns. At Lyons, it was brewed for each individual customer who ate from dainty china on marble tables and sat on red plush chairs. It was a roaring success

and queues formed outside, sitting on benches thoughtfully provided by the management as they waited for a vacant table. All the food and drink was prepared by Lyons' own cooks at **Cadby Hall, 62 Hammersmith Road, Hammersmith, London W14 0QH**. There were sixty-six items on the menu, including mutton pie (7d), iced Bovril and soda, egg rissoles and truffled foie gras sausage (3d). The twenty-six waitresses wore numbered brooches and customers were told to write to the head office with any complaints: "Postage will be refunded". Two more teashops were opened later that year and a dozen more appeared in 1895. By the end of their first year in business, the company announced a profit of £11,404 6s 4d. By 1900, there were thirty-seven Lyons teashops in London and branches in Bradford, Leeds, Liverpool, Manchester and Sheffield. J. Lyons also invested in classy restaurants and hotels, but it was the Corner Houses that captured the public imagination in the twentieth century. The first Lyons Corner House opened on Coventry Street on Monday 4 January 1909 and closed on Saturday 13 June 1970, initially seating 2,000 people until 1922, when it was enlarged to hold 4,500. Thanks to further expansion it had an All-Night Café (July 1923), a Brasserie in the basement (September 1936), Old Vienna Café (February 1940), Sandwich Meal Counter (September 1942), Vita Sun Café (October 1942), another brasserie called the Salad Bowl (April 1943) and a Wimpy Grill (May 1955). The Corner House served 25,000 meals in 24 hours. Unlike the teashops, every meal was cooked on site. Most of the Lyons Houses were over four or five storeys and employed around 400 staff. Each floor had its own restaurant style, and all had orchestras playing to the diners almost continuously through-out the day and evening – at one time they were open twenty-four hours a day. A large food hall usually took up the ground floor and sold normal as well as speciality foodstuffs. Lyons Corner Houses and Maison Lyons contained hair dressing salons, telephone booths, theatre booking agencies and a food delivery service to any address in London, twice a day. They were also pioneers of self-service dining: the Strand Lyons Corner House offered a fixed price meal, with the attraction of being able to fit as much as you could on your tray. There were three official Corner Houses and four Maisons Lyons in London, which were almost identical to the Corner Houses but came under a separate management structure. The Corner Houses were located at Coventry Street, Strand and Tottenham Court Road. The Maisons Lyons were at Oxford Street (opened Thursday 21 November 1912, closed Sunday 17 September 1916), Shaftsbury Avenue, a second Oxford Street (opened Monday 18 September 1916, closed Sunday 22 October 1933) and Marble Arch. The waitresses in their black uniforms with white hats and pinnies were called Nippys because of their ability to move speedily around the diners' tables. The first Nippys started work on Thursday 1 January 1925. It was reported by *Picture Post* that every year 800 to 900 Nippys got married to customers they "met on duty", and the publication reported that being a Nippy was good training for becoming a housewife. As tastes changed, the Corner Houses and Maisons Lyons lost custom. The Strand Corner House on the junction of Strand and Craven Street opened on Thursday 8 April 1915 and closed on Monday 28 February 1977. The Oxford Corner House on the junction of Tottenham Court Road and Hanway Street with entrances in Tottenham Court Road and **14-16 Oxford Street, London W1** was opened on Thursday 3 May 1928 by TRH the Duke and Duchess of York, serving 21,947 meals on its first day. It closed in May 1967 and never made a profit in its thirty-nine year history, The Maison Lyons, Marble Arch, at the junction of Oxford Street and Great Cumberland Place, opened on Monday 23 October 1933 and closed on Thursday 27 January 1977. The Maison Lyons, Shaftesbury Avenue – once a recruiting centre for Nippys – at the north side of Shaftesbury Avenue opposite the Trocadero Restaurant opened on Monday 16 August 1915 and closed on Thursday 14 November 1940. On Monday 22 June 1981, thanks to the work of company chairman Neil Salmon(b. Thursday 17 February 1921 d. Tuesday 8 August 1989), the Strand Lyons Corner House reopened. However, by that time Allied Breweries Limited had acquired Lyons. In 1994, Allied-Lyons decided to dispose of its food manufacturing operation and to change its name to Allied Domecq. It closed on Tuesday 14 June 1988 after initial enthusiasm waned. The individual companies were sold off and Lyons head office was closed the following year.

DID YOU KNOW?

In May 1944, the Salad Bowl brasserie opened in the Oxford Corner House. A little under a year later, it was the scene of a double homicide. Around 4pm on Friday 20 April 1945, 58-year-old Jean-Baptiste Tratsart, his daughter Claire, 29, and son Hugh, 17, boarded the number 49 bus from Streatham to Trinity Road Underground Station and then from there went to Tottenham Court Road. The family made their way to the Oxford Corner House where they met the other son Jacques Adrian and two more family members, sister Anne, 13, and an aunt, also called Claire. Jacques was an insomniac and a manic depressive – he had sought medical help but believed the psychiatrists were not helping him so stopped seeing them. Sister Claire was an epileptic and Hugh had cerebral palsy and was wheelchair-bound, so Jacques decided that they would be better off dead. At 5pm they sat down to dinner. Some time after, Jacques pulled a Browning automatic revolver, aimed at his sister and pulled the trigger, but nothing happened. Only Hugh saw what had happened and he sat in his wheelchair grinning at his brother, who put the gun under the table cloth. Ten minutes later, he pulled the gun out again and fired, but again nothing happened. This time Aunt Claire asked him what he was doing and he said it was a water pistol. Under cover of the linen, he fiddled with the gun and heard a click as the safety mechanism was released. For a third time he pulled the gun out, and this time shot Claire. The other diners fled in the mêlée and Tratsart shot his father twice before turning the gun on Hugh. He was also shot twice and then placed the weapon against his temple and pulled the trigger. Nothing happened. Furious, he threw the gun into the air and it landed in one of the upturned light bowls. Indeed, it was only when the lights were turned on later that day that an eagle-eyed policeman spotted the gun's outline. Jean-Baptiste was admitted to Middlesex Hospital but died five minutes after arrival. Claire died at the scene as a priest performed the Last Rites. Hugh survived the assault and died aged 61 in July 1988. On Monday 28 May 1945, Jacques appeared at the Old Bailey charged with two counts of murder, one count of attempted murder and one count of attempted suicide. He pleaded not guilty but he was found guilty by reason of insanity, and detained at **Broadmoor Psychiatric Hospital, Crowthorne, Berkshire RG45 7EG**. He died there having slit a vein on Friday 30 May 1947.

MARKS & SPENCER
Kirkgate Market, Leeds, West Yorkshire LS2 7HY

In 1884, Jewish émigré Michael Marks (b. at Slonim, Russia, June 1859 d. at Knoll House, 396 Bury New Road, Higher Broughton, Salford M7 3NG Tuesday 31 December 1907, aged 48) met Isaac Dewhirst while on the hunt for work. Dewhirst loaned Marks £5 to buy stock for a stall at Kirkgate Market in Leeds. Dewhirst's bookkeeper was Thomas Spencer (b. at Skipton, Yorkshire Friday 7 November 1851 d. at Whittington, Staffordshire Tuesday 25 July 1905, aged 53) and they formed a partnership on Friday 28 September 1894, with each partner making share contributions of £300 (£41,500 at 2022 values). In 1901, Marks and Spencer moved to the Birkenhead open market, where in 1903 they opened the Penny Bazaar at stall numbers eleven and twelve in the centre aisle. Marks remained in charge of all buying operations and retail, while Spencer focused on wholesale and the distribution of goods from their warehouse. It was at this time that Marks moved to Hulme, Manchester, living above the shop and also leasing a warehouse in the city that was to become the new focus of operations. By 1900, Marks & Spencer had expanded to include thirty-six Penny Bazaars as they called their shops – "Don't ask the price, it's a penny" – and a dozen high street stores. The following year, Marks & Spencer built a warehouse at Derby Street, Manchester, which became the company's first registered address and headquarters. The official first Marks and Spencer store opened in 1904 at **Cross Arcade, Boar Lane, Leeds**. In June 1926, the company went public and on Monday 5 November 1928, the St Michael trademark was registered by Simon Marks, 1st Baron Marks of Broughton (b. at Trafalgar Street, Leylands, Leeds, Monday 9 July 1888 d. at 47 Baker Street, London W1U 8AA Tuesday 8 December 1964), in honour of his father. Initially the name was only used on textile goods; in 1940, margarine became the first food product to use the trademark. The company stopped using St Michael in 2000. Frozen food was sold for the first time in 1972, and the following year, the company became the first to use sell-by dates on their foodstuffs. The flagship store was opened at **458 Oxford Street, London W1C 1AP** on Wednesday 5 November 1930. Work will begin on developing the site in 2023, with a new Marks & Spencer Marble Arch due to open in 2027.

MCDONALD'S
56-60 Powis Street, Woolwich, London SE18 6LQ
Telephone: 020-8317 0102

The first McDonald's hamburger emporium in Britain – the 3,000th worldwide – was opened here on Wednesday 13 November 1974 by disc jockey Ed Stewart and Mayor of Woolwich Len Squirrel. On its thirtieth anniversary, the restaurant celebrated by selling its fare at 1974 prices: you could buy a hamburger for 17p. The first manager, Ohio-born Paul S. Preston, 36, later became the president and chief executive officer of the UK division of the corporation, retiring in 2001. In 1986, the first franchise-operated restaurant opened in Hayes, Middlesex. On Saturday 12 October 1991, the 400th UK restaurant and the first in Northern Ireland opened in Belfast.

NATIONAL HEALTH SERVICE
Park Hospital, Davyhulme, Manchester M41 5SL
Telephone: 0161-748 4022

On Monday 5 July 1948, Aneurin Bevan, the Secretary of State for Health, opened the first National Health Service hospital, stating, "We now have the moral leadership of the world." It is now Trafford General Hospital. Bevin's NHS had a three prong plan – it met everyone's needs, it was free at the point of delivery and it was based on need, not ability to pay. Prior to the NHS, people usually had to pay for their own health treatment. The night before, Bevan blotted his copybook in a speech at a Labour rally in Belle Vue, Manchester, calling the Conservatives "lower than vermin". The speech earned him a reprimand from Prime Minister Clement Attlee and the lasting enmity of the Tories. The NHS story began when Bevan was 12 and still at school. London School of Economics co-founder Beatrice Webb (1858-1943) suggested the idea in the Poor Law Royal Commission in 1909. At the 1934 Labour Party Conference in Southport, Dr Somerville Hastings, the President of the Socialist Medical Association, passed a motion that Labour should introduce a national health service. The Beveridge Report was published on Tuesday 24 November 1942, recommending a "comprehensive health and rehabilitation service for the prevention and cure of disease". Following Clement Attlee's landslide win in the General Election of

1945, wheels were set in motion. The Conservatives voted against the idea that the NHS would own all the hospitals, but the Labour majority saw it through. Many doctors were opposed to the idea of a national health service and, in May 1948, the British Medical Association voted not to participate. Bevan persuaded the doctors to join, not least with financial incentives: "ultimately I had to stuff their mouths with gold," he said. In June 1948, the Central Office of Information for the Ministry of Health issued a leaflet explaining the new service: "It will provide you with all medical, dental and nursing care. Everyone – rich or poor, man, woman or child – can use it or any part of it. There are no charges, except for a few special items. There are no insurance qualifications. But it is not a 'charity'. You are all paying for it, mainly as tax payers, and it will relieve your money worries in time of illness." In 1951, Bevin resigned in protest when the Labour Government introduced charges for dentists, false teeth and spectacles, along with an up-and-coming MP called Harold Wilson. In 1952, the Conservatives under Winston Churchill brought in a fee of one shilling (£8 in 2022) for prescription forms. In December 1956, the cost was increased to one shilling per item. In 1965 they were abolished by Prime Minister Harold Wilson, but later reintroduced. The NHS currently employs more than a million and a half people.

NON-EXISTENT HOUSES
23–24 Leinster Gardens, London W2
To the casual passer-by, Leinster Gardens seems a perfectly ordinary street in Bayswater. However, closer inspection reveals that numbers 23 and 24 are merely a five-feet-thick façade containing eighteen blackened windows. When the Metropolitan Railway extension (now the Circle Line) was built in 1868, it used locomotives that puffed out smoke. To prevent the tunnels becoming clogged, short sections were exposed to the elements to allow the trains to "vent off". One such area was created at Leinster Gardens by demolishing two houses and creating the façade.

OXFAM
17 Broad Street, Oxford OX1 3AS
Oxfam opened Britain's first permanent charity shop here in February 1948. The organisation had been founded six years earlier as the

Oxford Committee for Famine Relief by Canon Theodore Richard Milford (1896-1987) and the Oxford Meeting of the Quakers. Their original mission was to send food through the Allied blockade to the people of German-occupied Greece. In 1943, the Oxford Committee for Famine Relief was registered as a charity. Its first appeal, Greek Week, raised £12,700 for the Greek Red Cross. The first paid employee, Joe Mitty (1919-2007), began working at the Broad Street shop on Monday 9 November 1949. The committee gradually became known by its abbreviated telegraph address, Oxfam, and that name was formally adopted in 1965.

PIZZA EXPRESS
29 Wardour Street, London W1D 6PS
The first Pizza Express was opened here on Saturday 27 March 1965 by Peter Boizot (b. at Peterborough Saturday 16 November 1929) who having returned from Italy, he wanted somewhere to buy a proper Italian pizza and decided to create such a place. He ordered a large pizza oven, but when it arrived it would not fit through the door so Boizot and his staff had to make a hole in the front wall. The first day of business was not successful – only £3 (£62 at 2022 values) went into the till. Slices of pizza cost 2s and were served on greaseproof paper with plastic cutlery and coffee in paper cups. The plastic cutlery was soon replaced by stainless steel because the heat of the cheese melted the plastic. The original pizza was square, as were the slices. Boizot found mozzarella from the only producer in London and was the first man to import Peroni to the UK. A second Pizza Express opened on Coptic Street, next to the British Museum, in 1967. Peter Boizot died aged 89 on Wednesday 5 December 2018.

PONTIN'S HOLIDAY PARK
Brean Sands, Burnham-on-Sea, Somerset TA8 2RJ
Fred Pontin (b. at 127 Edward Road, Walthamstow, Essex E17 6PA Wednesday 24 October 1906 d. at Blackpool Saturday 30 September 2000) opened his first holiday park on an eight-acre site in Brean Sands (an abandoned D-Day training camp). He borrowed £25,000 – half from City investors and half from Barclays Bank – and bought Ministry of Supply surplus stock to furnish the camp. By the end of the

following year he had six resorts, with the capacity for 1,300 holiday-makers. Unlike his rival Billy Butlin (see page 7), Pontin offered self-catering holidays. By 1963, he had twenty-two camps and also offered self-catering Mediterranean holidays: holidaymakers could go "Pontinental" at ten camps including Majorca, Tenerife and the Costa Brava. By 1975 he was making an annual profit of £3.6million (£32million at 2022 values). Pontin kept racehorses and gained publicity for his business with names like Go Pontin, Go Pontinental and Pontingo. On Saturday 3 April 1971, his horse Specify, ridden by John Cook and trained by John Sutcliffe, won the Grand National. Pontin was knighted in 1976 for services to charity. Aged 73, he sold his company to Coral Leisure for £56million (£302million, 2022) but was thrown off the board in 1981. There were thirty resorts in the portfolio at one point, but by the time the company went into administration on Friday 12 November 2010, there were just five left: Brean Sands in Somerset; Camber Sands in East Sussex; Pakefield, Lowestoft, Suffolk; Prestatyn Sands, Denbighshire; and Southport on Merseyside. Unlike Butlin's with its red coats, camp entertainers at Pontin's sported blue coats. Former Bluecoats include Shane Ritchie, Lisa Scott-Lee, Helen Chamberlain, Lee Mack and Bobby Davro. The 1973 film *Holiday On The Buses* was filmed at and set in the Pontin's Prestatyn resort.

PORT SUNLIGHT
Wirral, Merseyside CH62

This village was built by an employer for his staff. William Hesketh Lever was born at **16 Wood Street, Bolton, Lancashire BL1 1DY** on Friday 19 September 1851, one of the ten children of grocer James Lever (b. at Bolton Friday 25 August 1809 d. at Cheshire Wednesday 26 May 1897). Lever saw a world outside vegetables and he launched Lever's Pure Honey Soap tablets in 1874. He launched Lever Brothers ten years later, selling soap made mainly from vegetable oils rather than the usual tallow. The company registed the name Sunlight; their products stood out by being wrapped in paper. Lux soap powder and Vim household cleaner were also launched. Lever Brothers initially paid other companies to make Sunlight soap but the firm bought a soapworks at Warrington in 1885 and began to make their own. In

1887, the company bought fifty-two acres of land (later extended to 500 acres) on the Mersey near Bebington in Cheshire for the purposes of building a factory. Lever conceived the idea of a working village in which workers would be provided with a home near their place of work, which would engender loyalty both ways; it was called Port Sunlight, and 900 houses were eventually built there. Rents were taken straight from the pay packet – the Kitchen houses cost five or six shillings weekly, while the Parlour houses went from between seven and ten shillings. Male employees were paid between twenty and twenty-five shillings a week so the fees were eminently affordable. The staff ate in vast dining halls charged at thruppence a meal. Taking maintenance and rates into account, Lever Brothers ran Port Sunlight at a loss. A primary school was built along with shops and a post office, and residents could avail themselves of tennis courts, a football and cricket pitch, bowling greens, table tennis and an open-air swimming pool. Unmarried women were provided with classes in cookery, needlework and housewifery to prepare them for looking after their husbands. A pub, the Bridge Inn, opened in October 1900, although it was dry until 1903 and remained dry on a Sunday until 1973. Lever believed in the benefits of sleeping outdoors whatever the weather, and indeed the death rate in Port Sunlight's Cottage Hospital (opened in 1907), where two wards were open to the elements, was about fifty percent lower than Liverpool. He lived in a magnificent house, Thornton Manor, but the bedroom he shared with his wife was open to the elements all year round. Lever had a sort of profit-sharing scheme; of an annual bonus he said, "It would not do you much good if you send it down your throats in the form of bottles of whisky, bags of sweets, or fat geese at Christmas. On the other hand, if you leave the money with me, I shall use it to provide for you everything that makes life pleasant – nice houses, comfortable homes, and healthy recreation." People tended to stay at Port Sunlight, because if they left the company they also had to leave their homes. A weekly dance was organised which Lever attended; he often asked plain girls who had been overlooked to join him on the dancefloor. "He always danced with Ethel Williams, the hunchback," recalled one worker. In 1890, Lever Brothers became a limited company and was floated on the market in 1894 with a capital of £1½million (£207,735,000 at 2022 values). Lever eventually owned all the ordinary shares which had not been offered to the public. He began to buy up other soap brands and, in 1906, proposed more soap mergers. A dozen companies began to amalgamate, a move condemned by the *Daily Mail*, which saw its advertising income decrease. Such was the power and ferocity of the *Mail* attack that the Sunlight brand was harmed and some of the other soap manufacturers pulled out of the amalgamation idea. The *Mail* did not give up its campaign and, on Tuesday 4 December 1906, Lever sued for libel. The case was heard at Liverpool Assizes from Monday 15 July 1907. Lever was represented by Sir Edward Carson while the *Mail* hired Rufus Isaacs. Lever's performance in the witness box was so assured the *Mail* gave up on the second day and offered a settlement. Lever Brothers received £141,000 (£18million, 2022) from Lord Northcliffe's newspapers – the largest libel payment ever made at that time – which he gave to Liverpool University to establish schools of tropical medicine, town planning and civic design. In 1911, to ensure he had a regular supply of raw materials for his goods, he bought land in the Congo and built a town called Leverville where he opened Lever hospitals, but he overreached himself in 1920 and almost wrecked his own legacy. In December 1911, Lever was made a baronet and was raised to the peerage on Thursday 21 June 1917 as Baron Leverhulme, becoming Viscount Leverhulme in 1922. King George V visited Port Sunlight in 1914. In August that year, 700 men signed up to fight for King and Country. Four hundred and eighty-one – the Port Sunlight Pals – were killed on the Somme in 1916. Lever died from pneumonia at **The Hill, Hampstead, London NW11 7EX** at 4.30am on Thursday 7 May 1925, leaving £1,625,409 2s. 4d (£101,097,635, 2022). He was buried on Monday 11 May 1925 at Port Sunlight. In the 1980s, the first houses in Port Sunlight were sold privately. The school is now a working men's club and the hospital a hotel.

TELEPHONE EXCHANGE
36 Coleman Street, London EC2R 5EH

The first telephone exchange in Britain opened in August 1879 and was run by the appropriately named Telephone Company. It had just eight subscribers, most of whom were within walking distance of each other. By the end of the year, a further two exchanges had been opened at **101 Leadenhall Street, London EC3A** and **3 Palace Chambers, Westminster, London SW1**; there were now 200 subscribers, each paying £20 per annum (around £10,000 at 2022 prices) for line rental and equipment consisting of a large bell box, a microphone and a separate earpiece. There was no dial as each call was connected by the operator, whose attention was attracted by tapping the hook. There were no numbers either, as there were so few customers that callers asked the operator to connect them to the person they wished to speak to. They spoke for as long as they wished. Other businesses saw the potential and soon a dozen companies were vying for custom-ers. However, subscribers with one company were not able to speak to those with another, and trouble flared when unscrupulous businesses began cutting their opponents' lines. The solution – to nationalise the phones and put them all under one company umbrella – was dismissed by many in Government, who believed that telephones were a flash in the pan gimmick. A review by Richard Culley, the Post Office Engineer-in-Chief, commented, "The possibilities of the telephone appear to be even more limited than I first supposed it." It was not until Monday 1 January 1912 that nationalisation took place and the Postmaster-General became responsible for 9,000 employees, 1½ million miles of wire and 1,465 exchanges, of which 231 had more than 300 subscribers each, all at at a cost of £12,515,264. The Post Office operated a virtual monopoly on telephones except in Hull, Portsmouth and Guernsey. On Saturday 15 July 1922, the first direct dialling exchanges were introduced at Fleetwood, Lancashire. As with all new technology, there were fears – some believed that users could catch tuberculosis of the mouth and companies began selling products that would sterilise the phones after each use. Telephone companies produced a guide for new users that told them to answer with their title and full name and not to let the phone ring for too long: "Promptitude in answering is essential."

THURSDAY CLUB
Wheeler & Co, 19–21 Old Compton Street, Soho, London W1D 5JJ
Wheeler & Co was a specialist oyster merchants and continental fish supplier, with a cafeteria and deli from 1929. It was in a second-floor

room here on Thursdays from around 1947 that the all-male membership got together for lunch and to elect a Cunt Of The Month,
paying a fixed fee for lunch, wine and vintage port. There were no
social formalities observed and the fifty or so members included:
the actors James Robertson Justice, David Niven and Peter Ustinov;
Baron Nahum, the society photographer; the artists Vasco Lazzolo
and Feliks Topolski; the American writers Donald Ogden Stewart
and Harry Kurnitz; Larry Adler, the harmonica player; Arthur
Christiansen, the editor of the *Daily Express*; Frank Owen, the editor
of the *Daily Mail*; Prince Philip (who was introduced by Baron) and
David Milford Haven, the best man at his Thursday 20 November
1947 marriage to Princess Elizabeth. Adler wrote of the club in 1993,
"I, being blacklisted in the US at the time, was dubbed the Subversive
Country Member and, in my honour, whitebait, on the menu, was
changed to redbait." The club began to fizzle out as its members died
and when Wheeler's owner Bernard Walsh died in 1981, the club's
demise was inevitable.

TRAFFIC LIGHTS
Parliament Square, London SW1
The first traffic lights in Britain began operating in Parliament Square
on Thursday 10 December 1868, consisting of a manually operated
revolving lantern with red and green lights (no amber), invented by
the railway engineer J.P. Knight. Its crude construction resulted in
the world's first traffic light accident when it exploded on Saturday 2
January 1869, injuring the policeman operating it.

WHITE, MARCO PIERRE
Harvey's, 2 Bellevue Road, Wandsworth Common, London SW17 7EG
It was at this restaurant that the *enfant terrible* of the kitchen made his
name in 1987. White won his first Michelin star at Harvey's almost
immediately and was awarded his second in 1988. He then became
chef-patron of the Oak Room at **Le Meridien Piccadilly, 21 Piccadilly,
London W1J 0BH** and then the dining-room at the former Hyde Park
Hotel. Harvey's closed and the site has been occupied by Michelin-
starred restaurant Chez Bruce since 1995.

WILLIAM HILL
97 Jermyn Street, London SW1Y 6JE

On Wednesday 26 July 1933, the William Hill Organisation came into existence and William Hill opened his eponymous bookmakers – a one-room establishment above a hat shop – here in 1934 when gambling was illegal in Britain. The "Organisation" consisted of Hill and a young clerk, George Campesi. Born at **32 Henshaw Road, Small Heath, Birmingham B10 0TB** on Thursday 16 July 1903, one of eleven children, Hill left school when he was 12 and began working on his uncle's farm. He began illegal bookmaking and moved to London in 1929, beginning with the dogs before adding pony-racing at Northolt Park to his portfolio. By 1939, the firm had outgrown its Jermyn Street base and moved to **32 Park Lane, London W1K 1PN**. On Saturday 4 November 1944, William Hill moved into the football pools but sued Ladbrokes in 1962 for copyright infringement. The case went to the House of Lords and Hill won the £1 (plus costs) he had asked for. On Wednesday 1 May 1961, betting shops became legal but Hill hated them, calling them "a cancer on society". He did not open his first until Friday 30 December 1966, when he took over the Jack Swift betting shop chain. He died of a heart attack in the bathroom of room fourteen at the **Rutland Hotel, Newmarket CB8 8NB** on Friday 15 October 1971, leaving £1,014,803 (£16million in 2022 values).

WIMPY
Lyons Corner House, Coventry Street, London W1

London's first Wimpy Bar opened in 1953 as a fast food section in a Lyons Corner House. Eddie Gold of Chicago had created the Wimpy brand in the 1930s, the name deriving from the character of J. Wellington Wimpy in the *Popeye* cartoons created on Thursday 17 January 1929 by Elzie Crisler Segar. Despite the reservations of the J. Lyons & Co board, Wimpy in London quickly became a success; separate Wimpys were soon created and franchised. Some Lyons teashops were even converted to exploit the demand from the public for the new fast food. By the end of the 1960s there were nine Wimpy bars on Oxford Street alone. By the early 1970s, the business had expanded to more than 1,000 restaurants in twenty-three countries, with 461 in the UK. Hamburgers (or frankfurters) with French fries, washed down by the milkshake Whippsy (available in strawberry, chocolate or vanilla), was a modern, welcome alternative to the staid restaurants to which post-war Britons had become accustomed. In December 1976, as the Lyons era was coming to an end, Wimpy was sold to United Biscuits.

WOOLWORTHS
25-25a Church Street, Liverpool L11DA/8 Williamson Street, Liverpool L11EB

The first branch of F.W. Woolworth's store opened here (two entrances on different streets) at 2pm on Friday 5 November 1909. Initially, Frank Winfield Woolworth (1852-1919) invited shop managers in America to open stores in England, but received only two applications, rising to three by the time they set sail on Wednesday 19 May 1909. The first shop was formerly Henry Miles, a hat shop; Woolworth offered the landlord a year's rent in advance and a twenty-five-year lease which was signed on Friday 13 August 1909. The first shop opened with a fireworks display, an orchestral display and a circus performance. Nothing was sold on the first day, which was given over entirely to browsing as per an American tradition. The visitors were given free tea as they listened to a brass band in the café. The goods cost 3d or 6d and by the end of the first day of trading, everything had been sold. By 1914, the company had forty stores in Britain, from which fifty-seven employees signed up to fight for King and Country: most perished. By 1923, there were 130 stores. The 400th branch opened on Saturday 12 July 1930 in Southport, Lancashire. The following year, Woolworths was floated on the London Stock Exchange. The 600th store opened in Wallington, Surrey, in 1934; the 800th on Wilton Road, Victoria, London, in September 1953; and the 1,000th on Boundary Road, Hove on Thursday 22 May 1958. The company prospered during the 1960s but ran into trouble in the twenty-first century: the trading of shares was suspended on Wednesday 26 November 2008, the firm going into administration with debts totalling £385million. The staff did not learn they were losing their jobs from head office but from the BBC's Business Editor Robert Peston on the *Six O'Clock News*. A closing down sale began on Thursday 11 December 2008. The shops began closing on Saturday

27 December 2008, with the final 199 closing on Tuesday 6 January 2009 with the total loss of 27,000 jobs.

DID YOU KNOW?
Although founded in America, Woolworths shops lasted longer in Britain. In 1997, all 700 branches in America closed and the company name was changed to Venator.

Chapter II:
History and Tragedy

ABERFAN
Pantglas Junior School, Moy Road, Aberfan,
Merthyr Tydfil, Mid Glamorgan CF48

At 9.15am on Friday 21 October 1966, colliery waste tip number seven (a slag heap) slipped down Merthyr Mountain, destroying twenty houses and a farm before crashing onto Pantglas Junior School and part of the adjacent secondary school in the small Welsh village of Aberfan. Half a million tons of coal waste, forty-feet high engulfed the area. In total, 155 people were killed, 116 of whom were children mostly aged from 7 to ten. It was the last day before term and the children had just returned to their classrooms after singing *All Things Bright And Beautiful* at assembly. Although the emergency services worked tirelessly, no one was pulled out alive after 11am. The causes of death were typically found to be asphyxia, fractured skulls or multiple crush injuries. Many of the dead were buried together in Aberfan Cemetery on Thursday 27 October 1966, but the wishes of some parents who wanted individual ceremonies were respected. A memorial garden was built on the site of the school and the colliery closed in 1990. The Tribunal of Inquiry lasted seventy-six days, the longest in British history at that time; 136 witnesses were interviewed, 300 exhibits examined and 2½ million words heard. When the verdict was delivered on Thursday 3 August 1967, it concluded: "The Aberfan Disaster is a terrifying tale of bungling ineptitude by many men charged with tasks for which they were totally unfitted, of failure to heed clear warnings, and of total lack of direction from above. Not villains but decent men, led astray by foolishness or by ignorance or by both in combination, are responsible for what happened at Aberfan." The report made clear that it was a tale "not of wickedness but of ignorance, ineptitude and a failure of communications". No one faced criminal proceedings. The collapse was found to have been caused by a build-up of water in the pile – when a small rotational slip occurred, the saturated fine material of the tip liquefied and it flowed down the mountain.

AIR RAID VICTIMS
St Peter's Plain, Great Yarmouth, Norfolk

Samuel Smith and Martha Taylor became the first victims of the first air raid on Britain here at 8.30pm on Tuesday 19 January 1915. A German Zeppelin L3 dropped six 110-pound bombs and a number of incendiary devices over Great Yarmouth. The first bomb dropped just before 8.25pm "in a meadow at Ormesby", a second destroyed a stable at the rear of **78 Crown Road, Great Yarmouth NR30 2JH**. Samuel Smith, a 53-year-old cobbler, heard the explosions and left his workshop at St Peter's Plain to see what was happening. At 8.30pm, a third bomb fell on a house opposite and he was killed instantly by flying shrapnel. Simultaneously, Martha Taylor, a 72-year-old spinster, died as she was getting her supper.

ANDERSON SHELTER
Tober Street, Islington, London N1
Carlsbad Street, Islington, London N1

The first domestic bomb shelters were erected in these two London streets on Saturday 25 February 1939. Made of fourteen sheets of corrugated iron, they were six feet high, four and a half feet wide and six feet six inches long. They were buried four feet deep in the soil and then covered with a minimum of fifteen inches of soil above the roof. On Thursday 10 November 1938, Sir John Anderson, the Lord Privy Seal, asked the engineers William Paterson and Oscar Carl Kerrisonto design a shelter. Within a fortnight, the first prototype had been built and it was said that John Anderson promptly jumped on the model with both feet to test it. Anderson shelters were issued free to all householders who earned less than £250 a year, and cost £7 for anyone who earned more. In total,

2¼ million were erected and thousands of lives were saved. After the end of the Blitz, in the summer of 1941, an American journalist wrote that "there was a greater danger of being hit by a vegetable marrow falling off the roof of an air-raid shelter than of being struck by a bomb".

BLAIR-BROWN PACT
Granita, 127 Upper Street, Islington, London N1 1QP
Telephone: 020-7226 3222

It was here, a Mediterranean restaurant, that the two architects of New Labour supposedly formed a pact following the death of Labour leader John Smith. He had been expected to lead Labour to victory in the next general election – likely to be in 1997 – after four successive defeats. The Shadow Home Secretary Tony Blair and Gordon Brown, the Shadow Chancellor, were two of the most likely candidates to succeed Smith. It is alleged that at this meal, Brown agreed not to run for the party leadership and to allow Blair a clear run, on the condition that Blair stood down after two parliamentary terms and handed the leadership to Brown. On Thursday 21 July 1994, Tony Blair was elected Labour Party leader beating off challenges from John Prescott and Margaret Beckett. On Thursday 30 September 2004, Blair announced his decision to stand down after serving a full third term. In the end, he left office on Wednesday 27 June 2007, two years into his third term. Brown realised his lifetime ambition and led Britain into the worst recession in living memory as well as presiding over an administration rife with internal dissent. Granita has since closed.

BOSWORTH, BATTLE OF
Market Bosworth, Leicestershire LE

King Richard III was killed here on Monday 22 August 1485 – the third and last English king to die on a battlefield (after Harold II and Richard I). The battle lasted two hours, marking the end of the War of the Roses and the start of the House of Tudor. Henry Tudor had arrived at Milford Haven on Monday 7 August with an army of just 2,000 (most of whom were French convicts offered a free pardon if they fought for the usurper). It had swelled to 5,000 by the time he arrived at Bosworth, while Richard III had 8,000. Sir William Stanley commanded a third army, of 3-4,000; Richard held Stanley's son hostage to ensure his support. As the battle raged, Richard saw Henry cut off from his men, protected only by a few bodyguards. On his white horse Surrey, he urged his men forward, hoping to engage Henry personally. He even killed his standard bearer Sir William Brandon before Sir William Stanley decided to change sides and came to Henry's aid. Richard bravely fought on until he was pole-axed by a Welsh halberdier. Sir William Stanley found the crown under a hawthorn bush and placed it on the head of Henry Tudor, Henry VII. This was the beginning of 118 years of Tudor rule, and is why that family's emblem is a crown and bush.

CABLE STREET ANTI-FASCIST RIOTS
Cable Street, Whitechapel, London E1 0AE

On Sunday 4 October 1936, Sir Oswald Mosley (1896-1980) intended to march his British Union of Fascists through Cable Street in the East End, the home of a thriving Jewish community, to celebrate the fourth anniversary of the founding of the Party. In the run up, anti-Semitic slogans had been daubed on walls around the area. By 1pm, around 2,000 of Mosley's blackshirts had gathered around Cable Street, while around 500 Jews and anti-fascists congregated at Gardiner's Corner, the junction of Commercial Road and Whitechapel High Street. They rushed to Cable Street and, arming themselves with sticks, formed a barricade by overturning a lorry. At 3.30pm, Cable Street was the scene of some of the worse street fighting ever seen in England; when Mosley's Bentley drove into **Dock Street, London E1**, it was pelted with bricks. Mosley's supporters began chanting his name while the anti-fascists retaliated with the *Internationale*. Mosley then gave a stiff, right-arm salute and was advised by the police to drive back through the City of London rather than press ahead. Mosley gave a brief speech in which he accused the government of surrendering to "red violence and Jewish corruption". At 4pm, the remaining fascists dispersed, allowing the locals to claim victory.

CATO STREET CONSPIRACY
Cato Street, London W1H 5HG

On Saturday 29 January 1820, King George III died after a reign of almost sixty years and was succeeded by his son the Prince Regent, who had been ruling in his stead. It had been a time beset by civil unrest, including the Spa Fields riots in 1816 and the Peterloo Massacre three years later. A group called the Spencean Philanthropists, named after the radical Thomas Spence, began to foment revolution. At a meeting on Tuesday 22 February, George Edwards suggested they should assassinate the Cabinet at a dinner at the home of Lord Harrowby, the Lord President of the Council. Another member, Arthur Thistlewood, was then assigned the task of recruiting men to join the uprising, but only managed to find twenty-seven more. The conspirators met in the loft of a small house rented by John Harrison in Cato Street off Edgware Road. Thistlewood insisted that they attack the next night. Unbeknown to them, they were betrayed by the agent provocateur George Edwards, and, at 7.30pm on Wednesday 23 February, the Bow Street Runners stormed the house. Thistlewood killed a Runner in the mêlée by running him through with his sword. Some of the conspirators gave themselves up without a fight but Thistlewood, Robert Adams, John Brunt and John Harrison escaped and were captured a few days later. Eleven conspirators eventually stood trial and a further two gave evidence for the Crown. Guilty verdicts were handed down on Friday 28 April 1820 and John Brunt, William Davidson, James Ings, Arthur Thistlewood and Richard Tidd were hanged at Newgate Prison at 6.08am on Monday 1 May 1820. After they had been hanging for half an hour, a man in a black mask with a coloured handkerchief further obscuring his face walked onto the gallows and spent the next one hour and eight minutes beheading the five dead men. As each head was removed, an assistant executioner held it up by the hair and proclaimed, "This is the head of [name], a traitor." Tidd was bald and his head had to be held aloft by his cheeks. Davidson's skull poured blood and Brunt's was clumsily dropped. Charles Copper, Richard Bradburn, John Harrison, James Wilson and John Strange were sentenced to death, later commuted to transportation for life. The previous year, the Government had passed the Six Acts, gagging radical newspapers, preventing large meetings and reducing what the administration saw as the possibility of armed insurrection. Following the Cato Street Conspiracy, the government used the incident to justify the Act's imposition.

DAMBUSTERS
RAF Scampton, Scampton, Lincoln LN1 2ST

617 Squadron, the Dambusters, had their headquarters here, having been formed amid great secrecy on Sunday 21 March 1943. Their specific purpose was to bomb three major dams on the Ruhr in Germany: the Möhne, Eder and Sorpe. The operation – codename Chastise – was carried out on Sunday 16-Monday 17 May 1943. The squadron's motto was "Après moi le Deluge" ("After me the Flood") and its mascot was N****r, a black Labrador belonging to the original leader of the squadron, Wing Commander Guy Penrose Gibson (b. at Simla, India, on Monday 12 August 1918). The dog had been with Gibson since puppyhood, accompanied him on several flights and was not averse to a drop of alcohol. The night before the raid, N****r was run over and killed, which Gibson saw as a bad omen for the raid. The Operations Room for the mission was at 5 Group Headquarters in St Vincents Hall, a Gothic Revival mansion built in 1868 in Grantham, Lincolnshire. Each aspect of the mission had a code name that was transmitted in Morse code: Goner meant that the bombs had been released, N****r was the signal that the Möhne had been breached and Dinghy heralded the fact that the Eder had suffered a similar fate. 617 utilised a special "bouncing bomb" invented and developed by Barnes Wallis, the Assistant Chief Designer at Vickers. The mission took off at 9.39pm and flew at an altitude of around 100 feet to avoid being picked up by radar. The mission was only a partial success – the Möhne and Eder dams were breached, leading to flooding in the Ruhr and Eder valleys, causing the deaths of more than 1,600 people, including 749 French, Belgian, Dutch and Ukrainian prisoners of war and labourers. Two hydroelectric powerplants were destroyed and several more were damaged. The Sorpe dam sustained only minor harm. Of the nineteen planes that took off, nine returned to base from 3.11am, with Guy Gibson's plane landing at 4.15am and the last (commanded by Flight Sergeant Bill Townsend) at 6.15am. Eleven bombers reached their targets, although only seven hit them

and of those, only three caused any real damage. Fifty-three of the 133 aircrew who participated in the attack were killed, a casualty rate of 39.85 percent. Of the survivors, thirty-four were decorated at Buckingham Palace on Tuesday 22 June, with Guy Gibson awarded the Victoria Cross. Five were awarded Distinguished Service Orders; ten, Distinguished Flying Crosses and four bars; two, Conspicuous Gallantry Medals; and eleven, Distinguished Flying Medals and one bar. Barnes Wallis wrote after the operation, "I feel a blow has been struck at Germany from which she cannot recover for several years." Unfortunately for the Allies, the Germans effected quick repairs and the dams were back in action by September. Guy Gibson returned to operations and was killed on a Mosquito operation on Tuesday 19 September 1944 over Mönchengladbach. To prevent the Germans making propaganda of Gibson's death, it was kept secret until Friday 5 January 1945. The last pilot to die was Squadron Leader Les Munro, who died aged 96 on 4 August 2015.

Building Research Establishment, Bucknalls Lane, Garston, Watford, Hertfordshire WD25 9XX

It was here in May 1942 that the first tests were carried out when a plaster model dam was destroyed. The small scale model of the dam used for testing can still be found at Garston today.

Nant-y-Gro dam, Powys

In July 1942, 617 Squadron attacked this small dam, which had originally been built to provide water for the navvies working on the site. Barnes Wallis was determined to prove that explosive pressure could breach a dam wall. A bomb was set off at the bottom of the thirty-six-feet-high wall, breaching it. The dam, however, remained in the same state after the explosion.

Chesil Beach, Portland, Dorset DT4 9XE

The first full-scale trials took place on this eighteen-mile-long beach on Friday 4 December 1942, with a second round on Tuesday 15 December. At the first tests, a news camera flmed a Wellington bomber dropping non-explosive bombs that burst on impact. Tests in January 1943 proved slightly more encouraging, although the head of Bomber Command, Sir Arthur Harris, called the plan "just about the maddest proposition… that we have come across". Wallis, however, had power-ful supporters who were determined the plan should succeed.

DID YOU KNOW?

Barnes Wallis, the inventor of the Bouncing Bomb, married his 20-year-old cousin-in-law, Molly Bloxam, at St Luke's Church, Hampstead, London on Thursday 23 April 1925; they stayed together until his death in 1979. They had four children – Barnes, Mary, Elisabeth and Christopher. Mary married Harry Stopes-Roe, the son of Marie Stopes, the eugenicist. Abortion advocate Stopes, a heroine of feminists, disapproved of the marriage because Mary was short-sighted and she feared any grandchildren would have the same condition. Such was her disapproval of the match that she cut her son out of her will.

DIANA, PRINCESS OF WALES
60 Colherne Court, Old Brompton Road, London SW5 0EF
Telephone: 01-373 7462

This three-bedroomed flat in Earls Court was home to Lady Diana Spencer before her Wednesday 29 July 1981 marriage to the Prince of Wales. Coleherne Court, which looks out onto Old Brompton Road. The property was purchased for £50,000 and given to Diana by her divorced parents as a coming-of-age present in July 1979. She furnished it in simple Habitat style and lived there until the night before her engagement to the Prince was announced on Tuesday 24 February 1981, when she moved into Clarence House. Diana once said that the happiest time of her life was spent in Coleherne Court. She had promised her old schoolfriend Carolyn Pride a room when she got a place of her own, and Diana was as good as her word. Sophie Kimball and then Philippa Coaker made up a trio for a while. Anne Bolton and Virginia Pitman then joined Diana and Carolyn. She charged them £18 a week rent and, to remind them whose flat it was, a sign on Diana's bedroom door bore the legend "Chief Chick". She also imposed a strict cleaning rota. After the wedding, Diana's mother, Frances Shand Kydd, sold the flat to Japanese buyers for £100,000, twice the sum she had originally paid for it. It went on sale in May 1998, with the anonymous owners pledging to donate 10 percent of any money paid over the £450,000 asking price to the Diana, Princess of Wales Memorial Fund. An English Heritage blue plaque was placed on the building in September 2021 to mark what would have been Diana's sixtieth birthday.

Chelsea Harbour Club, Watermeadow Lane, London, SW6 2RR
Telephone: 020-73717700

It was here that Diana met Will Carling, the married England rugby captain. They began meeting regularly for coffee to discuss her workout technique, and then began to confide in each other. The *News Of The World* broke the story of the friendship in early August 1995. Carling promised publicly not to see Diana again and said, "It was flattering that the Princess of Wales was interested in me – and that is where I made my mistake." He also apologised for hurting his wife, Julia. In September, Julia announced her separation from her husband, saying, "Recent pressure and tensions have produced this situation… It hurts me very much to face losing my husband in a manner which has become outside my control."

Squidgygate Tape
Diana: Sandringham, Norfolk PE35 6EN
Gilbey: Unknown location in Oxfordshire in a parked car

On Sunday 31 December 1989, the Princess of Wales was chatting at home in Sandringham with her lover James Gilbey, who was on a Cellnet mobile. During the course of the thirty-minute discussion, Diana expressed worries about whether a recent meeting with Gilbey would be discovered. She also discussed a fear of becoming pregnant, referencing an episode of *EastEnders* where a character "had a baby. They thought it was by her husband. It was by another man." Gilbey referred to her as "Darling" fourteen times, and as "Squidgy" or "Squidge" (thought to be a reference to her vagina) fifty-three times. She also showed her ignorance of the meaning of the word heterosexuality (she wondered about the sexuality of Sir Jimmy Savile, the TV personality, see page 263) and the two discussed phone sex. Gilbey asked Diana what she was wearing. On Monday 24 August 1992, *The Sun* published edited extracts from the tape, removing the references to sex.

San Lorenzo, 22 Beauchamp Place, London SW3 1NH
Telephone: 020-75841074

This was one of Diana's favourite restaurants, if not the favourite. Owned and run by Mara and Lorenzo Berni, it opened in 1963. She dined *à deux* here with James Hewitt, and even received mail thanks to Mara's discretion.

St Mary Magadalene Church, Trimdon Village, Trimdon, County Durham TS29 6LA

It was in the grounds of this Grade II listed church that Tony Blair called Diana "the people's princess" at 10.30am, just before the service on Sunday 31 August 1997. He had scribbled notes on the back of an envelope and discussed what he was going to say with Alastair Campbell, his chief spin doctor. While his family went inside the church, Blair addressed the media. He said, "Our thoughts and prayers are with Princess Diana's family – in particular her two sons... We are today a nation in Britain in a state of shock, in mourning, in grief that is so deeply painful for us. She was a wonderful and a warm human being, although her own life was often sadly touched by tragedy. She touched the lives of so many others in Britain and throughout the world with joy and with comfort... How difficult things were for her from time to time, surely we can only guess at, but people everywhere, not just here in Britain but everywhere, kept faith with Princess Diana, they liked her, they loved her, they regarded her as one of the people. She was the people's princess and that is how she will stay, how she will remain in our hearts and our memories forever."

DOODLEBUG
V1: Grove Road, Mile End, London E3

The first V1, Vergeltungswaffe Eins (Vengeance Weapon One) or Doodlebug, fell on London next to a railway bridge on Grove Road at 4.25am on Tuesday 13 June 1944. The Germans launched ten V1s but five of them crash-landed shortly after take-off in Watten, France. One went missing and four reached England, but three of those fell short of their target, falling on Swanscombe, Kent at 4.13am, Cuckfield, Sussex at 4.20am and Platt, near Sevenoaks in Kent at 5.06am. The one that reached London killed six people – Dora Cohen, 55, Connie Day, 32, Willie Rogers, 50, Lennie Sherman, 12, Ellen Woodcraft, 19, and her son, Tom, eight months – badly injuring thirty and leaving 200 homeless. The V1 was designed (as the Fi 103) by Robert Lusser (1899-1969) of the Fieseler Company and Fritz Gosslau (1898-1965) from the Argus Engine Works. It had a top speed of 390mph and a range of around 150 miles, later increased to 250. The V1 was twenty five and a half feet long and weighed 4,800 pounds.

V2: Staveley Road, Chiswick, London W4

On Friday 8 September 1944, the first V2 – Vergeltungswaffe 2 – fell on West London, killing three people, demolishing six houses and leaving a crater thirty feet across and eight feet deep. Faster and bigger than its predecessor, the V2's top speed was 3,580mph with a range of 200 miles. It was forty-six feet long and weighed 27,576lb. The V2 was responsible for the deaths of 2,754 Britons (6,523 were injured) in the closing stages of the Second World War, but this number is dwarfed by the 20,000 slave labourers in Mittelbau-Dora, Germany, who died making the rockets. The last British civilian to be killed by a V2 was Mrs Ivy Millichamp, 34, who died at her home, **88 Kynaston Road, Orpington, Kent BR5 4JZ** at 4.54pm on Tuesday 27 March 1945.

EDWARD VIII, HM KING
Constitution Hill, London SW1A

It was here at noon on Thursday 16 July 1936 that an MI5 informant named George McMahon tried to assassinate King Edward VIII after Trooping the Colour. The King-Emperor had presented colours to three battalions of Guards at Hyde Park and, as he rode back towards Constitution Hill, a man in a brown suit aimed a pistol at him. Alice Lawrence, a housewife, grabbed his arm and a policeman punched him, causing the weapon to fly into the road and land at the horse's feet. Edward rode on unpeturbed. Taken into custody, McMahon was sent for trial at the Old Bailey where he alleged that a foreign country had paid him £150 to kill the King-Emperor and that he had missed deliberately. On Monday 14 September 1936 the jury took ten minutes to convict McMahon of producing a revolver near the person of the King with intent to alarm His Majesty. Sentencing him to twelve months' hard labour, Mr Justice Greaves-Lord said, "I am quite satisfied that you never at any moment had any intention of harming His Majesty. The conclusion that I have come to is that you are one of those misguided persons who think by notoriety they can call attention to their grievances." He was found not guilty of "unlawfully possessing a firearm and ammunition to endanger life" at the judge's direction. Unbeknown to the press and public, McMahon, who lived in a basement flat in Westbourne Terrace, Paddington, left an unpublished autobiography, *He Was My King*. He claimed that the Italian embassy in London had hired him to kill Edward. He had tried to warn MI5 and Home Secretary John Simon, but was ignored. To save the blushes of MI5 and the authorities, the incident was covered. Born at Govan, Lanarkshire, in 1902, McMahon was a petty fraudster and gun runner to Abyssinia, where the Italians offered him money for information about armaments. In late 1935 and early 1936, he had several meetings with MI5. There is a theory that, despite the warnings, MI5 were happy to let McMahon kill Edward and solve the Mrs Simpson problem. McMahon died in 1970. King George V had said, "After I am dead, the boy will ruin himself in twlve months." Sir Alan Lascelles, Edward's secretary, said, "I can't help thinking that the best thing that could happen to him, and to the country, would be for him to break his neck."

Fort Belvedere, Shrubs Hill, Englefield Green, Ascot, Surrey SL5 7SD
Fort Belvedere was built in the 1750s for the Duke of Cumberland, the Butcher of Culloden. It was given to Edward Prince of Wales by his father King George V in 1929. The King-Emperor did not understand why his son wanted "that queer old place? Those damn weekends I suppose." Socialite Lady Diana Cooper (1892-1986) called it "a child's idea of a fort". Edward fell in love with the house and wrote that he had "created a home at the fort just as my father and grandfather had created one at Sandringham... here I spent some of the happiest days of my life." In 1931 and 1932, he spent £21,000 (slightly under £1½million at 2022 values) adding a swimming pool, tennis court, a stable, bathrooms with showers near bedrooms, central heating and a steam room. Edward first entertained Mrs Simpson at the fort at the end of January 1932 and she became a regular weekend guest. She moved in permanently in 1936 after receiving death threats (some orchestrated by the press baron Lord Beaverbrook), and left for the last time on Thursday 3 December to go abroad. In the run-up to her departure, Edward had hosted many meetings with Prime Minister Stanley Baldwin to discuss Mrs Simpson, the twice-divorced American whom the King-Emperor had fallen in love with. On Monday 16 November, Edward summoned Baldwin to Buckingham Palace and told him that he intended to marry Mrs Simpson despite establishment opposition. With Mrs Simpson safely ensconced in France, the establishment thought Edward might give

her up. Baldwin thought the King-Emperor personally a perfectly pleasant fellow, but possibly mad and totally unsuited to the role of king. Eventually the pressure became too much for him and at Belvedere at 10am on Thursday 10 December 1936, King Edward VIII signed the instrument of abdication, after a false start – "There's no ink in the damn pot!" – witnessed by his three younger brothers: Prince Albert, Duke of York, Prince Henry, Duke of Gloucester and Prince George, Duke of Kent, to be "with the woman I love". The eldest son of King George V had been on the throne for only 326 days – King Edward V managed seventy-seven days in 1483. On Friday 11 December, he made a broadcast to the Empire explaining his decision, before retiring to his bedroom where he drank whisky and soda while a servant trimmed the royal toenails.

DID YOU KNOW?
As he left Fort Belvedere, the Duke of Windsor took the visitors' book with him. It was subsequently kept at every home he and the Duchess shared.

Fort Belvedere was mostly unused in the twenty years after Edward abdicated. Filming for the television series *Edward & Mrs Simpson* took place there in 1977. The Honourable Gerald Lascelles (1924–1998), the grandson of King George V and Queen Mary, bought a ninety-nine-year lease on the fort; he reported it was "falling to pieces" and needed extensive renovation. It was reduced from forty rooms to the "equivalent of an eight-bedroom house, including quarters for three or four staff. It will be a very manageable home." In 1976, following his divorce, Lascelles put the house on the market and it was taken on by a son of the Emir of Dubai. It became a listed building on 17 November 1986

FLODDEN, BATTLE OF
Branxton Heath, Northumberland TD12 4SL
It was here between 4pm and 6pm on Friday 9 September 1513 that the Battle of Flodden was fought – the largest battle ever fought between England and Scotland, with 26,000 Englishmen against more than 35,000 Scots. James IV of Scotland (b. at Stirling Castle

17 March 1473) became the last Scottish king to offer battle in England, and the last to die in battle. The English were commanded by the rheumatic 70-year-old Thomas Howard, 1st Earl of Surrey (b. 1443 d. 21 May 1524) while Henry VIII was fighting in France. The weather was wet and stormy which hindered the English archers, as their bow strings became soaked. It also made for poor visibility. The Scots were further hampered because few wore armour and the wet ground made it difficult for them to use their twenty-two-feet pikes. James bravely led his army from the front and was killed near Surrey's coach. More than 10,000 Scots were killed and it was said that there was not one family that had not lost a father, husband or son. They were commemorated in the song *The Flowers Of The Forest*. The battlefield is now fully enclosed, but remains agricultural land.

GREAT FIRE OF LONDON
Pudding Lane, London EC3R 8AB and Pie Corner, London

The Great Fire began on Sunday 2 September 1666 in a house in Pudding Lane belonging to Thomas Farynor, a baker to King Charles II. It burned for three days. It is likely that the fire started because Farynor forgot to extinguish his oven before retiring for the evening; some time shortly after midnight, smouldering embers from the oven set some nearby firewood alight. Farynor managed to get out of the burning building, along with his family, by climbing through an upstairs window. The Farynors' housemaid failed to escape and became the fire's first victim. Within an hour of the fire starting, Sir Thomas Bloodworth, the Lord Mayor of London, was awakened with the news. He was unimpressed however, declaring that "a woman might piss it out". It was one of the biggest calamities in the history of London, destroying 13,200 houses, eighty-seven parish churches, six chapels, forty-four Company Halls, the Royal Exchange, the Custom House, St Paul's Cathedral, Guildhall, the Bridewell Palace and other City prisons, the Session House, four bridges across the rivers Thames and Fleet and three City gates. 100,000 people were made homeless, one sixth of London's inhabitants at that time. While only between nine and sixteen people were reported as having died in the fire, Neil Hanson, in his book *The Dreadful Judgement*, believes the true death toll numbered in the hundreds or even thousands. He believes

most of the fatalities were poor people whose bodies were cremated by
the intense heat and thus never found. The Monument to the Great
Fire is constructed on the site of St Margaret, New Fish Street: the
first church to be destroyed. Standing at the junction of Monument
Street and Fish Street Hill, it is 202 feet high and, if laid on its side,
its tip would touch the point in Pudding Lane where the fire began.
Three hundred and eleven steps lead to the top. When James Boswell
climbed in 1763, he was scared to look down and suffered a panic
attack halfway up. When he reached the summit, he was frightened
that the traffic below "would make the tremendous pile tumble to the
foundation". The monument cost £13,450 11s 9d to build. In 2006,
£790,000 was spent to pedestrianise the area at the bottom.

HEATH, EDWARD
Keyser Ullman, 25 Milk Street, London EC2V 8AN
Telephone: 01-606 7070

In October 1964, Labour won the General Election and Harold
Wilson became Prime Minister. Conservative leader Sir Alec
Douglas-Home altered the party rules for electing the leader: MPs
would now be balloted. On Wednesday 28 July 1965, Edward Heath
was elected the Party's youngest leader, receiving 150 votes and seeing
off the challenges of Reginald Maudling (133 votes) and Enoch Powell
(fifteen votes). Heath led the Tories to defeat in 1966 but won the
Thursday 18 June 1970 General Election with a majority of thirty.
He took the country into the Common Market on Monday 1 January
1973 and into the Three-Day Week a year later when an oil crisis in
the Middle East coincided with a miners' strike. At a Cabinet meeting
on Wednesday 12 December 1973, Chancellor of the Exchequer
Anthony Barber warned that Britain faced "the gravest economic
crisis since the Second World War". The next day, Heath broadcast
to the country and explained that a three-day week would begin on
Monday 31 December. Measures included: television shutting down
at 10.30pm; street lights dimmed to half brightness; offices to be no
warmer than 65°F; a national speed limit of 50mph; no floodlights at
football or other outdoor events. Petrol rationing coupons were issued
but never used. Any breach of the restrictions would be "punishable
by a fine or imprisonment or both". By the end of the first two weeks

of January 1974, the New Zealand High Commission had received more than double the usual number of enquiries about emigrating. Members of the public began calling government offices to report their neighbours for not following the rules. Heath was lucky with the weather – although December was cold, the temperatures in January and February were almost double the average. The Cabinet began talking of a four-day week after mid-January, and even a five-day week for some important industries. The Middle East oil supplies which had been cut by 15 percent were restored in February. On Thursday 7 February 1974, Heath called a General Election to decide "who governs Britain". Britain decided that it was not the Tories and at the end of the month Harold Wilson returned to Number 10, albeit with a minority administration. In a bid to win public support, on his first day of campaigning Heath had dropped the three-day week and television had returned to its normal schedules. However, rather than galvanising support, people were left puzzled and wondering why the Tories were going to the country if the crisis was over. Wilson was unable to govern without a majority and called another election in October 1974, this time winning with a majority of three. Heath continued as leader but was losing the confidence of his party; on Thursday 17 October 1974, he wrote to the Chairman of the 1922 Committee Sir Edward du Cann (1924-2017) to see how the party would progress in opposition. Before that could happen, du Cann held a meeting of the pre-election committee of the 1922 at his home at **5 Lord North Street, London SW1**. Du Cann then went to see Heath and told him the committee had decided that he had to go. The Tory leader replied that the committee had no authority to make such a decision as it needed to be re-elected first. A second meeting took place at this address, the office of the merchant bank Keyser Ullman (1868-1981), where du Cann had been chairman from 1970 until 1975. Due to the street name, the attending MPs were nicknamed the "Milk Street mafia" by the *Evening Standard*. On Sunday 3 November, the 1922 Committee was re-elected and by Thursday 7 November, Heath had completed a reshuffle of his Shadow Cabinet. He agreed to a revision of the rules on electing a leader and, on Monday 25 November, Margaret Thatcher (see page 64) went to see Heath to tell him she was standing against him. He replied, "You'll lose"

– said to be the last words they exchanged. Four days earlier, Sir Keith Joseph, the favourite to take over from Heath, announced he would not stand, having blotted his copybook with some intemperate remarks that working class women should stop breeding to improve national stock. On Sunday 22 December 1974, Heath's three-storey, eight-room rented Georgian home at **17 Wilton Street, Belgravia, London SW1X 7AX** was bombed by the IRA. He was late back from a Christmas carol concert in Broadstairs and missed the attack by five minutes. The leadership election took place on Tuesday 4 February 1975 and Heath scored 119 votes to Mrs Thatcher's 130, with Hugh Fraser limping home with just sixteen. Heath immediately announced he would not stand in a second ballot. He refused to serve in Mrs Thatcher's Shadow Cabinet and rebuffed her offer to make him Ambassador to the United States when she became Prime Minister in May 1979. Thus began the Great Sulk – Heath's remaining time in the Commons – and when Mrs Thatcher was deposed in November 1990, he said, "Rejoice! Rejoice!"

HESS, RUDOLF
field next to Humbie Road, Eaglesham, Glasgow G76 0PT

Adolf Hitler's Egyptian-born deputy flew a Messerschmidt ME110 from Augsburg to the United Kingdom at 5.45pm on Saturday 10 May 1941 in a peace bid, and bailed out of his plane at 11.06pm; the plane crashed three minutes later, twelve miles west of **Dungavel House, Strathaven ML10 6RF**, the summer retreat of the dukes of Hamilton. Davy Maclean of Floors Farm Cottage, a local ploughman supposedly armed with a Welland Vale pitchfork, met Hess, who asked to see Douglas Douglas-Hamilton, the 14th Duke of Hamilton, hoping that the Eton and Balliol, Oxford-educated nobleman, a close friend since 1936 and known to have right-wing views, would arrange for him to meet King George VI. Hess believed he could persuade the King to sack Churchill and make peace in order to join forces against the Soviet Union. When he heard the news, Hitler was quick to issue a statement, pointing out "Hess did not fly in my name." Albert Speer, who was with Hitler when he heard the news, later reported that "what bothered him was the fact that Churchill might use the incident to pretend to Germany's allies that Hitler was extending a peace feeler".

Hess was taken away by the Busby Home Guard and then kept in the Tower of London until his trial at Nuremberg in October 1946. He was found guilty of actively supporting preparations for war and in participating in the aggression against Poland and Czechoslovakia. He was sentenced to life imprisonment and was still in Spandau Prison when he was found dead on Monday 17 August 1987. Officially, he committed suicide but grave doubts have been raised about the possibility of an arthritic 93-year-old in poor health being able to hang himself with an electrical extension cord without outside help. The Duke of Hamilton died in Edinburgh on Friday 30 March 1973.

DID YOU KNOW?

A marble and slate memorial stone was erected in 1993 by the Rudolf Hess Society near the site of the crash, bearing the legend, "This stone marks the spot where brave, heroic Rudolf Hess landed by parachute on the night of 10th May 1941 seeking to end the war between Britain and Germany." It was destroyed on Thursday 18 November 1993 by anti-fascists, before Eastwood District Council could remove it legally.

HURRICANE, FIRST FLIGHT
Brooklands Aerodrome, Brooklands Road, Weybridge, Surrey KT13 0SL

The aeroplane that was overshadowed in the public mind by the Spitfire in the Battle of Britain had its premiere flight on the morning of Wednesday 6 November 1935, flown by Paul Ward Spencer "George" Bulman (b. at Luton, Bedfordshire 8 April 1896 d. at Surrey Monday 6 May 1963), who was Hawker Aircraft's chief test pilot. He thought the plane flew comfortably. On Saturday 27 June 1936, the silver plane was named Hurricane. The aircraft was designed by (Sir) Sydney Camm (b. at 10 Alma Road, Windsor, Berkshire 5 August 1893 d. playing golf at Richmond Golf Club, Sudbrook Park, Sudbrook Lane, Surrey TW10 7AS Saturday 12 March 1966). The Air Ministry began using the Hurricane from December 1937. By September 1939 and the outbreak of war, the RAF had eighteen Hurricane-equipped squadrons in service, with 550 aircraft. It had a top speed of 318mph at 15,500 feet. The last Hurricanes left RAF service on Wednesday 15 January 1947.

INVASION OF BRITAIN, LAST
Llanwnda, Pembrokeshire SA64

It was here on Wednesday 22 February 1797 that General William Tate, a septuagenarian Irish-American, led the last invasion of mainland Britain. Commanding four ships and 1,400 men, Tate was sent by the French revolutionary government to foment revolution in Britain. His orders were to destroy Bristol and then march north and capture Chester and Liverpool. However, poor weather forced him to head for Fishguard where he was met by a single cannon report, which the locals used as an alarm signal. Believing himself to be under attack, Tate withdrew and sailed on until he found a beach at Llanwnda, where his men disembarked while their ships returned to France. Rather than wreaking havoc in Wales, the men enjoyed themselves with wine and eating local poultry. The invasion was defeated not by Lord Cawdor's 750 men but by the sight of several hundred local women wearing tall black felt hats and traditional scarlet cloaks, looking like very tall Redcoats. Tate surrendered at 2pm on Friday 24 February on the Goodwick Sands.

KELLY, DR DAVID
found dead at Harrowdown Hill, Longworth, Oxfordshire OX13

David Christopher Kelly (born at Llwynypia Hospital, Llwynypia, Glamorgan Sunday 14 May 1944) was a government scientist who was thrust into the public spotlight when the Ministry of Defence let it be known that he was the source for a report by BBC reporter Andrew Gilligan about Iraqi weapons of mass destruction broadcast on Radio 4 on Thursday 29 May 2003, a week after he had met Dr Kelly at the **Charing Cross Hotel, Strand, London WC2N 5HX**. Prime Minister Tony Blair had claimed that Iraq had weapons that could be launched in forty-five minutes; Dr Kelly expressed his doubts to Gilligan, as well as over the claims that Iraq possessed biological weapons. Gilligan said that the government had "sexed up" the dossier by including the forty-five minute claim while aware of its doubtful veracity. Gilligan also published an article in *The Mail On Sunday* on 1 June accusing Alastair Campbell, Blair's Director of Communications and Strategy, of insisting that the forty-five minute claim be included. The government demanded to know

Gilligan's source and the BBC stood by their story. At the end of June, Dr Kelly told his bosses that although he had met Gilligan, he was "convinced that I am not his primary source of information". When Dr Kelly was identified by journalists after an indiscreet Government statement, he was summonsed to appear before the House of Commons Foreign Affairs Select Committee on Tuesday 15 July and the Intelligence and Security Committee the following day. Dr Kelly faced extremely hostile questioning and his voice was so subdued that the air conditioning had to be turned off for him to be heard. He confessed to meeting Gilligan but denied saying what the journalist had reported. At 9am on Thursday 17 July, Dr Kelly was at his desk at his home, **Westfield, Faringdon Road, Southmoor, Abingdon, Oxfordshire OX13 5BH.** At 11am he took a brief coffee break and, getting back to his desk, sent eight jocular emails to friends and said that he was looking forward to his daughter's wedding and to returning to Iraq the following week. At some point during the morning, he received a telephone call and his mood darkened. At 12.30pm, he went to his sitting room and sat there in silence. Janice Kelly made her husband some sandwiches for lunch, which were eaten in silence. After lunch, Mrs Kelly went upstairs for a nap. Just before 3pm, the telephone rang and Mrs Kelly got up to answer it but when she went downstairs, her husband was talking on it. She went back to bed. When she went downstairs at 3.20pm, her husband had gone out – she never saw him alive again. The following day at 9.20am, two search volunteers found him under a tree, having committed suicide by cutting his left wrist and over-dosing on twenty-nine of his wife Janice's co-Proxamol painkillers. The next day, Tony Blair ordered an enquiry into the death under the chairmanship of Lord Hutton. The eventual report, published on Wednesday 28 January 2004, ran to 700 pages. Lord Hutton cleared the Government and Alastair Campbell of Gilligan's claim they had included the forty-five-minute claim despite knowing it was incorrect. The BBC was heavily criticised and chairman Gavyn Davies resigned, followed two days later by Director-General Greg Dyke and Gilligan. Many do not believe the official verdict regarding the circumstances of Dr Kelly's death; the establishment was not helped by the Hutton Report's insistence that Dr Kelly's post mortem results be kept secret for seventy years. At least two books have been written to date, claiming that the true details behind the scientist's death were covered up. Dr Kelly left £176,142.

LABOUR PARTY
Congregational Memorial Hall, 14 Farringdon Street
(now 5 Fleet Place), London EC4

Britain has always been a two-party state – one conservative and one radical. The Labour Party was formed at the beginning of the twentieth century and slowly began to replace the Liberals as the radical party. Prior to that, the Liberals had tried to embrace the new party in the hopes of not losing its own place. In a by-election on Thursday 17 February 1870 at Southwark, trade unionist George Odger (1813-1877) was the first Lib-Lab candidate, and lost to the Conservatives by only 304 votes. The Representation of the People Act 1884 increased suffrage but still left forty percent of men and all women without a vote. At the 1895 General Election, the Independent Labour Party put up twenty-eight candidates but won only 44,325 votes. Party leader Keir Hardie thought combining all the left-wing parties was the only way to achieve electoral success. The Labour Party as we know it was formed here on Monday 26 and Tuesday 27 February 1900. Two Labour Representative Committee – as it was then called – MPs were elected at the General Election in autumn 1900: Keir Hardie in Merthyr Tydfil and Richard Bell in Derby. It was a start. The Congregational Memorial Hall was built upon the site of the Fleet Prison in Farringdon Street. It opened in 1875 and was demolished in 1968.

LAWRENCE OF ARABIA
Tank Park Road, Bovington, Dorset BH20

Thomas Edward "Ned" Chapman was born at Woodlands, Tremadoc, Caernarvonshire in the early hours of Thursday 16 August 1888, the illegitimate second son of Eton-educated Sir Thomas Robert Tighe Chapman (b. at Delvin, County Westmeath, Ireland Friday 6 November 1846 d. at Oxford Tuesday 8 April 1919), a married Anglo-Irish landowner, and his mistress Sarah Junner (b. at Sunderland, County Durham Saturday 31 August

1861 buried at Oxford Thursday 19 November 1959, aged 98). The couple adopted the name Lawrence in 1887. Young Ned grew up to be a war hero, although he semi-fictionalised many of his exploits. During the First World War, he fought in the Middle East alongside King Feisal (from November 1916, he was permanently attached to him as a liaison officer, advising on strategy). On Wednesday 21 November 1917, Lawrence was captured during a raid in Deraa while in disguise and, after being identified, was flogged and raped. Lawrence told the tale in 1919 but his description has split biographers – some believe him while others doubt his story. Awarded the DSO in January 1918, in April of that year he wore women's clothes during a brief reconnaissance into the garrison town of Amman. On Tuesday 1 October 1918, he arrived in Damascus in a Rolls-Royce but was unable to maintain order; the Army arrived the next day and restored peace. Lawrence was utterly despondent when the area was carved up after the war, believing he had misled the Arabs. The creation of the legend of Lawrence began in August 1919 when the American journalist Lowell Thomas presented *With Allenby In Palestine* and *Lawrence In Arabia* at the Royal Opera House, London. Thomas referred to Lawrence as "The Uncrowned King of Arabia". Modest Lawrence was faintly embarrassed by Thomas's verbiage but privately loved it, believing it would help him lobby for the Arab cause. Lawrence went to the Versailles Conference in 1919 as Feisal's adviser and translator. On Wednesday 30 August 1922, Lawrence joined the RAF using the nom de guerre John Hume Ross at the recruiting centre on **4 Henrietta Street, London WC2 (Telephone: REGent 2755)**. The recruiting officer was Captain W.E. Johns, the author of the Biggles adventure series for boys. The enrolment was an accepted fiction – it was known who Ross was and his references were obviously forged, but after being rejected he returned with a letter signed by Lord Trenchard, the Chief of Air Staff. On Wednesday 27 December 1922, his deception was uncovered by the *Daily Express* and he left the Air Force in January 1923. On Monday 12 March 1923, he enlisted in the tank corps as 7875698 Private T.E. Shaw. In August 1925, following threats of suicide, Lawrence rejoined the RAF, where he remained until February 1935. In September 1923, Lawrence moved into a tiny cottage, **Clouds Hill, King George V Road, Bovington, Dorset BH20 7NQ**, buying the property for £450 (£30,460 at 2022 values) in 1929. By the spring of 1935, Lawrence was happy at Cloud Hills and began inviting friends to stay. He had matching sleeping bags, his marked Meum, his guest's Tuum. On Saturday 11 May 1935, Lawrence received a letter from Henry Williamson (1895-1977), the author of *Tarka The Otter* (1927), who said that he would be driving to London from Devon on 14 May and wanted to call in on Lawrence, unless it was raining. At 10.30am on Monday 13 May 1935, Lawrence set off to Wool's post office to send a telegram to Williamson which read, "Lunch Tuesday wet fine cottage one mile north Bovington Camp – Shaw." He also sent a package of books to Jock Chambers in London. On the way back, Lawrence was riding his Brough Superior GW2275 motocycle (which he had named Boanerges after the sons of thunder in the Bible) when, travelling at about 50-60mph, he swerved to avoid two 14-year-old boys, Frank Fletcher and Bertie Hargraves. As he went past, he clipped the back wheel of Hargraves's bicycle and went over the top of the handlebars. He hit his head and was knocked out. Lawrence remained unconscious at Wool Military Hospital, Bovington Camp, Dorset until his death aged 46 at 8.25am on Sunday 19 May 1935. Had he recovered, he would have been almost completely paralysed and lost his memory. Oddly, the only witness to the accident was Corporal Ernest Catchpole of the Royal Army Ordinance Corps who had been walking his dog; he was warned not to mention a black car he had seen at the time. Odder still, Catchpole committed suicide on Wednesday 10 July 1940 while serving in Egypt. The boys' fathers were told to keep their sons quiet about what they had seen. Lawrence's funeral was at 2.30pm on Tuesday 21 May 1935 in **St Nicholas's Churchyard, Moreton, Dorchester, Dorset DT2 8RH**. Among the mourners were Winston Churchill, Mrs Thomas Hardy, Nancy Astor, Jonathan Cape, Basil Liddell Hart, Augustus John and Siegfried Sassoon. Lawrence left £7,441 9s (£566,711 at 2022 values).

DID YOU KNOW?

Noël Coward gently mocked Lawrence's desire for privacy, writing to him on Friday 15 August 1930, "Dear 338171, may I call you 338?"

MANDELSON, PETER
1 Brick End Cottage (now Lower Stephlands Cottage), Foy, Ross-on-Wye, Herefordshire HR9 6QZ

For eight years, this three-bedroom cottage belonged to Labour politician Peter Mandelson and it was here that he spotted the tightly furled bud that inspired New Labour's red rose symbol. Mandelson, his then boyfriend Peter Ashby, a freelance writer, and Sue Robertson, the education secretary of the British Young Communists, bought the cottage from local farmer Jim Williams for £36,000 in 1984. Mandelson spent weekends at Foy. Gwen Meek bought the house from Mandeson in 1992 for £70,000, after haggling him down £20,000. It was last sold on Friday 20 June 1997, a month after New Labour's landslide, for £89,850. Even in 2018, Foy had no pub, no shop, no wine bar or private members' club – but it is perfect if you like bird watching, canoeing, fishing, walking or horse-riding. Mandelson sold the cottage to buy his constituency home at **30 Hutton Avenue, Hartlepool, County Durham TS26 9PN**.

9 Northumberland Place, Notting Hill, London W2 5BS

Despite his election as MP for Hartlepool on Thursday 9 April 1992, Mandelson was not a household name outside the world of political anoraks. In 1982, he went to work at London Weekend Television as a researcher on *The London Programme*. He left in 1985 to work for Labour leader Neil Kinnock as the party's Director of Campaigns and Communications. He held the job for five years until the two men's relationship weakened. The next Labour leader John Smith did not rate Mandelson highly and eschewed his talents. When Smith died, two young Labour MPs were spoken of as his successor: Gordon Brown and Tony Blair. Mandelson was a friend of both and decided to back Blair (see Blair-Brown Pact, page 36). Along with Blair, Brown, Alastair Campbell and Philip Gould, Mandelson was an architect of the New Labour movement, preparing for what was regarded as an inevitable Labour win in the 1997 General Election. Despite their closeness, Blair did not appoint Mandelson to a senior position, making him Minister Without Portfolio in the Cabinet Office: his hands were tied by Labour Party rules that meant the Shadow Cabinet had to be given the same roles in Government that they had occupied in opposition. Blair reshuffled his Cabinet the following year and, on 27 July 1998, Mandelson became

Secretary of State for Trade and Industry. He described his five months at the DTI as "in many ways the most fulfilling I had spent in politics", but it was all to come tumbling down. In 1992, Mandelson had bought a small home at **Flat 3, 18-21 Wilmington Square, Clerkenwell, London WC1X 0ER**, but as he moved up the political ladder, he decided he needed a bigger place. In May 1996, Mandelson had dinner at fellow MP Geoffrey Robinson's penthouse apartment at the **Grosvenor House Hotel, 86-90 Park Lane, London W1K 7TN**. As a result, Robinson agreed to loan Mandeleson £373,000 to buy a three-storey house in Northumberland Place, Notting Hill. Mandelson paid £465,000 in total for the house on Wednesday 23 October 1996. The solicitor who handled the sale was Stephen Wegg-Prosser, the father of Mandelson's bespectacled young assistant Benjamin Wegg-Prosser. Mandelson decided not to tell Blair, Anthony Phillipson, his then Principal Private Secretary, or the Britannia Building Society, his mortgage lender. Somewhat ungratefully, Mandelson did not invite his benefactor to the house-warming party. He took great joy in his new home, being photographed by Lord Snowdon for *Vogue* sitting on a tanned leather Balzac chair that cost £1,800. A makeover costing £50,000 was undertaken and original features were ripped out, leaving "a shrine of soulless minimalism". On the evening of Wednesday 16 December 1998, Mandelson was informed by Wegg-Prosser that a new biography of him by *Daily Mirror* journalist Paul Routledge would reveal the loan. "I think this could be trouble for you," said Wegg-Prosser. Mandelson rang the Permanent Secretary at the DTI, Sir Michael Scholar, but could not bring himself to tell Blair, so Wegg-Prosser rang Campbell. Both Blair and Campbell expressed horror at Mandelson's naïveté and on 23 December, Blair sacked his loyal lieutenant. On Wednesday 9 June 1999, Mandelson sold the three-bedroom house for £772,650.

PEEL, SIR ROBERT
Constitution Hill, London SW1A

At 11am on Saturday 29 June 1850, the former Conservative Prime Minister Sir Robert Peel attended a meeting about the forthcoming 1851 Great Exhibition. The meeting went on until 3pm and, when he returned home, he briefly worked in his study before going out for his usual ride at about 5pm. Sir Robert mounted an 8-year-old horse that had been bought recently; he had been warned the horse was temperamental but had ridden it for eight weeks without incident so ignored the caveats. After a visit to Buckingham Palace where he signed the visitors' book, Sir Robert rode the horse up Constitution Hill towards Hyde Park Corner. Near the top, he saw two young women he knew but had barely said hello when his horse began to buck, throwing him over its head while he was still holding the reins. The horse then fell onto the politician, its knees striking his back. Various bystanders rushed over to help, one offering her carriage to take Peel home to **4 Whitehall Gardens, Middlesex SW1A 2DD**. He was barely conscious, but revived when he reached home and was carried into the dining room where he was placed on the table supported by cushions and a water mattress. It was discovered that he had a fractured left collar bone and severe bruising. At 7pm, a press release was issued stating that Sir Robert had suffered a serious fall. When there was no improvement the following day, it became apparent he had a severe internal haemorrhage. Leeches and a mercury treatment were applied that evening but his condition worsened and on the Sunday he lapsed into delirium. As the news spread, many people came to visit or mounted a vigil outside. The police placed a guard at both ends of Whitehall Gardens to divert traffic and issue health bulletins. A journalist for the *Illustrated London News* called the crowd a "guard of honour accorded to the last hours of Sir Robert Peel – by the people". On Tuesday 2 July, Sir Robert rallied and ate some food for the first time since the accident. Supported on both sides, he walked around his dining room, but within two hours, his condition worsened and he fell unconscious once more. The doctors told the family that there was no hope and one by one they came into to say their goodbyes. Sir Robert Peel – twice Prime Minister, twice Home Secretary, the founder of the modern Conservative Party and the Metropolitan Police Force and the last Prime Minister not to be photographed – died at 11.09pm. He was 62 years old.

PERCEVAL, SPENCER, ASSASSINATION OF
Lobby of the House of Commons, Westminster, London SW1A 0AA
It was here that Spencer Perceval became the only British Prime Minister to be assassinated. Perceval assumed office on Wednesday 4 October 1809 after the Duke of Portland suffered a stroke. Born the seventh son of the 2nd Earl of Egmont, Perceval was educated at

Trinity College, Cambridge; he married his sister-in-law's older sister against family wishes and fathered thirteen children (twelve lived to adulthood). He was called to the Bar when he was 33 but sought a life in politics, becoming an MP on Monday 9 May 1796. It was a year before he made his maiden speech. On Thursday 26 March 1807, the Duke of Portland appointed him Chancellor of the Exchequer, although the Home Department was his preferred berth. When he moved into Number 10, he asked five colleagues to be his Chancellor and all five turned him down, which meant he had to combine the jobs of Prime Minister and Chancellor. Most of the Cabinet sat in the Lords and at one stage there was only one other minister on the Treasury Bench. At 5.15pm on Monday 11 May 1812, as he walked in the lobby of the House of Commons, Perceval was shot in the chest by John Bellingham, a mentally unbalanced salesman. On Saturday 16 May, Perceval was buried in Lord Egmont's family vault at St Luke's, Charlton, near to his birthplace. Bellingham was tried and condemned to death, his plea of insanity being rejected. On Monday 18 May 1812, he was hanged at Newgate Prison.

POWELL, ENOCH, "RIVERS OF BLOOD" SPEECH
Midland Hotel, 126 New Street, Birmingham B2 4JQ
Regarded as one of the most brilliant minds of his generation, it was here on Saturday 20 April 1968 that Enoch Powell's political career came to an abrupt end. At 2.30pm, he gave what was later called the "Rivers of Blood" speech (Powell referred to it as "the Birmingham speech") to the Conservative Political Centre, in which he warned of the perils of unchecked immigration from the Commonwealth. He said, "We must be mad, literally mad, as a nation to be permitting the annual inflow of some 50,000 dependants, who are for the most part the material of the future growth of the immigrant descended population. It is like watching a nation busily engaged in heaping up its own funeral pyre. So insane are we that we actually permit unmarried persons to immigrate for the purpose of founding a family with spouses and fiancées whom they have never seen… As I look ahead, I am filled with foreboding. Like the Roman, I seem to see 'the River Tiber foaming with much blood'. That tragic and intractable phenomenon, which we watch with horror on the other side of the

Atlantic but which there is interwoven with the history and existence of the States itself, is coming upon us here by our own volition and our own neglect. Indeed, it has all but come. In numerical terms, it will be of American proportions long before the end of the century. Only resolute and urgent action will avert it even now. Whether there will be the public will to demand and obtain that action, I do not know. All I know is that to see, and not to speak, would be the great betrayal." Powell referred to one of his constituents in Wolverhampton, the last white person in her street who, after refusing to let rooms to non-whites, was called a racist and had excrement put through her letterbox. The speech caused immediate anger. *The Times* called it "evil", adding, "This is the first time that a serious British politician has appealed to racial hatred in this direct way in our post-war history." Tory leader Ted Heath (see page 48) sacked Powell as Shadow Defence Secretary by telephone (it would be the last time the two men spoke). The public disagreed and Powell received almost 120,000 (predominantly positive) letters, and East End dockers went on strike in support of him. On Monday 22 April, Heath appeared on *Panorama*, telling presenter Robin Day, "I dismissed Mr Powell because I believed his speech was inflammatory and liable to damage race relations. I am determined to do everything I can to prevent racial problems developing into civil strife... I don't believe the great majority of the British people share Mr Powell's way of putting his views in his speech." Powell left the Conservatives in early 1974 in part due to the undemocratic way Heath took Britain into the Common Market, and was elected as the Ulster Unionist MP for South Down on Thursday 10 October 1974. He lost his seat in June 1987 by 731 votes, which was fortunate because he was on an IRA death list and marked for assassination had he been re-elected. John Enoch Powell died aged 85 at 4.30am on Sunday 8 February 1998 at the **King Edward VII Hospital, 5-10 Beaumont Street, Marylebone, London W1G 6AA**. The Midland Hotel is now the Macdonald Burlington Hotel.

RICHARD III, KING, BURIAL SITE OF
Greyfriars Car Park, New Street, Leicester LE1 5NR

The remains of the last Plantaganet king of England were found just two feet beneath the car park of Leicester Council social services in August 2012. Richard was killed at the Battle of Bosworth Field (see page 36) aged just 32 after two years on the throne; the victor, Henry Tudor, became King Henry VII. Richard was buried in the choir of the Greyfriars church which, much later, was covered by a council car park. On Monday 4 February 2013, academics from the University of Leicester revealed in a press conference that DNA had confirmed that the bones were indeed Richard's. In December 2017, the location was given ancient monument status by Historic England. His bones were interred in Leicester Cathedral in March 2015.

SECOND WORLD WAR FATALITY, FIRST
Harley Street, London W1
On Sunday 3 September 1939, the day war was declared on Germany, PC George Southworth was on patrol in Harley Street when he heard an air raid siren. He spotted a light showing in a third-floor window; realising the illumination could be seen by enemy bombers, he banged on the door to tell the owner to "put that light out". When he got no reply, he shinnied up the drainpipe to reach the room but lost his grip and fell to his death. Ironically, the air raid warning turned out to be a false alarm.

SECOND WORLD WAR PARLIAMENT
Church House, Great Smith Street, Westminster, London SW1P 3NZ
On Wednesday 6 November 1940, Prime Minister Winston Churchill announced that the Commons would meet at Church House rather than the Palace of Westminster. MPs were unhappy with the decision and made their feelings known, but on Saturday 10 May 1941, a bomb destroyed the House of Commons chamber. Commissioned in 1902, Sir Herbert Baker designed the present Church House in the 1930s, replacing the original building which was created to commemorate Queen Victoria's 1887 Golden Jubilee. Queen Mary laid the foundation stone on Saturday 26 June 1937, and King George VI officially opened the building on Monday 10 June 1940. The first meetings of both the United Nations Security Council and the United Nations Preparatory Commission both took place in the Hoare Memorial Hall on Tuesday 27 November 1945.

SEDGEMOOR, BATTLE OF
Westonzoyland, Bridgewater, Somerset TA7

The last pitched battle on English soil was fought here at 1.30am on Monday 6 July 1685. James Scott, 1st Duke of Monmouth (1649-1685) was the favourite illegitimate son of King Charles II (1630-1685) and his prostitute mistress Lucy Walter (1630-1658). When Charles died without legitimate issue, his brother James II, a devout Catholic, became king. Monmouth, in exile in Holland, decided to return to take the throne. On Thursday 11 June 1685, he landed on the beach near the Cobb at Lyme Regis, Dorset, with three ships and eighty-three men, and accused James of poisoning Charles and usurping the throne. Within hours, 1,500 anti-Catholic men had rallied to Monmouth. He marched through the West Country and had gathered 3,500 peasants by the time he arrived at Bridgewater. They faced 3,500 fully armed and trained soldiers of the king. The royalists, led by Louis de Duras, 2nd Earl of Feversham (1641-1709) and Lord John Churchill (1650-1722), camped at Westonzoyland. Monmouth decided to mount a surprise attack and managed to get within 150 yards of the royalist camp before one of their guns accidentally discharged and they were discovered. Monmouth's cavalry and infantry both ended up in the same irrigation ditch, where they made easy targets for the royalist marksmen. The royalists picked off the rebels for ninety minutes until Lord Feversham called a halt. The rebels lost 400 men in the battle and a further 1,000 as they tried to flee; the royalists lost just eighty. The captured rebels were tried at Judge Jeffreys's Bloody Assizes: 333 were sentenced to death and 814 to transportation. The day before his execution, Monmouth wrote begging letters to King James II and Queen Mary, pleading for his life, but to no avail. He was beheaded for treason on Wednesday 15 July 1685 on Tower Hill. Despite paying the executioner Jack Ketch six guineas to do the job properly, it took five strokes of the axe plus a butcher's knife to remove his head. After the first stroke inflicted only a flesh wound, Monmouth was said to lift his head in anguish, and, according to diarist John Evelyn, the crowd of onlookers were so angry that "they would have torne" the executioner "in pieces" if not for the heavy guard. It was only realised after the execution that no official portrait existed, so his head was sewn back on and Sir Godfrey Kneller painted his picture.

SPITFIRE, FIRST FLIGHT
Eastleigh Aerodrome, Wide Lane, Southampton SO18 2NL

The Supermarine Spitfire 224 was designed by R.J. Mitchell (1895-1937) after the Air Ministry put out a request for a fighter aeroplane that could reach 250mph. It made its first flight in February 1934, but Mitchell was not pleased with the design. The team worked on the Spitfire 300, but the design was rejected in July 1934. In November that year, Mitchell began another redesign, and a £10,000 contract was signed on Saturday 1 December. The eight-minute maiden flight took place here at 4.35pm on Thursday 5 March 1936 with Captain Joseph "Mutt" Summers, the 32-year-old chief test pilot for Vickers, at the controls. After more modifications, the Air Ministry ordered 310 Spitfires on Wednesday 3 June 1936. The public first saw the Spitfire at the RAF Hendon air display on Saturday 27 June. Full production did not begin until 1938 and the plane entered service on Thursday 4 August 1938 when 19 Squadron, Duxford took delivery.

THATCHER, MARGARET
19 Flood Street, Chelsea, London SW3 5ST

Britain's first woman prime minister lived here when she was elected the first woman leader of a major British political party. The Thatchers bought the house in 1967 and sold it in 1986. The three-storey house, worth about £28,000 when they bought it, has four bedrooms, three reception rooms and parking space to the rear. Mrs Thatcher led the Conservative Party to three election victories before being toppled by her colleagues because of her opposition to the European Union and not, as is usually thought, the Poll Tax. On Thursday 23 November 1989, the little known pro-European backbench MP Sir Anthony Meyer stood against her for the party leadership but was easily defeated on Tuesday 5 December by 314 votes to 33 (although 27 abstained). The following year, discontent continued to grow within the party and on Thursday 1 November, Deputy Prime Minister Sir Geoffrey Howe, the last remaining member of Mrs Thatcher's original 1979 Cabinet, resigned over her refusal to lay out a timetable for joining the European Exchange Rate Mechanism, giving a devastating resignation speech in the Commons twelve days later. The night before, Monday 12 November, Mrs Thatcher had given a speech at the Lord Mayor's Banquet at Guildhall in the City of London in which she said, "Since I first went into bat eleven years ago the score at your end has ticked over nicely. You are now the 633rd Lord Mayor. At the Prime Minister's end we are stuck on forty-nine. I am still at the crease, although the bowling has been pretty hostile of late... The bowling is going to be hit all around the ground. That is my style." Howe kept the cricket metaphor going in his resignation statement: "It's rather like sending your opening batsmen to the crease only for them to find the moment that the first balls are bowled that their bats have been broken before the game by the team captain." He finished the speech with, "The time has come for others to consider their own response to the tragic conflict of loyalties with which I myself have wrestled for perhaps too long." The next day, Michael Heseltine, who had left the Cabinet four years earlier over the Westland helicopter affair (the first Cabinet minister to resign during a Cabinet meeting since Joseph Chamberlain and G. O. Trevelyan on Friday 26 March 1886 over home rule for Ireland), threw his hat into the ring. Mrs Thatcher foolishly placed her confidence in the lazy, effete and ineffectual Peter Morrison, her Parliamentary Private Secretary, who took her victory for granted and did not bother to campaign for votes. On Monday 19 November, Alan Clark, the acidic diarist, womaniser and Thatcherite loyalist, found Morrison asleep in his office at the Commons. Morrison told him that arm twisting was counter-productive and that, in any case, he estimated that Heseltine had at most 124 votes. Morrison added that some MPs would abstain in the first ballot to give Mrs Thatcher a fright but would come good in the second. Clark dismissed this strategy as "balls". Some of her other natural allies were not even asked to campaign for her: MP Tristan Garel-Jones, the real Prince of Darkness, later said, "I'd have got the old bat in." Mrs Thatcher completely failed to realise just how dangerous her situation was and went to an unimportant Conference on Security and Co-operation in Europe summit in Paris on the night of the vote (Tuesday 20 November) rather than staying in Westminster. Party rules meant that the winner had to obtain a clear majority and a margin of 15 percent of all those entitled to vote – fifty-six votes. Mrs Thatcher failed by just four votes, winning 204 votes to Heseltine's 152, with 16 MPs spoiling their ballot papers.

In the courtyard of the British Embassy where she was staying, she told journalists that she intended to let her name go forward for the next ballot. Back in London, however, Mrs Thatcher made another mistake when she assembled her Cabinet. Rather than holding a joint meeting at which, perhaps, they could have been cajoled into a display of mass public support, she saw them individually; each minister told her that although he would support her, he did not think that she could win and did not want to see her humiliated. However, Heseltine lost the party leadership contest to John Major, although he was given the position of Deputy Prime Minister and President of the Board of Trade as a sop.

Grand Hotel, 97-99 Kings Road, Brighton, East Sussex BN1 2FW

Each autumn the major political parties gather for their annual conference, usually at a seaside venue; the Conservatives chose Brighton in 1984. The Party bigwigs, apparatchiks and faithful decamped to the seaside town and the Tory grandees booked into the Grand Hotel. Unbeknown to them, the IRA was planning a murderous campaign to assassinate the Prime Minister and Cabinet, aiming to plunge the country into political chaos and force it out of Northern Ireland. Patrick Magee had planted a bomb under the bath in his room (629) in the hotel when he stayed there on the weekend of 14-17 September under the name Roy Walsh. On Friday 12 October at 2.54am, Mrs Thatcher was in her suite at the Grand when the bomb exploded. Ten minutes earlier, she had finished her conference speech with speechwriter Ronnie Millar and John Selwyn Gummer, the Party Chairman. As they left, Robin Butler came in with a last letter to sign. Had it not been for that, Mrs Thatcher might have been seriously injured or even killed, as her bathroom was wrecked. Her sitting room and bedroom escaped damage. The news came through that five people had been killed, including Roberta Wakeham, the wife of Chief Whip John Wakeham, and Sir Anthony Berry, the member for Enfield Southgate. Norman Tebbit was badly injured and his wife, Margaret, paralysed for life. At an impromptu press conference, Mrs Thatcher insisted that the conference should begin as scheduled. Tory party treasurer Lord McAlpine (1942-2014) persuaded Marks & Spencer to open early at 8am so those whose clothes had been destroyed could buy new ones. The hotel reopened on Thursday 28 August 1986. Patrick Magee was arrested in Glasgow in 1985 and, in September 1986, received eight life sentences with a recommendation that he serve at least thirty-five years. As with so many other thugs, terrorists and murderers, Magee was freed under the Good Friday Agreement in 1999.

VICTORIA, HM QUEEN
Constitution Hill, London SW1A

It was on this road that connects the western end of The Mall with Hyde Park Corner, bordered by Green Park to the north and Buckingham Palace Gardens to the south, that three assassination attempts were made on the life of Queen Victoria. The first was in 1840 by Edward Oxford, a manic depressive with a violent temper. He was unable to keep a job and was sacked on 30 April 1840 from the Hog In The Pound pub on Oxford Street because of his hysterical laughter, which upset the customers. He was given £5, three months' wages; four days later, he spent £2 of it on pistols. He then spent time practising his shooting and reading novels about seafaring, but would fly into a rage if interrupted. On Wednesday 3 June, he went to buy some percussion caps and gunpowder at a shop at **10 Westminster Bridge Road, Lambeth, London SE1 7QX,** but finding they only sold gunpowder in large tubs, he then went to a different emporium on Parliament Street because he only wanted a quarter of a pound. A week later, Oxford told his sister Susannah after an early dinner that he was going to the shooting gallery. With a pistol in each trouser pocket, Oxford went to a coffee shop to check the *Court Circular* to ensure Victoria's presence, drinking the coffee but leaving without paying. He hung around Marble Arch (then in its original position as the gate leading to Buckingham Palace) before making his way up Constitution Hill. At around 6pm, Victoria and Albert left the Palace in a low carriage that left them entirely visible. Crowds clapped and waved and the future artist John Everett Millais, then 11, standing with his brother and father, doffed his cap and was pleased when the Queen bowed to him. Standing six paces from them, Oxford raised his gun and fired at the royal couple. Victoria was looking the other way and did not see her would-be assassin. Expecting the Queen to be terrified, Oxford was momentarily at a loss; Albert began to dismount until he saw a second pistol and thought better of this folly. When

Victoria spotted Oxford, she pulled Albert to her but the carriage stopped, awaiting instructions. As the crowd descended on Oxford, Albert finally told the carriage driver to get them out of there, but the carriage went forward rather than turning around and heading for the safety of the Palace. The move did the couple an enormous amount of good, as it showed they had confidence in the public, which was returned to them in spades. The couple went to Victoria's mother's house in Belgrave Square to tell her the news before resuming their carriage ride. On the second day of his Old Bailey trial, which began on 9 July, Oxford was found not guilty by reason of insanity. The guns had contained no bullets, only gunpowder. Oxford was ordered to be held "until Her Majesty's pleasure be known" and sent to the State Criminal Lunatic Asylum in Bethlem, Southwark, where he stayed for the next twenty-four years. He was moved to Broadmoor in 1864. He was released on condition that he go overseas and lived out his life in Melbourne, Australia under the name John Freeman. He died on Monday 23 April 1900, five days after his 78th birthday. The second assassination attempt was made two years later. John Francis worked in showbusiness with his father in Covent Garden until 1841, when the two men fell out. On 14 July 1841, he was arrested for stealing more than thirty-two sovereigns from an old-aged pensioner, and spent three days in prison before being released for lack of evidence. On Sunday 29 May 1842, the Queen was being driven up The Mall after returning from a church service when Francis pointed a small pistol at her. Accounts vary as to whether he fired or not, but he vanished into Green Park. The next day, the Queen and Albert took the same route in an attempt to flush out the perpetrator. The royal party set out at 6pm, rushing at 11mph with the equerries crowding the carriage. Victoria and Albert did not wave to or acknowledge the crowds as was their wont. As the carriage approached Buckingham Palace, a gunshot rang out. The shot missed but a policeman, William Trounce, and Henry Allen, a private in the Scots Fusilier Guards, pounced on Francis. He was questioned from 8pm until 10pm that night before being taken to the cells and was returned to Whitehall the next day for further questioning. He was charged with high treason and put in a cab to Newgate. Francis went on trial at the Old Bailey on Friday 17 June, the prosecution being led Attorney

General Frederick Pollock, Solicitor General William Webb Follett and three other senior lawyers. After thirty minutes of deliberation, the jury found him guilty of two out of three charges, including high treason. Chief Justice Nicholas Tindal then donned the black cap and sentenced Francis to death: "afterwards your head be severed from your body, and your body divided into four quarters, and be disposed of as Her Majesty may think fit". Francis collapsed in tears, fainted and had to be dragged away by the warders. On Saturday 1 July, the sentence was commuted to transportation for life with hard labour. In August 1856, Francis was freed on condition he never returned to England; he died aged 63 in 1885. Seven years later, unemployed Irishman William Hamilton became the third would-be assassin on Constitution Hill. Around 6.20pm on Thursday 19 May 1849, Prince Albert and an equerry returned to Buckingham Palace as Hamilton was standing at the bottom of the hill. The royal carriage was not far behind; as it approached, Hamilton asked the woman standing next to him if it was the Queen. When she said yes, he pulled out a pistol and fired. The Queen saw the outstretched arm and told the carriage driver to stop, giving Hamilton a better target. When she asked a servant what had happened, he replied, "Your Majesty has been shot at." The Queen sat down and told the driver to move on. George Mulder, Green Park's head keeper, grabbed Hamilton, but when many in the crowd, assuming Victoria had been assassinated, called for Hamilton to be killed, he was quickly bundled into a cab and taken to a police station. At 10am on 14 June, Hamilton pleaded guilty at the Old Bailey and was sentenced to seven years' transportation. He was freed from prison in Australia in August 1854 and vanished into obscurity.

WILSON PLOT
2 Kinnerton Street, London SW1X 8AE

It was here, Lord Mountbatten's Knightsbridge home, on Wednesday 8 May 1968 that Mountbatten, the press barons Cecil Harmsworth King and Hugh Cudlipp, and Sir Solly Zuckerman, the chief scientific adviser to the government, held a meeting about deposing Prime Minister Harold Wilson and placing Mountbatten at the head of a military government. King was convinced that Wilson was leading the country to anarchy and civil war and that only a cabal of business leaders, politicians and soldiers could prevent the coming storm, saying that Wilson was "a liar, an untrustworthy man and ruining the country". He believed that the Labour Party would collapse but did not see the Conservatives as a viable alternative after leader Edward Heath sacked Enoch Powell (see page 60). While on a business trip to France, King went to see Sir Oswald Mosley on Tuesday 23 April 1968 to sound him out about leading a military-led government. Although he described Mosley as "a most fascinating man", he decided he was not right to be the dictator of Britain. He turned to Mountbatten, who he believed that, as both a member of the royal family and a former chief of the defence staff, would be able to command public support as leader of a non-democratic government. Mountbatten insisted that Zuckerman should be present at the meeting. (For his part, Zuckerman later claimed that he was urged to attend by Mountbatten's son-in-law, Lord Brabourne, who was worried about King's influence over Mountbatten.) After King explained his view that the country was headed toward civil collapse, he asked Mountbatten if he would be willing to head an emergency government. The accounts of Mountbatten, King and Cudlipp tally: Zuckerman's does not. All agree that Zuckerman left early but differ as to why. King claimed that Zuckerman left in embarrassment after Mountbatten described him as one the "greatest brains in the world". According to Zuckerman, he said that the idea was treachery and told Mountbatten to have nothing to do with it. Mountbatten took his friend's advice and turned down King. Two days later, King published an article in the *Daily Mirror* under his own name entitled "Enough is enough". It read: "Mr Wilson and his Government have lost all credit and we are now threatened with the greatest financial crisis in history. It is not to be resolved by lies about our reserves but only by a fresh start under a fresh leader." The City was aghast and three weeks later, on Thursday 30 May 1968, King was sacked as the head of the International Publishing Corporation. Details of the meeting did not become public until 1975 when they were hinted at in *Private Eye*. Accusations that King was a spy were dismissed by Cudlipp, who claimed he was unable keep a secret. Documents released in the 1990s show that Cecil King had indeed been an agent of British Intelligence.

YORK HRH THE DUKE OF, SPEECH THERAPY OF
146 Harley Street, London W1G 7LF

It was here at 3pm on Tuesday 19 October 1926 that a remarkable friendship began between the second son of HM King George V and an Australian speech therapist. Lionel Logue (b. at College Town, Adelaide, South Australia 26 February 1880) had arrived in England with his wife and three sons in 1924 with no formal qualifications but he helped the Duke of York (later King George VI) to virtually overcome the stammer that had blighted his public appearances. The first appointment card in Logue's tiny writing reveals that the future king was: "Mental: Quite Normal, has an acute nervous tension which has been brought on by the defect. Physical: well built, with good shoulders but waistline very flabby." The visit lasted two hours and Logue commented, "When he left at 5 o'clock, you could see that there was hope once more in his heart." The duke visited the Harley Street practice eighty-two times between October 1926 and December 1927, and Logue was constantly by his side whenever he had to make an important speech as duke and then, from December 1936, as king. The men remained friends until George died on Wednesday 6 February 1952. Queen Elizabeth wrote to Logue, "I know perhaps better than anyone just how much you helped the king, not only with his speech, but through that his whole life & outlook on life. I shall always be deeply grateful to you for all you did for him." Logue, a freemason like the king, died at his home, **68 Princes Court, Brompton Road, Knightsbridge, London SW3**, on Sunday 12 April 1953. The story was told in the film *The King's Speech* (2011), starring Colin Firth as the duke and Geoffrey Rush as the therapist. It contains a number of historic inaccuracies, including: Winston Churchill supporting the Duke of York when he became king, when his allegiance actually lay with King Edward VIII; Logue advising the duke to swear as part of his therapy; crowds gathered outside Buckingham Palace at the end of the Second World War, not the start.

Chapter III
Crime, Murder and Assassination

AITKEN, JONATHAN
Conservative Central Office, 32-34 Smith Square, London SW1P 3EU

It was here that Tory MP Jonathan Aitken held a press conference that would result in him being jailed for perjury. Elected MP for Thanet East (Thanet South from 1983) in 1974, he is the great-nephew of the *Daily Express* proprietor Lord Beaverbrook. Aitken never achieved high office under Margaret Thatcher because, it was said, he made her daughter Carol cry when they were in a relationship. He thrived under her successor John Major and, on Wednesday 20 July 1994, he joined the Cabinet as Chief Secretary to the Treasury, succeeding Michael Portillo. He had earlier been Minister for Defence Procurement and had developed a close relationship with Saudi Arabia. On Thursday 28 January 1993, he and Major went to Saudi Arabia to meet King Fahd, who promised to buy large quantities of British weapons. On Friday 17 September, a secret meeting was scheduled at the Ritz in Paris between Aitken, Prince Mohammed and Lebanese businessman Mohammed Said Ayas; it was cancelled and rearranged for the next day in Geneva, at which Ayas promised to help with arms deals. Ayas paid the hotel bills. Agreements were struck with GEC and the helicopter firm Westland in 1994 and 1995. Then everything began to fall apart. On Monday 10 April 1995, *The Guardian* splashed on Aitken's connections with Prince Mohammed. At 5pm, Aitken held a press conference at Smith Square slamming the report, which was a joint venture with Granada TV's current affairs programme *World In Action*, who were due to air an episode entitled "Jonathan of Arabia" at 8pm. Aitken declared, "If it falls to me to start a fight to cut out the cancer of bent and twisted journalism in our country with the simple sword of truth and the trusty shield of British fair play, so be it. I am ready for the fight. The fight against falsehood and those who peddle it. My fight begins today. Thank you and good afternoon." When the programme claimed that the MP broke ministerial rules by letting Ayas pay for his hotel stay at the Ritz, Aitken issued a writ for libel and resigned from the Cabinet to fight the action. Aitken claimed Lolicia, his wife, had paid the hotel bill and had his 14-year-old daughter Victoria and Ayas write confirmatory statements to that effect. In May 1997, Aitken lost his seat in the New Labour landslide that brought Tony Blair to power. The terrier-like QC George Carman (1929-2001) represented the *Guardian* and Granada TV at the trial. The coup de grâce came on Friday 20 June 1997 when Carman proved Mrs Aitken had been in Switzerland at the time she was supposedly paying her husband's bill. Aitken dropped his libel action and was charged with perjury and perverting the course of justice. On Tuesday 8 June 1999, he was sentenced to eighteen months' imprisonment, serving almost seven months. Upon his release he found God and was ordained a Church of England priest. At **St Matthew's, 20 Great Peter Street, Westminster, London SW1P 2BU**, he married Elizabeth Harris (b. at Cardiff, Wales Friday 1 May 1936 as Elizabeth Rees-Williams d. at Chelsea and Westminster Hospital Friday 15 April 2022 at 11.10pm), the ex-wife of actors Richard Harris and Sir Rex Harrison.

ASBO
Taunton Deane Shopping Centre, Taunton, Somerset TA1

Taunton Deane Magistrates' Court issued the first Asbo in the UK on Friday 17 September 2004 to Thomas Harcombe. The 38-year-old was ordered not to loiter within fifty yards of any school in England and Wales with pupils under the age of 15, having been arrested on 2 August for exposing himself in the town centre.

BALCOMBE STREET SIEGE
22b Balcombe Street, London NW1 6ND

On Saturday 6 December 1975, four IRA terrorists responsible for the bombing campaign that had plagued London with forty attacks in a year (including the pub bombings in Guildford (8.30pm on Saturday 5 October 1974 in the Horse & Groom, killing four soldiers, one civilian and injuring fifty-seven others; and at 9.25pm in the nearby Seven Stars pub, causing injuries to eight people, mainly staff, because the manager had cleared the pub after the Horse and Groom explosion) and Woolwich (on Thursday 7 November 1974, a 6lb bomb packed with bolts exploded in the King's Arms, injuring twenty-six people including five soldiers) and the murders of cancer specialist Professor Gordon Hamilton-Fairley (killed on Thursday 23 October 1975 along with his two poodles when he bent to examine a suspicious device under the Jaguar XJ6 of anti-Common Market Tory MP Sir Hugh Fraser) and campaigning writer and journalist Ross McWhirter (see page 177) burst into the council flat home of John Matthews and his wife Sheila, who were watching an episode of *Kojak*. Earlier that evening, the Irishmen had sprayed the front of **Scott's Restaurant, Oyster Terrace and Bar, 20 Mount Street, Mayfair, London W1K 2HE** with machine gun fire from their stolen car. (They had thrown a bomb through the window on Tuesday 12 November and were furious because Scott's refused to close). That night, 6,000 policemen were on the lookout for the terrorists. Two plainclothes officers spotted the car because it was driving so slowly; when the four men got out, the policemen gave chase. The terrorists shot at the unarmed officers (who did not even have a truncheon between them) and ran into the flats near Dorset Square. Thus began the Balcombe Street siege. Detective Chief Superintendent Peter Imbert, a future Metropolitan Police commissioner, oversaw the police operation. The siege continued for six long days. At 2.54pm on Thursday 12 December, shortly after Mrs Matthews's negotiated release, police sent in hot sausages, Brussels sprouts and potatoes and peaches and cream, the first food the terrorists had eaten since the siege began. At 4.15pm, they agreed to surrender, leaving the flat one by one with their hands in the air. The siege had lasted 138 hours. The gang members, Hugh Doherty, 27, , Eddie Butler, 28, Harry Duggan, 25 and Martin O'Connell, 22, were given forty-seven life sentences at the Old Bailey in February 1977. All four were released on Wednesday 14 April 1999 under the Good Friday Agreement and were greeted as heroes by Gerry Adams and Martin McGuinness.

BAMBER, JEREMY
White House Farm, Pages Lane, Tolleshunt D'Arcy, Essex CM9 8AA

At 3.25am on Wednesday 7 August 1985, Jeremy Bamber (b. at St Mary Abbot's Hospital, Marloes Road, Kensington, London W8 Friday 13 January 1961 as Jeremy Paul Marsham) called Chelmsford police station to tell them that his adoptive sister Sheila Caffell (b. Thursday 18 July 1957) had gone mad and murdered their family: adoptive father and mother (Ralph) Nevill (b. Sunday 8 June 1924) and June Speakman Bamber (b. Tuesday 3 June 1924), and her 6-year-old sons, Nicholas and Daniel (b. Friday 22 June 1979), at White House Farm in Tolleshunt D'Arcy, Essex. Bamber claimed that his father had just telephoned him to say that Sheila had gone mad with a gun. Twenty-five minutes later, Bamber arrived at the farm where three policemen met him. Armed police arrived at 4.48am but waited until 7.35am before entering the farm. They found 6ft 4in Neville Bamber on the kitchen floor, shot eight times; his wife June lay in her bedroom doorway, shot seven times, including once between the eyes; nearby was daughter Sheila, and, across the hall in their beds, the twins, both shot as they slept. The initial investigation asserted that Sheila, a former model with psychiatric problems and known as Bambi, had murdered her family before committing suicide; much forensic evidence was lost. Subsequently, Bamber displayed an arrogance that led his remaining family to believe that he was the killer. He sold his parents' furniture to fund his playboy lifestyle, supplying friends with drink and drugs. When money ran short, he sold soft-porn photographs of his sister. A month after the killings, Bamber split from his girlfriend Julie Mugford who went to the police after discovering that he had slept with one of her friends; she told them that Bamber had confessed to killing his parents. On Sunday 8 September 1985, Bamber was arrested and went on trial at **Chelmsford Crown Court, New Street, Chelmsford, Essex CM1 1EL** thirteen months later on 2 October 1986. When prosecuting lawyer Anthony Arlidge QC suggested Bamber was lying, he replied, "That is what you have got to establish." Julie Mugford was a star witness, although defending counsel Geoffrey Rivlin QC attempted to portray her as a scorned woman. The police investigation had been inept to say the least – a family member, not the police, had found the silencer the killer used on the .22 Anshutz automatic. Mr Justice Maurice Drake (1923-2014) summed up and sent the jury out at 12.49pm on Monday 27 October to consider their verdict. Rivlin was furious at what he saw as the judge's biased summation. The next day, the jury asked for clarification on the blood evidence. After lunch, when the jury sent Drake a second question, he said that he would accept a majority verdict as long as at least ten jurors agreed. At 2.35pm, after a total of 9½ hours of deliberation, the jury returned a guilty verdict by ten votes to two. The judge sentenced Bamber to a minimum of twenty-five years' imprisonment, calling him "evil almost beyond belief". Bamber continues to proclaim his innocence but successive appeals have all failed. The key to Bamber's guilt was provided by a telephone: White House Farm had four phones, all on the same line. One was in the kitchen, one in the office and one in Nevill and June's bedroom. The fourth, a cordless, was away for repair. Police photographs showed that the ivory dial-type bedroom phone was in the kitchen and the receiver was off the hook. The device had been taken from the bedroom and plugged into a kitchen socket. The kitchen phone had been unplugged and hidden under a stack of magazines. On the night of the murders, Bamber left the farm around 10pm and drove to his own home at **9 Head Street, Goldhanger, Maldon, Essex CM9 8AY** – less than three miles away, about seven minutes by car. He returned to the farm on his mother's bicycle and, on entering, took the kitchen phone off the hook, thus disabling all the phones in the house. He was probably wearing a wetsuit or some kind of protective clothing. Taking Nevill's gun, Bamber climbed the stairs and in all likelihood shot the children first. Then he walked across to his parents' bedroom, but Nevill was awake and waiting for him. He tried to call 999 but Bamber had of course planned ahead for this. Nevill was shot four times but was still alive when Bamber unloaded the rest of the magazine into June. He managed to make a break for the door, but Bamber had to stop his father from reaching the phone. With no time to reload, he battered his father into submission with the rifle, before reloading and pumping four bullets into Nevill's face and head. Returning to the bedroom, he came across Sheila tending to their injured mother. He shot June again before turning his attentions to his sister. He had to shoot her in such a way that suggested suicide. The first bullet did not kill her so Bamber had to shoot again: unlikely for a suicide to shoot themselves twice. To make it look as if a madman – or, indeed, a mad woman – had committed the atrocity, Bamber unloaded more bullets into his tiny nephews. He realised that the police might ask why his parents had not called for help from their bedroom. And what was Nevill's body doing in the kitchen? Bamber unplugged the bedroom phone, placed it in the kitchen and hid the kitchen phone. If anyone asked why the kitchen phone was unplugged, Bamber intended to tell them it was broken. It would also explain why Nevill was discovered downstairs. If Sheila were the murderer, there would be no need for the phones to have been moved. As Mr Justice Drake said, Jeremy Bamber truly is "evil almost beyond belief".

> **DID YOU KNOW?**
> In September 1984, a notice announcing the birth of Prince Harry was posted on the gates of Buckingham Palace by Major Leslie Marsham, a senior courtier – and the father of Jeremy Bamber.

BEHEADING, LAST
Broad Street, Stirling, FK8

At 2.49pm on Friday 8 September 1820, before a crowd of 6,000 people, Andrew Hardie and John Baird became the last people to be judicially beheaded in Britain. They were also the last to be executed for high treason in Scotland and the last to be hung, drawn and quartered (although it was later reduced to hanging and quartering). The two men had been ringleaders in a failed insurrection in Glasgow on Saturday 1-Sunday 2 April 1820. After their heads were covered with hoods, Hardie seized Baird's hand and they dropped through the trap hand-in-hand. After hanging for half an hour, the headsman began his gruesome task. He was a delicate, young man of about 20 who wore black crepe over his face, a black serge gown and a boy's hairy cap. Using axe and block, it took three strokes to sever Hardie's head and two strokes to decapitate Baird. In 1847, with the Home Secretary's permission, Baird's and Hardie's corpses were exhumed from Stirling and carried to Glasgow, where they were given honourable burials beneath a large memorial in Sighthill Cemetery.

BENTLEY, DEREK
Barlow & Parker Ltd, Croydon House, 27–29 Tamworth Road,
West Croydon, Surrey CRO 1XT
Telephone: CROydon 0027

At 9.15pm on Sunday 2 November 1952, Derek William Bentley (b. at 13 Surrey Row, Blackfriars Road, Blackfriars, London SE1 0QA Friday 30 June 1933, a twin whose brother died aged two hours), a subnormal youth with an IQ of 66, and Christopher Craig (b. at Croydon, Surrey Tuesday 19 May 1936), a young thug, broke into a wholesale confectioners' warehouse here. The police arrived and the youths were trapped on the roof. Detective Constable Frederick Fairfax (b. at Westminster, London Sunday 17 June 1917) climbed up and arrested Bentley. The police claimed that Bentley shouted, "Let him have it, Chris!" and Craig fired a Colt New Service .455 Webley calibre revolver, wounding DC Fairfax and hitting PC Sydney George Miles, 42 above the left eyebrow, killing him. Craig then unleashed a few more bullets before flinging himself off the roof, breaking his pelvis. In a trial lasting two and a half days in December that year at the Central Criminal Court, Old Bailey, before the Lord Chief Justice of England and Wales, Lord Goddard, Bentley's mental state was not revealed and he was sentenced to death after the jury spent seventy-five minutes deliberating. The jury recommended mercy for Bentley, and Craig was sentenced to be detained during Her Majesty's Pleasure. Craig was released from prison in May 1963 and he settled in Buckinghamshire, married and worked as a plumber. Sir David Maxwell Fyfe, the Home Secretary, refused to recommend that the Queen exercise the prerogative of mercy and Bentley was executed at HM Prison Wandsworth at 9am on Wednesday 28 January 1953 as a crowd waited outside. His older sister Iris began a campaign to clear his name. In 1966, Bentley's corpse was disinterred from the grounds of Wandsworth prison and reburied in Croydon cemetery on Friday 4 March. Initially a headstone was not permitted but the Government changed its mind in July 1994 and the tombstone bears the words "A victim of British justice". On Thursday 29 July 1993, Home Secretary Michael Howard granted a partial pardon, admitting that Bentley's execution had been wrong, but maintaining the guilty verdict. Five years later and a year after Iris's death, Derek Bentley's conviction was quashed on Thursday 30 July 1998. The Barlow & Parker factory was demolished in 1977 and replaced by houses.

BIBLE JOHN
Barrowland Ballroom, 244 Gallowgate, Glasgow G4 0TT
Telephone: 0141-552 4601

In a twenty-month period in Glasgow in the late 1960s, an unknown killer who was given the nickname Bible John because he liked to quote from the holy book, murdered three women. The only link between the victims seemed to be a love of dancing. Patricia Docker, a 25-year-old nursing auxiliary employed at Mearnskirk Hospital (opened Friday 9 May 1930 closed Thursday 28 February 2019) and the separated mother of Sandy, a 4-year-old son, became the first victim. She was strangled and her naked body was found near a garage in **Carmichael Lane, Langside, Glasgow G42** on Friday 23 February 1968. The night before, she had told her parents with whom she lived at **29 Langside Place, Battlefield** she was going to the **Majestic Ballroom, Hope Street, Glasgow G2 2UG (Telephone 041-332 2166)** (demolished 1972). When it closed at 10.30pm, she went to the Barrowland Ballroom. Police believe she met a man and left with him but refused to have sex with him because she was menstruating. In frustration, he killed her. A year and a half later, on Saturday 16 August 1969, 5ft 7in mother of three Jemima McDonald was found at **23 Mackeith Street, Glasgow G40 1HE** a few yards from where she lived at **15 Mackeith Street**; she too was strangled. The police discovered that she had still been at the Barrowland Ballroom at midnight and had been seen with a man aged around 35. Living at **129 Earl Street, Scotstoun, Glasgow G14 0DE,** 5ft 8in Helen Puttock, a 29-year-old mother of two, her sister Jeannie and two friends went dancing on Thursday 30 October 1969 at the Barrowland Ballroom. Helen's husband babysat the children. Jeannie was chatted up by a man called John and spent the rest of the evening with him. Helen was also approached by a man called John. They talked about a number of subjects and he mentioned the Bible several times. "My father says these places are dens of iniquity," he said, adding he disapproved of married women going out dancing. When the ballroom closed at 11.30pm, the two couples left the club together. "Bible John" called a taxi and got in with the two women, while the other John made his own way home. After dropping Jeannie off, the cabbie left Helen and "Bible John" at Earl Street. Her body was found outside a tenement block at 7am the next day by a man walking his dog. Jeannie was interviewed by the police and was able to give a detailed description of "Bible John". Newspapers printed a photofit with appeals, leading to Scotland's biggest manhunt. In 1995, Donald Simpson wrote a book naming furniture salesman John Irvine McInnes as Bible John. The police had questioned McInnes at the time of the killings but took no further action. He died in 1980. In 1996 McInnes's body was exhumed; his DNA was compared to stains left on the third victim and his teeth compared to bite marks. The investigation took five months but the evidence was inconclusive. The Bible John murders remain unsolved.

BLACK PANTHER

Donald Neilson was born Donald Nappey on Saturday 1 August 1936 in Dewsbury, West Yorkshire. An unhappy childhood (he was bullied because he was short – 5ft 6in – and because of his surname) was made worse when his 33-year-old mother died when he was 10-years-old. He joined the King's Own Yorkshire Light Infantry for his National Service and married 20-year-old Irene Tate in April 1955 at St Paul's Church, Morley; their daughter Kathryn was born in early 1960. In 1964, he changed his surname to Neilson to prevent his daughter receiving the same bullying. He left the Army but remained obsessed with military life. Living at **1129 Grangefield Avenue, Thornbury, Bradford, West Yorkshire**, he was unable to hold down a legal job and turned to robbery in 1965. By the time he came to trial, he had committed more than 400 burglaries and murdered four people. In 2008, an appeal to reduce his sentence to thirty years was rejected. In March 2009, Neilson was diagnosed with motor neurone disease and moved to a special prison hospital unit. In the early hours of Saturday 17 December 2011, Neilson was discovered in his cell at Norwich Prison having difficulty breathing. He was taken to **Norfolk and Norwich University Hospital, Colney Lane, Norwich, Norfolk NR4 7UY**, where he died at 6.45pm the following day.

Sub-Post Office, 22 Rochdale Road East, Heywood,
Lancashire OL10 1PX
Telephone: 01706 360962

On Wednesday 16 February 1972, Neilson broke into a sub post office run by Leslie Richardson, who woke to find a hooded man in the bedroom he shared with his wife. Mr Richardson went to tackle the intruder while his wife telephoned the police. Neilson pulled out a sawn-off shotgun and, speaking in a West Indian accent, told the Richardsons, "This is loaded." The sub-postmaster spotted that the gun was pointing upwards and flung himself at the intruder, shouting, "We'll find out if it's loaded." Mr Richardson found out that it was when Neilson pulled the trigger, opening two holes in the bedroom ceiling. He pulled off the intruder's black hood and, instead of a black man, saw a white man with dark, staring eyes. Neilson stamped on Mr Richardson's foot, breaking his toes, and kneed him in the groin before he escaped empty-handed. Neilson would not allow the situation to repeat itself – if challenged, he would shoot immediately.

New Park Post Office, 324 Skipton Road, Harrogate,
North Yorkshire HG3 2XS
Telephone 01423 565487

Donald Lawson Skepper was born on 7 December 1923 and served in the Fleet Air Arm during the Second World War. He had kept the corner shop-cum-sub post office in Harrogate for ten years, taking over from his father. He attended the local Methodist chapel and had three children. – a doctor daughter, a 22-year-old son at Manchester University and a second son, Richard, 18, who lived at home. It was here at 5am on Friday 15 February 1974 that Neilson committed his first murder. He broke in and went to Richard's room where he gagged him and demanded the keys to the safe. Unable to find them following the teenager's instructions, he forced Richard into his parents' room. Johanna Skepper woke before her husband. He made to lunge at Neilson and was shot once fatally in the chest. Police were called after 5am following a 999 call from Richard. The police flooded the area but Neilson had made good his escape.

Higher Baxenden Post Office, 523 Manchester Road,
Accrington, Lancashire BB5 2QJ
Telephone: 01254 233017

On Friday 6 September 1974, Neilson broke into the sub post office run by Derek Astin (b. Saturday 14 June 1930), 44. Marion Astin awoke around 4am to see her husband confronting a stranger and picked up a vacuum cleaner to try to help him. The noise woke their children Susan, 13, and Stephen, 10. Mr Astin tried to force the intruder down the stairs and then two shots rang out – one from a shotgun and the other from a .22. Susan, who had seen everything, rushed to her mother's side and the two tried to staunch the flow of blood from Mr Astin's body. Neilson had cut the telephone line so Susan and Stephen ran into the street and began banging on neighbours' doors until one opened and the police were summoned. Mr Astin died in hospital soon after. It was at this time that Neilson was given the nickname "Black Panther" after Marion Astin described Neilson as "so quick, he was like a panther".

Langley Sub Post Office, High Street, Langley, Oldbury, West Midlands B69 4SN

Neilson waited only two months before striking again. Sub postmistress Margaret Frances Grayland was assisted by her husband Sidney (b. Thursday 28 November 1918), who had given up his job as a bread round manager to help her. Their shop was to be demolished in a few months to make way for a new development. At 10.55pm on Monday 11 November 1974, PCs Roger Toghill and Philip Rich were on patrol when they spotted lights still on in the Graylands' shop. They found Mrs Grayland in a pool of blood, one wrist bound and bleeding profusely from the head. A subsequent examination found three depressed skull fractures. Nearby lay the dead body of Sidney Grayland – he had been shot in the stomach with a .22. Neilson had escaped with £800 (some sources say £1,000).

Beech Croft, Bridgnorth Road, Highley, Bridgnorth, Shropshire WV16 6JT

Bathpool Park, Westmoreland Avenue, Kidsgrove, Stoke-on-Trent, Staffordshire ST7 4EF

George Whittle (b. 1905 d. Wednesday 23 September 1970) ran the Whittle coach business, based at Highley and Kidderminster, one of Britain's biggest private coach firms which was formed in 1926 and sold in January 2015 to Johnsons Coach Travel of Henley-in-Arden. He lived in a four-bedroom detached house called Beech Croft with his girlfriend Dorothy – whom he had met on a bus twenty-five years before – and had two children by her, Ronald and Lesley (b. Friday 3 May 1957). Ronald ran the company and Lesley was studying geography O-level and A-levels in pure and applied maths at Wulfrun College, Wolverhampton in the hope of joining her boyfriend at Sheffield University. Before his death, George gave Ronald £107,000 and Lesley £82,500 which was put into a trust. He left a further £106,000 to Ronald in his will. George's estranged wife Selina knew nothing of this financial arrangement and, believing she had been cheated of money, launched a legal battle in May 1972 to demand £1,500 a year backdated to September 1970. The case was featured in an article about the will in the *Daily Express* on Wednesday 17 May 1972. Donald Neilson read the story and decided to kidnap either Ronald or Dorothy Whittle and demand a £50,000 ransom. He spent three years planning his crime and, on Tuesday 22 October 1974, he stole a Connaught green Morris 1300 car. On the night of Monday 13 January 1975, Neilson drove to the Whittle home. Dorothy had gone out with friends, leaving Lesley alone in the house. At 1.30am, Dorothy returned and peeked in on her daughter, who was asleep. She took a couple of sleeping pills and took to her own bed. Once outside, Neilson cut the telephone line before entering the house through the garage. He came across Lesley's room and gagged the terrified teenager and took her to his car, where he bound her and put her on the back seat. She was wearing only a dressing gown and her mother's slippers. He drove sixty miles to Bathpool Park in Kidsgrove, Staffordshire, where he had arranged a hideout. He put Lesley in a drainage shaft off the nearby reservoir, where he had placed a sleeping bag and mattress. He put a hood over her head and pulled off her dressing gown, leaving her naked, and tied her to the shaft by a wire noose. Later that day at 7am, Dorothy went down for breakfast, calling for Lesley. When she realised she wasn't there, she went to ring Ronald but, with no dialling tone, she drove over to his house on the other side of Highley. Ronald was already at work so his wife Gaynor accompanied Dorothy back to Beech Croft, where they found three messages on Dymotape. The first read: "No police £50,000 ransom to be ready to deliver wait for telephone call at Swan shopping centre telephone box 6pm to 1pm (sic) if no call return following evening when you answer call give your name only and listen you must follow instructions without argument from the time you answer you are on a time limit if police or tricks death". The second read: "Swan shopping centre Kidderminster deliver £50,000 in a white suitcase", while the third said: "£50,000 all in old notes £25,000 in £1 notes and £25,000 in £5 notes there will be no exchange only after £50,000 has been cleared will victim be released". The police were contacted and Detective Chief Superintendent Robert Booth of West Mercia Police took charge. Remarkably, the news of the kidnapping leaked almost immediately and was broadcast on local radio station BRMB at 8pm and on the main BBC News bulletin an hour later. That night Neilson was doing a final recce of the route he expected Ron Whittle to take to deliver the ransom. He parked his car and walked into British Rail Freightliners Limited railway yard in Dudley, where he was confronted by security guard Gerald Smith (b. Wednesday 20 August 1930), 45. Neilson fired six bullets into Mr Smith and made his escape. Despite the excruciating pain, the guard crawled to a hut and summoned help. Mr Smith survived the initial attack but died from his injuries on Thursday 25 March 1976. Forensics were able to prove that the gun used in this attack was the same that had been used to kill Sidney Grayland in Langley. The policeman whose job was to answer the phone left his post after the news broke, so when it rang at midnight there was no one to answer it. The next night, Ron waited for several hours but no call was made. At 11.45pm on 16 January, the phone rang at Beech Croft and was answered by Len Rudd, the firm's transport manager. He heard Lesley's tape-recorded voice assuring her family she was okay and directing someone to go to a phonebox in Kidsgrove, Staffordshire, where there would be a second message behind the back-board. Ron went to Bridgnorth police station for instructions and left between 1.15am and 1.30am on 17 January. Carrying £50,000 in used banknotes, he set off for Kidsgrove but, not knowing the area, he was late and did not reach the phonebox until 3am, taking an additional half an hour to find the Dymotape message. Eventually locating it, he was sent to Bathpool Park, about 1½ miles away. The message read: "GO TO THE TOP OF THE LANE AND TURN INTO NO ENTRY GO TO THE WALL AND FLASH LIGHTS LOOK FOR TORCHLIGHT RUN TO TORCH FURTHER INSTRUCTIONS ON TORCH." By a terrible stroke of misfortune, at 2.45am Peter Shorto, a nightclub DJ, and his girlfriend parked in the exact place Neilson was expecting Ron Whittle. The DJ saw a flashing torch but ignored it. Worse, a Panda car pulled into the park, the driver stopped for a cigarette and then left. When Ron arrived, he flashed his lights and waited, but nothing happened. He got out of his car and shouted, but when there was no reply, he left Bathpool Park and went to meet the police. Neilson, watching, panicked and may have killed Lesley that night. On 5 March, Ronald and Detective Chief Superintendent Robert Booth of West Mercia Police made a television appeal for help. The next day, the headmaster of **Maryhill Primary School, Gloucester Road, Kidsgrove, Staffordshire ST7 4DJ** (closed Saturday 31 August 2013) told police that two of his pupils had found an orange piece of Dymotape bearing the legend "DROP SUITCASE INTO HOLE", and a torch. The discovery had been made several weeks earlier but no one had thought to connect it to the kidnapping. The police launched a major search of Bathpool Park the next day. Two drainage shafts were examined, but a search of the third was halted for health and safety reasons. At 4.15pm the next day, SOCO Detective Constable Philip Maskery climbed down the third shaft and found a broken police torch on the first landing, twenty-two feet down. A cassette tape recorder was discovered on a second landing another forty-five feet down. Maskery descended to the third landing a further fifty-four feet down and discovered a rolled up sleeping bag, a yellow foam mattress and a blanket. Shining his torch down and putting his head under the platform, Maskery came virtually face to face with the naked body of Lesley Whittle, hanging by wire around her neck about six inches from the bottom of the shaft. The area was sealed off and Lesley was examined and photographed in situ. Her body was brought up the next day and taken away in a plain coffin. An autopsy carried out by Dr John Brown revealed that Lesley had died of vagal inhibition – in other words her heart had stopped beating due to the shock of falling (or being pushed). She was emaciated and had not eaten for at least three days, perhaps meaning that she had fallen and not been pushed by Neilson the day after the failed ransom delivery. Lesley's funeral took place on Friday 14 March 1975 at St Mary's, Highley, where she had been christened. The service was conducted by the Reverend John Brittain and 500 mourners attended, 200 inside the thirteenth-century church and the rest outside listening on loudspeakers. Lesley was then cremated at Bushbury Crematorium, Wolverhampton. Plain clothes policemen mingled with mourners hoping that the killer might make an appearance, but he did not.

Months went by until, at 11pm on Thursday 11 December 1975 in Mansfield, a man was seen acting suspiciously outside the Four Ways pub by PCs Stuart McKenzie and Tony White. When they stopped him, he told them his name was John Moxon before pulling a shotgun on PC McKenzie, whose understandable response was "Fucking hell". He forced them to drive to Blidworth, near Mansfield. PC McKenzie realised the road led out into the country and, fearing for their lives, he swung the car to the right over the white line, then back to the left and braked hard. The car finished up outside a fish and chip shop at **289 Southwell Road East, Rainworth, Mansfield, Nottinghamshire NG21 0BL (Tel 792472),** where Roy Morris and Keith Wood were buying their dinner. When they saw the two policemen struggling with a man with a gun, they dashed out to help. The four men struggled to restrain him and Mr Morris grabbed his wrists until he could be handcuffed. He was moved over to some railings to be searched; a crowd gathered, some of whom began to hit the prisoner. Taken into custody with a black eye, Neilson refused to reveal any information about himself for two days before finally cracking and revealing his true identity. Neilson's trial began on Monday 14 June 1976 at Oxford Crown Court. His barrister claimed that Lesley had fallen accidentally and Neilson had looked after her, feeding her chicken soup, spaghetti and meatballs, fish and chips and chicken legs. On Thursday 1 July 1976, Neilson was convicted of the kidnapping and murder of Lesley Whittle after the jury deliberated for ninety minutes. There was a gasp from the public gallery and then a brief burst of applause. On Wednesday 21 July, Neilson was found guilty of the murders of the three postmasters and sentenced to life in prison. The shooting of security guard Gerald Smith remained on file. DCI Robert Booth was demoted from the CID and reduced to the ranks. The Neilson family home remained empty until 1979, when it was bought for £6,000 by ex-soldier Jack Hiley.

CALVI, ROBERTO
Blackfriars Bridge, London SE1

"God's banker", so-called because he ran the Banco Ambrosiano whose biggest shareholder was the Vatican, Roberto Calvi, 62, was found hanging from Blackfriars Bridge on Friday 18 June 1982. In

1978, a Bank of Italy report on Ambrosiano discovered that several billion lire had been exported illegally, leading to criminal investigations. In May 1981, Calvi received a four-year suspended sentence and a $19.8million fine for taking $27million out of Italy in violation of currency laws. After a prison suicide attempt, he was released on bail pending an appeal and kept his job at the bank. The bank collapsed in June 1982 owing between $700million and $1½billion; much of the money had been siphoned off via the Vatican Bank (*Istituto per le Opere Religiose*, or Institute of Religious Works). On Thursday 10 June 1982, Calvi disappeared from his Rome apartment, having fled the country on a false passport under the name of Gian Roberto Calvini. He fled initially to Venice and from there he apparently hired a private plane to London. Eight days later, a passing postman found his body hanging from scaffolding beneath Blackfriars Bridge. There were stones in his clothes and he had around $15,000 worth of cash in three different currencies. The conspiracy theories began: Calvi had been a member of Licio Gelli's secretive masonic lodge P2, and Blackfriars Bridge was allegedly a significant location in freemasonry, since members of P2 referred to themselves as *frati neri* or "black friars". On the day before his body was found, Calvi was sacked from the Banco Ambrosiano by the Bank of Italy, and his 55-year-old private secretary Graziella Corrocher had jumped to her death from a fifth-floor window, leaving a note condemning the damage that Calvi had done to the bank and its employees. The first inquest on Calvi in July 1982 returned a verdict of suicide. A year later, a second inquest recorded an open verdict. The Calvi family insisted that he had been murdered. In December 1998 his body was exhumed and an independent forensic report published in October 2002 concluded that he had been murdered. The injuries to his neck were inconsistent with hanging and he had not touched the stones found in his pockets. Additionally, there would have been rust and paint on his shoes from the scaffolding he would have needed to climb over in order to hang himself. In September 2003, the City of London Police reopened their investigation as a murder inquiry. In Rome on Wednesday 5 October 2005, the trial began of five men charged with Calvi's murder. After twenty months of evidence, all five were acquitted on 6 June 2007.

CHRISTIE, JOHN
Ground Floor Flat, 10 Rillington Place, London W11 1RB
John Reginald Halliday Christie was born on Saturday 8 April
1899 at his parents' home, Black Boy House, near Halifax. In July
1918, while serving with the British Expeditionary Force in France,
he lost his voice and was invalided out of the Army in March 1919.
On Monday 10 May 1920, he married Ethel Simpson Waddington,
a typist. He spent much of the next few years in and out of prison for
theft and, on Monday 13 May 1929, was sentenced to six months'
hard labour for malicious wounding. In 1938, the Christies moved
into the ground floor flat at 10 Rillington Place in Notting Hill, west
London, where Christie found work as a clerk. In 1939, despite his
criminal record, he became a war reserve policeman and won two
commendations. On Sunday 28 March 1948, an illiterate van driver,
Timothy John Evans, 23, and his pregnant wife Beryl, 18, moved into
the upstairs flat. The Evans's marriage was not a happy one even after
the birth of Geraldine on Sunday 10 October 1948. In 1949, Beryl
found that she was pregnant again and the tensions in the marriage
bubbled to the surface. Not wanting the second child, the couple were
offered an abortion by Christie. When Evans returned from work
on Tuesday 8 November, Christie told him that the operation had
gone wrong and Beryl had died at 3pm. The men decided to store the
body in the middle flat, which was unoccupied because the tenant,
a Mr Kitchener, was in hospital. Christie said that he would dispose
of the body and arrange for Geraldine's care, suggesting that Evans
should leave London. He left Paddington on 14 November for Cardiff
to stay with his aunt, Mrs Lynch, briefly returning to Rillington
Place before going back to Wales. On Wednesday 30 November, he
admitted at a Merthyr Tydfil police station that he had killed his wife.
Geraldine and Beryl's bodies were discovered on 2 December. That
night, Evans also confessed to murdering his daughter (on Thursday
10 November). He went on trial at the Old Bailey for Geraldine's
murder on Wednesday 11 January 1950; Beryl's murder remained on
file. Christie and his wife were key prosecution witnesses. The jury
retired only briefly before returning a guilty verdict on Friday 13
January. Evans was hanged by Albert Pierrepoint at Pentonville on
Thursday 9 March 1950. In the summer of 1950, 10 Rillington Place

was purchased by a Jamaican, Charles Brown. Three years later, on Saturday 21 March 1953, Christie left Rillington Place, and three days later Beresford Dubois Brown, a new tenant, found six bodies in the garden, kitchen and under the sitting room floor. They were identified as Ruth Margarete Christine Fuerst, a waitress, missing since August 1943; Muriel Amelia Eady, who had worked with Christie, missing since Saturday 7 October 1944; Christie's wife, Ethel, on Sunday 14 December 1952; two prostitutes, the pregnant Rita Elizabeth Nelson and Kathleen Maloney (February 1953); and pregnant Hectorina MacLennan, who was rumoured to be a prostitute despite scant evidence. All had been strangled and raped. Christie was arrested on Tuesday 31 March by PC Thomas Ledger on the Embankment near Putney Bridge and went on trial at the Old Bailey on Monday 22 June, charged only with his wife's murder. He was convicted and hanged at Pentonville on Wednesday 15 July 1953, also by Albert Pierrepoint. After Christie went to his death, disquiet was raised over Evans's conviction. In 1961 Ludovic Kennedy published a book about the case and, on Tuesday 18 October 1966, Evans received a royal pardon, exonerating him of the murder of Geraldine but not Beryl. Who killed Beryl and Geraldine? Christie's modus operandi was to render his victims unconscious with carbon monoxide before strangling them during sex. There were no signs of carbon monoxide or semen in Beryl's body, but there was significant bruising and evidence of rape from a few days before. Christie was not known to be physical whereas Evans was. If Christie had raped Beryl, why did she not go to the police or tell her husband? If Evans was the perpetrator, then it was somewhat characteristic of his violent nature. On the night of the murder, the Christies had left for the cinema at 5.30pm and Evans returned an hour later. If Christie was the killer, he must have left the body in the flat (Ethel was around so he could not carry it to the outhouse), so why didn't Evans go to the police then? That night, while in bed, the Christies heard a loud bump from upstairs (likely Evans moving the body to the middle flat). There was no reason why Ethel should have made this up, so it is likely that Evans did murder his wife and daughter. If Christie had not killed Beryl, he had no reason to kill the baby. Thus Timothy Evans is the only killer to receive a royal pardon for a murder he actually committed. Rillington Place was renamed Ruston and became a tourist attraction until the 1970s when it was torn down and rebuilt as Bartle Road, most likely after the nearby Bartle James Iron Works.

CRIPPEN, DR
39 Hilldrop Crescent, Camden Road, Lower Holloway, London N7

The first murderer to be caught by wireless telegraphy was Hawley Harvey "Peter" Crippen (b. at Coldwater, Michigan 11 September 1862). After qualifying as a doctor at the Homoeopathic Hospital in Cleveland, Ohio, he moved to New York, where he married an Irish girl and had a son, Otto. In 1882, his wife, pregnant for the second time, suddenly and unexpectedly died of apoplexy. In 1892 he met and married the 19-year-old would-be music hall singer Cora Turner. Five years later, the couple embarked for London, where Crippen opened an office selling patent medicines. The marriage was stormy – Mrs Crippen frequently belittled her husband and would often bring men home for sex as well as making heavy financial demands on him. Crippen began an affair with his secretary, Ethel Le Neve, twenty-one years his junior. Unable to stand Cora's behaviour any longer, Crippen poisoned her with hyoscine after a dinner party on Tuesday 1 February 1910. (The only time hyoscine or, more correctly, hydrobromide of hyoscine – an extract of the deadly plant henbane, used in small doses to quieten mental patients – has been used to commit murder.) Crippen buried the body in the cellar and told his wife's friends that she had gone abroad. Later, he informed them she had died of pneumonia while travelling and had been cremated. Suspicious, they went to Inspector Walter Dew at Scotland Yard, who interviewed Crippen and his "housekeeper" Le Neve on Friday 8 July 1910. Crippen said that his wife had left him for another man but he had been too embarrassed to admit this so he said that she had died instead. Dew accepted the story but he did wonder why she had left so much of her wardrobe behind, and why Le Neve was wearing one of her brooches. Thinking the jig was up, Crippen and Le Neve decided to flee the country. On the Monday morning, Dew returned to Hilldrop Crescent and found the house deserted. A thorough police search uncovered human remains, and Dew immediately issued descriptions of Crippen and Le Neve. The pair had fled to Antwerp in Belgium where, on Wednesday 20 July, they boarded the steamship SS Montrose, bound for Canada. Crippen had shaved off his moustache, Ethel had cropped her hair and bought boys' clothing, and they were travelling together as Mr Robinson and his son, who was supposedly ill and travelling to Quebec for his health. Captain Kendall, *Montrose*'s skipper, recognised Crippen from a newspaper photograph and telegraphed the ship's owners, who alerted Scotland Yard. On Saturday 23 July, Dew set sail on a faster ship, SS Laurentic. At 9am on Sunday 31 July, Dew, dressed as a pilot, boarded *Montrose* from the pilot's launch and arrested Crippen and Le Neve, who fainted. Crippen was tried at the Old Bailey on Tuesday 18 October and sentenced to death four days later; Winston Churchill rejected his petition for a reprieve. On Tuesday 25 October, Le Neve was tried before the same judge and acquitted. The night before his execution, Crippen attempted to cheat the gallows by committing suicide but was foiled by the death-watch warder, who discovered that he had removed an arm from his glasses, apparently intending to cut himself with it and painlessly bleed to death. His last request, which was granted, was to die with a photo of Le Neve in his top pocket. John Ellis hanged him in Pentonville Prison at 9am on Wednesday 23 November 1910. In his memoirs, Ellis recalled, "I could see him smiling as he approached, and the smile never left his face up to the moment when I threw the white cap over it and blotted out God's light from his eyes forever." On the same day, Ethel Le Neve, under an alias, boarded a ship for America. The Crippens' house was destroyed in a German air raid during the Second World War. Ethel Le Neve died in Croydon on Wednesday 9 August 1967.

CUMMINS, GORDON
Room B, Flat 27, St James's Close, Regents Park, London NW8

Gordon Frederick Cummins was born at New Earswick, north of York, on Friday 18 February 1914 and joined the RAF on Monday 11 November 1935. He married Marjorie Stevens on Monday 28 December 1936. From 1936 until 1939, he was posted to the north. His fellow trainee officers nicknamed him "The Count" because of his imperious manner. Despite being married he behaved as if he was single, getting drunk and cavorting with women. On Wednesday 25

October 1939 he was transferred to 600 Squadron at Helensburgh, Dunbartonshire, where his carousing continued and his nickname was upgraded to "The Duke". Indeed, when he was transferred to Colerne, Wiltshire, in April 1941, the 5ft 7in Cummins told people he was the Honourable Gordon Cummins, the son of a peer and the black sheep of the family. He often socialised in Bath; while he was there, three women were assaulted although the perpetrators were never identified. On Monday 10 November 1941, he was sent to Predanneck, Cornwall, where, although his comrades soon tired of his boasting, the local women lapped up his charm, although one who gave him a job as a barman later sacked him when she found him handing out free drinks to his friends. She later found £35 (£2,002.02 at 2022 values) of jewellery was missing from her home. The police suspected Cummins but were unable to prove anything against him. By February 1942, Cummins decided that he wanted to become a pilot and was billeted at St James's Close during his training. From here he became the Blackout Ripper, killing four women in the space of just six days at the start of 1942.

Evelyn Hamilton: air raid shelter on Montagu Place, Marylebone, London W1H

Evelyn Hamilton was born on Friday 8 February 1901 and qualified with a chemist and druggist diploma from Edinburgh University in October 1938. In mid-1941, she joined a pharmaceutical company in Leicestershire and travelled the northwest selling their products. In November 1941, she moved to Surrey to work in a hospital but left after a few days when she discovered it was a mental institution. Her last job was as manageress of a pharmacy on **High Street, Hornchurch, Essex RM12** on £5 a week. At 10.30pm on Sunday 8 February 1942, she checked into the boarding house **The Three Arts Club, 76 Gloucester Place, London W1U 6HJ**. She went up to her room and twenty minutes later was back in reception asking manageress Catherine Jones if she knew of somewhere she could get something to eat. Mrs Jones directed her to the Lyons Corner House at Marble Arch (see page 18). She left and never returned. She was found dead at 8.40am on Monday 9 February 1942 in an air raid shelter, one of several on Montagu Place. She was clad in a green jumper and a camel-hair coat and her skirt had been pulled up to expose her thighs. Her underwear was bloodstained. Her handbag containing £80 had been taken. At 9.10am, Dr Alexander Baldie arrived and declared strangulation as the cause of death. Detective Chief Superintendent Frederick Cherrill, the head of Scotland Yard's Fingerprint Division, arrived and began his own investigation. He deduced that the murderer was left-handed. The autopsy was conducted by Professor Sir Bernard Spilsbury, who found no evidence of rape.

Evelyn Oatley: 153 Wardour Street, Soho, London W1F 8WE

Born in 1907, Evelyn Oatley arrived in London in 1936 to try to make a career as an actress on the London stage. Blonde, slim and busty, she found work as a nude at the Windmill Theatre. She married on Thursday 25 June 1936. Realising her career was probably going nowhere, she moved up north with her husband and worked on his poultry farm for eighteen months. He was a good man but she missed the bright lights. They went their separate ways and she made her way back to London where she again tried to make a living on the stage, but the war interrupted her career and to make ends meet she turned to prostitution. She shared a flat with Ivy Poole, 49, but the sleeping quarters were one large room separated only by two folding doors. Every night, from Tuesday 3 February until Saturday 7 February 1942, Mrs Oatley entertained a different man in her room. On the night of Monday 9 February, she went out looking for trade. She went into the **King's Arms, Gerrard Street, London W1** where she ordered scotch. When no one made a move, she left and walked to the Monico Restaurant near Regent Street where she picked a handsome younger man in an RAF uniform. They went back to Wardour Street and chatted. At 12.20am on Tuesday 10 February, Mrs Poole went to bed, but just as she was dropping off, Mrs Oatley's wireless was turned up as loudly as it would go. Mrs Poole was minded to get up to complain but did not like the idea of seeing her flatmate and her gentleman caller, so she closed her eyes until the music stopped. At 8am, two men arrived to empty the electricity meters. To their horror, they discovered the body of Mrs Oatley – her throat had been cut, she had been mutilated with a tin opener and a torch had been pushed inside her. More left-handed fingerprints were found. At 8.50am, Dr Alexander Baldie arrived; when he opened the blackout curtains, he saw a line of blood stretching five feet from her neck.

Margaret Florence "Pearl" Lowe: Flat 4, 9/10
Gosfield Street, Marylebone, London W1W

In 1932, Fred Lowe died, leaving a 5-year-old daughter Barbara and wife Margaret Florence "Pearl" Lowe in their small home in Southend-on-Sea, Essex. Whether the Lowes were really Mr & Mrs remains open to speculation. Fred Lowe's brother William did not believe they were legally married and suspected his "sister-in-law" worked as a prostitute. To make ends meet, Mrs Lowe had to sell their household goods and she moved to London in 1934 to try to find a job, leaving her daughter behind. She worked in Charing Cross Road and Oxford Street from 11pm each night, rarely mixing with the other prostitutes, who called her "The Lady". On the night of Tuesday 10 February 1942, there was an enhanced police presence because of the two murders. Just before 1am on Wednesday 11 February 1942, a well-spoken man approached Mrs Lowe on Piccadilly and asked if she did business. She nodded and took him to her Marylebone flat, arriving there at 1.15am. The man was heard leaving a little while later, whistling to himself. At 4.30pm on Friday 13 February 1940, Barbara Lowe arrived to visit her mother, but went for a walk when she received no reply. When she returned, the police had arrived after being alerted by an uncollected parcel. A silk stocking had been tied around Mrs Lowe's neck and her body had been mutilated with a razor blade, and a knife and a candlestick had been thrust inside her. Pathologist Sir Bernard Spilsbury called her attacker "a savage sexual maniac".

Doris Jouannet: 187 Sussex Gardens, Paddington, London W2 2RH

Doris Jouannet was born in about 1907. In September 1935, she was standing at a bus stop on Oxford Street when she caught the eye of Henry Jouannet, a retired hotelier thirty years her senior. He took the opportunity to introduce himself and after a brief chat they repaired to her flat at **240 Edgware Road, London W2 1DW** where they had sex. They quickly became friends and married in November 1935. He asked her to come off the game and she agreed, moving into his home **at 14 Bathurst Street, London W2 2SD**. The couple lived in apparent happiness for three years, but Doris became bored of domestic life and yearned for the touch of other men. When Henry's mother died and left him £1,300 (£90,500 at 2022 values), he used the money to buy a café and install his wife as co-manageress. It was not a success and they sold up after four months and moved to Eastbourne. On Monday 26 January 1942 they rented the flat in Sussex Gardens. On Sunday 1 February Henry became the manager of the **Royal Court Hotel, Sloane Square, London SW1W 8AS**. The job required him to spend nights away from his wife but he would return between 7pm and 9.30pm for vegetable soup. On Thursday 12 February, he returned home as usual and ate his soup before going back to Sloane Square. With her husband out of the way, Doris changed into an outfit she thought might attract men, despite the inclement weather that night. She fell into conversation with two other prostitutes before they went their separate ways. Henry Jouannet returned from work to find the bedroom locked. He called the police and PC William Payne arrived at 7.31pm. He broke the door down and found Mrs Jouannet laying naked on the bed. Her left hand had been placed between her legs, her genitals had been slashed and stabbed, her left breast cut off and a stocking had been tied around her neck. The bedsheets were soaked with blood and there was an empty condom on the floor. On 14 February, Cummins propositioned Greta Hayward in a Piccadilly bar; against her better nature, she followed him outside where he pulled her into a doorway and they kissed. She did not object until he tried to put his hands up her skirt. She pushed him away but he started to strangle her until she lost consciousness. A night porter, John Shine, 18, was passing, heard the altercation and saw a man running away. He went to her aid and found on the floor next to her handbag an RAF gas mask case, serial number 525987. An RAF policeman rang the billet and was told the number had been allotted to L.A.C. Cummins. He requested Cummins be detained, as the Met wanted a word with him.

Kathleen King: 29 Southwick Street, Tyburnia, London W2 1JQ

On Saturday 14 February, Kathleen King, also known as Mrs Mulcahy, was waiting for business outside **Oddendino's, 54-62 Regent Street, London W1B 5RE**. Cummins approached her and asked her to go with him. "£2," she said and he agreed. They caught a taxi and, inside, he put his head up her skirt, much to her annoyance. They went past Marble Arch, got out and walked to a flat she sometimes used. Once there they both stripped naked, although she kept her boots and a necklace on. When he put his hands around her neck and began to squeeze, she raised her knees and heaved him off her and onto the floor. She ran outside and banged on a neighbour's door, begging for help. Cummins threw his clothes on, went to the door and threw £8 in one-pound notes at the prostitute. When Cummins returned to his billet on Friday the 13th, he realised he had lost his gas mask so stole one belonging to another airman. He was arrested on Monday 16 February and when his billet (in St John's Wood) was searched, police found a number of items belonging to the victims. On Tuesday 17 February, Cummings appeared at Bow Street charged with three murders and was tried at the Old Bailey before Mr Justice Asquith on Thursday 27 April 1942 for the murder of Evelyn Hamilton. The jury retired at 4pm the next day and took just thirty minutes to return a guilty verdict. Asked to speak, Cummins said, "I am completely innocent, sir." The court chaplain placed the black cap on the head of Mr Justice Asquith, who pronounced the death sentence. Cummins was hanged by executioner Albert Pierrepoint in Wandsworth Prison on Thursday 25 June 1942. As his body was taken down, an air raid began.

ELLIS, RUTH
Magdala Tavern, 2a South Hill Park, Hampstead, London NW3 2SB
Telephone: 020-7435 2503
It was outside this Hampstead pub on Easter Sunday 10 April 1955 that Ruth Ellis committed the murder that would lead to her becoming the last woman in Britain to be judicially hanged. The 28-year-old good-time girl pumped four bullets into her lover David Blakely. On being sentenced to death she simply said, "Thanks". Ruth Ellis spent just twenty-three days in the condemned cell and was Albert Pierrepoint's sixteenth female client.

GREAT TRAIN ROBBERY
Leatherslade Farm, Thame Road, Brill, Aylesbury,
Buckinghamshire HP18 9SG
Ay 6.50pm on Wednesday 7 August 1963, the Glasgow to London Royal Mail train pulled out of Glasgow Central station, due to arrive at Euston Station at 4am the next day. Just after 3am, the train was stopped at Bridego Railway Bridge (Number 127), Ledburn, near

Mentmore, Buckinghamshire. Fifteen hooded men in blue boiler suits led by Bruce Reynolds (b. at Charing Cross Hospital, Strand, London WC2 Monday 7 September 1931 d. at Croydon Thursday 28 February 2013) stormed the train and escaped with 120 Royal Mail sacks containing £2,595,997 10s, (£57million at 2022 values) in 636 packages. The train driver, 57-year-old Jack Mills (b. 1 September 1905), was badly injured by being struck over the head with a cosh. He was never the same again and died on Saturday 28 February 1970. The majority of the money was never recovered. The gang retired to Leatherslade Farm – twenty-seven miles away – after the robbery, where they famously played Monopoly with real money. Each of the main participants was given approximately £150,000 each. The alarm was raised at about 4.20am and the gang listening in on shortwave radios heard a policeman say, "A robbery has been committed and you'll never believe it – they've stolen the train!" Reginald Bevins, the Postmaster General, offered a £10,000 (£220,000, 2022) reward to "the first person giving information leading to the apprehension and conviction of the persons responsible for the robbery". On Tuesday 13 August 1963, after a a police sergeant and constable visited Leatherslade Farm after a tip-off, they found many clues left behind by the robbers; the farm was supposed to have been burned down but that plan was bungled and fingerprints were found. Two informants provided eighteen names they said were linked to the robbery. Roger Cordrey was the first gang member to be caught: he had been staying with a friend, William Boal, in a rented, furnished flat above a florist in **Wimborne Road, Moordown, Bournemouth, Dorset BH9 2AA**. Despite having nothing to do with the robbery, Boal (b. Wednesday 22 October 1913) was jailed for twenty-four years in a miscarriage of justice, and died in prison in 1970. The robbers were rounded up not long after and went on trial before Mr Justice Edmund Davies at Aylesbury Assizes, Buckinghamshire, on Monday 20 January 1964. The local court was too small so the offices of Aylesbury Rural District Council were converted for use instead. The trial ran for fifty-one days, heard from 240 witnesses and saw 613 exhibits. It ended on Wednesday 15 April 1964, and Mr Justice Davies jailed Ronnie Biggs, 34, Gordon Goody, 34, Charlie Wilson, 31, Tommy Wisbey, 34, Bobby Welch, 34, Big Jim Hussey, 34 and Roy

James, 28, to thirty years behind bars (twenty-five years for conspiracy to rob and thirty years for armed robbery, the sentences running concurrently). Roger Cordrey, 42, was sent down for twenty years for conspiracy to rob and various receiving stolen goods charges; Brian Field, 29, got twenty-five years (twenty years for conspiracy to rob and five for obstructing justice); Lennie Field (no relation), 31, received the same sentence and solicitor John Wheater received three years for aiding and abetting a crime. On Monday 13 July 1964, the appeals by the Fields against the charges of conspiracy to rob were upheld and their jail terms were reduced to five years. The next day, Cordrey and Boal's convictions for conspiracy to rob were quashed by Mr Justice Fenton Atkinson. On Wednesday 12 August 1964, Charlie Wilson broke out of **Winson Green Prison, Winson Green Road, Birmingham B18 4AS**. In July 1965, Ronnie Biggs, a minor member of the gang despite his subsequent infamy, escaped from **Wandsworth Prison, Heathfield Road, Wandsworth, London SW18 3HU** and remained on the run, latterly in Rio de Janeiro, until May 2001, when he returned to England voluntarily. He was jailed but released on compassionate grounds on Thursday 6 August 2009, two days before his 80th birthday. He died at the **Carlton Court Care Home, 112 Bells Hill, Barnet EN5 2SQ** on Wednesday 18 December 2013, aged 84. Jimmy White stayed at large in Britain until he was arrested in April 1966. He was tried at Leicester Assizes in June 1966 before Mr Justice Nield, who jailed him for eighteen years. Buster Edwards fled to Mexico in July 1965 to join Bruce Reynolds, but returned voluntarily to England in 1966, where he was sentenced to fifteen years. Charlie Wilson moved to Canada and lived under the name Ronald Alloway; he was arrested on Thursday 25 January 1968. On Saturday 6 June 1964, Bruce Reynolds arrived in Mexico but left for Canada in 1966. He later returned to England where he was arrested by Tommy Butler, the unmarried Flying Squad detective who lived with his mother. Butler greeted him with "Hello, Bruce, it's been a long time" and Reynolds replied, "C'est la vie". Brian Field was released from prison in 1967 and changed his name to Brian Carlton. On Friday 27 April 1979, he and his second wife were killed in a car crash on the M4 motorway. Charlie Wilson was the last Great Train Robber to be released. On Tuesday 24 April 1990, he was slicing cucumbers for a salad at his villa in Llanos de Nagüeles, near Marbella, Spain, when a young man in a baseball cap turned up on a mountain bike and asked Wilson's wife Pat if he could have a word with her husband. He then shot Wilson and Bobo, the family alsatian, before escaping over the back wall. Buster Edwards became a flower seller outside Waterloo station after his release and committed suicide on Monday 28 November 1994 by hanging himself in his lock-up on **Greet Street, Lambeth, London SE1 8NP**. Roy James was released in August 1975. After various criminal enterprises, he died on Thursday 21 August 1997. Bruce Reynolds, the last to be caught, was released from jail on Tuesday 6 June 1978. He died aged 81 at his flat on **Addiscombe Road, Croydon, Surrey** on Thursday 28 February 2013. Jim Hussey was released in November 1975. Tommy Wisbey and Hussey were imprisoned in July 1989 for cocaine dealing. Wisbey died on Friday 30 December 2016 aged 86, while Hussey died on Monday 12 November 2012 aged 79 after apparently making a deathbed confession claiming that he was the gang member who had coshed Jack Mills. Bob Welch was released on Monday 14 June 1976. Gordon Goody was released from prison on Tuesday 23 December 1975. He died at Mojacar, southern Spain on Friday 29 January 2016.

HANRATTY, JAMES
Deadman's Hill, A6, near Clophill, Bedfordshire

At 9.30pm on Tuesday 22 August 1961, married father-of-two Michael Gregsten, 36, was in his parked grey Morris Minor in a cornfield in Dorney Reach, Buckinghamshire, with his 22-year-old lover Valerie Storie, when a man approached with a gun. He told Gregsten to drive and, thirty miles later, in the early hours of Wednesday 23 August, they pulled to a halt in a layby on the A6 in Bedfordshire known as Deadman's Hill. At 3am, the man shot Gregsten and then raped Storie before shooting her five times and driving away, eventually dumping the stolen car in Ilford, Essex, where it was found at 6.30am. Storie survived her appalling injuries to describe her assailant, and an identikit was issued. Two cartridge cases belonging to the gun were found in a room in the Vienna Hotel in Maida Vale: the occupant the night before the murder had been the petty crook James Hanratty (b. in Kent Sunday 4 October 1936). A man called Peter Alphon stayed in the room the following night. On Monday 9 October 1961, Hanratty was arrested in Blackpool and identified as the A6 killer. At first, Hanratty claimed he was in Liverpool, then changed his story and said that he was in a boarding house: **Ingledene, 19 Kinmel Street, Rhyl LL18 1AH**. Changing his alibi probably cost him his life as he was convicted and hanged at Bedford Prison at 8am on Wednesday 4 April 1962. There was little confidence in the soundness of Hanratty's conviction and a public campaign began to clear his name, involving, amongst others, John Lennon, Yoko Ono and the campaigning journalist Paul Foot. On Friday 12 May 1967, Peter Alphon confessed to the crime, saying he had been paid to end the relationship between Gregsten and Storie. The Hanratty family continued to campaign for a pardon and their hopes were raised with the advent of DNA testing. On Thursday 22 March 2001 Hanratty's body was exhumed, and a sample of his DNA was taken and compared to that found at the crime scene. The results were not what the Hanratty family and supporters were hoping for. The results showed there was a $2\frac{1}{2}$million to one chance that the samples came from someone other than Hanratty. On Friday 10 May 2002, Lord Woolf, the Lord Chief Justice, said, "In our judgment... the DNA evidence establishes beyond doubt that James Hanratty was the murderer."

HOSEIN BROTHERS, KIDNAPPING OF MURIEL MCKAY BY
St Mary's House, 20 Arthur Road, Wimbledon, London SW19 7DZ

It was from this house at about 6pm on Monday 29 December 1969 that Trinidad-born Muslims Arthur Hosein, 34, and his younger brother Nizamodeen abducted Muriel McKay (b. Adelaide, South Australia Wednesday 4 February 1914), 55, mistakenly believing she was 25-year-old Anna Murdoch, the wife of the newspaper tycoon. After an unsuccessful stint in the Army where he was court-martialled, Arthur Hosein became a tailor in Hackney before buying Rooks Farm, a remote, twelve-acre dilapidated pig farm at Stocking Pelham on the Essex-Hertfordshire border in 1967. Unable to make ends meet, he hatched the kidnap plot after seeing Rupert Murdoch being interviewed on television by David Frost. Arthur Hosein followed Murdoch's Rolls-Royce to the Wimbledon house, unaware that it had been loaned to the tycoon's deputy chairman,

Alick McKay, while the Murdochs were on holiday in Australia. Arthur Hosein telephoned Alick McKay: "We are Mafia M3. We tried to get Rupert Murdoch's wife. We couldn't get her so we took yours instead. You have a million by Wednesday night or we will kill her." When DSC Smith, leading the inquiry, was asked if police were sure they were investigating a genuine ransom demand he replied, "How do we know? We've never had one before." Forty-one days later, police raided Rooks Farm and arrested Arthur Hosein after his Volvo was seen repeatedly driving past the briefcases that held the ransom demand. His fingerprints were found on the ransom note. Mrs McKay's body was never found. During their trial at the Old Bailey on Monday 14 September 1970 the brothers blamed each other, but neither confessed. Arthur was sentenced to life imprisonment and twenty-five years for kidnapping, fourteen years for blackmail and ten years for sending threatening letters. Nizamodeen received the same sentence, except ten years less on the kidnap charge. It was generally believed Mrs McKay had been drugged, shot, butchered and fed to the Hoseins' herd of Wessex Saddleback pigs. Arthur died in 2009 in prison and Nizamodeen returned to Trinidad on his release. In December 2021 in an interview for a television documentary, Nizamodeen claimed that far from being fed to pigs, Mrs McKay had collapsed and died while watching a news report about her kidnapping. He then buried her body on the farm.

IRANIAN EMBASSY SIEGE
16 Princes Gate, London SW7 1PT
Telephone: 01-584 8101

At 11.30am on Wednesday 30 April 1980, six men calling themselves the Democratic Revolutionary Movement for the Liberation of Arabistan took control of the Iranian embassy in central London. They wanted autonomy for Khūzestān, a petrol-rich area in southern Iran. They then demanded the freeing of ninety-one political prisoners. They took twenty-six hostages – twenty men and six women – including PC Trevor Lock, who had been guarding the building, and two BBC employees, journalist Chris Cramer, 32 and Sim Harris, a sound recordist. The corporation broadcast an appeal from the terrorists, who released five of their hostages. Cramer was released on the second day because he was suffering from acute dysentery, although he later admitted that he had exaggerated his illness. At 7pm on Bank Holiday Monday 5 May 1980, the sixth day, the terrorists killed press attaché Abbas Lavasani and threw his body outside. Twenty masked members of the Counter Revolutionary Warfare (CRW) wing of the SAS had been sent to the embassy on the first day. The five four-man teams had rehearsed the mission in a mock-up of the building in a nearby Army barracks in central London. The SAS went into action at 7.23pm, twenty-three minutes after Mr Lavasani had been thrown from the building, with an explosive charge in the second floor stairwell at the rear of the building. At the same time the power to the building was cut and stun grenades were thrown. Five of the six terrorists were killed in Operation Nimrod and nineteen hostages were saved. One hostage, Ali Akbar Samadzadeh, was killed by a terrorist during the attack. The remaining terrorist, Fowzi Nejad, pretended to be a hostage and was taken outside. When the SAS realised their error, one soldier wanted to take him back inside, but the presence of the world's media stopped him.

JACK THE RIPPER

The unknown killer struck five times between Friday 31 August and Friday 9 November 1888. Theories about his identity abound – he was either a cricketer (Montague John Druitt), a prince (Albert Victor, Duke of Clarence), a cotton merchant (James Maybrick), a Jewish slaughterman (unnamed), a confidence trickster (Michael Ostrog), a former lover of Mary Kelly (Joseph Barnett), a directory compiler (Thomas Cutbush), a hairdresser (Aaron Kosminksi), a surgeon (Sir William Withey Gull), a killer (James Kelly), a plumber (Frederick Deeming), a poisoner (Dr Thomas Neill Cream), a cobbler (John Pizer, otherwise known as "Leather Apron"), a painter (Walter Sickert), another surgeon (Vassily Konovalov), a quack doctor (Francis Tumblety), a philanthropist (Dr Thomas Barnardo), a shopkeeper (Edward Buchan), a military historian (Sir George Arthur), another doctor ("Dr Stanley"), a Cambridge University Fellow (James Kenneth Stephen), a journalist and sacked doctor (Robert Donston

Stephenson), an insurance salesman (G. Wentworth Bell Smith), a coroner (Dr William Wynn Westcott), a butcher (Jacobs), a sawdust seller (William Henry Bury), another doctor (Dr Cohn), yet another doctor (Frederick Chapman), still another doctor (John Hewitt), a former soldier (William Grant Grainger), a vagrant (Alfred Gray), a traveller (Frank Edwards), a barber (Severin Klosowski otherwise known as George Chapman), another surgeon (Oswald Puckeridge), a hairdresser (Charles Ludwig), a landlord (John McCarthy) and even a woman (Olga Tchkersoff).

Mary Ann "Polly" Nichols
Bucks Row, London E1

The first victim of the Whitechapel murderer, Polly Nichols was last seen alive, drunk, at 2.30am on Friday 31 August 1888 on the corner of Osborne Street and Whitechapel High Street. At 1.20am she had been turned away from a doss house at 18 Thrawl Street because she did not have the requisite 4d. She told the deputy lodging house keeper, "I'll soon get my doss money, see what a jolly bonnet I have now." At 3.45am her corpse was discovered with her skirt pulled up. The body was taken to the mortuary at the Old Montague Street Workhouse Infirmary. The 5ft 2in Nichols, five days past her 43rd birthday when she was murdered and a mother of five, was buried in grave 49500, square 318 of Ilford Cemetery on the afternoon of Thursday 6 September. Thousands watched the cortège pass. In late 1996, the cemetery authorities decided to mark the grave with a plaque. Bucks Row is now Durward Street, and runs between Brady Street and Vallance Road.

"Dark Annie" Chapman
29 Hanbury Street, London E1 5JR

On Saturday 8 September 1888, "Dark Annie" Chapman – so-called because she had wavy, dark-brown hair – became the Ripper's second victim. Short (5ft) and stout, she was discovered shortly before 6am in the rear yard of 29 Hanbury Street, a three-storey house built in about 1740. Chapman's dress was pulled up over her knees and her intestines lay over her left shoulder. Her throat was cut deep to the spine and there were two cuts on the left side of the spine. On Friday 14 September 1888 she was buried secretly in Manor Park. She was 48.

"Long Liz" Stride
Dutfield's Yard, 40 Berner Street, London E1

Long Liz was the third victim, and the first to be killed on Sunday
30 September 1888. At 1.05am, Louis Diemschütz, a 26-year-old
Russian Jew and seller of cheap jewellery, discovered Long Liz's body
as he turned his pony trap into Berner Street from Commercial Road.
The pony shied and Diemschütz saw what he first thought was a pile
of dirt. When it didn't move after he had prodded it with his whip,
he lit a match and saw the corpse. He believed that the murderer was
still present, and went to raise the alarm at the nearby International
Workingmen's Educational Association at 40 Berner Street, where he
was the steward. The body was not mutilated, so it is assumed that the
Ripper was disturbed. Long, 44, was buried on Saturday 6 October
1888 in grave 15509, square 37 at **East London Cemetery, Grange
Road, Plaistow, London E13 0HB**. Berner Street is now Henriques Street
(named after the Jewish philanthropist Sir Basil Henriques (1890-1961)).

Catherine Eddowes
Mitre Square, London EC3A

Eddowes was the fourth victim, the second to be murdered on Sunday
30 September 1888, and the only victim to come under the aegis of the
City of London rather than the Metropolitan Police. Eddowes had been
disembowelled, and a piece of her ear, her left kidney and part of her
entrails were missing. Less than three-quarters of an hour before her
death, 46-year-old Eddowes had been released at 1am by the City of
London Police, who had arrested her for being drunk and disorderly.
At 1.45am PC Edward Watkins discovered her body in the south-west
corner of Mitre Square; it was taken to Golden Lane Mortuary. There
is no direct evidence that Eddowes was a prostitute. She was interred in
grave 49336, square 318, in **Manor Park Cemetery, Sebert Road, Forest
Gate, London E12** on Monday 8 October 1888. Square 318 has since been
reused as part of the Memorial Gardens for cremated remains. Eddowes
now lies beside the Garden Way in front of Memorial Bed 1849. In late
1996, the cemetery authorities marked the grave with a plaque.

Mary Jane Kelly
13 Miller's Court, 26 Dorset Street, Christchurch, London E1

On Friday 9 November 1888, 5ft 7in Mary Kelly became the fifth
and final victim of the Ripper – she was also the youngest and

the only victim to be killed indoors. At 11.45pm on 8 November she returned home, drunk, accompanied by a man, and told her neighbour she was going to sing. For the next hour she sang *Only a Violet I Picked from My Mother's Grave*, despite being told at 12.30am to keep the noise down. At 2am she was seen in Commercial Street where she picked up a client. At just before 4am a cry of "Murder!" was heard from Kelly's room, but no one went to investigate. Her brutally mutilated body was found at 10.45am by Thomas "Indian Harry" Bowyer who had come to collect the rent on behalf of his boss, John McCarthy. Mary Jane Kelly, who was 25 years old, was buried on Monday 19 November in grave number 66 in row 66, plot 10 of **St Patrick's Roman Catholic Cemetery, Langthorne Road, London E11 4HL**. Oddly, four of the five victims had links to Dorset Street. Annie Chapman had lodged with Jack Sivvy at 30 Dorset Street and was living at number 35 when she was murdered. Liz Stride had lived at 38 Dorset Street with Michael Kidney, and Catherine Eddowes is thought to have occasionally dossed at number 26. Dorset Street was later renamed Duval Street, but is now an unnamed service road between Crispin Street and Commercial Street. Miller's Court was demolished in 1929. The site of the murder is now a multi-storey car park.

The Ten Bells
84 Commercial Street, London E1 6LY
Telephone: 020-7366 1721
A Spitalfields pub supposedly frequented by at least two of the Ripper's victims. From 1976 until 1988 it was called the Jack the Ripper, until feminists insisted it reverted to its former name.

JACK THE STRIPPER

A series of six unsolved murders occurred between Sunday 2 February 1964 and Tuesday 16 February 1965 and were also known as "the Hammersmith Nudes Murders". Jack the Stripper's victims were all prostitutes from the Notting Hill-Bayswater area; they were all between 5ft and 5ft 3in tall; they had all suffered from some form of venereal disease; they all disappeared between 11pm and 1am and their bodies were thought to have been dumped between 5am and 6am.

Hannah Tailford
Pontoon by Hammersmith Bridge

On Sunday 2 February 1964, 30-year-old Hannah Tailford's naked body was found under a pontoon by Hammersmith Bridge by two brothers preparing for a weekend's sailing. Tailford (b. at Heddon-on-the-Wall, Northumberland Saturday 19 August 1933) had drowned; her knickers were in her mouth and her stockings were around her ankles. She had last been seen alive on Friday 24 January 1964 at her home in **Pembridge Villas, Notting Hill, W11** that she shared with her boyfriend Alan Lynch and her 3-year-old daughter Linda. It was initially believed that she had been killed because of her reputation for hosting kinky parties and may have been blackmailing someone. This was later discounted. At the autopsy it was discovered she was pregnant.

Irene Lockwood
Duke's Meadow, Upper Mall, London W6 9TA

The second victim's naked body was found at 8.30am on Wednesday 8 April 1964 at Duke's Meadow, about 300 yards from Hannah Tailford. The location was known both as a spot for courting couples and a place where prostitutes took their clients. 26-year-old Lockwood's (b. at Walkeringham, Nottinghamshire Thursday 29 September 1938) speciality was stealing a client's wallet as he removed his trousers. She had also appeared in porn films and, like Hannah Tailford, 5ft Irene, of **Denby Road, Ealing, London W13**, was pregnant when she was murdered. On 27 April Kenneth Archibald, a 54-year-old bachelor caretaker, walked into Notting Hill police station and confessed to the murder. After a six-day trial beginning on Friday 19 June 1964 he was found not guilty. He had retracted his confession, claiming to have made it while drunk, and was scared he was going to be accused of theft at **Holland Park Tennis Club, Addison Road, Notting Hill W11** where he was the caretaker.

Helene Barthelemey
Swyncombe Avenue, Brentford, Middlesex W5 4DS

On Friday 24 April 1964 the body of convent-educated Helene Catherine Barthelemey (b. at Ormiston, East Lothian 9 June 1941), 22, was discovered in a driveway near Swincombe Avenue in Brentford. She was naked and four of her front teeth were missing. There were traces of spray paint on her body and semen in her throat.

Mary Fleming
Berrymede Road, London W4 5JD

On Tuesday 14 July 1964 the Stripper's fourth victim, Mary Fleming (b at Clydebank Saturday 16 September 1933), 30, was found naked outside a garage in a cul-de-sac in Chiswick. She was in a sitting position and was initially mistaken for a shop dummy. Her false teeth were missing; she had paint on her body and semen in her mouth. She had last been seen alive at 1am on Saturday 11 July. She lived in one room in **Lancaster Gardens, London W11** with her two children. Not long before the discovery of Fleming's body, a van had pulled out sharply in Acton Lane (which adjoins Berrymede Road), almost causing a collision with another motorist.

Margaret McGowan
Hornton Street, London W8 4NR

Victim number five, a 21-year-old Glaswegian, was found naked in a car parked in a car park opposite High Street Kensington Tube station in west London on Wednesday 25 November 1964. Again there were traces of paint in her body and semen in her mouth. A front tooth had been forcibly removed. A mother of three illegitimate children, she had used a number of aliases, one of which was Frances Brown, which she had used when giving evidence at the trial of Stephen Ward the previous year. She was born on Sunday 3 January 1943 and had disappeared on Friday 23 October.

Bridie O'Hara
Westpoint Trading Estate, Westfield Road, London W3

The final victim, 27-year-old Bridie O'Hara (b. Dublin Wednesday 2 June 1937), had last been seen alive on Monday 11 January 1965 in the Shepherd's Bush Hotel. From the post mortem it appeared that her corpse had been kept for some time before being dumped in undergrowth in Acton, where it was discovered by Ernest Beauchamp on Tuesday 16 February 1965. Again there was semen in her mouth and some of her teeth were missing. Police discovered that paint flecks on the women's bodies matched those from a paint-spraying shop on the Heron Factory Estate. This was likely where the women's corpses were kept prior to being dumped. It seemed that they had all choked to death while performing fellatio on their killer. The removal of the teeth led some to believe that further oral relief was performed post mortem.

John du Rose, in charge of the case, waged a war of nerves with the killer. He announced that twenty suspects had been whittled down to three. One of them, a married security guard from Putney, committed suicide in June 1965, saying that he could not "stand the strain any longer". However, despite intensive searches of the man's home, police found nothing to link him to any of the murders. Two unlikely suspects were the boxer Freddie Mills (see page 182) and Tommy Butler, the detective who investigated the Great Train Robbery (see page 96). Butler was a small, bald, unmarried man who lived with his mother near Hammersmith Bridge. Born in Shepherd's Bush, he knew the area well and as a senior policeman would have been aware of detection methods. However, there is no real evidence linking either Mills or Butler to the murders, which remain unsolved.

KRAY TWINS
178 Vallance Road, London E2 6HR

This two-up, two-down Victorian terraced cottage was the Bethnal Green home of the Kray family. The road was known as "Deserters' Alley" because of the number of fit men there who refused to serve their country in the Second World War, including Charlie Kray, the twins' father. The twins were born on Tuesday 24 October 1933 at **68 Stean Street, Hoxton, London E8** and, encouraged by brother Charlie, began boxing when they were young, perhaps to hide their homosexuality. When Reggie was released from a lunatic asylum in 1959, he spent most of his recovery time in Vallance Road. He found it difficult to adapt to normal life and spent his first few months of freedom sitting by the fire in the front room. He had put on weight in the asylum, began to slurr his speech and now walked with a stiff gait. He only went out at night, when he always carried a .32 Beretta and a sword stick. Later that year Reggie was jailed for eighteen months, leaving Ronnie in charge of their criminal empire. It was a disaster, and business suffered until Reggie was freed. Both brothers lived at Vallance Road until 1963, when they moved to Flat 1 (Reggie) and Flat 8 (Ronnie), **Cedra Court, Cazenove Road, Clapton, London N16 6AT**. Each day a barber arrived there to massage surgical spirit and olive oil into their hair, and tailors visited to make bespoke clothes for them. Every night, Ron bathed his feet in a bowl of milk and rosewater. Despite being barely able to read, write or count, the twins became successful businessmen and developed an unfounded reputation that they "only killed their own kind" – "Yus," said the cockney actor Arthur Mullard, "Ooman beings". In 1967, the twin's parents, Violet and Charles, left and moved to **Flat 43, Braithwaite House, Bunhill Row, London EC1Y 8NE** when redevelopment of the area began. The Vallance Road house was knocked down in 1968. A housing association property now stands on the site.

The Blind Beggar, 337 Whitechapel Road, London E1 1BU
Telephone: 020 7247 6195

The Blind Beggar pub is named for Henry de Montford, who was wounded at the Battle of Evesham on Tuesday 4 August 1265. A nobleman's daughter discovered de Montford blind and dressed as a beggar, and nursed him back to health. The pub opened in 1894. It was here on Wednesday 9 March 1966 that Ronnie Kray shot and killed George Cornell, a member of the south London Richardson gang. Kray and his associate Ian Barrie walked into the pub and saw Cornell sitting on a stool by the U-shaped bar sipping a light ale. Kray, carrying two guns – a Luger and a Mauser – fired three shots, but only one hit Cornell. The song on the pub's record player (not jukebox) at the time was "The Sun Ain't Gonna Shine Anymore" by the Walker Brothers. The usual reason given for the murder is that Cornell had called Ronnie a "fat poof" but, in 1989, Ronnie said Cornell had threatened to kill him. The two guns were disposed of – the Mauser was discovered in the River Lea in 1993 and is now in Scotland Yard's Black Museum. The Luger has never been found. Cornell did not die immediately, but was admitted to the London Hospital at 8.49pm and at 9.30pm he was taken, unconscious, to **Maida Vale Hospital, 4 Maida Vale, London W9 1TL**, where he died at 10.29pm before an operation could be performed on him. When Cornell's wife, Olive, learned that he had been murdered, she went to Vallance Road and threw a brick through the window. Not long after, her cottage burned down.

Esmeralda's Barn, 50 Wilton Place, London SW1X 8RH

This was a gambling club that the Krays took a controlling interest in for £1,000 thanks to slum landlord Peter Rachman (see page 200). When Ronnie learned of Rachman's rent racket, he decided that he wanted a piece. After some trouble, Rachman was persuaded to pay protection money to stop the Krays' henchmen from interfering with his own thugs. Rachman paid the first instalment with a cheque which bounced and went to ground before Ronnie could take personal revenge. However, Rachman's thugs found their rounds disrupted and were met with violence; as Reggie said, "His rent collectors were big, but our boys were bigger." Rachman did not want to become beholden to the Krays so he put them in touch with Stefan de Faye, who owned a gaming club called Esmeralda's Barn. The Esmeralda of the title was Esmeralda (sometimes Esme) Noel-Smith, who accidentally gassed herself and another hostess in her bed in February 1955. De Faye stayed on as director and manager of the club. Esmeralda's Barn was one of the first beneficiaries of the Gaming Act, which legalised gambling. It had attractive croupiers, top staff to take care of the needs of the patrons and a fine bar and restaurant. The Krays' friend Leslie Payne restructured the legal ownership of the club so the executive director owned 50 percent, with the twins and Payne sharing the other half. The Krays were said to earn £100,000 a year for their stake in the club for doing nothing. However, when Reggie was sent back to prison after losing an appeal, Ronnie ran riot and the club was soon owed thousands in debts that were never paid. Ronnie was offered £1,000 a week to stay away, but when he refused, the management left. Esmeralda's Barn closed at the end of 1963 and has since been demolished.

Frank Mitchell, the Mad Axeman
206a Barking Road, East Ham, London E6 3BB

Frank Mitchell was born in Canning Town, East London on Sunday 19 May 1929, one of seven children. He was described as a giant psychopathic simpleton with "the mind of a child of 13 or under" and began his criminal career aged 9 when he stole a bicycle, for which he was put on probation. He was sent to prison for the first time on Monday 9 February 1948 and spent much of his life locked up. In 1955, he was declared "mentally defective" and sent to **Rampton Hospital, Woodbeck, Retford, Nottinghamshire DN22 0PD**, a maximum-security psychiatric facility. He escaped with fellow prisoner Richard Maskell on Friday 18 January 1957 and terrorised the local villages, attacking police with meat cleavers before being captured and sent to Broadmoor. He escaped again in July 1958 and held a married couple hostage with an axe, earning the nickname

"The Mad Axeman" in the media. In October 1958, he was jailed for life for robbery with violence and was sent to Dartmoor Prison in 1962. Mitchell had become friendly with Ronnie Kray when they were both in Wandsworth Prison in the 1950s. As with many of Ronnie's mad ideas, he thought breaking Mitchell out of prison would enhance the Krays' underworld reputation. On Monday 12 December 1966, Mitchell asked the guard if he could feed some ponies while on a work party in the moors. He walked over to a car parked nearby and climbed in. Inside were Kray associates Albert Donoghue, Billy Exley and "Mad" Teddy Smith, who drove him to this flat, owned by Lennie Dunn. A huge manhunt was launched to recapture him. The Krays' plan did not go smoothly, as Mitchell quickly went stir crazy and was not placated by the arrival of blonde prostitute Liza Prescott. The Krays decided that they had to get rid of him. On Saturday 24 December 1966, Mitchell was taken to a van by Albert Donoghue, believing he was on his way to a safe house in the countryside to meet Ronnie. A further complication arose when Mitchell insisted Liza Prescott, with whom he had fallen in love, come with him. Donoghue persuaded him it would be safer for all concerned if she came later. The engine was started and the men in the back of the van, who included Freddie Foreman and Alfie Gerrard, opened fire on Mitchell. It took twelve bullets to kill him. Whether dumped in the sea off Newhaven or used to prop up Bow flyover, his body was never found.

Frances Kray

34 Wimbourne Court, Wimbourne Street, Islington, London N1 7HD

It was here that Frances Shea, Reggie's first wife, committed suicide, unable to cope with life with her violent, homosexual husband. Frances was born at **57 Ormsby Street, Hoxton, London E2 8JG** on Thursday 23 September 1943 and began walking out with Reggie in 1960. He proposed the following year at Steeple Bay in Essex but she turned him down. In February 1965 she said yes when Reggie again proposed, and they married on 19 April 1965 at **St James The Great Church, Bethnal Green Road, Bethnal Green, London E2 0AG**; Frances was 22, Reggie 31. David Bailey was the official photographer (the only wedding he ever worked at) and many celebrity guests attended, including the actress Diana Dors who arrived at the church in a Rolls-Royce. The congregation was lacklustre in the hymn singing, so

Ronnie patrolled the aisles hissing, "Sing you fuckers, sing." Frances's mother Elsie, who was fiercely opposed to the marriage, wore black to the ceremony in protest. The marriage was never consummated and Frances left her husband after only three months. On Tuesday 22 March 1966, Frances visited **Lowe & Company, Kingsland High Street, Dalston, London E8** to change her name from Kray back to Shea by deed poll. In June 1966, she was admitted to a psychiatric ward at **Hackney Hospital, Homerton High Street, London E9 6BE** and was kept in until September of that year. On Monday 17 October 1966, she was admitted to **St Leonard's Hospital, 85 Nuttall Street, Kingsland Road, London N1 5HZ** after taking an overdose of barbiturates. On Monday 30 January 1967, Frances locked herself in the front room of her parents' house at Ormsby Street, turned on the gas fire and took another barbiturate overdose. Rushed to hospital, she was discharged on Tuesday 7 February 1967. Her brother Frankie, 27, offered to put her up in his home with his wife Bubbles and their daughter. Reggie visited his estranged wife and Frances agreed when he suggested a second honeymoon in Ibiza at the end of June. On Monday 5 June, Frances explained to her psychiatrist, Dr Julius Silverstone at Hackney Hospital, that she was going on holiday with her husband and needed some tablets for the flight. She was given a prescription and the next day she and Reggie booked their tickets. On the morning of Wednesday 7 June 1967, Frankie Shea made his sister a cup of tea and left it beside her bed when he left for work. Some intuition played on Frankie's mind and at 2pm he went home from work to find his sister dead in bed. An inquest opened at St Pancras Coroner's Court on Tuesday 13 June where coroner Ian Milne said Frances had suffered "a personality disorder" and killed herself. Ignoring her family's wishes, Reggie took complete control of everything after the suicide – her clothes, jewellery, letters and mementos – and organised the funeral, insisting she be buried as a Kray, not a Shea. The service was at the same church where she had been married. She was buried at **Chingford Mount Cemetery, 121 Old Church Road, Chingford, London E4 6ST** – also the resting place of Charles, Violet, Reggie, Ronnie and Charlie Kray. Charlie Kray senior was born in Shoreditch on Sunday 10 March 1907 and died in Islington on Tuesday 8 March 1983. Charlie junior was born at **26 Gorsuch Street, Shoreditch, London E2** on Friday 9 July 1926 and died at **Parkhurst Prison, 53 Parkhurst Road, Newport, Isle of Wight PO30 5RS** on Tuesday 4 April 2000. Ronnie Kray died from a heart attack in **Wexham Park Hospital, Wexham Park, Slough, Berkshire SL2 4HL** on Friday 17 March 1995. On Saturday 26 August 2000, Home Secretary Jack Straw freed Reggie Kray from Wayland Prison, Norfolk on compassionate grounds. He died thirty-five days later in the honeymoon suite at the **Beefeater Town House Hotel, 18–22 Yarmouth Road, Thorpe St Andrew, near Norwich, Norfolk NR7 0EF** on Sunday 1 October 2000. Frank Shea senior died of a heart attack at Homerton Hospital in March 1987. He was 75. Elsie Shea died in Hackney in 2002, aged 85. Like his sister, Frankie Shea killed himself with a drugs overdose aged 71 on Friday 5 August 2011.

Jack "the Hat" McVitie

Basement Flat, 97 Evering Road, Stoke Newington, London N16 7SL

With Ronnie having killed George Cornell, the pressure was on Reggie to prove his mettle. Jack Dennis McVitie was born on Tuesday 19 April 1932 and became involved with the Krays' firm more as a freelancer than a fully fledged gang member. He was supposedly known as Jack the Hat because of the trilby he wore to cover his baldness. A drug runner in the 1960s, McVitie was given £500 (£9,500 in 2022 values) in 1967 by Ronnie to kill former business partner Leslie Payne, with another £500 when the job was done. McVitie took his friend Billy Exley with him, but they kept the £500 when they arrived at Payne's home and were told by his wife that he was out. On Saturday 28 October 1967, McVitie was invited to a party with the promise of "booze" and "birds" in Stoke Newington at a flat occupied by "Blonde Carol" Skinner, 27. Reggie intended to shoot McVitie as he arrived but the pistol jammed. A quick fight followed before the 6ft 2in, sixteen-stone McVitie tried to leap through an open window; he was too big and became wedged, with just his head and shoulders making it through. He was yanked back inside and Reggie produced a carving knife. Ronnie encouraged his brother, telling him, "Kill him, Reg, kill him." The first stab wound was to McVitie's face, just below his eye. Then he stabbed McVitie repeatedly in the face, chest and stomach, finishing him off by thrusting the blade into McVitie's throat. The twins left the party quickly and the Lambrianou brothers (Chris and Tony), Keith Askem and Ronnie Bender wrapped the corpse in an eiderdown and dumped it outside **St**

Mary's Church, St Marychurch Street, Rotherhithe, London SE16. When the Krays heard what had happened, they ordered the body to be removed, and it was never recovered. Tony Lambrianou later said that he had disposed of McVitie by locking his body in a car and crushing the vehicle into a 3ft square cube. The house remains the same today as it was in 1967. The Krays were eventually caught thanks to the work of Detective Chief Superintendent Leonard Ernest "Nipper" Read (b. at Nottingham on Tuesday 31 March 1925, died Tuesday 7 April 2020 from Covid-19) and his incorruptibles at their office at **Tintagel House, 92 Albert Embankment, London SE1 7TY**. On Tuesday 4 March 1969 at the Old Bailey, the twins were found guilty of murder. Mr Justice Melford Stevenson sentenced them to life, with a recommendation that they should each serve a minimum of thirty years behind bars, saying, "In my view, society has earned a rest from your activities." He said the twins had only told the truth on two occasions during the trial – firstly, when Reggie referred to a barrister as "a fat slob" and secondly, when Ronnie said the judge was biased. The jury had taken six hours and fifty-five minutes to reach their unanimous verdict. Nipper Read said of them, "They were courteous and always referred to me as Mr Read during interviews. But I was never in any doubt of what they were capable of. They were killers and I was often in fear of my life. I find it odd that people think of the Krays as criminal masterminds. They were not clever. If they had been, they would never have been caught."

LAMPLUGH, SUZY
37 Shorrolds Road, Fulham, London SW6 7TP
It was outside this Fulham house at 12.45pm on Monday 28 July 1986 that the 25-year-old brunette estate agent arranged to meet "Mr Kipper" to show him around the property. Lamplugh drove from her office at Sturgis Estate Agents to Shorrolds Road in her B-registration white Ford Fiesta and was never seen again. Her car was discovered at 10pm outside a house for sale in **Stevenage Road, Fulham, London SW6** approximately 1½ miles away. The ignition key was missing and her purse was found in a door storage pocket. During police investigations, witnesses recalled a man arguing with a woman in Shorrolds Road, but no one intervened and they got into a car. In 1994, Suzy Lamplugh was declared legally dead. The chief suspect is

a convicted killer called John Cannan, although he had consistently denied having anything to do with the abduction.

LUCAN, LORD
46 Lower Belgrave Street, Belgravia, London SW1W 0LN

It was in this six-storey house on Thursday 7 November 1974 that the 7th Earl of Lucan (b. as the Honourable Richard John Bingham at 19 Bentinck Street, Marylebone, London Tuesday 18 December 1934) murdered Sandra Rivett, his children's nanny, who had begun work for the family less than three months earlier on Monday 26 August, mistaking her for his estranged wife. Lucan, a gambler nicknamed "Lucky", had become increasingly angry with his wife and had told several of his friends at the **Clermont Club, 44 Berkeley Square, London W1J 5AR** that he wanted to murder her. The club was then a bastion of middle-aged, upper-class men who viewed women with little affection or use other than for breeding purposes. Knowing that Thursday was the nanny's night off, Lucan let himself into the house and removed the light bulb from the kitchen staircase so his victim would not see him. Just before 9pm a woman came down the stairs to make some tea and Lucan struck her over the head with a 2ft piece of lead piping. Unfortunately, the intended victim was not the Countess of Lucan but 29-year-old Sandra Rivett, who had changed her day off. Hearing a commotion, Lady Lucan came downstairs and was attacked by Lucan. She managed to grab him between the legs. Incredibly, he apologised to the woman he had just tried to murder and began to tend her wounds. When he went upstairs to fetch a towel to stem the bleeding, Lady Lucan made her escape.

DID YOU KNOW?

Oddly, in January 1985, a second Lucan nanny was killed. Christabel Martin began working for the Lucans in January 1973 and returned after Sandra Rivett's murder. In October 1985, her husband Nicholas Boyce was convicted of her manslaughter after the jury heard that he had strangled and then dismembered her before roasting and boiling her corpse, which he then dumped around London in skips and dumps in more than 100 plastic bags. He encased her skull in concrete and threw it off Hungerford Bridge while out walking with their 3-year-old son.

The Plumbers Arms, 14 Lower Belgrave Street, Victoria, London SW1W 0LN
Telephone: 020-7730 4067

It was to this pub that Lady Lucan ran, bursting into the saloon bar at 9.50pm on that cold November 1974 day screaming, "Help me, help me, help me! I've just escaped from being murdered. My children, my children! He's murdered my nanny, he's murdered my nanny." So began the biggest manhunt in British history, spanning several continents.

Grants Hill House, Church Street, Uckfield, Sussex TN22 2BN

Lucan fled here, the home of his friends Ian and Susan Maxwell-Scott; he was given a drink by Mrs Maxwell-Scott, as her husband was staying in London after having too much to drink. Lucan rang his mother and then wrote two letters to his brother-in-law Bill Shand Kydd. At 1am after another Scotch and water, he left and disappeared. Lucan's car was discovered in Norman Road, Newhaven two days later, but there was no trace of the missing earl. In 2005, the respected author John Pearson propounded the theory that Lucan had been smuggled out of the country to Switzerland. The shadowy figure who had helped Lucan to escape became fearful that he would return to England and begin a custody battle for his children. Several members of Lucan's social circle might then have been implicated in the events of 7 November. With no other choice, Lucan was murdered and his corpse buried in Switzerland. The house was knocked down and flats built on the site in 2019.

5 Eaton Row, Belgravia, London SW1W 0JA

It was to this mews house that Lord Lucan moved on Sunday 7 January 1973 after he separated from his wife. However, it proved too small for him and within months he had moved to a larger flat nearby.

72a Elizabeth Street, Belgravia, London SW1W 9PD

This was Lucan's home at the time of his disappearance. Police found his passport, wallet, credit cards and some money here. In October 1999, Lord Lucan was officially declared dead by the High Court, but when his son Lord George Bingham attempted to take his seat as the 8th Earl of Lucan, he was told by the Lord Chancellor's office that there was no proof that "the Right Honourable Richard John Bingham, 7th Earl of Lucan" was actually dead. On Wednesday 31 March 1976, Lucan's family silver, ceremonial robes, watch and gambling chips were auctioned at Christie's to help settle his gambling debts, which stood at £61,000.

METROPOLITAN POLICE FORCE
4 Whitehall Place, London SW1A 2BD
The first uniformed police force, the Metropolitan Police Force, went on patrol here at 6pm on Tuesday 29 September 1829. The initial force consisted of around 1,000 men with instructions to patrol the streets within a seven-mile radius of Charing Cross. They were on the streets twelve hours a day, seven days a week and wore blue uniforms to distinguish them from the military red, with a top hat which was useful for standing on to see over walls. They also carried a rattle and a twenty-inch truncheon. In the first six months, half of the recruits were sacked – usually for drunkenness. Their main task was not to catch criminals but to prevent crimes from happening in the first place. In the first four years, they reduced the monetary loss from robberies from £1million to £200,000. The police also had a social effect: shopkeepers began to display their wares in their windows.

METROPOLITAN POLICE DEATH, FIRST ON DUTY
Smith's Place, near Skinner Street, Somers Town, London
The first Metropolitan policeman to die on duty was PC Joseph Grantham on Tuesday 29 June 1830. Whilst patrolling Somers Town, he spotted two very drunk Irishmen quarrelling over a woman. It transpired the two men had started fighting after one of them had been beating his wife. When Grantham intervened, he was kicked to death by all three, a kick to the temple from young bricklayer Michael Duggan the cause of Grantham's death a few minutes later. However, the coroner's jury exonerated Duggan, claiming that Grantham had caused his own death by "over-exertion in the discharge of his duty". The day before he was murdered, Grantham's wife gave birth to twins.

MOORS MURDERERS
Millwards Merchandise, Levenshulme Road, Gorton, Manchester M18
Telephone: EASt 1261
It was at this company that Ian Brady landed a job on Monday 16 February 1959. Millwards held the Lancashire distribution contract for ICI and Brady worked in the stock control department. His colleagues thought of him as intense. None of the women caught

his eye apart from the married receptionist who had been in the Hitler Youth. That changed on Monday 16 January 1961 when Myra Hindley joined the firm as a shorthand typist on £8 a week (£190 at 2022 values). Later, she said, "When I met Ian Brady I was emotionally immature, relatively unsophisticated and sexually inexperienced – I was a virgin and intended to be so until I got married… I can only describe my reaction [to him] as an immediate and fatal attraction, although I had no inkling then of how fatal it would turn out to be." While Brady took very little notice of his colleague, she began to keep a diary of her feelings for him that she locked in her office drawer. The entries included the days when he looked at her or spoke to her and her love for "Ian all over again". Hindley discovered where Brady lived and began taking her baby cousin down his road in the hope she would bump into him, but she never did. At the Millwards Christmas party on Saturday 23 December 1961, Brady kissed all the typists and, as she walked through the door, Hindley too. As the others gradually left, Brady and Hindley left together, and as they walked down Levenshulme Road, he asked her out. After a drink at the **Three Arrows pub, 1 Hyde Road, Gorton, Manchester M18** (the pub has since been demolished and the land is occupied by a self-storage company's car park) they went to the Deansgate cinema where they watched *King Of Kings* starring Jeffrey Hunter as Jesus Christ. On the way home they stopped at the Thatched House for more drinks before they began kissing and caressing each other. Hindley was wearing a girdle and Brady told her he did not like them – she never wore one again. The next night, Christmas Eve, they went to see *El Cid* (premiered at the **Metropole Theatre, 160 Victoria Street, London SW1E 5LB** Wednesday 6 December 1961; demolished March 2013) starring Charlton Heston and Sophia Loren. They ended up going to Midnight Mass but on leaving, Brady urinated against the church wall. They went to her grandmother's house, **7 Bannock Street, Gorton, Manchester M18**, where Hindley lost her virginity to Brady. They continued to date until July 1963 when the discussion of the perfect murder arose.

Pauline Reade: Froxmer Street, Gorton, Manchester M18 8EF

Pauline Catherine Reade (b. Tuesday 18 February 1947) lived at 9 Wiles Street, Gorton, Manchester with her parents Joan (b. Monday 23 April 1928 *née* Hadfield d. 30 May 2000) and Amos (b. Thursday

11 March 1926 d. 23 November 1995). She was 16-years-old and a
practising Roman Catholic. Hindley knew of her because Pauline
went to school with her younger sister Maureen (b. Wednesday 21
August 1946 d. Wednesday 9 July 1980) and had had a brief dalliance
with David Smith, who would go on to marry Maureen. On Friday
12 July 1963, Pauline wanted to go to a dance at the **Railway Workers'
Social Club, 250 Chapman Street, Gorton, Manchester M18 8WQ**,
ten minutes' walk from her home. Two of her friends could not go
because alcohol would be served, but Pauline convinced her mother
that she would be fine. She left home at 7.45pm and eventually came
to Froxmer Street, where she saw a black van parked. The window
was open and as Pauline walked by, Myra Hindley told the teenage
girl that she had lost her glove on Saddleworth Moor and, pointing
to some LPs, told her she could have her choice if she helped to find
the glove. Pauline agreed and they drove to the moor, whereupon
Brady arrived on his motorbike. They led her further onto the moor
where they began undressing and sexually assaulting her despite her
pleas to be left alone. Once they had taken their pleasure, Brady told
the girl to get dressed. He returned to the van, leaving Hindley alone
with Pauline. When he returned, he found that Hindley had tried to
stab Pauline but the blade had bent. She had then punched her in the
face and head. Brady pulled a knife and slit Pauline's carotid artery;
the girl bled out in seconds and was buried on the moor. Joan Reade
rang the police at 2.30am to report her daughter missing. At Bannock
Street, Brady and Hindley burned their clothes.

John Kilbride
Ashton Market, Bow Street, Ashton-under-Lyne,
Lancashire OL6 6BZ
John Kilbride (b. 15 May 1951), 12, lived with his parents, Sheila (b. 15
April 1932 d. Saturday 27 July 2002) and Pat (b. Monday 1 July 1929
d. Monday 3 May 1999), and his five siblings at **262 Smallshaw Lane,
Ashton-under-Lyne, Lancashire OL6 8RW**. Like Pauline Reade, John
Kilbride was a Roman Catholic and had recently started at **St Damian's
Secondary Modern School, Lees Road, Ashton-under-Lyne, Lancashire
OL6 8BH** as part of its first intake. On Saturday 23 November 1963,
the day after President John F. Kennedy was assassinated in Dallas,
Texas, by Lee Harvey Oswald, John went to the cinema with friend

John Ryan to see *The Mongols* starring Jack Palance and Anita Ekberg. The two boys then went to Ashton Market where they earned some pocket money helping the stallholders. Stories vary as to how John was lured into Hindley's hired Ford Anglia car, but he was driven to Saddleworth Moor where he was sexually assaulted then strangled by Brady. He was buried in a shallow grave on **Sail Bark Moss, Oldham, Lancashire OL3 7NN**.

Keith Bennett
Longsight, Manchester M24

Keith Bennett (b. Saturday 12 June 1952), 12, lived with his mother and stepfather, Winnie (b. Thursday 14 September 1933 d. Saturday 18 August 2012) and Jimmy Johnson, and three siblings at **29 Eston Street, Longsight, Manchester M13 0FF**. On Tuesday 16 June 1964, he waved to his pregnant mother on his way to visit Gertrude Bennett, his 65-year-old grandmother, on **Morton Street, Longsight, Manchester M24**. She never saw him again. Hindley waylaid the boy and asked him for some help with putting boxes into her Mini pick-up, after which she said that she would drive him home. She then asked him if he could help her find a glove. When he agreed, she drove the boy to Saddleworth Moor where he was sexually assaulted and strangled at Shiny Brook. Brady photographed the remains before he and Hindley buried him.

Lesley Ann Downey
16 Wardle Brook Avenue, Hattersley, Hyde SK14 3JB

Six months later, 10-year-old Lesley Ann Downey became their fourth victim. Lesley Ann (b. Saturday 21 August 1954). She lived in a first floor maisonette in **Charnley Walk, off Varley Street, Miles Platting, Ancoats, Manchester M40 7AT** with her mother (Gertrude) Ann, (b. Wednesday 11 September 1929 d. at Fallowfield, Manchester Tuesday 9 February 1999 of liver cancer) 36, her boyfriend Alan West and Anne's children by Terry Downey: Terry, 14, Tommy (b. 1956 d. at Princess Eoad, Manchester Monday 31 December 2001), 8 and Brett, 4. On Friday 25 December 1964, 4ft 10in Lesley Ann received a toy sewing machine and some white beads for Christmas. She was never to play with the sewing machine and would be buried with the white beads, a present from her big brother Terry. The next day, Lesley Ann was due to visit a fairground with Terry but he came down with flu and was unable to go. A neighbour offered to take Lesley Ann along with her own offspring, but in the end the small children went alone. When their money ran out, they wandered home – all except Lesley Ann who wanted one more look around the fair. Brady and Hindley were also there and dropped some boxes to attract Lesley Ann's attention. She then got into their car. Brady later claimed that Hindley was in the car alone with Lesley Ann and that he got in a few streets away. Hindley drove the nine miles to Wardle Brook Avenue. Once there, the little girl was stripped, gagged, made to pose for pornographic photographs, raped and killed. As "Jolly Old St Nicholas" and "The Little Drummer Boy" played, Lesley Ann begged for her life, calling Hindley "Mummy" and Brady "Daddy" to try to appeal to their parental side. For at least sixteen minutes the torture continued – we know because Brady and Hindley taped the little girl's last moments on earth. On Sunday 27 December 1964, Brady and Hindley drove Lesley Ann's naked body to Saddleworth Moor and buried her.

Edward Evans
16 Wardle Brook Avenue, Hattersley, Hyde SK14 3JB

The Moors Murderers' fifth and final victim was the only one not buried on the moors. Edward Evans, born on Saturday 3 January 1948, lived with his parents Edith (b. 1921 d. Thursday 20 September 2007) and John Edward Evans (b. at Manchester Wednesday 16 March 1910 d. at Manchester Thursday 17 August 1967), brother Allan and sister Edith at **55 Addison Street, Ardwick, Manchester**. On Wednesday 6 October 1965, Edward left home between 6.15 and 6.30pm. Around 10pm, he stopped at Central Station for a drink, but the bar in the buffet was shut so he went to a gay bar nearby, where he was approached by Ian Brady and invited for a drink. Brady drove the teenager eleven miles to Wardle Brook Avenue, Hattersley. There, Brady and Evans had sex and Hindley went to fetch her brother-in-law David Smith (b. at Withington Hospital, Manchester 9 January 1948 d. at Oughterard, County Galway, Ireland Saturday 5 May 2012) and insisted he come to the house. Once there, he saw Brady attack Evans with an axe, smother him with a cushion and strangle him with an electrical cable. Hindley's grandmother was upstairs in the house at the time. Brady had sprained his ankle, so Smith agreed to return the next day with his baby's pram to help with the corpse. He got home at 3am and told Maureen what had happened. At 6.10am, Smith rang the police from a phone box on his estate. He was taken to Hyde police station where he made a full statement. Superintendent Bob Talbot and Detective Sergeant Alexander Carr went to Wardle Brook Avenue where they arrested Brady on suspicion of murder. On 11 October, Hindley was arrested, charged as an accessary to the murder of Evans and remanded at HMP Risley. On 16 October, the body of Lesley Ann Downey was discovered. Five days later, the police unearthed the "badly decomposed" body of John Kilbride.

Number 2 Court, The Castle, Castle Square, Grosvenor Street, Chester CH1 2DN

The trial of Brady and Hindley began at The Castle, Chester at the Spring Assizes before Mr Justice Fenton Atkinson on Tuesday 19 April 1966. Prosecuting was the Attorney-General (Sir Frederick Elwyn Jones QC, MP) aided by William Lloyd Mars-Jones QC and Ronald Gough Waterhouse. Brady was defended by Hugh Emlyn Hooson QC, MP and David Trevor Lloyd-Jones, while Godfrey Heilpern QC and Philip Curtis represented Hindley. Smith, the chief prosecution witness, sold his story to the *News Of The World* for £1,000 (£20,000 at 2022 values). Brady was in the witness box for more than eight hours, Hindley for six, both pleading not guilty. The trial ended after fourteen days and, at 4.56pm on Friday 6 May 1966, the twelve-man jury filed back into court after deliberating for two hours and sixteen minutes. Brady was found guilty of the murders of Edward Evans, Lesley Ann Downey and John Kilbride. Hindley was found guilty of the murders of Edward Evans and Lesley Ann Downey and not guilty of the murder of John Kilbride. She was found guilty of receiving, comforting, harbouring, assisting and maintaining Brady, knowing that he had murdered John Kilbride. Both were sentenced to life in prison. At the end of the trial, all the windows at 16 Wardle Brook Avenue were smashed. The house was demolished in autumn 1987, as the local council could not find any tenants willing to live in it. The Millwards building was demolished in the 1970s. Though the case was over, public interest in the pair remained high. In 1969, Lord Longford began an ultimately unsuccessful campaign to free Hindley. In the mid-1980s, the pair's co-operation with the police led to the recovery of Pauline Reade's body after 100 days of searching on 1 July 1987. She had been buried three feet below the surface of Hollin Brown Knoll, 100 yards from Lesley Ann Downey. Keith Bennett's body remains missing. In 1997, Piers Morgan asked the new Home Secretary Jack Straw about the possibility of parole for Hindley at a dinner. Straw replied, "Officially, I fully intend to afford her the same rights as any other prisoner in Britain. Unofficially, if you think I'm going down as the Home Secretary who released Myra Hindley, then you must be fucking joking." Hindley died of respiratory and heart failure at **West Suffolk Hospital, Hardwick Lane, Bury St Edmunds, Suffolk IP33 2QZ** on Friday 15 November 2002. Brady (b. at Rottenrow Maternity Hospital, Rottenrow, Glasgow (demolished 2001) Sunday 2 January 1938 as Ian Duncan Stewart) never applied for parole during his time behind bars. He died of restrictive pulmonary disease at **Ashworth Hospital, Parkbourn, Liverpool L31 1HW** on Monday 15 May 2017.

NILSEN, DENNIS

The Scottish former policeman murdered around fifteen men at two addresses in North London. Dennis Andrew Nilsen was born at 10 High Street, Strichen, Fraserburgh, Aberdeenshire on Friday 23 November 1945. When his parents divorced in 1950, he was sent to live with his grandparents. He returned to his mother after his grandfather died aged 62 of a heart attack on 31 October 1951. In 1961, Nilsen left school and in September that year enrolled in the Army Catering Corps, where he cooked for troops in South Yemen, Cyprus, Berlin and, nearer to home, the Shetland Islands. He was discharged in November 1972 and, the following month, joined the Metropolitan Police Force and was posted to Willesden, London as PC Q287. However, a policeman's lot was not a happy one for Nilsen and he left in December 1973 after eight months. In 1974, he landed a job as a civil servant in a jobcentre in **Denmark Street, London WC2**, better known by its nickname Tin Pan Alley because of the music publishers based there.

195 Melrose Avenue, Cricklewood, London NW2 4NA

In November 1975, Nilsen moved here with David "Twinkle" Gallichan whom he had rescued from being hassled outside one of the capital's iconic gay pubs, **Champion, 1 Wellington Terrace, London W2 4LW**. He moved out in 1977 and the following year Nilsen began his killing spree. He picked on gay men and tramps, inviting them to his home offering food and drink. He then strangled or drowned them but kept their bodies for company, often having sex with the corpses. He committed the first murder on Saturday 30 December 1978. The night before, Nilsen had met Stephen Holmes in the **Cricklewood Arms, 75 Cricklewood Lane, London NW2 1HR**, a tough Irish pub, and invited him to Melrose Avenue. In the morning Nilsen strangled him with a tie and then, when unconscious, drowned him in a bucket of water. Nilsen assumed Holmes was about 17 but it turned out he was just 14 and had been on the way home from a gig. On Saturday 11 August 1979, Nilsen burned the remains in his garden. He was never charged with the murder. On Thursday 11 October 1979, Nilsen met Andrew Ho, a student from Hong Kong, in **The Salisbury, 91-93 St Martin's Lane, Covent Garden, London WC2N 4AP**. They went back to Nilsen's where Ho wanted either to be tied up or to tie up Nilsen himself, but Nilsen feared he would be robbed. Nilsen met his second victim, 23-year-old Canadian student Kenneth Ockenden (b. Thursday 9 February 1956), in a pub on Monday 3 December 1979; Nilsen showed him the sights before taking him back to Cricklewood. They got on well, having ham, eggs and chips for dinner before going to an off licence for beer, rum and whisky. Then, as Ockenden listened to a record, Nilsen strangled him with the headphones cord. On Saturday 17 May 1980, 16-year-old runaway Martyn Duffey (b. at Birkenhead Saturday 6 July 1963) went to Nilsen's home where he was strangled in Nilsen's home and drowned in the kitchen sink. In August 1980, Nilsen met 24-year-old Scottish father-of-one and rentboy Billy Sutherland in a pub before strangling him. In October 1980, Nilsen met a Thai rent boy in the Cricklewood Arms and later murdered him. Around the same time, and in the same pub, Nilsen met an Irish labourer who he also killed. His seventh victim was a hippy he found sleeping in a doorway in Charing Cross. They went back to Melrose Avenue where Nilsen strangled him, putting the corpse under the floorboards. On Monday 10 November 1980, Nilsen picked up Douglas Stewart, a Scottish barman, at the gay pub the **Golden Lion, 51 Dean Street, Soho, London W1D 5BH**. Back at

Melrose Avenue, Stewart fell asleep and awoke to find his host trying to throttle him. When called, the police were uninterested, writing it off as a domestic tiff. In late autumn 1980, Nilsen took each of his victims' bodies, built a bonfire and burned them on waste ground behind his flat. In November or December 1980, he murdered his eighth victim after meeting him in the West End, cutting the body up and hiding it under the floorboards. In January 1981, Nilsen picked up and murdered a young Scot he had seen in the Golden Lion, calling in sick so he could spend the day cutting up this body and another he had murdered the year before. In February 1981, Nilsen picked up and murdered another young Scot he had met in the West End. In April 1981, Nilsen picked up his eleventh victim in Piccadilly Circus, an English skinhead who had bragged about how hard he was. Nilsen got him drunk and killed him. On Thursday 17 September 1981, Nilsen found 24-year-old Malcolm Barlow leaning against a garden wall near his home. He took Barlow back, gave him a cup of coffee and called an ambulance. After a night in Park Royal Hospital, he was released and went to see Nilsen to thank him for his kindness. Nilsen invited him for food and drink. That night, Barlow became his last Melrose Avenue victim. On Sunday 4 October 1981, Nilsen took the remains of his last five victims and burned them all on a bonfire, complete with an old car tyre to disguise the smell.

Top Floor, 23d Cranley Gardens, Muswell Hill, London N10 3AA

The next day, Monday 5 October 1981, Nilsen moved to Cranley Gardens in Muswell Hill, which had neither garden nor floorboards. Ever resourceful, he had to improvise and stored the body parts in a wardrobe, chests and cupboards. On Monday 23 November 1981, Nilsen met University of London student Paul Nobbs, 19, at the Golden Lion, and the two men went back to Muswell Hill. It was Nilsen's 36th birthday. The next morning, feeling out of sorts, Nobbs went to see his GP who told him that it looked as if he had been strangled and suggested that he go to the police. Not wanting his sexual preferences to become public, Nobbs did nothing. In December 1981, Nilsen met John Howlett at a pub called **Princess Louise, 208 High Holborn, London WC1V 7EP.** Howlett became the first of Nilsen's victims to die in Muswell Hill in March 1982. Nilsen cut him up, put his body parts around the flat and flushed other bits down the lavatory. In April 1982,

Nilsen met drag queen Carl Stottor at the gay pub **The Black Cap, 171 Camden High Street, London NW1 7JY**. He awoke in Muswell Hill to find Nilsen attempting to strangle him. He lost consciousness and then awoke again to find Nilsen trying to drown him. Then, in a total volte face, Nilsen let him go. On 28 June 1982, he was posted to the job centre in Kentish Town. In September 1982, Nilsen met 27-year-old father of one Graham Allen in **Shaftesbury Avenue, London WC2**. Back at Muswell Hill, as Allen ate an omelette, Nilsen strangled him. He put the body in the bath where he left it for three days before carrying out the same operation as with John Howlett's body. It was remnants of Allen that blocked the drains at Cranley Gardens; the drain-cleaning company Dyno-Rod called and Mike Cattran set out to investigate. Before that, Nilsen committed one more murder in Muswell Hill. Alcoholic drug addict Stephen Sinclair, 20, was on Oxford Street when Nilsen saw him on Wednesday 26 January 1983. He chatted him up and bought him a burger before suggesting they repair to Nilsen's home. In Cranley Gardens, Sinclair drank alcohol and used heroin before Nilsen strangled him and cut up his corpse. To try to escape detection, Nilsen visited **Kentucky Fried Chicken, 278 Muswell Hill Broadway, London N10 2QR** (now a pizzeria), bought chicken, washed away the mystical blend of eleven herbs and spices and flushed the chicken down the drains. The lumps of white flesh led to the police being called, and pathologist Professor David Bowen identified them as human. Detective Chief Inspector Peter Jay went to Cranley Gardens and waited until Nilsen returned from work at 5.40pm. With two other policemen, Detective Inspector Steve McCusker and Detective Constable Geoffrey Butler, DCI Jay went up to the flat and was met by a sickly smell. When Nilsen was told of the human flesh in the drains, he replied, "Oh my God, how awful." Jay lost patience and snapped, "Now, don't mess about, Nilsen. Where's the rest of the body?" Nilsen indicated his wardrobe, which contained two plastic bags. He was arrested on Wednesday 9 February 1983 and when asked on the way to the station how many bodies were involved, gave the shocking answer "Fifteen or sixteen, since 1978." The police had thought only one or two. Nilsen went on trial at the Old Bailey on Monday 24 October 1983 and was found guilty of six murders and two attempted murders and sentenced to life behind bars on Friday 4

November 1983. In 2001, in **HMP Whitemoor, Longhill Road, March, Cambridgeshire PE15 0PR,** he sued over being denied access to gay porn – he lost the case. In December 1994, Home Secretary Michael Howard imposed a whole life tariff, which was ruled illegal on Saturday 13 July 2013 by the European Court of Human Rights. On Thursday 10 May 2018, Nilsen was taken from **HMP Full Sutton, Moor Lane, Full Sutton, East Riding of Yorkshire YO41 1PS** to York Hospital after complaining of severe stomach pains. He died two days later of pulmonary embolism and retroperitoneal haemorrhage.

PAYNE, CYNTHIA
32 Ambleside Avenue, London SW16 1QP

The luncheon vouchers madam. Cynthia Payne (b. at Bognor Regis, Sussex 24 December 1932) came to public attention in 1980 when she was convicted of running a brothel here. In 1978, police raided her premises and found fifty-three men who had paid to be spanked by young women – what made the situation unusual was that they paid with luncheon vouchers. Payne was jailed for eighteen months, reduced to six months and a fine on appeal. She served four months in Holloway prison. A film of her life, *Personal Services*, was made in 1987 starring Julie Walters, and Payne held a party to celebrate. It, too, was raided by the police. Payne appeared on various television shows but her party-giving career was over. On Thursday 14 July 1988, Payne stood for Parliament in the Kensington by-election as a candidate for the Rainbow Alliance – Payne and Pleasure Party. She came sixth (out of fifteen candidates) with 193 votes. In the 1992 General Election, she stood in her own constituency of Streatham and again came sixth, this time with 145 votes. Payne died, aged 82, at King's College Hospital on 15 November 2015.

PIERREPOINT, ALBERT
Help the Poor Struggler, 303 Manchester Road,
Hollinwood, near Oldham, Lancashire OL8

Albert Pierrepoint (b. at 5 Green End, Clayton, Bradford, West Yorkshire BD14 6BS Thursday 30 March 1905) was, by far, the most prolific hangman of the twentieth century, having executed an estimated 433 men and seventeen women in his twenty-four-year-long career. On Thursday 13 December 1945, he hanged thirteen

German war criminals at Hameln jail, including Irma Greese, Elizabeth Volkenrath and Juana Boreman, and ten men including Josef Kramer, the "Beast of Belsen". He is thought to have hanged around 200 Nazis in all. On his return to Britain, Pierrepoint opened a public house with his wife Anne called Help the Poor Struggler. He denied rumours that he had put up signs reading "No hanging about the bar", although the actress Diana Dors claimed he had told her this while she was filming *Yield to the Night*, a 1956 film based on the story of Ruth Ellis (see page 96), whom Pierrepoint had hanged. He resigned as hangman on Wednesday 29 February 1956 in a dispute over expenses. He had gone to Strangeways in January 1956 to hang Thomas Bancroft but arrived only to find that Bancroft had been reprieved. Pierrepoint claimed the full fee of £15 (more than £400 at today's prices), but was offered just £1 in out-of-pocket expenses by the Under Sheriff of Lancashire. Pierrepoint appealed to his employers, the Prison Commission, but they refused to get involved. The Under Sheriff sent him a cheque for £4 in final settlement. Pierrepoint never told his wife that he was a hangman until after they were married, and he claimed that she never asked him a single question about his other life. He retired to Southport, where, suffering eventually from Alzheimer's disease, he died of bronchopneumonia at **1 Westbourne Road, Southport, Merseyside PR8 2JU** on Friday 10 July 1992, aged 87. The pub closed in 1972 and was later demolished when construction began on the M60 motorway.

RATTENBURY, ALMA
Villa Madeira, 5 Manor Road, Bournemouth, Dorset BH1 3ET

On Wednesday 26 September 1934, an advert appeared in the *Bournemouth Echo*: "Daily willing lad, 14-18, for house-work; Scout-trained preferred. Apply between 11-12, 8-9 at 5 Manor Road, Bournemouth." The house, better known as the Villa Madeira, belonged to the retired architect Francis Mawson Rattenbury, (b. at Leeds Friday 11 October 1867) 67, where he lived with his 47-year-old third wife Alma (b. at London Friday 23 September 1887), Christopher Pakenham (b. at Queens, Queens County, New York, USA Friday 8 July 1921 d. at Raritan Township, Barnes County, North Dakota, USA Monday 30 October 1995) her 13-year-old son from a previous marriage, their 5-year-old son John (b. at Victoria, Capital Regional District, British Columbia, Canada Thursday 27 December 1928 d. at Scottsdale, Maricopa County, Arizona, United States of America Sunday 28 March 2021), and Alma's live-in companion-housekeeper Irene Riggs. Two months later, 5ft 6in 18-year-old George Stoner moved in in response to the advertisement, and not long after began an affair with the mistress of the house. Francis Rattenbury was impotent and had not had sexual relations with his wife since John's birth. He drank whisky and slept on the settee downstairs while his wife entertained her lover in the marital bed. Despite his age and infirmity, Rattenbury became the object of Stoner's jealousy, and the younger man was furious when Alma spent time with her husband. On the weekend of 23/24 March 1935, Stoner and Alma enjoyed time away in London. On the evening of Sunday 24 March 1935, Stoner bashed Rattenbury over the head with a wooden mallet he had borrowed from his grandparents supposedly to erect a screen in the garden. Francis Rattenbury was taken to hospital where he hovered between life and death. Early the next day the police arrived at the Villa Madeira to find Alma incoherent through drink and babbling that that she had "done him in". They arrested her for attempted murder. On Wednesday 27 March, Stoner confessed to Irene Riggs and he too was taken into custody. When Francis died of his injuries, the charges were altered to murder. Alma and Stoner went on trial in Court Number One at the Old Bailey before Sir Travers Humphreys KC on Monday 27 May 1935. The Prosecution was led by Reginald Powell Croom-Johnson KC and Anthony Hawke. Alma was represented by Terence James O'Connor KC, Ewen Montagu and Mr Midford. Stoner, who was represented by Joshua David Casswell, refused to say anything other than answer to his name. His former lover was more loquacious and was found not guilty and released on Friday 31 May 1935. Stoner was found guilty of murder and sentenced to death. Alma was bereft and, on Tuesday 4 June 1935, bought a kitchen knife, took a train to Bournemouth and stabbed herself on the Avon riverbank at Three Arches railway bridge near Christchurch, three of the cuts penetrating her heart. She had written, "If I only thought it would help Stoner I would stay but it has been pointed out too vividly that

I cannot help him – and that is my death sentence." Stoner, when informed of her death, broke down and wept. Meanwhile, more than 300,000 people signed a petition demanding clemency, and the Home Secretary commuted Stoner's sentence to penal servitude for life. He was released after seven years and fought in the Second World War. In September 1990, Stoner was again in the news when he was given two years' probation for indecently assaulting a 12-year-old boy in a public lavatory. He died of dementia and a brain tumour at **Christchurch Hospital, Fairmile Road, Christchurch, Dorset BH23 2JX**

> **DID YOU KNOW?**
> Terence Rattigan's last play, *Cause Célèbre*, was based on the case. Although Alma Rattenbury's name was retained, Stoner's was changed to George Wood. The play was first created for the wireless and broadcast on Monday 27 October 1975, starring Diana Dors as Alma. Rattigan was asked by the London impresario John Gale to turn the events into a stage play. *Cause Célèbre* opened on Monday 4 July 1977 at Her Majesty's Theatre, London, and ran for 282 performances. Rattigan died four months later on Wednesday 30 November 1977 in Bermuda.

on Friday 24 March 2000 aged 83, not much more that half a mile from where Alma died and on the sixty-fifth anniversary of Francis Rattenbury's murder.

RICHARDSON, CHARLIE
Peckford Scrap Metal Ltd, 50 New Church Road, Camberwell, London SE5

It was to these premises that those who had offended or upset Charlie and Eddie Richardson were often brought to see the error of their ways. The Richardsons ran what became known as the Torture Gang, with "Mad Frankie" Fraser one of their main enforcers. On one occasion, Richardson and Fraser stripped naked a man who owed them money and tied him to a chair before proceeding to beat him for nine hours using their fists, feet and a pole. The punishment stopped only when the torturers became hungry and thirsty and ordered sandwiches and beer, which were consumed in situ. Afterwards, the victim was made to clean up the blood-spattered room with his own underpants. On another occasion a glass of orange squash was poured over a man to provide better conductivity for the electrodes attached to his body. Charlie Richardson always denied these stories, including nailing feet to the floor or removing toes with bolt cutters. As the firm had a number of bent policemen on their payroll, Charlie boasted that he would be told almost immediately when people went to the police to grass him up; give him another half hour and he would even know what was in their statements. As their power in London grew, the Richardsons began to clash with the Krays in east London. At a Christmas 1965 party in a club, one of the Richardson gang members, an unstable criminal called George Cornell, supposedly called the homosexual Ronnie Kray a "fat poof". A fight ensued and the bad blood remained. Three months later, the feud worsened when the two sides fought again at a Catford nightclub for which the Richardsons were providing security. This time, guns and bayonets were used. An associate of the Krays was shot dead and "Mad Frankie" Fraser was wounded in the thigh. The following evening, Cornell was in the Blind Beggar pub in Whitechapel bad-mouthing the Krays. Ronnie Kray arrived with two henchmen. Cornell remarked, "Well, look what the dog's brought in!" and was shot through the head (see page 108). The Richardson gang was now in a corner, with Cornell dead and two other leading members behind bars. "Mad Frankie" had been cleared of the Catford club murder but he and Eddie Richardson were both jailed for five years for affray. The end came when two people talked – one in England, the other in a South African court-room. Businessman James Taggart went to the police after he was savagely beaten by Richardson and Fraser because his company owed £1,200 to a gang associate. It was he who was made to clear up his own blood with his underwear. Then, in June 1965, a mineral prospector called Thomas Waldeck was shot dead on the doorstep of his home in Johannesburg. Lawrence "Johnny" Bradbury, a former barrow boy who lived in Peckham, was arrested and confessed to being the getaway driver. It transpired that a "London scrap dealer" called Charlie Richardson was the murdered man's business partner in a perlite mining company which controlled a claim in the Ghost Mountains of Transvaal. Huge riches were anticipated, but there had been "friction over voting rights". Bradbury had been at school with

Richardson. Facing the death sentence at his trial, the thug cracked
and told the court what many people in London already knew but
were too afraid to say publicly: Richardson was a major gangland
boss. He had enforced Bradbury's loyalty as much through fear as
old school ties, once having Bradbury held over a bar counter while
his arm was slashed with a broken bottle. Bradbury claimed he
took part in the Richardson-ordered murder through fear. He was
sentenced to death, later commuted to life imprisonment. In public,
Richardson responded with hurt bewilderment: "I was amazed
at what happened at the trial," he told one newspaper. "Bradbury
claimed that I was a London gang boss. The truth is that Tom's death
cost me a lot of money. There is no reason on earth why I should
want him killed." British detectives flew out to speak to Bradbury in
May 1966 and the net began to close around the Richardson gang.
Most of its key members were snapped up in a series of dawn raids
on Saturday 30 July 1966, which was described as one of the most
carefully planned operations in police history. Given the Richardson
penetration of Scotland Yard, it had also to be discreet. Significantly,
the investigation and raids were not led by a policeman from the
Met but by Gerald McArthur, the Assistant Chief Constable of
Hertfordshire and head of the regional crime squad. He had played a
major role in the capture of the Great Train Robbery gang. When the
accused appeared at Bow Street Magistrates' Court for a committal
hearing, twenty-five uniformed police officers ringed the dock. The
court heard from so many victims that the trial became known as
the "torture case". The evidence was sensational and shocking: one
victim, Benjamin Coulston, told how he had been attacked outside
a pub then driven to Camberwell, where Charlie placed a gun on a
table and ordered him to be stripped. Then Frankie Fraser appeared
with a pair of pliers. "He put them into my mouth and started to try
to pull out my teeth," Coulston said. "He slipped and pulled a lump of
my gum out. Then he tried again and pulled part of a top tooth out."
The court heard that the witness was then beaten before Richardson
held an electric fire against his genitals. Cigarettes were applied to
his arms and chest before he was wrapped in tarpaulin and "taken
for a ride" before being dumped. At the end of his ordeal, he had the
dubious consolation of being told by Eddie Richardson that they had

got the wrong man and that he was sorry. Another victim, Derek Harris, described how he was invited to the Camberwell HQ and was asked about the whereabouts of Jack Duval, a swindler who had set Richardson on the road to gangland crime. "Charles Richardson came up and stuck a thumb in each of my eyes and ordered me to take my shoes and socks off," he recalled. "Leads were attached to my toes and I got some violent shocks." He was getting dressed afterwards when Richardson plunged a knife through his foot and into the floor beneath. A witness called Cyril Green told the court that his toes were broken with pliers. He could hear the screams of another man being tortured. One businessman said that when he heard that Richardson wanted to speak to him, he fled to Heathrow but was so terrified he was unable to form the words to buy an air ticket. The torture case went to trial at the Old Bailey in April 1967. Eight gang members were in the dock, including the two Richardson brothers and Frankie Fraser. Opening the prosecution, Sebag Shaw QC said the case was "about violence, not sudden violence committed on the spur of the moment but brutal violence, systematically carried out with utter and callous ruthlessness." Charlie Richardson described the allegations of torture as "something out of a storybook". The jury, which resisted determined attempts at intimidation by Richardson associates, did not believe him. He got twenty-five years, his brother ten. Mr Justice Lawton told him: "One is ashamed to think that one lives in a society that contained men like you." Richardson, "with a click of his heels and a gentle bow", was gone. Charlie Richardson died on Wednesday 19 September 2012.

SAVUNDRA, EMIL

Describing himself as "God's own lounge lizard", Emil Savundra (formerly Marion Emil Anacletus Pierre Savundranayagam) was one of those characters who rose and quickly burned out in the Sixties. Much of the truth about him has been lost in the mists of time, or was fake news in the first place. He was born on 6 July 1923 in Ceylon, the youngest son of a devoutly Roman Catholic judge, Anthony Peter Savundranayagam, who died on 17 September 1941. Despite not attending university, he was awarded a doctorate of civil law from the Greek Apostolic Church of St Peter. As Savundranayagam, his life was a series of frauds. He conned the Chinese out of $1¼million in 1950; fraudulently obtained $750,000 from a Belgian bank in 1954 for a non-existent cargo of rice to the Government of Portuguese Goa (for which he served fifteen months of a five-year prison sentence in Belgium); in 1958 he was deported from Ghana after the Camp Bird mineral rights scandal; in 1959 he conned the Costa Rican Government in a coffee bean swindle. Savundranayagam became a British citizen on Wednesday 10 February 1960 and began calling himself "Dr Emil Savundra PhD, DCL". In October 1962, he began renting a room from Stephen Ward (see Profumo Affair page 187), where he met Mandy Rice-Davies (1944-2014), who became his mistress after the death in 1962 of her Svengali, the slum landlord Peter Rachman (see page 200). For some reason Savundra was given anonymity during Ward's trial, and was referred to only as "the Indian doctor" – odd, because he was neither Indian nor a doctor.

Fire, Auto and Marine Insurance Company Ltd, Jacqueline House, North Circular Road, Harlesden, London NW10 Telephone ELGar 4020

The firm was founded on Thursday 14 February 1963 in three rooms in **Baker Street, London W1** just as the motoring boom was beginning in Britain. Savundra kept a low profile, leaving the limelight to managing director Stuart de Quincey Walker (b. Friday 11 January 1924 d. at Highgate, London Thursday 14 April 2011). Savundra was careful who he would and would not offer insurance to – responsible family motorists were okay, but no fleets, young drivers or motorcyclists. He would not pay out if a car was driven "in an unsafe or unworthy condition or manner", which one Lloyd's broker said "ruled out everything but an act of God". FAM operating out of **Orchard House, 26 Orchard Street, London W1H 6HG (Telephone: HYDe Park 5703)** with other offices in **Hesketh House, 43-45 Portman Square, London W1H 6HN (Telephone HUNter 2586)** and **5 Crawford Street, London W1U 6BF (Telephone WELbeck 8323)** offered brokers a 20 percent commission (the usual was 10 percent) and soon policies began flooding into the office. Rather than hiring qualified actuaries, Savundra often hired people based not on their ability but on their star sign. It also helped if you had social connections – he appointed the Honourable Maurice Howard the 20th Earl of Suffolk's younger brother as head of the claims department. FAM hired dozens of staff but most of them had nothing to do, so clocked on then went to another job before clocking out and taking two wage packets. The Board of Trade began taking an interest in FAM, but was unable to intrude because of a deal that allowed companies two years' freedom from state interference. The authorities knew that FAM could not remain solvent while continuing to pay out large commissions and cutting premiums. Savundra needed a public name to head FAM, so he appointed Cecil H. Tross Youle (b. Friday 6 August 1909 d. Saturday 23 April 1988), a Royal Navy veteran and friend of Lord Astor (see Profumo Affair page 187), as chairman. Savundra introduced computerisation to the company and, in January 1964, opened the eight-storey Jacqueline House, named after his only daughter. He signed a deal to pay rent of £36,500 (£783,000 at 2022 rates) a year for the first seven years, which worked out as 12s 6d for each of the 63,000 square feet. At their previous office, Orchard House, staff had been crowded together but they now had room to spread out and were also given one free three-course meal each day. Savundra and de Quincy Walker had luxury offices on the top floor accessed by a private lift that was forbidden to all other staff. Savundra's office boasted a photograph of him and Lord Mountbatten; on one side of the floor was a polar bear skin, while on the other was a tiger skin. In 1964, the money coming in for the policies was sent to Liechtenstein, where Savundra had created the Merchant Finance Trust (MFT). He borrowed £500,000 from MFT at a fixed interest of 3 percent non-repayable for twenty years, while de Quincy Walker was loaned £224,848 on the same terms. Ego was a problem for Savundra: he was not legally involved with FAM but he wanted people to know of his involvement in its great success. He had himself elected vice-chairman. In 1965, he asked the company lawyer how he would go about getting a knighthood.

White Walls, 57 The Bishops Avenue, London N2 0BJ

A man of the stature of Dr Emil Savundra should own property commensurate with his importance and in 1964 he bought this house on Millionaires' Row in Hampstead, paying £72,000 in cash (£1,500,000 at 2022 values). Not long after he bought White Walls, Savundra had IBM install a second computer in his office, which allowed brokers to issue a policy in sixty-seven seconds. In December

1965, he spent £40,000 on Christmas bonuses for all the workers and then booked the banqueting room of the Grosvenor Hotel for a staff party. A downside to working for Savundra was that the staff were expected to stand up and bow if he passed by their desks. He spent lavishly on whatever he wanted. The problem that he faced was that claims were beginning to be made. In March 1965, Leslie Cocke, the chief accountant, was ordered to restrict claims payments to £10,000 a week. Cocke, Winter and Savundra were the only employees who knew the true financial state of FAM. Savundra came up with a novel solution – he sacked his accountant – but when his replacement went through the books, he discovered that FAM was operating insolvent. When auditors arrived, Savundra produced fake documents to convince them the company had assets of £510,000. Claims continued to pour in and were stored in shoeboxes on the floor. In March 1966, company morale at Jacqueline House was low so Savundra summoned all the senior staff for a pep talk where he insisted everything was fine. In April 1966, more fake assuraces were given to the auditors and then Savundra suffered a heart attack. He entered **The London Clinic, 20 Devonshire Place, London W1G 6BW**, where he was diagnosed with a blocked artery complicated by the diabetes he had contracted in 1956. Savundra sold his shares in FAM and resigned his directorship on Wednesday 22 June 1966. He told the Board of Trade that he had left the company and it was now the sole responsibility of Stuart de Quincey Walker. In early July 1966, the staff believed the company was safe and was experiencing nothing more than temporary financial difficulties. A deputation of workers went to see the senior managers and offered to forego a month's pay to help FAM. On Friday 8 July, the staff were paid before being told to not bother coming back on the Monday: they did not know that the company had gone into liquidation on Saturday 2 July, leaving 400,000 motorists with worthless car insurance policies and 43,000 unsettled claims exceeding £300,000. On Saturday 9 July 1966, Savundra flew to Ceylon where he was hidden by relatives at Barnes Place, Cinnamon Gardens, Colombo 00700. The local government refused to extradite him to Britain. FAM was finally wound up on Sunday 24 July 1966. On Saturday 14 January 1967, Savundra returned to Britain of his own volition and two days later he went to sign on at the Labour Exchange in Regent's Park Road. On Monday 23 January, the Official Receiver issued writs to Savundra (£386,534; £7,475,520 at 2022 values) and de Quincey Walker (£216,762; £4,192,150, 2022). Savundra received hate mail and also a job offer to work in a petrol station "to give him a chance to talk with any former policy holders". After a week in Barnet Hospital, Savundra returned to White Walls to recuperate and turned on the television to watch *The Frost Programme*, which featured an item about car insurance. After the show Savundra rang to congratulate the production office. An invitation to appear on the show was declined, but such was Savundra's consummate self-belief that he rang back ten minutes later to accept the offer to be interviewed by David Frost in the last in the series (Rediffusion London) on Friday 3 February 1967. Savundra was paid forty-five guineas for the show, which he donated to a children's charity. Frost's team tracked down several victims but he was disappointed to learn the average loss was only £80 (£1,525, 2022); they then lucked out and found two widows who had not been compensated. The trap was set. In the programme, recorded at **Wembley Park Studios, 128 Wembley Park Drive, Wembley, Middlesex HA9 8HP**, Savundra gave a bravura performance amid some hissing from the audience and boasted, "I am not going to cross swords with peasants. I came here to cross swords with England's finest swordsman." The "peasants" were the audience. It became known as the first trial by television. Frost later said that he had never been so angry in a television studio as he was that night. On Saturday 4 February 1967, Savundra left White Walls and moved into his rarely used other home, **12 Ouseley Road, Old Windsor, Berkshire SL4 2SQ**, which he had bought in 1960. White Walls was rented out to a Moroccan princess for £100 (£1,900, 2022) a week. At 6.20pm on 10 February, as he returned from visiting friends, Savundra was arrested along with Stuart de Quincey Walker. The trial began in Court Number One of the Old Bailey on Thursday 12 January 1968. The case went on and on until Monday 4 March when judge Alan King-Hamilton began his summation, which went on for almost two days. The jury convicted Savundra and Walker on Wednesday 6 March. Savundra was found guilty of four charges and Walker two, the jury foreman telling the judge that Walker was under

Savundra's influence. The following day Savundra was sentenced to eight years in jail and fined £50,000 (£925,000, 2022), with two additional years if he did not pay the fine. Walker was jailed for five years and fined £3,000 (£55,000, 2022), again with two additional years. Judge King-Hamilton said of the pair, "They had been ruthless as they had been unscrupulous. You did not rob and were not armed, but in fact you stole, and instead of arms you used more subtle ways, lies, forgery, and all the techniques of a confidence trickster." On appeal, Walker's fine was dropped and Savundra made no attempt to pay his £50,000 penalty. The appeal was quashed by Lord Justice Salmon, who made clear his displeasure at the Frost programme: "On any view the television interview was deplorable... Savundra was faced by a skilled interviewer whose object was to establish his guilt before millions of people. None of the ordinary safeguards of a court of law were observed." He added, "Trial by television will not be tolerated in a civilised country." He went on to say that if television companies produced another such interview, they would do so at their own risk. Savundra was sent to **HMP Wormwood Scrubs, 160 Du Cane Road, London W12 0AN** as prisoner 9630. He never spoke to Walker again and spent so much time in the prison hospital that he was nicknamed "The Howard Hughes of Wormwood Scrubs". Released from **HMP Brixton, Jebb Avenue, Brixton Hill, London SW2 5XF** on Friday 4 October 1974, he had served six years, seven months and three days of his sentence. It was raining heavily when he returned to Ouseley Road. He lived a quiet life although he had one more deal in him. He offered the American Government the vast estates owned by his wife Pushpam (b. at Ceylon Monday 28 November 1927 d. Sunday 3 February 1985) in northern Sri Lanka, as an airbase on condition she was made Queen of Jaffna. It all came to nought as on Tuesday 21 December 1976, Savundra collapsed at his home and by the time he got to **King Edward VII Hospital, St Leonards Road, Windsor, Berkshire SL4 3DP**, a little over two and a half miles away, he was dead. He was 53. His death certificate described him as a retired banker. Savundra was buried in **Windsor Cemetery, 4 Gatehouse Close, Windsor, Berkshire SL4 3DB**. White Walls was later changed to Eliot House and became two exclusive flats. The press speculated at the time of Savundra's trial that he had one last secret – a million pounds stashed away somewhere. It was never found but, perhaps interestingly, the files at the National Archive relating to Fire Auto and Marine Insurance Co Ltd, Emil Savundra and Stuart de Quincy Walker are closed until Saturday 1 January 2039.

7/7 BOMBINGS
Liverpool Street Station, Liverpool Street, London EC2M 7QH
Edgware Road Station, Chapel Street, Marylebone, London NW1 5DH
Russell Square Station, 7–11 Bernard Street,
Bloomsbury, London WC1N 1LG
Tavistock Square, London WC1H 9JP

On Wednesday 6 July 2005, the International Olympic Committee announced that the 2012 Games had been awarded to London. Little could anyone know that the next day – Thursday 7 July 2005, 7/7 – would witness the deadliest single act of terrorism in the United Kingdom since Lockerbie, and the deadliest bombing in London since the Second World War. At 8.50am, a bomb exploded on the packed train number 204 on the Circle Line about 100 yards from Liverpool Street tube as it headed for Aldgate. Within less than a minute, bombs also went off on train number 216 which had just left platform 4 on the Circle Line at Edgware Road and was heading for Paddington, and on a southbound Piccadilly Line train, number 311, travelling between King's Cross St Pancras and Russell Square. The bomb exploded about one minute after the train had left King's Cross, by which time it had travelled about 500 yards. At 9.47am, an explosion occurred in Tavistock Square outside the headquarters of the BMA on a number 30 double-decker bus travelling from Marble Arch to Hackney Wick. The bombings were the first to be perpetrated by suicide bombers in Western Europe. The terrorists were all Muslims: the Edgware Road bomber was Mohammad Sidique Khan of **51 Stratford Street, Dewsbury, West Yorkshire LS11 6JG** (b. at St James's University Hospital, Leeds Sunday 20 October 1974), the ringleader and oldest of the terrorists, who killed six people; the Aldgate atrocity, which killed seven people, was carried out by Shehzad Tanweer of **49 Colwyn Road, Beeston, Leeds LS11 6LQ** (b. at St Luke's Maternity Hospital, Bradford on Wednesday 15 December 1982); Germaine Maurice Lindsay of **15 Norfolk Terrace,**

Aylesbury, Buckinghamshire HP20 1BL (b. at Jamaica Monday 23 September 1985) was responsible for murdering twenty-six people on the Russell Square tube; and Hasib Mir Hussain of **7 Colenso Mount, Holbeck, Leeds LS11 0DQ** (b. at Leeds General Infirmary Tuesday 16 September 1986) carried the bomb that killed thirteen people on the number 30 bus. Early on the morning of 7 July, Khan, Tanweer, Lindsay and Hussain picked up their bombs from a house in the Burley area of Leeds and drove to Luton in a red Nissan Micra hired a few days earlier by Khan. CCTV footage shows them entering the station at 7.21:54am. They boarded the 7.48am Thameslink train to King's Cross, arriving at 8.26am before each going on their separate deadly missions. It is believed that Hussain had intended to get on the Northern Line but discovered it was suspended (from 6.29am due to a defective train at Balham) that day. He was captured on CCTV in a Boots store on the concourse of King's Cross station after the other bombs had gone off, and mobile phone records indicate that he had tried to call the other terrorists. About fifty minutes afterwards, Hussain boarded the number 30 bus and detonated his bomb. The remnants of his skull, driving licence and credit cards were found in the wreckage on Tavistock Square. Hussain's remains were buried in a Muslim cemetery in Leeds on Wednesday 2 November 2005. In total, fifty-two people were killed and more than seven hundred injured.

SHIPMAN, HAROLD
Donneybrook Medical Practice, Clarendon Street, Hyde, Cheshire SK14 2AH

It was here that Dr Harold "Fred" Shipman began work on Saturday 1 October 1977. The 31-year-old had begun practising as a GP three years earlier in Todmorden, West Yorkshire but after just a year of practice he was forced to enter rehab after being caught forging prescriptions of pethidine for his own use. During the 1980s Shipman worked in and around Hyde, before opening his own practice on Market Street in 1993. Shipman became a popular local figure and was featured on *World In Action* talking about the mentally ill. Suspicions arose in March 1998 when Dr Linda Reynolds of the Brooke Surgery in Hyde was alerted by Deborah Massey, an undertaker, to the seemingly high proportion of deaths among Shipman's patients, many of whom were cremated. Miss Massey thought that Shipman was killing those in his care – although she was unsure whether it was down to incompetence or malice. The police were informed but dropped the case on Friday 17 April 1998 due to lack of evidence. Between then and his arrest Shipman killed another three people, the last being Kathleen Grundy, a former Mayor of Hyde, who was found dead at her home on Wednesday 24 June 1998. Shipman, the last person to see her alive, recorded her death as "old age". When Mrs Grundy's daughter discovered that her mother had left her entire £386,000 estate to Shipman, she went to the police and an investigation began. Mrs Grundy's corpse was exhumed and an autopsy revealed traces of diamorphine. Shipman was arrested on Monday 7 September 1998 and the police began to look into fifteen other deaths where Shipman had signed the death certificate: a trail of forged medical notes was found in them all. On Tuesday 5 October 1999, Shipman went on trial charged with the murders of Marie West, Irene Turner, Lizzie Adams, Jean Lilley, Ivy Lomas, Jermaine Ankrah, Muriel Grimshaw, Marie Quinn, Kathleen Wagstaff, Bianka Pomfret, Norah Nuttall, Pamela Hillier, Maureen Ward, Winifred Mellor, Joan Melia and Kathleen Grundy. On Monday 31 January 2000, he was found guilty of all fifteen murders and sentenced to life imprisonment, with a recommendation that he should never be released. The Shipman Inquiry believed that he had killed around 250 people, although 459 died under his care. On Tuesday 13 January 2004, one day before his fifty-eighth birthday, Shipman hanged himself in his cell at Wakefield Prison.

SIEGE OF SIDNEY STREET
100 Sidney Street, Stepney, London E1

The Siege of Sidney Street began on Tuesday 3 January 1911. The early twentieth century saw an untrammelled influx of immigrants from Russia and the Balkans into the East End of London, much to the consternation of the indigenous population. Crime levels began to rise among the immigrants and a group of Latvian anarchists under the leadership of Peter Piatkow – known as Peter the Painter – attempted a wages snatch at Schnurmann's rubber factory on Chestnut Road on Saturday 23 January 1909, an incident that became known as the Tottenham Outrage. On Friday 16 December 1910, they killed three policemen – Sergeant Robert Bentley, 40, PC Walter Choate, 32 and 46-year-old Sergeant Charles Tucker – in a jewellery robbery at **119 Houndsditch, London EC3A 7BT** (currently a coffee shop). A large manhunt resulted in several of the gang being arrested; an informant revealed that other members of the gang were hiding at 100 Sidney Street. By 2am on 3 January, 200 police surrounded the house and cordoned off the street. As the gang were better armed than the police, a contingent of Scots Guards arrived from the Tower of London, the first time armed soldiers had been seen on the streets of the capital since Bloody Sunday in 1887. Home Secretary Winston Churchill was in the bath when he was informed. He quickly dressed and hastened to Sidney Street, where he was met by chants from the crowd of "Who let 'em in?" He suggested that the house should be bombarded and then stormed by the police and Army – a suggestion that was not acted upon as smoke began billowing from the top floor. Churchill refused to let the fire brigade in to extinguish the flames and within a few minutes, the upper floors had collapsed. When the police entered the building they found the charred remains of Fritz Svaars and William Sokolow. Of Peter the Painter, there was no sign. Churchill was heavily criticised for his role in the siege. The police later captured five more members of the gang, but they were acquitted when their prosecution was bungled.

SPILSBURY, SIR BERNARD
University College, Gower Street, London WC1E 6BT
Born at 35 Bath Street, Leamington Spa, Warwickshire CV31 on Wednesday 16 May 1877, Bernard Spilsbury was the leading honorary Home Office pathologist of his day. His word was regarded as gospel in many courtrooms and the evidence he gave in the Crippen case (see page 90) brought him fame. Spilsbury's testimony sent Frederick Seddon (1912), George Joseph Smith (1915), Major Herbert Rowse Armstrong (1922) and Norman Thorne (1925) to the gallows. At his most productive in the 1930s, Spilsbury was performing between 700 and 1,000 post-mortem examinations

per year and performed more than 25,000 autopsies during his career. In 1940, he suffered the first of a series of minor strokes that would gradually impair his skills; he also began to develop arthritis which made him lose the adroitness in the fingers of one hand. In addition, he suffered the deaths of two sons (Alan (b. Saturday 5 April 1913) from tuberculosis on Tuesday 27 November 1945 and Peter (b. Friday 28 May 1915) killed at **St Thomas' Hospital, 20 St Thomas Street, London SE1 9RS** on Sunday 15 September 1940 in a bombing raid during the Blitz. On Wednesday 17 December 1947, Spilsbury returned to his lab at University College where he turned on the gas taps. At 8.10pm, a colleague saw a light was on in Spilsbury's lab and smelled gas. When he discovered the door was locked, he called a janitor. The door was opened but Spilsbury could not be revived and was pronounced dead at 9.10pm. An inquest was heard on Friday 19 December and on Monday 22 December he was cremated at Golders Green Cemetery. Spilsbury left £9,932 4s. 10d (£425,400 at 2022 values). His home, **20 Frognal, London NW3 6AG** is now a hotel.

TYBURN
Marble Arch, London W1

For 600 years all kinds of villains were despatched at Tyburn. The first recorded hanging occurred in 1196 when William FitzOsbert, or Osborn, was executed after leading a rebellion against taxes imposed on Londoners to pay the ransom of King Richard the Lionheart, who had been captured by the Holy Roman Emperor Henry VI. FitzOsbert's revolt was swiftly quelled, and when he fled to the sanctuary of St Mary-le-Bow, his pursuers set fire to the church to force him out. After a summary trial he was found guilty and dragged naked by horse to Tyburn, where he was "hanged on a gibbet with nine of his accomplices who refused to desert him". The first hanging on the infamous Triple Tree occurred on Friday 1 June 1571: it consisted of a horizontal wooden triangle supported by three legs so that two dozen criminals could be hanged at once. The first victim was 67-year-old Dr John Story, the Roman Catholic First Regius Professor of Civil Law at Oxford University, who refused to recognise Queen Elizabeth I and was accused of plotting against her. Story was hanged, drawn and quartered, and his head placed on London Bridge while his quarters were set on four of the city gates. Story "did not only roare and cry like a helhound, but also strake the executioner doing his office, and resisted as long as strength did serve him, beinge kept downe by three or foure men, until he was deade".

WEST, FRED AND ROSE
25 Cromwell Street, Gloucester GL1

Fred West, an illiterate labourer, lived here with wife Rose. They were married on Saturday 29 January 1972 and she was his second wife. From the age of 12, Fred West had had a sexual relationship with his mother. On Thursday 9 November 1961, he appeared in court accused of sex with a 13-year-old girl, but the trial collapsed when his victim refused to give evidence. On Saturday 17 November 1962, West married prostitute Catherine "Rena" Costello, who was pregnant by an Asian bus driver: her daughter Charmaine was born on Friday 22 March 1963. West began an affair with Anna McFall, but when she asked him to divorce Rena, he murdered her in August 1967 and cut up her body, even though she was eight months' pregnant. On Saturday 6 January 1968, he murdered Mary Bastholm, 15, after abducting her in Gloucester. On Friday 29 November 1968, he met Rosemary Letts on her fifteenth birthday; he was pleased when she agreed to participate in his perverted sexual desires. She, too, became a prostitute. On Saturday 17 October 1970, she gave birth to Heather. On Friday 4 December, West was jailed for theft and motoring offences and was sent to prison until Thursday 24 June 1971. Just before West was released, Rose killed Charmaine. Not long after, West murdered Rena. In September 1972, eight months after their wedding, they moved into 25 Cromwell Street. Over the next few years the Wests killed Lynda Gough (April 1973), Carol Ann Cooper (November 1973), Lucy Partington (abducted in December 1973), Therese Siegenthaler (April 1974), Shirley Hubbard (kidnapped in November 1974), Juanita Mott (April 1975), prostitute Shirley Robinson (pregnant by West when she died in May 1978) and Alison Chambers (August 1979). Finally, on Friday 19 June 1987, West murdered his daughter Heather. In May 1992 he raped a 13-year-old girl, who told a friend. The police arrived on Thursday 6 August to search for evidence of child abuse. Both Wests were arrested but the case collapsed when their victim refused to testify. The search for Heather began and West was arrested for her murder on Friday 25 February 1994. In custody, he denied that Rose had anything to do with any of the murders. The next day, Heather's remains were found and the Wests were charged with murder on 13 December 1994. On Sunday 1 January 1995, Fred West hanged himself in his cell at **Winson Green Prison, Winson Green Road, Birmingham, B18 4AS**. On Wednesday 22 November, Rose West was found guilty of ten counts of murder and sentenced to life. On Monday 7 October 1996, 25 Cromwell Street was demolished.

YORKSHIRE RIPPER
Bingley Cemetery, Bailey Hills Road, Bingley, West Yorkshire BD16 2RJ

It was here at the grave of Bronislaw Zapolski (who died on Saturday 19 June 1965, aged 49) that gravedigger Peter Sutcliffe first heard the "Voice of God" that told him to murder prostitutes. After being sacked for poor time keeping, he began work as a lorry driver. Between Saturday 5 July 1975 (Anna Rogulskyj) and Monday 17 November 1980 (Jacqueline Hill), he brutally murdered thirteen women and attempted to murder seven more. Despite his "orders" from God, several of Sutcliffe's victims were not prostitutes. He died at the age of 74 from Covid-19 on Friday 13 November 2020 at **University Hospital of North Durham, North Road, Durham DH1 5TW**. He had been locked up since his arrest in January 1981.

First victim
St Paul's Road, near Manningham Park, Bradford, West Yorkshire BD8

In September 1969, 23-year-old Peter Sutcliffe and his friend Trevor Birdsall were sitting in Birdsall's mini-van in St Paul's Road looking for a prostitute who Sutcliffe believed had conned him out of £10. Sutcliffe opened the van door and walked up St Paul's Road and disappeared. Ten minutes later, he returned out of breath and told Birdsall to quickly drive off. Sutcliffe told his friend that he had hit a prostitute (not the one he was looking for) over the head with a stone hidden in a sock. The next day police arrived at Sutcliffe's home, **57**

Cornwall Road, Bingley, West Yorkshire BD16 4DL to question him. Sutcliffe admitted that he had struck the woman, but said he only used his hand. The woman did not want to press charges.

Anna Rogulskyj

Alley off North Queen Street, Keighley, West Yorkshire BD21 3DL

Anna Rogulskyj, 42 (b. at Tralee, Co Kerry, Ireland Tuesday 21 March 1933 as Anna Brosnan d. at Airedale General Hospital, Skipton Road, Steeton, Keighley, West Yorkshire BD20 6TD April 2008 of breast cancer), became the first recognised victim of the Ripper when he attacked her on Saturday 5 July 1975. On the night of 4 July, she had been out drinking. On the way home, she changed her mind and decided to call on her boyfriend, Geoffrey Hughes, with whom she had a stormy relationship, at his home in North Queen Street. As she walked towards Hughes's home, a male voice asked if she "fancied it". She replied, "Not on your life", and quickened her pace. At 2am, Rogulskyj banged on Hughes's front door but he was not home. Twenty minutes later, she was discovered in an alleyway near the Ritz Cinema fifty yards from Hughes's home, her handbag undisturbed by her side. She was taken to Airedale hospital and then transferred to Leeds General Infirmary, where she underwent a twelve-hour operation. She was given the Last Rites at one stage (like Sutcliffe, Rogulskyj had been raised a Catholic). Sutcliffe had hit her three times on the head with a ball pein hammer before lifting her blouse and slashing her across the abdomen. A man in nearby Lord Street heard the commotion and called out before Sutcliffe could finish the job. As Rogulskyj recovered, her auburn hair grew back grey.

Olive Smelt

Off Woodside Road, Halifax, West Yorkshire HX3

At 11.45pm on Friday 15 August 1975, Sutcliffe attacked Olive Smelt, a 45-year-old office cleaner. She had been socialising in the Royal Oak, a pub in Halifax town centre, with her friend Muriel Falkingham. Her routine was to pick up a late chippy tea for herself and husband Harry. By coincidence, Sutcliffe was also drinking in the Royal Oak that night with his friend Trevor Birdsall. The two men were driving home to Bradford when Sutcliffe saw a woman walking down Woodside Road and recognised her. Sutcliffe stopped his car and attacked Smelt, hitting her twice on the head with a hammer. He had made two cuts to her back and side when a car's headlights disturbed him. Smelt was rushed to Halifax Infirmary and then Leeds Infirmary, where she had brain surgery and stayed in for ten days. She told the police that her attacker was about 30, 5ft 10in, slightly built, with dark hair and some beard or growth on his face. The next evening, Trevor Birdsall read in the *Bradford Telegraph & Argus* about the attack on Olive Smelt; he wondered if Sutcliffe might be responsible but did not act on his suspicions. Mrs Smelt died on Wednesday 5 April 2011 in Huddersfield Royal Infirmary after contracting pneumonia. She was 82.

Tracey Browne
Upper Hayhills Farm, Horne Lane, Silsden, near Keighley, West Yorkshire BD20 9JJ

It was not until 1992 that Sutcliffe confessed to the hammer attack on 14-year-old Tracey Browne on a lonely farm road at 10.30pm on Wednesday 28 August 1975. Tracey and her twin sister Mandy had been out. As Tracey made her way home, a man began talking to her. She described him as having dark, Afro-like crinkly hair and beard. As they reached the gateway to her family's farm, he brutally attacked her from behind. "He hit me five times on the head. I heard him grunt like Jimmy Connors serving, each time he struck. I kept saying to him 'Please don't.'" She believed that she was being attacked by the Black Panther (see page 80) and called out that name to attract attention. Another passing car saved her life and Sutcliffe threw her over a fence. Surgeons at Chapel Allerton Hospital in Leeds operated on Tracey for four hours to save her life and removed a sliver of bone from her brain.

Wilma McCann
Prince Philip Playing Fields, Chapeltown, Leeds, West Yorkshire LS7

Peter Sutcliffe attacked Wilma McCann (b. at Dumbarton Tuesday 1 July 1947 as Williamina Newlands), a 28-year-old prostitute, at 1.30am on Thursday 30 October 1975. At around 7.30pm on Wednesday 29 October, she walked out of her council house, **65 Scott Hall Avenue, Chapeltown, Leeds, West Yorkshire LS7**, leaving her four children, Sonia Maree (b. October 1968), 7, Richard (b. 1969), 6, Donna (b. 1970), 5, and 3-year-old Angela (b. 1972) alone. She walked past the Prince Philip Playing Fields and headed for the pub. Just before 1am, drunk, she decided to go home and bought a carton of curry and chips to eat on the way. Peter Sutcliffe was also out drinking in Leeds that night and he saw McCann thumbing a lift. When he stopped his lime-green Ford Capri GT, she got in and asked him if he "wanted business". They parked next to the Prince Philip Playing Fields, about 100 yards from her home. Impatiently, she said, "Well, what are we waiting for! Let's get on with it" and told him that the price was £5. He suggested sex on the grass. As he put his coat on the ground, he hid a hammer in his right hand. McCann sat on the coat and began to undo her trousers, saying again, "Come on, get it over with". Sutcliffe replied, "Don't worry, I will", and struck her several times with his hammer. Her battered body was found at 7.41am the next day by milkman Alan Routledge and Paul, his 10-year-old brother. McCann was found lying on her back, her trousers down by her knees and her brassiere lifted to expose her breasts. She had been stabbed in the lower abdomen, chest and neck. She was the first known murder victim of the man who would soon be known as the Yorkshire Ripper. McCann's son Richard, wrote a best-selling book, *Just A Boy: The True Story of a Stolen Childhood* (2004) about his traumatic upbringing that ended in prison for dealing drugs. A follow-up, *Into the Light*, was published in February 2006. On Tuesday 18 December 2007, McCann's daughter, Sonia Newlands, texted her sister to say there were crocodiles in her room. The next day, unable to cope with the tragedy that had befallen her when she was just seven, she committed suicide by hanging herself in the bathroom of her home in Armley, Leeds. She had become an alcoholic and the year before her death had said, "Before I die I want to meet Peter Sutcliffe. I want to ask, 'Why did you kill my mum? Why her? What happened that night? Are you sorry?' All I want is to be happy. I haven't been happy since I was seven – since mum was taken from us." Sonia Newlands was 39.

Emily Jackson

Manor Street, Sheepscar, Leeds, West Yorkshire LS7 1PZ

On Tuesday 20 January 1976, Emily Jackson (b. at Hemsworth, West Yorkshire Wednesday 30 March 1932 as Emily Monia Wood), a 43-year-old part-time prostitute, was killed by Peter Sutcliffe. Sydney Jackson ran a roofing company and his wife sorted out the paper-work because he was illiterate. With money in short supply around Christmas 1975, Jackson suggested to her jealous husband that she become a prostitute and use their dark blue Commer van to pick up clients. On 20 January, they went to the Gaiety pub on Roundhay Road, Leeds, where Sydney went in for a pint while Emily went looking for business. At 7pm, she met Peter Sutcliffe and told him that sex would be £5. She got into his car and drove to a piece of derelict land where he hit her twice with his hammer and then pushed up her sweater, cardigan and bra, and pulled down her pants. Taking a Phillips screwdriver and "seething with hate for her", he viciously stabbed her fifty-two times in the neck, breasts, lower abdomen and back. At 8.10am the following day, a workman found Emily Jackson's body.

Marcella Claxton
Soldiers' Field, Roundhay Park, Princes Avenue, Leeds, West Yorkshire LS8 2ER
Telephone: 0113-266 1850

At 4am on Sunday 9 May 1976, Marcella Claxton, a 20-year-old prostitute, was attacked. The police did not link the attack to the Yorkshire Ripper inquiry until after the next murder in February 1977. On Saturday 8 May, Claxton had gone to a party in Chapeltown and left drunk at 4am. Sutcliffe was cruising through the area when he spotted her, and stopped the vehicle. She got in the car with him and Sutcliffe drove to Soldiers' Field in Roundhay Park. When he stopped the car, he offered Claxton £5 to get out, take her clothes off, and have sex on the grass. She said that she did not want to, but went behind a nearby tree to urinate. Sutcliffe also left the car and smashed her head eight or nine times with his hammer before driving off at speed. Claxton was to claim later that as she lay on the ground, he masturbated and then pushed a £5 note into her hand, telling her not to call the police. Sutcliffe always denied Claxton's version of events: he told police, "I didn't want sex wi' any of them. And certainly not that one. Even t'police said she were like a gorilla." A policeman had said privately that Claxton, educationally subnormal with an IQ of only fifty, was regarded as "just this side of a gorilla". She required extensive brain surgery and needed fifty-two stitches to close the wounds in her head. After the attack on Claxton, the Yorkshire Ripper did not strike again for 271 days.

Irene Richardson
Soldiers' Field, Roundhay Park, Princes Avenue,

Leeds, West Yorkshire LS8 2ER
Telephone: 0113-266 1850

At 11.30pm on Saturday 5 February 1977, 28-year-old Irene Richardson (b. at Glasgow Sunday 28 March 1948, née Osborne) was murdered at almost exactly the same spot as Marcella Claxton. Roundhay Park comprises more than 700 acres of parkland, lakes and woodland and was purchased by the City in 1872 and opened as a public park by HRH Prince Arthur on Thursday 19 September that year. Richardson had gone to a club called Tiffany's, formerly the Mecca ballroom, while Sutcliffe had spent the night kerb crawling and saw Richardson near the Gaiety pub (Emily Jackson's local). When he stopped the car, Richardson jumped into the passenger seat. Sutcliffe drove her to Soldiers' Field in Roundhay Park. Like Claxton, Richardson needed to relieve herself and Sutcliffe hit her on the head three times with his hammer while she did so. One of the blows was so fierce that it pushed fragments of her skull three-quarters of an inch into her brain. He then slashed and stabbed her with a Stanley knife. Richardson's bloodied remains were found at 7.30am the next day by jogger John Bolton. She was lying face down, her hands under her stomach and her head turned to the left, with her long hair hiding the stab wounds to her neck and throat.

Patricia Atkinson
Flat 3, 9 Oak Avenue, Bradford, West Yorkshire BD8 7AQ

In 1975, Patricia "Tina" Atkinson (b. Sunday 9 July 1944) was arrested for soliciting – the only published photograph of her dates from that time. Two years later, at 11.15pm on St George's Day 1977, Sutcliffe murdered her in her flat – she was 32. It was the only murder that Sutcliffe committed indoors. That night, Atkinson had drunk about twenty measures of spirits in the Perseverance pub on Bradford's Lumb Lane. Sutcliffe spotted her banging on the roof of a parked car and screaming obscenities at passers-by. He approached her and they went to her flat. Once inside, he hit her on the head four times with a claw hammer and stabbed her six times in the stomach. When he got home to **Tanton Crescent, Clayton, Bradford, West Yorkshire BD14**, Sutcliffe noticed that he had blood on his jeans so he washed them in the kitchen sink. He also wiped blood off his boots. Atkinson's body was discovered the next day when a friend called round. Police found a bloody footprint on a sheet from a size seven Dunlop Warwick Wellington, which matched footprints found at the Emily Jackson murder scene.

Jayne MacDonald
Reginald Street, Leeds, West Yorkshire LS7 3HL

At 16, Jayne Michelle MacDonald was the youngest of Sutcliffe's murder victims – she was born on Tuesday 16 August 1960. A keen Bay City Rollers fan, Jayne began work in April 1977 as a shop assistant in the shoe department of **Grandways Supermarket, 243 Roundhay Road, Leeds, West Yorkshire LS8**. On Saturday 25 June, Jayne went with some friends from work to Hofbrauhaus, a German bierkeller-themed bar on the top floor of the city's **Merion Centre, Merrion Way, Leeds, West Yorkshire LS2 8NG** where she met 18-year-old Mark Jones, with whom she became friendly. At 10.30pm, the pair and some friends set off for Briggate, the main shopping street. Jayne said that she was hungry and wanted something to eat, but by the time they found a chippy, Jayne's last bus had gone. The couple said their goodbyes at 1.30am outside **St James Hospital, Beckett Street, Leeds, West Yorkshire LS9 7LS**, making a date to have sex the following Wednesday (Jayne was on her period when she died). The teenager began walking home and passed near the Grandways supermarket and then the Gaiety, where Emily Jackson had last been seen. She continued along Chapeltown Road towards her home at **77 Scott Hall Avenue, Leeds, West Yorkshire LS7 2HJ**. Sutcliffe spotted Jayne walking on Chapeltown Road near the Hayfield pub and followed her into Reginald Street. He struck at 2.15am on Sunday 26 June 1977 near an adventure playground, hitting her with a hammer before pulling her clothes up and stabbing her twenty times in the chest and back with a kitchen knife. She was discovered by two children at 9.45am. Jayne's father, Wilf MacDonald, a former railwayman, died aged 60 in October 1979. His family believe that he died of a broken heart. He was buried next to Jayne.

Maureen Long
Bowling Back Lane, Bradford, West Yorkshire BD4 8SE

At 3.20am on Sunday 10 July 1977, 42-year-old Maureen Long became the fourth woman to be attacked by Sutcliffe in 1977 but the first that year to live to tell the tale. The previous evening, Mrs Long had left her home in Farsley, Leeds, for a night on the town in Bradford. She met her estranged husband in a pub and agreed to stay at his home in Laisterdyke, Bradford. She ended her night at the Mecca ballroom, renamed Tiffany's, in **Manningham Lane, Manningham, Bradford, West Yorkshire BD8**. Then she went to the Bali Hai discotheque, where she danced with lots of men and drank lots of alcohol before leaving shortly after 2am. Sutcliffe spotted her leaving and watched as she walked past a queue of people waiting for cabs. When he offered her a lift, she got into his car. Mrs Long asked if he found her attractive and when Sutcliffe said that he did, she told him to drive to Bowling Back Lane. Once again, Sutcliffe hit her on the back of the head with a hammer as she was relieving herself. Once on the ground, he began ripping her dress and stabbing her but was scared off by a patrolling night watchman. Mrs Long was found at 8.30am when two women heard her cries.

Jean Jordan

Princess Road, Chorlton, Manchester M14 4RB

At 9:30pm on Saturday 1 October 1977, 20-year-old prostitute Jean Jordan (b. at Motherwell Maternity Hospital 11 December 1956), aka Jean Royle, aka Scotch Jean, was murdered by Sutcliffe. Jordan lived with her boyfriend Alan Royle and their two children in a Moss Side flat on Lingbeck Crescent. On Monday 26 September, Peter and Sonia Sutcliffe had moved into their new home at **6 Garden Lane, Heaton, Bradford, West Yorkshire BD9 5QJ**. Five days later, Alan Royle went for a drink with some friends but returned to find his sons were asleep and alone. He assumed that Jordan had gone to see friends or relatives in Scotland but in fact she was out working the streets. Sutcliffe spotted her and she got into his car at 9pm. Another car driver wanted her but she changed her mind and climbed into Sutcliffe's. "I supposed this was the biggest mistake she ever made. She told me she was going to go with the other man until she saw me," Sutcliffe later said. They haggled over the price until Sutcliffe agreed to the standard charge of £5, to be paid in advance. She told him to go to Princess Road, Chorlton, near the Southern Cemetery, a popular spot for Moss Side prostitutes and their clients, as well as courting couples. Sutcliffe used a hammer that the previous owner of his new home had left in the garage, hitting her eleven times before he was disturbed and drove away. It was only when he was on the way home that he realised that the £5 he had used to pay her was a brand

> ## DID YOU KNOW?
> Ian Jones later changed his first name to Bruce and found fame as Les Battersby in the television soap *Coronation Street* from Friday 4 July 1997 until Sunday 6 May 2007. He rang the police when he discovered Jean Jordan's body, but to his horror found himself a suspect. This led to the breakdown of his first marriage.

new note from his pay packet from Clark's Haulage Company just two days previously. On Sunday 9 October, the night of his house-warming party, he decided to retrieve the note; when he could not find it, he began stabbing at the decomposing corpse. He decided to cut her head off but gave up after two hours of trying. At 10.30am, the body was found by Jimmy Morrisey and Ian Jones, two friends who owned an allotment.

Jordan's handbag was finally found 189 feet from her body on Saturday 15 October, with a crisp fiver inside. Sutcliffe was questioned on Thursday 2 November, but too much time had passed and the house-warming party gave him an alibi.

Marylyn Moore
Leeds, West Yorkshire LS7

Sutcliffe attacked Marylyn Moore, a 25-year-old prostitute, at 8.30pm on Wednesday 14 December 1977, seventy-three days after his last attack. She was plying her trade that night on Gipton Avenue in the red light district of Chapeltown, Leeds. Sutcliffe stopped her and asked if she was doing business: he told her he was called Dave and she said she was Susan. After the usual £5 fee had been agreed, Sutcliffe drove to Scott Hall Road, turned on to Buslingthorpe Lane and headed towards some waste ground behind a mill, around 200 yards from the Prince Philip Playing Fields where he had killed Wilma McCann. Sutcliffe told Moore to get into the backseat, but the car door was locked and he hit her with a hammer as he pretended to unlock it, striking her eight times before leaving. Moore was taken to Leeds Infirmary for emergency surgery.

Yvonne Pearson
Drummond's Mill, Arthington Street, Bradford, West Yorkshire BD8

At 9.30pm on Saturday 21 January 1978, Yvonne Pearson, a

21-year-old prostitute, was murdered by Sutcliffe, thirty-seven days after he had attacked Marylyn Moore. Pearson had left her two children in the care of a 16-year-old neighbour whom she told she was visiting her mother in Leeds for two hours. She went instead to the Flying Dutchman pub. She left around 9.30pm to earn some money; she was up before the beak at Bradford Magistrates' Court on Thursday 26 January charged with soliciting and was facing a jail sentence. Sutcliffe was cruising Lumb Lane when Pearson tapped on his car window and opened the door. The usual £5 was agreed and Sutcliffe went to the back of Drummond's Mill. As Pearson got out of the car, Sutcliffe hit her with a heavy walling hammer. He then pulled down her trousers, exposed her breasts and jumped up and down on her chest before leaving. Pearson's body was not found until Easter Sunday, March 26 1978.

Helen Rytka
Garrard's Timber Yard, Great Northern Street, Huddersfield, West Yorkshire HD1 6BR

Ten days after Yvonne Pearson's killing, Sutcliffe murdered 18-year-old prostitute Helen Rytka at 9.25pm on Tuesday 31 January 1978. Elena Maria De Mattia "Helen" Rytka and her twin sister Rita Rosemary (b. at St Mary's Hospital, Green Hill Road, Leeds, West Yorkshire LS12 3QE Tuesday 3 March 1959), were neophyte prostitutes and had worked out a system they hoped would keep them safe. They would entertain clients simultaneously but only for twenty minutes, before meeting at an agreed place, a block of public lavatories at the market end of Great Northern Street, Huddersfield. At 8.30pm on 31 January, the Rytkas left their bedsit **Enderley, Flat 3, 13 Elmwood Avenue, Highfields, Huddersfield, West Yorkshire HD1 5DA** to go to work. At around 9.10pm, Rita watched as her sister got into a dark-coloured car, before finding a client with a Datsun. Helen got back first and was spotted by Sutcliffe. When he approached, she got into his car and they drove to a wood yard. As he began to undo her trousers, he became aroused and told her he needed to relieve himself. When he returned, she agreed to get into the backseat and he swung his hammer as she went to the back door. The blow only brushed Helen and hit the roof of the car instead. She thought Sutcliffe had hit her with his hand. "What was that?" she asked. Sutcliffe said, "Just a small sample of one of these" and struck her much harder. When she collapsed, he pulled her by the hair to the end of the yard. She was still alive and bleeding but he had sex with her – the only one of his victims he was intimate with. Then he took a knife and plunged it into her heart and lungs several times. He covered her corpse with a sheet of asbestos and placed it behind some timber. Despite their system, Rita did not report her sister missing for three days. Helen's naked body was found at 3.10pm on Friday 3 February 1978. The inquest coroner said the murder was "of the utmost callousness and brutality. If the full details could be released they would shock even our modern, brutal society."

Vera Millward
Manchester Royal Infirmary, Oxford Road, Manchester M13 9WL

Sutcliffe killed Vera Millward, a 40-year-old prostitute from **8 Greenham Avenue, Hulme, Manchester M15 4HD** on Tuesday 16 May 1978 at 11pm. Millward (b. at Madrid, Spain Thursday 26 August 1937) was a sick woman with only one lung and chronic stomach pains. At 10pm she told Cyrenous Birkett, her Jamaican boyfriend, that she was going out to "buy cigarettes". Having been let down by a regular, she waited for clients; the first one to come along was Peter Sutcliffe. She got into his car and he drove for about two and a half miles to the Manchester Royal Infirmary's car park where prostitutes frequently took their clients. Sutcliffe attacked Millward with a hammer and knife, leaving her body by a fence to be found the next day at 8am by six gardeners. He had hit her three times with a hammer and repeatedly stabbed her. Vera Millward`was the last known Sutcliffe attack in 1978, and also the last murder of or attack on a prostitute.

Josephine Whitaker
Savile Park, Calderdale, Halifax, West Yorkshire HX1

At 11.55pm on Wednesday 4 April 1979, 322 days after the attack on Vera Millward, Sutcliffe killed Josephine Whitaker (b. at Halifax, West Yorkshire Saturday 19 December 1959), a 19-year-old building society clerk, after she visited her grandparents, Tom and Mary Priestley. Mrs Priestley suggested that her granddaughter stay the night, but Miss Whitaker had to be up for work the next day and had left her contact lens case at home. She left the Priestleys at 11.40pm and headed towards

Savile Park, which led to **10 Ivy Street, Bell Hall, Halifax, West Yorkshire HX1 3EH** where Miss Whitaker lived. Sutcliffe had been drinking that night with Trevor Birdsall and, after dropping him off, headed for Halifax. He arrived in Savile Park and spotted Miss Whitaker walking alone. Sutcliffe parked and locked his car. He had with him a ball pein hammer and a large, rusty Phillips screwdriver, which he had

---

DID YOU KNOW?

The boot imprints found next to Josephine Whitaker's body were the same as those left at the murder scenes of Emily Jackson and Tina Atkinson. In 1980, Sutcliffe was interviewed by police, who had a photograph of his boot print from the scene of the Josephine Whitaker murder. Sutcliffe later said that he was wearing the same boots during the interview. "I stayed dead calm, and as I got into the wagon I realised I was standing on the steps, which were mesh, and they could look up and see for themselves that I was wearing those boots. But they didn't. They couldn't see what were in front of their own eyes."

---

sharpened into a bradawl. Sutcliffe caught up with the teenager and engaged her in conversation. Thirty or forty yards from the main road, he attacked her from behind with his hammer, and, after dragging her thirty feet into the darkness away from the road, proceeded to stab her twenty-one times in the chest with the screwdriver. Sutcliffe pulled her clothing back, turned her over and stabbed her six times in the right leg, also thrusting the screwdriver into her vagina. The ferocity of the attack had fractured her skull from ear to ear.

Barbara Leach
13 Ash Grove, Bradford, West Yorkshire BD11 2JP
Barbara Leach (b. at Kettering, Northamptonshire Monday 5 January 1959), a 20-year-old university student, about to start her third and final year studying Social Psychology, was murdered at 1am on Sunday 2 September 1979 just west of Bradford city centre. She had been with some friends at the **Mannville Arms, 31-33 Great Horton Road, Bradford, West Yorkshire BD7 1AT** where there was a lock-in until 12.45am. It was raining as they left the pub but Barbara Leach decided to clear her head and go for a walk. None of her friends wanted to go with her. Sutcliffe watched her saying goodbye to them. He drove past her and

turned into Ash Grove. As she walked past him, he attacked her from behind with a hammer and dragged her into a backyard. He pushed up her shirt and bra to expose her breasts and undid her jeans before stabbing her with the same screwdriver that he had used on Josephine Whitaker. He then put her body in an area where the bins were usually kept, covering her remains with an old piece of carpet and putting some stones on top of it. The following day at 3.55pm, PC Simon Greaves found her body, around 200 yards from where she had left her friends.

Marguerite Walls
Claremont, New Street, Farsley, Pudsey, West Yorkshire LS28 5BF

Marguerite Walls (b. at Lincoln Saturday 17 December 1932) was a 47-year-old civil servant who worked at the Department of Education and Science office in Pudsey. On Wednesday 20 August 1980, she worked late because she was due to attend a friend's funeral on the 22nd before going on a ten-day walking holiday in the Lake District. She was unmarried and a very private woman, never telling her work colleagues about her personal life. Between 9.30pm and 10.30pm she left her office for the thirty-minute walk home to **7 New Park Croft, Farsley, Pudsey, West Yorkshire LS28 5TT**. Sutcliffe happened to be driving past that night en route to Chapeltown when he saw Miss Walls. He parked up and prepared to attack. As she walked past a driveway with high pillars, he struck her on the back of the head and screamed, "Filthy prostitute" as he hit her again and again. He wrapped a length of rope around her neck and dragged her into the back garden. Sutcliffe knelt on her chest as he strangled her. Once she was dead, he stripped her naked apart from her tights and threw some leaves and grass over her. Her body was found at 9am by two of Claremont's residents when they went out to tidy the garden. Sutcliffe had changed his modus operandi to put the police off, and it worked. DCS James Hobson, after speaking to forensic experts said, "We do not believe this is the work of the Yorkshire Ripper." Like Jayne MacDonald's father, Miss Walls's father was also heartbroken by her death and died four months later. Claremont is now a care home.

Uphadya Bandara
Chapel Lane, Headingley, Leeds, West Yorkshire LS6 3BW

Dr Upadhya Bandara, 34, arrived in Leeds from Singapore in August 1979. She spent a year studying at the Nuffield Medical Centre and was preparing to return to her home country. She had spent the evening of Wednesday 24 September 1980 with some friends in Cottage Road, a mile from her digs on Cardigan Road, Headingley. She began the walk home through lit streets. As she turned into Chapel Lane, a shortcut to Cardigan Road, she heard footsteps behind her and moved to let the person pass. But as she turned, she caught a brief glimpse of a bearded man before he launched his attack, hitting her twice on the head before tieing a rope around her neck and dragging her up the street. Fortunately for Dr Bandara, Valerie Nicholas, a lady who lived in the house backing on to where the attack happened, heard a commotion outside and went to investigate before calling 999. Disturbed, Sutcliffe fled the scene and Dr Bandara awoke to find a policeman standing over her. In October 1980, she flew back to Singapore and never spoke about her attack again. She died aged 60 in 2006.

Teresa Sykes
Park path leading to Willwood Avenue, Oakes, Huddersfield, West Yorkshire HD3 4YB

Bonfire Night 1980 was a wet and windy night. Theresa Sykes, 16, lived with her fitness fanatic millworker boyfriend Jim Furey, 25, and their three-month-old son, Anthony. The pair had just sat down to watch *Coronation Street* when they realised that they had no cigarettes. Theresa nudged her boyfriend to go out and get some but he was happy to wait until the morning when the weather was better. Theresa went out instead; on the way back, Sutcliffe struck her on the head from behind. Jim Furey saw the attack and gave chase, but Sutcliffe eluded him. Theresa spent five weeks in hospital before she was released. She survived the attack but her relationship did not – she and Jim Furey split not long after, as she could not bear to be around men anymore.

Jacqueline Hill
Alma Road, Leeds, West Yorkshire LS6 2AH

Just like Bonfire Night twelve days earlier, Monday 17 November 1980 was a wet, rainy evening. Jacqueline Hill (b. Sunday 22 May 1960), aged 20, was in the third year of her English degree at the University of Leeds and lived in an all-women students' hall of residence, **Lupton Court, Alma Road, Headingley, Leeds, West Yorkshire LS6 2PG**. That day, she had attended a seminar for probation officers on Cookridge Street in Leeds city centre. She was on her way home and, at 9.23pm, she got off a bus across from the Arndale Shopping Centre and began to walk up Alma Road, around 100 yards from her residence. Sutcliffe was sitting in his car eating Kentucky Fried Chicken and chips when he saw Jacqueline Hill and drove ahead of her on Alma Road before stopping his Rover car. He let her walk by and then followed her before hitting her on the head. He dragged her to some land behind the Arndale where he stripped her before stabbing her multiple times in the chest and once in the right eye with a yellow-handled screwdriver.

Olive Reivers
Driveway of Light Trades House, Melbourne Avenue, Sheffield, South Yorkshire S10 2QH

This was where PC Robert Hydes, 31, and Sergeant Robert Ring, 47, arrested Sutcliffe on Friday 2 January 1981 while he was in the company of a 24-year-old Jamaican prostitute called Olivia Reivers. He had picked her up and given her £10 for sex, but when it came to it Sutcliffe was unable to achieve an erection. They gave up after ten minutes, and as Sutcliffe was doing up his trousers, the inside of his car was illuminated by the headlights of another car that had pulled directly in front of him. Sutcliffe told Reivers to leave the talking to him. He told the police that his name was John Williams but when they did a PNC check on his Rover, they found it had false number plates – HVY 679N – which belonged to a Skoda instead of the real FHY 400K. As the police took Reivers to their car, Sutcliffe disappeared behind an oil storage tank, re-emerging to say he had needed to relieve himself. In fact, he had disposed of his ball pein hammer and knife. At the Hammerton Road police station he dropped a second knife into a lavatory cistern. All the weapons were later found. Sutcliffe's trial opened at the Central Criminal Court of the Old Bailey on Wednesday 29 April 1981. He claimed to be suffering from paranoid schizophrenia but on Friday 22 May 1981, he was found guilty of murder by a majority verdict of ten to two. Later, when Sutcliffe was asked by his brother to explain his actions, he said, "I were just cleaning up the streets, our kid," he replied, "just cleaning up the streets."

Chapter IV
Celebrity Deaths &
Infamous Celebrity Events

ANDREW, PRINCE
Pizza Express, 65-67 Goldsworth Road, Woking, Surrey GU21 6LJ

Born at Buckingham Palace, London SW1 on Friday 19 February 1960, Prince Andrew is said to be the favourite child of the Queen. After serving in the Royal Navy during the Falklands War (1982), he later became a trade envoy for the United Kingdom. In 1999, he met the American billionaire financier Jeffrey Epstein (b. Brooklyn, New York Tuesday 20 January 1953 d. Metropolitan Correctional Center, 150 Park Row, New York NY10007 USA Saturday 10 August 2019). In March 2005, the stepmother of a 14-year-old girl had alleged that Epstein had sexually abused the teenager. An FBI investigation revealed Epstein had been involved sexually with dozens of teenage – and younger – girls. It was claimed that French 12-year-old triplets were flown in for Epstein's birthday, sexually abused and returned to France the next day. He was arrested on Thursday 27 July 2006 and later pleaded not guilty to one felony charge of solicitation of prostitution. In Florida on Monday 30 June 2008, Epstein pleaded guilty to procuring a child for prostitution and of soliciting a prostitute. He agreed to spend a year and a half in prison, sign the sex offenders' register and pay compensation to three dozen victims. Epstein served his sentence in a private wing of the Palm Beach County Stockade and was allowed out on "work release" after three and a half months. Epstein used his own chauffeur to ferry him between prisons and his office. Despite Epstein's conviction, Andrew maintained their friendship and he was seen with Epstein in Central Park in December 2010 and stayed at Epstein's house, 9

East 71st Street, Lenox Hill, New York, NY10021. The following year, Andrew stepped down from his trade envoy role. Nine years earlier, Epstein and his girlfriend Ghislaine Maxwell (b. at Maisons-Laffitte, Île-de-France, France Monday 25 December 1961), the daughter of disgraced media tycoon Robert Maxwell (1923-1991), had been spending time in Britain with Prince Andrew, who was her longtime friend. It was claimed that on Saturday 10 March 2001, Andrew, Epstein, Maxwell and 17-year-old Virginia Roberts went to the nightclub **Tramp, 40 Jermyn Street, St James's, London SW1Y 6DN**. Later that night, they went back to Maxwell's mews house at **44 Kinnerton Street, Belgravia, London SW1X 8ES**, where it was claimed Andrew had sex with Roberts in the bathroom. A photograph was taken that night, supposedly by Epstein, showing Andrew with his arm around Roberts's waist and Maxwell grinning in the background. Maxwell paid £290,000 for the property on Wednesday 22 January 1997. On Monday 19 April 2021, it was sold for £1,750,000. On Saturday 6 July 2019, Epstein was arrested on federal charges for the sex trafficking of minors in Florida and New York and committed suicide in his prison cell just over a month later. On Saturday 16 November 2019, Andrew sat down for a one-on-one interview with the BBC's Emily Maitlis in a bid to clear his name. He said that he had no recollection of meeting Virginia Roberts, that he always wore a jacket and tie when he went out and that since the Falklands War, he had been unable to sweat and so could not have perspired with Roberts in Tramp. He also claimed that on the night he allegedly had sex with her, he was actually at a pizza restaurant in Woking with his daughter. He said, "I was with the children and I'd taken Beatrice to a Pizza Express in Woking for a party at I suppose sort of 4 or 5 in the afternoon. And then because the Duchess was away, we have a simple rule in the family that when one is away the other one is there. I was on terminal leave at the time from the Royal Navy so therefore I was at home." Far from clearing his name, the interview exposed Andrew to even more scrutiny. In August 2021, Virginia Roberts, later Mrs Giuffre, sued Andrew in the US, accusing him of sexual assault. On Monday 29 November 2021, Maxwell went on trial in the US federal court on sex trafficking charges and was later convicted on five counts and acquitted on one more. On Tuesday 28 June 2022, she was sentenced to 20 years in prison. After saying time and again that he would fight in court to clear his name Andrew capitulated and, on Tuesday 15 February 2022. settled with his accuser, reputedly paying £12million.

BARNETT, LADY
The White House, 80 Main Street, Cossington, Leicestershire LE7 4UW
Telephone: Sileby 222

One of the leading television personalities of the 1950s (a member of the original panel on *What's My Line?*), Isobel Barnett was arrested in August 1980 for shoplifting (a tin of tuna fish and a carton of cream worth 87p) from a local shop. At her trial, which began on Wednesday 15 October 1980, she was found guilty, fined £75 and ordered to pay costs of £200. As she left court, she said to reporter Mary Griffiths of *The Sun*, "Please help me – I can't stop stealing." Found guilty on Thursday 16 October, she was discovered dead in her bath – clad in a floral nightgown with her head under the water – on the following Monday. She was 62 and had taken between twenty and twenty-six Distalgesic tablets that had been prescribed for her arthritis. There was no alcohol in her body and a two-bar electric fire found in the bath with her had played no part in her death. Of all her showbiz friends, only David Jacobs turned up to her funeral on Friday 24 October 1980 at **St Mary Magdalene Church, Church Lane, Knighton, Leicestershire LE2 3WG**. Lady Barnett's ashes were scattered over the grave of her husband who had died ten years earlier. Thieves ransacked her home shortly after her death. The road next to the house is now called Barnett Close.

BINDON, JOHN
Ranelagh Yacht Club, 74 Station Approach, London SW6

Thug-turned-actor John Bindon was a well-known face on the London underworld scene. Nicknamed "Biffo", he was not slow to use his fists. On Tuesday 21 November 1978 a cocaine deal went disastrously wrong at the Ranelagh Yacht Club, a seedy Fulham drinking den, and a gangster and police informer named Johnny Darke, 40, was stabbed nine times and killed. Bindon was also stabbed, his heart nicked in the fight. Bindon's friend Lennie Osborne dragged him, semi-conscious, away from the Ranelagh. Bindon's girlfriend, the model Vicki Hodge, and his younger sister, Geraldine, helped to dispose of his bloodstained clothes. Leaning on Hodge, the heavily bleeding Bindon made his way to Heathrow and boarded Aer Lingus flight EI179 to Dublin, intending to stay at an IRA safe house to avoid the police. After four days, Bindon was taken to St Vincent's Hospital where a priest administered the Last Rites. On Saturday 2 December 1978, Detective Chief Superintendent George Mould of F Division announced that Bindon was his chief suspect. Bindon didn't fancy a life on the run, so he rang DCS Mould and told him where he was. On Friday 8 December, Bindon flew back to London and gave himself up to DCS Mould who charged him with Darke's murder. At his trial at the Old Bailey, which began on Tuesday 23 October 1979, the prosecution alleged that Bindon had been paid £10,000 (£63,700 at 2022 values) to kill Darke, while the defence claimed that Bindon had gone to help a man who Darke had stabbed in the face. The actor Bob Hoskins appeared as a character witness for Bindon and told the court that his nickname came from *The Beano* comic character Biffo the Bear, and was nothing to do with his propensity for hitting people. On Tuesday 13 November 1979, after twelve hours' deliberation, Bindon was acquitted on grounds of self-defence. The judge, Mr Justice Mars-Jones, said that he believed the truth had not been told in his courtroom. Bindon's life took a downward turn after the case. He would often use his fists on Vicki Hodge but was careful never to mark her face. He would often get down on all fours in pubs and bang the floor, shouting, "What's it like down there, Darkey?" In 1982, a year after he and Hodge split up, he pleaded guilty to using a piece of pavement as an offensive weapon against a "short and weedy" man who had bumped into him while Bindon was celebrating his birthday. He was fined £100. On Tuesday 18 September 1984, he appealed successfully against a conviction for threatening an off-duty detective constable with a carving knife in a Kensington restaurant. In 1985, he was charged with possessing an offensive weapon and then cleared of threatening to firebomb the home of a mother of three. Bindon spent his final years living alone and on the dole in his flat, **20 Chesham Mews, Belgravia, London SW1X 8HS**. He died of Aids-related broncho-pneumonia a week after his fiftieth birthday. The Ranelagh Yacht Club is now derelict.

BOLAN, MARC
Queens Ride, Barnes Common, London SW15 5RH

At just after 5am on Friday 16 September 1977, the dyslexic pop star Marc Bolan, who still managed to write four Number One hits, was killed in a car crash on Queens Ride near the junction with Gypsy Lane in Barnes Common. His girlfriend Gloria Jones lost control of her purple mini (registration FOX 661L) as she drove over a hump-backed bridge, and the car smashed into a horse chestnut tree. A monument at the site was unveiled by Rolan Bolan on the twentieth anniversary of his father's death. Unfortunately, the tree on which fans leave their tributes is not the one that killed Bolan. The local council removed it long ago because it was so badly damaged. Bolan's funeral was held at Golders Green Crematorium on Tuesday 20 September 1977.

BOWLLY, AL
Duke's Court, 32 Duke Street, St James's, London SW1Y 6DF

The popular singer was in bed here at 3.10am on Thursday 17 April 1941 when a bomb exploded in Jermyn Street, blowing out the windows of his flat and killing him instantly. He was 43. Ironically, he had been performing at the **Rex Theatre, Oxford Street, High Wycombe, Buckinghamshire HP11** (closed Saturday 30 January 1965) the previous evening and had decided to catch the train back to London at the last minute. His last recordings were made with guitarist Jimmy Mesene a fortnight before his death. Bowlly was buried in a communal grave at **City of Westminster Cemetery, 38 Uxbridge Road, Hanwell, London W7 3PP** on Saturday 26 April.

BRAMBELL, WILFRID
Public lavatory, Shepherd's Bush Green, London W12

In 1955, the television actor divorced his wife of seven years, Molly Josephine, after she became pregnant by their lodger, Roderick

Fisher, and gave birth to a son. Brambell then claimed that he forsook sex for ten years. However, on Thursday 22 November 1962, he was arrested outside a public lavatory here for importuning for immoral purposes. At his trial in December, Brambell denied that he was gay (although his homosexuality was well-known to the police and in showbusiness circles), claimed that he got drunk at a BBC cocktail party and decided to walk a quarter of a mile to find a taxi to take him home to **10 Lynton Court, Horn Lane, Acton, London W3 6PN**. He visited two lavatories in quick succession because he was "extremely fuddled" and "it was necessary". Luckily for him, the magistrates believed his defence and he received a conditional discharge, paying twenty-five guineas in costs. From 1969 until his death on Friday 18 January 1985 at the Westminster Hospital, he lived with Yussof Ben mat Saman, his boyfriend, at **22 Moreton Place, Pimlico, London SW1V 2NP**.

CLEVELAND STREET SCANDAL
19 Cleveland Street, London, W1T 4HY

On Thursday 4 July 1889, telegraph messenger boy Charles Swinscow was questioned by the police over the theft of money from a room in the General Post Office at St Martin's-Le-Grand in the City of London. The 15-year-old had eighteen shillings about his person, far too large a sum for him to have saved from his wages. Swinscow claimed he had received the money for doing some "private work" for a man named Hammond who lived at 19 Cleveland Street, north of Oxford Street. Swinscow revealed a post office clerk named Henry Newlove, also 15, had introduced him to Cleveland Street after the two boys had been intimate together in the basement lavatory of their office. Swinscow had been to bed with a gentleman in Cleveland Street who gave the boy half a sovereign after anal sex. Swinscow gave the money to Hammond, who then gave him back four shillings. This became a regular occurrence. Swinscow revealed that other GPO employees George Wright and Charles Thickbroom, both 17, had also visited Cleveland Street. Newlove had been busy, because he had also visited the bathroom with Wright, At Cleveland Street, Wright went to bed for four shillings with a "foreign-looking chap", while Thickbroom got his four shillings for some mutual masturbation. On Friday 5 July, Newlove warned 32-year-old Charles Hammond that the police were on to him. Hammond, his French wife and their two sons fled to France. When Newlove was taken to the police station by Jack the Ripper (see page 102) investigator Detective Chief Inspector Frederick Abberline, he moaned that it wasn't fair he (Newlove) was under arrest while the top people were getting away with it. When Abberline asked him to explain, Newlove revealed that Lord Arthur "Podge" Somerset, the Earl of Euston and Colonel Jervois were all regulars at the male brothel. Newlove pleaded guilty at Bow Street Magistrates' Court and was sentenced to four months in prison with hard labour. The scandal was covered up as the establishment did not want the big names to be identified, especially another, huge name which had been revealed by Lord Arthur Somerset's solicitor. The case would have rested here had it not been for the press. On Saturday 16 November 1889. Ernest Parke of *The North London Press*, an obscure radical weekly, named Lord Arthur Somerset and the Earl of Euston and hinted at "a far more distinguished and more highly placed personage [who] was inculpated in these disgusting crimes". Euston issued a writ for libel and Parke appeared at the Old Bailey on Wednesday 15 January 1890; he was in a vulnerable position as he had falsely claimed that the earl had fled to Peru. Still, Euston admitted that he had been to Cleveland Street by mistake – he had thought it would be full of naked girls. However, a number of witnesses testified that he had been there on several occasions and rentboy John Saul claimed that he had been to bed with Euston who was "not an actual sodomite. He likes to play with you and then 'spend' on your belly." In his summation to the jury, the judge described Saul as a "loathsome creature" and Parke was found guilty of libel and sentenced to a year in prison without hard labour. Lord Arthur Somerset went abroad for four months after his second police interview, returning to England only to flee again when he was told he was about to be charged. He eventually settled in France where he lived with his boyfriend James Neale, until he died aged 74 in Hyères on Wednesday 26 May 1926. Charles Hammond moved from France to America, where he lived under an assumed name and remained a free man. Henry FitzRoy,

Memorial Park, 4471 Lincoln Avenue, Cypress, Orange County, California 90630. At the Bristol Assizes in June 1960, the driver George Martin was fined £50 for dangerous driving and banned from the road for fifteen years. A plaque marks the site of the crash on Rowden Hill. Ironically, in 2002, Sharon Sheeley was involved in another serious car crash. She died, aged 62, on Friday 17 May 2002 at Sherman Oaks Hospital Medical Center in Los Angeles, five days after suffering a brain haemorrhage. Gene Vincent died, aged 26, on Tuesday 12 October 1971 of heart failure, a ruptured ulcer and a haemorrhage.

> ### DID YOU KNOW?
> One of the policemen who attended the scene was a cadet called David Harman. He later became Dave Dee of the pop group Dave Dee, Dozy, Beaky, Mick and Tich.

CONNERY, SEAN
MGM Studios, Elstree Way, Borehamwood, Hertfordshire WD6 1SD

For Sean Connery, it was a chance to appear with a beautiful star. In *Another Time, Another Place* (released Friday 2 May 1958), Lana Turner was cast as Sara Scott, an American reporter working in London during the final year of the Second World War, who falls for British journalist Mark Trevor (Connery). Although some scenes were filmed in Cornwall, the major set was at MGM's studios in Borehamwood. At the time, Turner, 36, was seeing a short-tempered, jealous gangster named Johnny Stompanato, 32. Rumours reached him in Los Angeles that the relationship between his girlfriend and Connery, 27, had moved beyond the merely professional. He caught a flight to London to confront his love rival. Turner managed to calm him down at the flat she rented in Hampstead, but because she refused to allow him to come to the studio, he was convinced she was hiding something. Stompanato acquired a gun and then bribed his girlfriend's chauffeur to take him to the studio. As he arrived on set, he saw Turner and Connery embrace. In a jealous rage, he pulled the gun out and pointed it at Connery. Before he could pull the trigger, the 6ft 2in Scotsman yanked the gun from his grasp and punched him in the face, knocking him down. Stompanato was later quietly deported from the United Kingdom.

> **DID YOU KNOW?**
> A month before the film was released, Stompanato was stabbed to death with a nine-inch butcher's knife by Lana Turner's lesbian teenage daughter Cheryl Crane, on Friday 4 April 1958 at the family home, 730 North Roxbury Drive, Beverly Hills, California 90210, three days after they had moved in. Although Cheryl was charged, convicted and jailed, many believe that it was actually her mother who killed Stompanato, and she persuaded her daughter to take the blame.

COOPER, TOMMY
Her Majesty's Theatre, Haymarket, St James's, London SW1Y 4QL
Telephone: 020 7087 7762

Regarded as one of Britain's most loved comedians, it was said Tommy Cooper had "funny bones". He was a regular on television where he performed tricks that went wrong, which made the 6ft 3in Welshman's performances even funnier. On Sunday 15 April 1984, he appeared on the television show *Live From Her Majesty's*. One of his tricks was to don an oversize cloak and pull unlikely objects like a ladder or a hosepipe from between his legs. Sandy Lawrence, a glamorous blonde dancer, helped him on with the garment and began to leave the stage. Cooper put his hand on her back and, as she walked off, slumped to his haunches. The audience laughed, believing it was part of the act. He stayed where he had collapsed for some time, and the broadcast continued until he fell backwards. The show's producer David Bell, Cooper's personal assistant Mary Kay,and his son Thomas were in the wings. Bell asked, "Is that a joke?" Mary said it was but Thomas disagreed: "No, my dad's got a bad back and if he fell like that he wouldn't be able to get up again." When a loud, snore-like noise emanated from Cooper, the gallery staff realised something was amiss and went to a commercial break as Alyn Ainsworth's orchestra struck up the theme tune. The stage curtain was pulled around him. As the audience of 12½ million at home watched the advertisements, medical staff frantically worked on the stricken comedian. The next act, comedy duo Les Dennis and Dustin Gee, assumed the show would be stopped, but were surprised when David Bell came over and told them that they had to go on. Gee was reluctant. Following the maxim the show must go on, compère Jimmy Tarbuck welcomed the audience back and, without mentioning what had happened, introduced Les Dennis and Dustin Gee. The shock made him forget Dustin Gee's name and Dennis had to shout out his partner's name. Cooper was taken to Westminster Hospital, London, where he was pronounced dead on arrival, aged 63. A nine-feet statue of him was unveiled by Sir Anthony Hopkins in Caerphilly on Saturday 23 February 2008.

DANDO, JILL
29 Gowan Avenue, Fulham, London SW6 6RH
Television presenter Dando was shot and killed by a single bullet on the doorstep of the Fulham home that she rarely lived in. At the time of her death she was spending most of her time at the home of her gynæcologist fiancé Alan Farthing in nearby Chiswick. She had returned to Gowan Avenue to check her fax messages when she was ambushed at 11.33am on Monday 26 April 1999. Oddball loner Barry George, a fantasist who lived at **2b Crookham Road, Fulham, London SW6 4EQ**, about 400 yards from the murder scene, and who claimed to be the cousin of the late singer Freddie Mercury (he was listed on the electoral roll as Barry Bulsara) was arrested and eventually convicted of her murder. He was sentenced to life imprisonment. George's conviction was judged unsafe by the Court of Appeal (Criminal Division) and quashed on Thursday 15 November 2007. On Friday 1 August 2008, he was cleared of the murder. Barry George was twice refused compensation for wrongful imprisonment. The case remains unsolved.

DRIBERG, TOM
5 Queen's Gate Place Mews, South Kensington, London SW7 5BQ
Born at Uckfield Lodge, Crowborough, Sussex on Tuesday 22 May 1905, Thomas Edward Neil Driberg was thrown out of Lancing College after making sexual advances to another boy. His lifelong passion was fellating handsome, lean, intelligent, working-class men. Driberg became a newspaper gossip columnist, Labour MP and a member of the House of Lords. In November 1935, Driberg appeared in court charged with indecent assault. On Wednesday 30 October, he had been stopped on a street corner by two unemployed Scottish miners, Alexander Livingstone and James Kitchener Reid. Driberg invited them to his home in Queen's Gate Place Mews, where all three

shared a single bed. In the morning, both men accused Driberg of attempting to seduce them. The jury found him not guilty but, years later, Driberg revealed to the Labour MP, later Tory peer, Woodrow Wyatt, that he had lied in court. To the surprise of everyone who knew him, on 30 June 1951 Driberg married Ena Mary Binfield (1902-1977) but the marriage was never consummated. The new Mrs Driberg was rather plain of looks, causing Winston Churchill to comment, "Well, buggers can't be choosers."

GARLAND, JUDY
4 Cadogan Lane, London SW1X 9DP

It was here that Judy Garland died on Sunday 22 June 1969. On the night of Saturday 21 June, Judy and her fifth husband Mickey Deans were at their Chelsea home with Deans's close friend Philip Roberge, watching *The Royal Family*, a documentary about the House of Windsor, when Judy and her husband began to argue. She ran into the street shouting and, after a time, he went after her. Unable to find her, he returned to the house and went to bed. At approximately 10.40am the next morning, the telephone rang for Judy. Deans scoured the house and when he discovered the bathroom door was locked, he banged on it but received no reply. He climbed in through the bathroom window and found Judy dead sitting on the lavatory. Rigor mortis had already set in. She was only 47. The official cause of death was given as "Barbiturate Poisoning (quinalbarbitone), incautious self-overdosage, accidental." The house, a mews terrace, was hardly befitting of a Hollywood icon and as the years went by, it fell into disrepair. Demands for a Blue Plaque to commemorate Judy were ignored. Having lain empty for some time, it was finally demolished in the spring of 2016.

GIELGUD, SIR JOHN
Dudmaston Mews, Chelsea, London SW3 6JH

On Wednesday 21 October 1953, while he was rehearsing for his role as the fastidious prig Julian Anson in N.C. Hunter's play *A Day By The Sea* at London's Haymarket Theatre, and five months after he was knighted in the Coronation Honours List, Gielgud was arrested in a Chelsea public lavatory near the Royal Brompton Hospital and charged with importuning. That night, at home at **16 Cowley Street, Westminster, London SW1P 3LZ**, he contemplated suicide. The next morning, he turned up to the magistrates' court and pleaded guilty to the offence, but lied to the court about his occupation, telling the Bench that he was a self-employed clerk who earned £1,000-a-year and giving his name as Arthur Gielgud. The magistrate, E.R. Guest, fined him £10 and told him to visit a doctor. The follow-up story – although undoubtedly apocryphal – has it that when Gielgud turned up at the theatre there was an embarrassed silence until Dame Sybil Thorndike approached him and said, "Oh John, you *have* been a silly bugger!"

HASSALL, IMOGEN
17 Crooked Billet, Wimbledon Village, London SW19 4RQ

The "Queen of Cleavage" had a privileged background and was named after Shakespeare's *Cymbeline* heroine. She attended the Royal Ballet School and the London Academy of Music and Dramatic Art before joining the Royal Shakespeare Company. She began appearing on television including roles in *The Saint* (1964, 1966 and 1968), *The Avengers* (1967), *The Persuaders!* (1971), *Jason King* (1972) and *And Mother Makes Three* (1972). She played ugly duckling turned beautiful swan Jenny Grubb in *Carry On Loving* (1970). However, her private life did not go as she wished: her daughter Melanie died aged four days in 1972; two marriages ended in divorce; she suffered a miscarriage; and work dried up. Depression set in and she was found dead here aged 38 at 2pm on Sunday 16 November 1980 after taking a drugs overdose. She had been due to go on holiday to Mombasa with her actress friend Suzanna Leigh. Hassall's body was found naked in her four-poster bed by her house sitter. Her right hand was on the telephone and an empty bottle of Tuinal barbiturates was beside her.

HILL, BENNY
7 Fairwater House, 34 Twickenham Road, Teddington, Middlesex TW11 8AY

Alfred Hawthorn Hill was born at Bridge Street, Southampton, Hampshire on Monday 21 January 1924. His father, once a circus clown, later became the manager of a surgical appliance shop. Benny (he took the name from the American comedian Jack Benny) worked as a milkman and, in 1948, he appeared as a straight man to Reg Varney in the show *Gay Time* in summer season at Cliftonville, Kent. Hill made his name and his money on television, although he was uninterested in the financial rewards that came with his success. On Monday 29 May 1989, Hill was sacked from Thames Television after a ten-minute interview with Head of Light Entertainment John Howard Davies. He was very upset, believing it was unfair considering the millions of pounds he had made for the company. In 1990, *The Benny Hill Show* was shown in ninety-seven countries around the world, but not Britain. On Sunday 19 April 1992, the comedian Frankie Howerd died, aged 75. Among the tributes, Benny Hill said that he was "very upset", adding "We were great, great friends." They were friends but the quote did not come from Hill, who was already dead, but from Dennis Kirkland, his former producer. Hill had died, unmarried, of heart failure here on Saturday 18 April 1992. His body lay undiscovered until the following Tuesday when a neighbour called Kirkland, who climbed a ladder and peeped through the window of the second-floor flat. Hill was laying on the settee in front of two televisions, with dirty plates, glasses, videotapes and piles of papers scattered around him. Hill's corpse was bloated, distended and had turned blue. Dried blood trickled from an ear. The solitary comedian left £7,548,192 (£16,590,000 at 2022 values).

JAMES, SID
Sunderland Empire, 4-5 High Street West, Sunderland SR1 3EX

Sid James was born on Hancock Street, Newcastle, Natal, South Africa, on Thursday 8 May 1913 (although his death certificate lists the date as 6 May). He arrived in London, virtually penniless, on Wednesday 25 December 1946, his determination seeing him cast in a film within days of his arrival; he never looked back. He was quickly on his way to becoming a stalwart of British films in the 1950s. On Saturday 13 May 1967 while filming the sitcom *George And The Dragon*, Sid suffered a massive heart attack. His health was poor during the making of *Carry On Doctor* (1968), so it was fortunate that all his scenes required him to be in bed. Sid was a dedicated philanderer who attempted to seduce as many woman as possible, usually successfully. One of his conquests was his *Carry On* co-star Barbara Windsor. When the affair petered out, Sid began to lose the will to live. He told friends that if the affair ended he'd be dead within a year. He drank a bottle of whisky a day and preferred to work rather than spend time at home with his wife Val. On Monday 26 April 1976, he began a tour of the play *The Mating Season*: "an uproarious family comedy by Sam Cree". He suffered a fatal heart attack on stage at the Sunderland Empire Theatre on the opening night and died on the way to hospital. He was 62 years old.

LESLIE, JOHN AND ABI TITMUSS
Edinburgh House, 5 Uplands Close, London SW14 7AS

It was here that television presenter John Leslie and his University College Hospital nurse girlfriend Abi Titmuss took various videos of themselves and others in sexual situations in 2000. They had met in a Fulham bar in April 1999 and split up in 2004. Titmuss stood by her boyfriend when he was accused of sexual assault or impropriety by a number of women. However, the relationship was to falter and Leslie was sacked from ITV's *This Morning* in 2002. As his star waned, Titmuss's had an incredible rise. Her 2005 calendar was a best-seller and she guaranteed additional sales whenever she appeared on the cover of a lads' magazine. She began concentrating on acting, appearing on television and stage. In 2014, she relocated to Hollywood where she married Ari Welkom in 2017 and gave birth to a daughter.

LUCAN, ARTHUR
Theatre Royal, 5 Wellington Street, Barnsley, South Yorkshire S70 1SS
Telephone: Barnsley 2103

This is where on Friday 14 May 1954, Arthur Lucan, playing Old Mother Riley, was last seen on stage in *Old Mother Riley In Paris* as part of a national tour. He was born Arthur Towle on Wednesday 16 September 1885 in Sibsey, Lincolnshire. Determined to go into showbiz from an early age, he left home because his parents disapproved of his ambition. In 1910, he wrote his own version of *Little Red Riding Hood* for the Queens Theatre, Dublin. 13-year-old Kitty McShane was chosen to play the lead after Towle (then calling himself Clifton) spotted her at the penny arcade song booth in Henry Street. Towle adopted the name Lucan after a visit to the village of that name (owned the peer of that name). Three years later, at Dublin on Tuesday 25 November 1913, Lucan married 16-year-old Kitty McShane. They formed a professional as well as a personal double act, performing in South Africa, New Zealand and Australia as well as the British Isles. Their sketch, *Bridget's Night Out*, was selected for the 1934 Royal Variety Performance at the London Palladium before TM King George V and Queen Mary. From 1936 until 1951, they starred in fifteen low-budget films. Lucan became Old Mother Riley in 1937; in 1941, he and McShane had their own wireless series on the BBC: *Old Mother Riley Takes the Air*. Behind the scenes not everything was plain sailing – it was an open secret in showbusiness that they argued, and the comedian Max Wall thought Lucan was a battered husband. During filming, their scenes were shot separately before being edited together. In much the same way as Beryl Formby ruled husband George, Kitty McShane had much the same relationship with Lucan. She managed their business and hired and fired their support acts. One of their co-stars said that she told him to drop dead so often that he eventually did. Lucan died of a heart attack in his dressing room at the Tivoli Theatre, Paragon Street, Hull on Monday 17 May 1954 after collapsing in the wings. Kitty McShane died, an alcoholic, in London on Tuesday 24 March 1964, aged 66. The Theatre Royal is now a lap-dancing club.

MAMA CASS
Flat 12, 9 Curzon Place (now 1 Curzon Square),
Shepherd Market, Mayfair, London W1J 7FZ

It was here that the Mamas and the Papas singer (born Ellen Naomi Cohen). died aged 32. She arrived in England on Wednesday 10 July 1974 and appeared in a less-than-successful two weeks of concerts at the London Palladium. The audiences dwindled after the first show on 15 July, much to Mama Cass's embarrassment. She had lost six stone in the run-up to the trip but still found herself breathless during the shows. In England, she fell off the dieting wagon and her self-esteem took a hit. During her final show on Saturday 27 July she left a good luck message in lipstick on her dressing room mirror for the next occupant, her friend Debbie Reynolds, before going to a party for Mick Jagger's 31st birthday, where she chatted to Rod Stewart and Pete Townshend. Staying until the early hours, she then went to a brunch thrown for her by the singer Georgia Brown. At the event, other guests noticed that Cass was obviously unwell: coughing, blowing her nose and struggling to breathe. That night she went to a cocktail party hosted by American TV writer Jack Martin. She left around 8pm, saying that she needed some sleep, and was still asleep on Monday mid-afternoon when her English PA Dot McLeod went in to wake her up. Cass was naked and dead. Professor Keith Simpson, who carried out the post-mortem, put her death down to heart failure: "There was left-sided heart failure. She had a heart attack which developed rapidly." He also said there was no trace of drugs or alcohol in her system. This seems highly unlikely – the chances of her not drinking at Jagger's birthday party, Georgia Brown's brunch or Jack Martin's cocktail party seem unlikely in the extreme. The official verdict was a kindness, and Cass's biographer Eddi Fiegel wrote that it was "virtually impossible not to believe this was a drugs-related death".

MCWHIRTER, ROSS
50 Village Road, Enfield, Middlesex EN1 2ET

It was here on the doorstep of his home on Thursday 27 November 1975 that the campaigning journalist and co-founder and co-editor of *The Guinness Book of Records* was murdered, aged 50, by the IRA. Following the accidental murder of cancer specialist Professor Gordon Hamilton-Fairey (b. at 73 Harley Street, London W1 Sunday 20 April 1930) in Campden Hill Square on the morning of Thursday 23 October 1975 (the car bomb was intended for his next door neighbour Sir Hugh Fraser MP), Ross McWhirter offered £50,000 to anyone who provided information leading to the capture of the Irish bombers then plaguing London. On 27 November, McWhirter and his wife Rosemary were intending to go to the theatre with some friends. Mrs McWhirter drove off to fill their car with petrol. As she returned home at 6.50pm, two men ambushed her and took her car keys. She rang her front doorbell to get help from her husband. As he opened the door, she pushed past him into the hallway and he stood outlined in the doorframe. An IRA gunman shot him in the body and then again in the head with an Astra Magnum revolver. Mrs McWhirter was later told that the shot to the body alone would not have been fatal. Ross McWhirter was pronounced dead on arrival at **Chase Farm Hospital, The Ridgeway, Enfield, Middlesex EN2 8JL**. He was buried in an unmarked grave at Southgate Cemetery in north London. He left £137,082 (£1,225,275 at 2022 values). The house in Village Road has since been demolished. The gunmen were later arrested after their involvement in the siege of Balcombe Street (see page 73).

MEEK, JOE
304 Holloway Road, London N19 4DJ

Robert George "Joe" Meek was a record producer who was ahead of his time. He was born on Friday 5 April 1929 at 8 Market Square, Newent, Gloucestershire; because his mother had wanted a girl, he was dressed in female attire until he was four. After a stint in the RAF as a radar technician, Meek started to record local musicians and singers. He moved to London in 1953 or 1954 for his safety as much as anything: he had been beaten up several times because of his homosexuality. Meek landed a job in a studio but proved difficult to work with, such was his insistence on perfection and a diet of pills. He also had a propensity to violence. In January 1960, he created his own label, Triumph, and recorded the first concept EP, *I Hear A New World*. Space travel was capturing the public imagination at that time and Meek jumped on the bandwagon. Tracks on the album included such out-of-this world titles as "Entry Of The Globbots" and "March Of The Dribcots". Meek included sound effects such as bubbling water, lavatories flushing, radio interference and speeded-up voices over weirdly distorted Hawaiian guitar. Only 100 copies of the album, finished in May 1960, were ever pressed. With the help of a mysterious backer named Major Wilfred Alonzo Banks, a maker of Christmas decorations, Meek set up RGM Sound in a flat owned by his landlady Violet Shenton above A.H. Shenton, a leather-goods shop in Holloway, where he would create some of his most lasting music. He would also murder his landlady there. The flat was rather small, so string sections played huddled together on the stairs, singers recorded their vocals in the bathroom and whole bands crammed into the minuscule recording room. Loose wires were held in place with chewing gum and matchsticks, and some of the equipment was homemade. Meek once threw the young Rod Stewart out with a well timed raspberry, because he thought the London-born Scot was rubbish; he didn't rate The Beatles either. Meek tried to launch Geoff Goddard to fame as Anton Hollywood, but discovered that Goddard's real talent was as a songwriter. In 1961 Goddard wrote "Johnny Remember Me" "off the top of my head in ten minutes", a melodramatic song about a man hearing the voice of his dead lover. The song, performed by John Leyton, entered the UK Charts on Thursday 3 August 1961 and spent fifteen weeks there, including three at Number One. The bass was played by Chas Hodges, later to find fame as one half of Chas'n'Dave. When the song appeared on *Juke Box Jury*, the panel voted it a miss. Meek also recorded Screaming Lord Sutch but his own "Telstar", composed after watching the first transatlantic broadcasts from the Telstar satellites on television, became his biggest hit. Performed by the Tornados it topped the charts on both sides of the Atlantic, selling more than four million copies and making the Tornados the first all-British band to reach Number One in the USA. Meek who, remarkably, was tone deaf as well as dyslexic, would probably have been horrified if he had learned that Margaret Thatcher would reveal that "Telstar" was one of her favourite records. Meek hired Heinz Burt (b. at Dettmold, Lippe, Germany Friday 24 July 1942 d. at Eastleigh, Hampshire Friday 7 April 2000 of motor neurone disease) as lead singer of the group, and persuaded the former bacon slicer from Southampton to dye his hair peroxide blond. Heinz moved in with Meek but he denied that they were lovers. On Monday 11 November 1963, Meek was arrested for cottaging in the gents in **Madras Place, Holloway, London N7** (Joe Orton was another regular, see page 185). He was fined £15 on Tuesday 12 November for "persistently importuning for an immoral purpose". Meek believed that he had been set up – not least because his accuser was an old man – moaning, "I don't go chasing old men with watch chains dangling from their waistcoats – I go after young trade. Who wants a fucking old man?" Meek soon fell victim to several blackmailers as word got round that he would dish out fivers and tenners when accused of sleeping with someone, usually someone he had never even met. The hits continued but Meek became more and more paranoid, convinced that he was being spied on by other record companies. On Monday 16 January 1967, the dismembered body of rent boy Bernard Oliver was found in a suitcase on a farm in Tattingstone, Suffolk. Meek had been a client and was convinced that the police would try to blame him for the murder. The hits were drying up and he was facing financial worries. On Friday 3 February, Meek burned several paintings and documents. While his friend Patrick Pink was visiting him, a young boy called Michael turned up, but Meek told Pink to tell him to "Fuck off" and to send Violet Shenton up from her downstairs flat. Afterwards, Pink said that he heard shouting and scuffling: "I was in the office when I heard a big bang. It was such a fucking big bang. I was stunned. I rushed out and Violet was falling downstairs and I sort of grabbed her as she came to the bottom, and felt her. I was sitting on the stairs with her flapped over me... I saw the blood pouring out of these little holes in her back. And she died in my arms – I'm bloody positive she went still. I had quite a bit of blood over me. Her back was just smoking." Then Meek reloaded the gun and shot himself. Police found barbiturates, amphetamines and dexadrine in the flat. At his inquest, which recorded a suicide verdict, it was revealed that traces of amphetamines had been found in his body. Meek was buried in Newent cemetery on Friday 10 March. Despite interviewing more than 100,000 people, the Suffolk police never caught the suitcase murderer.

MERCURY, FREDDIE
Garden Lodge, 1–2 Logan Place, Kensington, London W8 6QN

It was here on Sunday 24 November 1991 that Freddie Mercury died of Aids aged 45. The Zanzibar-born Faroukh Bulsara had been one of the most flamboyant figures in pop music. He and his parents Bomi (b. at Bulsar, Maharashtra, India Monday 14 December 1908 d. at Basford, Derbyshire Friday 26 December 2003) and Jer Bulsara (b. at Gujarat, India Monday 16 October 1922 d. Sunday 13 November 2016), arrived in England in 1964, having fled the Zanzibar Revolution. Mercury joined the band Smile in April 1970, whose members included guitarist Brian May and drummer Roger Taylor. In February the following year, bassist John Deacon joined and the band became Queen (see page 243). In 1982, Mercury began to exhibit the first signs of the infection that would kill him nine years later. It seems most likely that he contracted the virus in New York at some point between Monday 26 July and Friday 13 August 1982 but nobody knows from whom. Indeed, Mercury had no idea he was infected and continued to party his way around New York, Munich and on tour. Mercury's boyfriend Jim Hutton (1949-2010) said that the singer was diagnosed with Aids in late April 1987. Mercury's last recording was in May 1991 at Mountain Studios in Montreux, Switzerland, more than a year after his final stage appearance at the 1990 Brit Awards held at the **Dominion Theatre, 268-269 Tottenham Court Road, London W1T 7AQ** on Sunday 18 February 1990. On Saturday 23 November 1991, Queen's manager Jim Beach released the following statement from Mercury: "Following the enormous conjecture in the press over the last two weeks, I wish to confirm that I have been tested HIV positive and have Aids. I felt it correct to keep this information private to date to protect the privacy of those around me. However, the time has come now for my friends and fans around the world to know the truth and I hope that everyone will join with me, my doctors and all those worldwide in the fight against this terrible disease. My privacy has always been very special to me and I am famous for my lack of interviews. Please understand this policy will continue." Mercury died a little over twenty-four hours later. He left an estate worth £8,649,940 (£19,787,500 at 2022 values).

MILLIGAN, STEPHEN
64 Black Lion Lane, Hammersmith, London W6 9BE

It was here, at his £160,000 house, on Monday 7 February 1994 that Milligan, bachelor Tory MP for Eastleigh, was found dead by his secretary Vera Taggart after failing to answer calls. He was tied up with electric flex and naked apart from stockings and suspenders. He had a satsuma in his mouth and a bin liner over his head. Milligan, 45, was found to have died from auto-asphyxiation. A death by misadventure was recorded. Milligan left an estate worth £846,860. The Conservatives lost the seat to the Liberal Democrats in a June by-election.

> **DID YOU KNOW?**
> The Eastleigh by-election was fought on Thursday 9 June 1994. Milligan's majority of 17,702 was overturned by David Chidgey of the Liberal Democrats, pushing the Tories, represented by Stephen Reid, into third place. The candidate finishing fourth was an aspiring politician by the name of Nigel Farage, standing for the United Kingdom Independence Party in his first Westminster election.

MILLS, FREDDIE
Goslett Yard, Soho, London WC2

Champion boxer Freddie Mills was found dead aged 46 in his car on Sunday 25 July 1965 in this side street off Charing Cross Road. His death remains a mystery. In 1959, Mills, who had won the British and European lightweight boxing championships seventeen years earlier, was having an affair with a much younger chorus girl he'd met while they were both appearing in summer season. The affair, which never became public, lasted three years. On Thursday 9 May 1963, Freddie Mills's Nitespot opened at **143 Charing Cross Road, London WC2H 0EE,** the venue for Mills's previous enterprise, an unsuccessful Chinese restaurant. On Sunday 5 July 1964, the *Sunday People* ran an exposé of the club, claiming prostitutes worked there as hostesses. Mills was shocked and instituted legal proceedings, but dropped them when the editor showed him evidence that the girls had been arrested numerous times for soliciting. Mills's death was shrouded in mystery. Various theories have been promulgated, including murder. A few days before, he borrowed a .22 rifle from an old friend, saying he wanted to dress as a cowboy at a fête he was opening in Esher on Saturday 24 July. There was no fête. On Tuesday 20 July 1965, he was fined £50 for allowing an illegal fruit machine on his premises and supplying alcohol to non-dining customers. On Saturday 24 July, he arrived at his club at 10.30pm but was disappointed to find it virtually empty. He told a young staff member that he would have a sleep in his car and asked to be woken in thirty minutes, when he was informed that the club was even emptier; he went back to sleep. That was officially the last time anyone saw him alive. At 1am, Mills was discovered with a wound in the corner of his right eye. An ambulance was called, but needed a push to get going on its journey to the hospital. Mills left just £387 in his will. When coroner Gavin Thurston recorded a verdict of suicide, Mills's widow refused to accept it and hired private detectives to find her husband's "killers". One unlikely theory has it that Mills was the unknown killer of prostitutes known as Jack the Stripper (see page 105). In April 1992, Mills's former sparring partner Fred "Nosher" Powell claimed that Mills had been arrested for cottaging in **Chandos Place, London WC2** and killed himself because he could not stand the public shame. It was also claimed that Mills was having a gay affair with gangster Ronnie Kray (see page 108) and was also close to singer Michael Holliday, who killed himself with a drugs overdose. Powell said, "Freddie certainly went bent in the last years of his life. Mills had a lot of friends in showbusiness and quite a few of them gave him the elbow because he went poof." Goslett Yard, previously George Yard was named after A. Goslett & Co, builders' merchants, who were based in a nearby building on Charing Cross Road.

MISS WORLD
Royal Albert Hall, Kensington Gore, London SW7 2AP
The annual beauty pageant before an audience of 5,000 was hosted here by Bob Hope on Friday 20 November 1970 and was interrupted by about fifty feminists throwing flour, stink and ink bombs and shouting "Women's liberation!" and "We are liberationists. Ban this disgraceful cattle market". The audience booed the protesters and Hope, who walked off the stage, said that "Anyone who would disrupt a beautiful occasion like this must be on some kind of dope." "None of them are pretty," he told journalists afterwards, "because pretty women don't have these problems." The protesters included: Sally Alexander, now a professor emerita of modern history at Goldsmiths College, University of London; Mair Davies, an artist from Wales; Jo Robinson, now an art teacher, who sprayed a bouncer with blue ink from a water pistol; Jenny Fortune, now an architect who lives with her daughter Maya in a semi-collective household; and Jan Williams, a physiotherapist. The show was hosted by Michael Aspel and the judges were the actress Joan Collins, film producer Nat Cohen, Sir Eric Gairy, the prime minister of Grenada, singers Nina van Pallandt and Glen Campbell, the Maharaja of Baroda, the Indonesian ambassador, the High Commissioner for Malawi and

BBC executive Peter Dimmock, the chairman of the judging panel. Miss World 1970 was the single most-watched television show of the year, with more than twenty-three million people tuning in. The pageant was won by 5ft 7in Jennifer Josephine Hosten, Miss Grenada, (b. at St George's, Grenada Friday 12 March 1948) a 22-year-old flight attendant and radio announcer with a 36-24-38 figure, who later became High Commissioner for Grenada to Canada. She was the first black winner and the runner-up was also black (Pearl Jensen, Miss Africa South).

MOON, KEITH
Flat 12, 9 Curzon Place (now 1 Curzon Square), Shepherd Market, Mayfair, London W1J 7FZ

It was here in the flat on the top floor of 9 Curzon Place that The Who drummer Keith Moon died, aged 32 (not 33 as his death certificate states). He had moved into the flat, which was owned by Harry Nilsson, in the middle of 1978, despite Nilsson's misgivings about renting it to him. Four years earlier, Mama Cass of The Mamas And The Papas had also died in the same flat (see page 176). Dr Geoffrey Dymond had prescribed 100 Heminevrin (clomethiazole, a sedative) pills for Moon to help him overcome his alcohol addiction., telling him he should take one pill every time he felt like a drink, but shouldn't take more than three a day. On Wednesday 6 September, Moon and his model girlfriend Annette Walter-Lax were hosted by Paul and Linda McCartney at the preview of *The Buddy Holly Story* (1978), starring Gary Busey as the ill-fated pop star. After the film, the two couples ate at Peppermint Park in Covent Garden before going their separate ways. Moon and Walter-Lax returned to Curzon Street. He awoke at 7.30am the next day and watched *The Abominable Dr Phibes* (1971). He asked Walter-Lax to cook steak and eggs but when she demurred, he shouted, "If you don't like it, you can fuck off!" He then took thirty-two Heminevrin tablets and went to sleep. When she woke at 3.40pm and wondered why the flat was so silent, she went to check on Moon and found him unresponsive. Paramedics were unable to restart his heart and a post mortem by Professor Keith Simpson revealed that six of the thirty-two pills had been absorbed in his system, enough to cause death. The coroner recorded an open verdict. On Wednesday 13 September, Moon was cremated at Golders Green Crematorium in London. The flat was last occupied in 2001. In 2011, the

Greek billionaire John Latsis bought the flat and neighbouring properties to turn them into a £120million development of houses, flats and offices.

ORTON, JOE
Flat 4, 25 Noel Road, London N1 8HQ

The gay playwright was murdered by his boyfriend Kenneth Halliwell here on Wednesday 9 August 1967. Halliwell, six years older than Orton and prematurely bald, met his future lover at Rada in 1951. Halliwell became a mentor to the Leicester-born Orton, encouraging him, guiding him, teaching him and loving him. Halliwell bought the studio flat in Islington in 1959 and he and Orton moved in the following year, at a time when homosexuality was still a criminal offence. Soon, however, Orton outgrew his boyfriend and, in the words of Orton's biographer, John Lahr, "edited Halliwell out". In 1963, Orton became a media star and Halliwell was left even further behind. Orton also led an excessively promiscuous sex life and recorded all the sordid details in his diaries that he left open for Halliwell to read. (They were published posthumously in 1987, edited by Lahr.) It all became too much for Halliwell and he took a hammer and smashed Orton's skull in before committing suicide with a dose of Nembutal. Halliwell left a note: "If you read his diary all will be explained. KH. PS: Especially the latter part." The final pages were, however, missing. Some people believed Orton's agent Peggy Ramsay took the diary to protect someone's identity. It has been reported that Orton was having an affair and was about to desert Halliwell, but the man in question has never been named. The author Michael Thornton was told by the police that he was mentioned in those pages, and that they were taken because they "contained sensitive information about persons still living". At Orton's funeral his favourite song "A Day In The Life" (see page 224) was played.

> ### DID YOU KNOW?
> Kenneth Leith Halliwell was born on Wednesday 23 June 1926 at Bebington, Wirral, Cheshire. When he was 11, he watched his mother die after being stung by a wasp. In 1944, he became a coal miner rather than serve in the armed forces. Halliwell's father committed suicide in 1949 by putting his head into a gas oven. Halliwell found the body. He inherited the family money which allowed him to move to London.

PLATH, SYLVIA
**Upstairs Maisonette, 23 Fitzroy Street,
Primrose Hill, London NW1 8TP**

On Monday 11 February 1963, the poet and wife of fellow poet Ted Hughes killed herself in this Primrose Hill flat by putting her head in a gas oven. She sealed up the children's bedroom door and left them milk and biscuits before she committed suicide. Plath had long been plagued by mental instability: she had a nervous breakdown in the summer of 1953 and was treated with electro-convulsive therapy. On Monday 24 August of that year, she attempted suicide with an overdose of sleeping pills. She was just 20. She met Hughes on Sunday 26 February 1956 while studying at Cambridge and they married at St George's Church, Bloomsbury, on Saturday 16 June 1956. Their daughter, Frieda Rebecca, was born on Friday April Fool's Day 1960 at **3 Chalcot Square, Primrose Hill, London NW1 8YA**. The couple moved to the West Country and, on Wednesday 17 January 1962, their second child, Nicholas Farrar, was born at **Court Green, North Tawton, Devon**. The marriage came under strain and Hughes began an affair with Assia Wevill (b. at Berlin, Germany Sunday 15 May 1927) in the summer of 1962. In December of that year, Plath and the children moved back to Primrose Hill, taking a five-year lease on an upstairs maisonette in a house that W.B. Yeats had once lived in. On Wednesday 23 January 1963, *The Bell Jar*, Plath's autobiographical novel about her mental breakdown, was published under the pseudonym Victoria Lucas. The critical reception was unenthusiastic. Plath was prescribed anti-depressants by her doctor, and both she and the children suffered from flu that winter. Hughes continued his affair with Assia Wevill and their daughter, Alexandra Tatiana Elise, known as Shura, was born on Wednesday 3 March 1965. He moved them into his Devon house, but early in 1968 Wevill moved back to London. Like Plath, she became depressed, and although Hughes fought to keep the relationship going, it was not to be. They argued on Sunday 23 March 1969. Later that day Wevill waited until 4-year-old Shura fell asleep and then carried her to the kitchen. She took pills washed down with whisky and turned on the taps of her Mayflower cooker before opening the oven and laying down beside her daughter to die. Ted Hughes had to identify both bodies at Southwark Mortuary. On Monday 16 March 2009, Nicholas Hughes, an unmarried, childless ecologist, hanged himself in his home in Fairbanks, Alaska. According to his sister Frieda and his former colleagues at the University of Alaska Fairbanks, where he earned a PhD in 1991, he had been depressed for many years.

PROFUMO AFFAIR, THE
In June 1963, a few years after Prime Minister Harold Macmillan assured Britain that they had never had it so good, his administration was rocked by a sex scandal that still fascinates almost sixty years later. In the summer of 1961, John Profumo, the Minister for War, met and became briefly involved with good-time girl Christine Keeler (1942-2017), who had appeared in a bikini in the magazine *Titbits*, aged 16, on Saturday 22 March 1958. Just over a year later, on Friday 17 April 1959, she gave birth to a son in King Edward VII Hospital in Old Windsor, but the child was premature and died after just six days. The father was an American soldier based at nearby Laleham Air Force Base at Staines, Middlesex. When Keeler left hospital, she found a room in St John's Wood. Two years later, she met Profumo and they had a short fling. On Friday 22 March 1963, Profumo made a personal statement in the chamber of the House of Commons: "I understand that in the debate on the Consolidated Fund Bill last night, under the protection of parliamentary privilege, the Honourable Gentlemen the Members for Dudley (George Wigg) and for Coventry, East (Richard Crossman), and the Honourable Lady the Member for Blackburn (Barbara Castle), opposite, spoke of rumours connecting a minister with a Miss Keeler and a recent trial at the Central Criminal Court. It was alleged that people in high places might have been responsible for concealing information concerning the disappearance of a witness and the perversion of justice. I understand that my name has been connected with the rumours about the disappearance of Miss Keeler. I would like to take this opportunity of making a personal statement about these matters. I last saw Miss Keeler in December 1961, and I have not seen her since. I have no idea where she is now. Any suggestion that I was in any way connected with or responsible for her absence from the trial at the Old Bailey is wholly and completely untrue. My wife and I first met Miss Keeler

at a house party in July 1961, at Cliveden. Among a number of people there was Dr Stephen Ward whom we already knew slightly, and a Mr Ivanov, who was an attaché at the Russian Embassy. The only other occasion that my wife or I met Mr Ivanov was for a moment at the official reception for Major [Yuri] Gagarin at the Soviet Embassy. My wife and I had a standing invitation to visit Dr Ward. Between July and December 1961, I met Miss Keeler on about half a dozen occasions at Dr Ward's flat, when I called to see him and his friends. Miss Keeler and I were on friendly terms. There was no impropriety whatsoever in my acquaintanceship with Miss Keeler. Mr Speaker, I have made this personal statement because of what was said in the House last evening by the three Honourable Members, and which, of course, was protected by privilege. I shall not hesitate to issue writs for libel and slander if scandalous allegations are made or repeated outside of the House." The pressure mounted on the minister and during a trip to Venice, Profumo told his actress wife Valerie Hobson that he had not been entirely truthful to her, his Party, the public or the House of Commons. On Tuesday 4 June Profumo confessed that he had misled the House and wrote a resignation letter: "Dear Prime Minister You will recollect that on 22 March, following certain allegations made in Parliament, I made a personal statement. At the time rumour had charged me with assisting in the disappearance of a witness, and with being involved in some possible breach of security. So serious were these charges that I allowed myself to think that my personal association with that witness, which had also been the subject of rumour, was by comparison of minor importance only. In my statement I said that there had been no impropriety in this association. To my very deep regret I have to admit that this was not true, and that I misled you, and my colleagues, and the House. I ask you to understand that I did this to protect, as I thought, my wife and family, who were equally misled, as were my professional advisers. I have come to realise that, by this deception, I have been guilty of a grave misdemeanour and despite the fact that there is no truth whatever in the other charges, I cannot remain a member of your Administration, nor of the House of Commons. I cannot tell you of my deep remorse for the embarrassment I have caused to you, to my colleagues in the Government, to my constituents, and to the Party which I have served for the past twenty-five years." Prime Minister Harold Macmillan, replied the next day from **Ardchattan Priory, Connel, Oban, Argyll PA37 1RQ**, where he was on holiday, although giving the impression that he had not actually read the letter: "Dear Profumo, The contents of your letter of 4 June have been communicated to me, and I have heard them with great regret. This is a great tragedy for you, your family, and your friends. Nevertheless, I am sure you will understand that in the circumstances, I have no alternative but to advise the Queen to accept your resignation." He made no mention nor thanks for Profumo's public service. On Thursday 20 June, the House of Commons formally censured him. *The Denning Report* compiled by Lord Denning into the affair was published on Wednesday 25 September 1963 but anyone expecting salacious details would be seriously disappointed.

Murray's Cabaret Club, 16-18 Beak Street, London W1F 9RD

Murray's Cabaret Club, an intimate Soho basement with space for 110 guests, opened (in the iteration that concerns us) in 1933. It was the first British venue to stage a nude cabaret. Membership was one guinea (£25 at 2022 values) and the entrance fee was a similar amount. It was here that Christine Keeler began working on Wednesday 26 August 1959 as a topless dancer, earning £8 10s a week (£205 at 2022 values) after leaving a job as a waitress at a Greek nightclub in Baker Street. She later recalled that her main task at Murray's was to "walk around naked" in a low-lit room with deep-red carpets and gilt furniture. She was hired when Maureen O'Connor, a fellow waitress, introduced Keeler to the owner, Percy "Pops" Murray. As was expected of his showgirls, Keeler was soon sitting with the customers between acts, encouraging them to buy more drinks. It was also here that she met Mandy Rice-Davies (b. at The Lynch, Mere, Wiltshire Saturday 21 October 1944 as Marilyn Rice Davies d. at Wexham Park Hospital, Wexham Street, Slough SL2 4HL Thursday 18 December 2014 of lung cancer and chronic obstructive pulmonary disease) and it was hatred at first sight. They eventually became firm friends after they went to the same parties and realised that they could make some money – Rice-Davies had a head for finances; Keeler did not, and was generally disorganised. They also worked well in the bedroom, earning them money for expensive clothes and lifestyles. After a few nights, a wealthy Arab came to the club accompanied by a woman and Dr Stephen Ward (b. at Lemsford Vicarage, Hatfield, Hertfordshire Saturday 19 October 1912), a society osteopath. Ward charmed Keeler and she soon moved into his flat at **11 Orme Court, Bayswater, London W2 4RQ**. "His flat was tiny and on the top floor but there was a lift. There was a bed-sitting room with two single beds pushed close together, and an adjoining bathroom. We would share the bed but only as brother and sister; there were never to be any sexual goings-on between us," Keeler later recalled. Murray's closed in 1975 in the face of competition from more explicit strip clubs and peep shows. Percy Murray died in 1979, aged 81.

Spring Cottage, Cliveden, Taplow, Berkshire SL6 0JF

Spring Cottage was originally built as a secluded summer house by the Countess of Orkney in 1813, and takes its name from the spring that emerges from the nearby cliffs. It was at a pool party here on Saturday 8 July 1961 – the first day of the hottest weekend of the year – that Profumo encountered a naked Christine Keeler. From 1956, Stephen Ward had a standing invitation from William Waldorf Astor, the 3rd Viscount Astor (b. Tuesday 13 August 1907 d. Tuesday 8 March 1966), the owner of Cliveden, to use his swimming pool. After cooking dinner for Keeler, her friend Leo Norell and Joy, a girl hitchhiker Keeler and Norell picked up en route, Ward and Keeler made their way to the pool (about a mile from Spring Cottage) between 10pm and 11pm. Keeler's swimming costume did not fit so Ward suggested she skinny dip. Their frolics were quite noisy and attracted the attention of Astor's thirty dinner guests, which included President Ayub Khan of Pakistan, Lord Mountbatten, Sir Isaac and Lady Wolfson, David and Pamela Hicks, Johnnie and Jane Dalkeith, Mr and Mrs Nubar Gulbenkian, Felix Kelly, Mary Roxburgh and several Tory MPs who wandered down to the pool. Astor and Profumo were the first to appear and Mrs Profumo handed Keeler a towel to protect her modesty. One of Astor's servants, however, later said that Ward and Keeler were already at the house and a group then set off for the pool. Was the servant mistaken, or was this done to put distance between the Astor party and the Ward group? The waters are further muddied because in his book *Bringing The House*

Down, the Profumos' son David revealed that Lord Astor took Ward to the Profumos' bedroom, where he massaged Valerie Hobson's stiff neck. She apparently "found him creepy". However it happened, the Ward party went to the house and Profumo gave Keeler a guided tour around Cliveden and dressed her in one of the suits of armour. To add to the confusion of the initial meeting, David Profumo said that his father told him that he had met Keeler before at Murray's and had a drink with her but Profumo *fils* wondered if *père* had confused Keeler with another dark-haired beauty. Keeler did not stay at Spring Cottage that night but returned to London. The next day, she was back at Cliveden with two more women and Soviet Naval attaché Yevgeny "Eugene" Ivanov (b. at Pskov, USSR Monday 11 January 1926 d. at Moscow, Russia Monday 17 January 1994), a friend of Ward. That afternoon, another pool party was held and the War Minister and the Russian spy vied for Keeler's attentions. An arms-only swimming race was won by Profumo after he cheated by using his legs. "That'll teach you to trust the Government," said Profumo. He asked for Keeler's telephone number and she told him to ask Ward. That night, she ended up in bed with Ivanov at Wimpole Mews after he gave her a lift home.

38 Devonshire Street, London W1G 6QB

This was Stephen Ward's consulting rooms. Ward began studying osteopathy at Kirksville College, Missouri in the autumn of 1934 and stayed there for four years. In 1938, he began practising in Torquay, Devon. In March 1944, he was posted to India, where later that year he treated Mahatma Gandhi for headaches and a stiff neck. In 1946, following demob, he began working at the **Osteopathic Association Clinic, 25 Dorset Square, London NW1 (Telephone AMBassador 1128)** at a salary of £10 a week. He soon took himself to Cavendish Square where he took over a practice before relocating to Devonshire Street, just half a mile away. His clients included Lord Astor (from 1950), John Profumo (from 1956), American ambassador Averell Harriman, King Peter of Yugoslavia, Elizabeth Taylor, Ava Gardner, Frank Sinatra, several maharajahs, six members of the Churchill family including Sir Winston, Mary Martin, Mel Ferrer, Danny Kaye and many more. Since 1972, the building has housed a dental practice.

17 Wimpole Mews, London W1G 8PG
Telephone: WELbeck 6933

Ward moved here in March 1961 with Keeler. She started sleeping with John Profumo on Sunday 16 July 1961; he gave her a bottle of perfume, a Flaminaire cigarette lighter and £20 to "buy your mother a little something". On Monday 4 September 1961, the West Indian thug Aloysius "Lucky" Gordon (b. at Kingston, Jamaica Sunday 5 July 1931; his parents won the lottery the day he was born, he had a brother called "Psycho", d. at London Wednesday 15 March 2017) arrived back in London, having been deported from Denmark for stabbing a woman. In October 1961, Ward, Keeler and the society portrait painter Vasco Lazzolo went to the **El Rio Café, 127 Westbourne Park Road, Notting Hill, London W2 5QL** to buy some cannabis. The two men stayed in the car while Keeler went inside to make the deal with a ten shilling note provided by Ward, buying the drugs from Lucky Gordon. She gave him her phone number because she thought he might be able to fix up Ward with a West Indian girl. Two days later, Gordon rang to tell Keeler he had sorted a girl for Ward at a forthcoming party at the El Rio. The party did not go to plan and Gordon tried to take advantage of a drunk and stoned Keeler. Ward intervened and took Keeler home alone, but only after he gave Gordon their address. The West Indian became obsessed with the show girl and turned up uninvited at Wimpole Mews several times; finally, she agreed to meet him at a café on Westbourne Park Road. He told her that he had some stolen jewellery at his flat in nearby **St Stephens Gardens, London W2**, which he wanted her to see. When she foolishly went back there, he raped her at knifepoint; the assault continued for twenty-four hours until she persuaded him to let her go. Back at Wimpole Mews, she told Ward what had happened but he convinced her not to report the rape to the police. In October 1961, Keeler received £50 (£1,200 at 2022 values), for sex from a man identified only as "Charles" in the later court case. "Charles" was later revealed to be the financier and retail magnate Charles Clore (1904-1979). The next month, Gordon attacked Keeler outside number seventeen as Ward looked on. In December 1961, Keeler's affair with Profumo ended and she left Wimpole Mews to move in with Mandy Rice-Davies in **Dolphin Square, Chichester Street, London SW1V 3LX**. In January

1962, Keeler, now alone after Rice-Davies moved out, underwent an illegal abortion at Dolphin Square and was taken to **The Chelsea Hospital for Women, Dovehouse Street, Chelsea, London SW3 6LT** by Peter Lewis, a childhood friend. In March or April that year, Gordon again raped Keeler, holding her and another woman captive until Keeler engineered an escape. This time she did call the police and pressed charges, but Gordon's family badgered her until she withdrew the allegation. Gordon's stalking campaign continued even when Keeler returned to Wimpole Mews. In May 1962, Keeler met, fell in love and got engaged to Old Etonian and former Guards officer turned publisher Michael Lambton, and they moved into **Kinnerton Street, Knightsbridge, London SW1X** (see also Prince Andrew p160).

DID YOU KNOW?

Michael Lambton (b. Saturday 24 November 1934), a cousin of the disgraced politician Lord Lambton (1922-2006), loved one thing more than Christine Keeler – alcohol. He used to keep a potty on the back seat of his Bentley in case he found himself too far from a public convenience. He would steer with one hand and ask his passenger to "pass the potty, dear".

Lambton was working in Philadelphia in the summer so Keeler returned to 17 Wimpole Mews. In September, she encountered Paula Hamilton-Marshall and Johnny Edgecombe (b. at St John's, Antigua and Barbuda Saturday 22 October 1932 d. at London Sunday 26 September 2010), another West Indian thug. Keeler, a friend and Edgecombe moved into Sheffield Terrace. Believing she was still in danger from Lucky Gordon, Keeler bought a Luger pistol for £20. She and Edgecombe began an affair as Rice-Davies moved into 17 Wimpole Mews with Ward. When Keeler and a friend, Jackie Brown, went to a hairdresser near Comeragh Road in October, Gordon appeared and thumped Keeler, leaving her on the ground. On Thursday 25 October, Keeler asked Ward if she could move back in. One of the claims made in the case was that Ward was a spy for the Soviets, but was he actually working for peace? On Saturday 27 October, Ward took Ivanov to the home near Kings Langley of

Lord Arran, the Permanent Under-Secretary at the Foreign Office, because the Soviet attaché "wished to get a message to the British Government by indirect means asking for them to call a summit forthwith". Nothing came of it.

DID YOU KNOW?

Eton and Balliol College, Oxford-educated Arthur Kattendyke Strange David Archibald Gore, the 8th Earl of Arran, later became an advocate for homosexual law reform, supposedly because his elder brother committed suicide because he was gay. Nine days after succeeding their father, the 6th Earl, "Pauly", the 7th Earl, killed himself on Sunday 28 December 1958. Arran sponsored Labour MP Leo Abse's 1967 private member's bill which sought to decriminalise homosexual acts between consenting men over the age of 21. Arran also kept a pet badger and spoke in favour of an ultimately unsuccessful bill to protect the black and white animals. When asked why his badger bill failed but his homosexual one succeeded, he replied, "There are not many badgers in the House of Lords."

On the night of 27-28 October, Gordon and Edgecombe had a fight over Keeler at the All-Nighters Club in Wardour Street; Gordon needed seventeen stitches after Edgecombe slashed him. Ward arranged a dinner between Keeler and solicitor-turned-restaurateur Michael Eddowes, but he was too old to be of sexual interest to her, 59 to her 20. On Wednesday 31 October, Keeler called it a day with Johnny Edgecombe. That same month, Ward let Keeler's room to Emil Savundra, who would be referred to only as the "Indian doctor" at Ward's subsequent trial. Savundra (see page 133) used the room to entertain women – including Rice-Davies – to whom he would pay £20 for sex. On Thursday 1 November, Keeler moved into **Third Floor, 63 Great Cumberland Place, London W1H 7LJ** with her friend Rosemary Wells. Rice-Davies took up residence at Wimpole Mews again; not long before Christmas, Keeler came to visit. Around 1pm on Friday 14 December 1962, a furious Edgecombe showed up at Ward's home and fired seven shots at the door after Keeler and Rice-Davies refused to let him in. Neighbours raised the alarm and Wimpole Mews was quickly swarming with police and journalists.

Edgecombe managed to make off in a taxi but was later arrested at his Brentford flat. The press had no inkling of the story that was about to be unleashed. Rumours began to circulate in Fleet Street but strict libel laws prevented any paper hinting at the gossip. The police began to take a more than healthy interest in Keeler, pulling her in for questioning every fortnight or so about the shooting and Ward. Two days before Chrstmas, Keeler and Paul Mann, a friend and bridge partner of Ward, met the former Labour MP John Lewis (b. Saturday 14 December 1912 d. at St Marylebone, London Saturday 14 June 1969) at a party for old friends from Murray's Club in **Rossmore Court, Park Road, Marylebone, London NW1 6XX**. Lewis offered help with the Gordon situation, but Lewis had been burning with hatred for Ward since 1952, when he was convinced Ward had slept with his wife Joy. He was determined to exact his revenge and Keeler had just provided him with the ammunition. A few days later, Lewis invited to Keeler his St John's Wood flat where he unbeknown to her taped their conversation. Keeler told Lewis about her fling with Profumo and said that Ward has asked her to quiz the War Minister about "when the 'Bomb' would come to Germany". Lewis then made a pass at Keeler which she rebuffed, and they never saw each other again. Gordon would still not leave Keeler alone and they met in January 1963 at **The Flamingo Club, 33-37 Wardour Street, London W1D 6PU**, where Keeler agreed to meet Gordon once more, at his brother's flat in Leytonstone. Keeler gave evidence at Johnny Edgecombe's committal proceedings in mid-January. On Friday 18 January, Gordon was fined £5 (which Keeler paid) at Marlborough Street Magistrates' Court for possession of an offensive weapon. On Saturday 26 January, Detective Sergeant John Burrows interviewed Keeler about the Edgecombe trial and she told him about her relationship with Profumo. The following day, Keeler met Gordon at Leytonstone and stayed with him until Tuesday 29 January, when she returned to Wimpole Mews. the same day that Ivanov was recalled to the Soviet Union. Four days earlier, Keeler had signed a deal with *The Sunday Pictorial* to sell her story. That month, John Lewis told Labour MP George Wigg about the Keeler-Profumo liasions. On Monday 4 February, Ward's home was broken into and a photograph of him with Keeler, Grundie Heiber and Sally Norrie at Cliveden was stolen.

Ward left Wimpole Mews and moved to Bryanston Mews as Keeler became more frightened about Edgecombe's trial; her nerves weren't helped when Gordon broke into their new home on Edgware Road. Managing to give him the slip, she arrived in France on Saturday 9 March. The next evening, the subject of Profumo's affair with Keeler came up at party attended by Labour leader Harold Wilson, George Wigg and Barbara Castle. On Friday 15 March Edgecombe was acquitted of slashing Lucky Gordon's face but was sent down for seven years for possessing a firearm with intent to endanger life. Andrew Roth, an American journalist with his finger on the pulse of Westminster goings on, published Profumo's letter to Keeler in his newsletter *Westminster Confidential*. The War Minister thought the circulation of the journal was so small that very few people would actually see it; as a consequence, he decided not to sue. On Thursday 21 March, Wigg and Castle both referred to the affair in the House of Commons chamber; Profumo, who had taken a sleeping pill, was roused from his bed at 3am to be quizzed by five of his colleagues. Iain Macleod, the Leader of the House, said to him, "Look, Jack, the basic question is, 'Did you fuck her?'" Profumo denied that he had and Bill Deedes, the Minister Without Portfolio and later editor of *The Daily Telegraph*, wrote a draft statement for Profumo to read to the House, which he did later that day (see above).

DID YOU KNOW?

In 1955 Andrew Roth (1919-2010) began producing *Westminster Confidential*, a well-informed but small circulation newsletter about shenanigans in Whitehall, which published the story of the Profumo Affair. The *Queen* magazine hinted at the goings-on; its gossip columnist and associate editor Robin Douglas Home (1932-1968) had a section called "Sentences I'd like to hear the end of" and, on Tuesday 31 July 1962, published the following delitescent snippet: "... called in MI5 because every time the chauffeur-driven Zis drew up at her *front* door, out of the *back* door into a chauffeur-driven Humber slipped..."

House of Commons, London SW1 0AA

It was here on Wednesday 27 March 1963 that a meeting was held between Henry Brooke, the Secretary of State for the Home

Department, Sir Joseph Simpson, the Commissioner of the Metropolitan Police Force and Roger Hollis, the head of MI5, who would later be accused of spying for the Soviets. The decision was taken to "get" Stephen Ward. The investigation began, perhaps appropriately, on Monday, April Fool's Day. The police put a tap on Ward's phone, a watch on his home and surgery and interviewed 140 of his friends and clients, forcing them to back away from him. On Tuesday 23 April, having refused to make a statement about Ward, Mandy Rice-Davies was arrested for possessing a false driving licence. Her spirit broken after a week in Holloway, she spoke to the police about her relationships with Ward and Rachman. On Sunday 19 May, Ward wrote to Home Secretary Henry Brooke to complain about police persecution, especially since he had "shielded" Profumo. The next day, Brooke replied saying that the police do not come under his purview, so Ward sent a copy of his letter to every national newspaper editor; fearing libel, none of them published the story. Ward also wrote to Labour leader Harold Wilson telling him that Profumo had lied.

Basement Flat, 13 Hyde Park Square, London W2 2JP

It was here on Saturday 9 December 1961 that the Man In The Mask orgy was held, hosted by antiques dealer Hod Dibben and his wife Mariella Novotny. It was said that Novotny, who called the party the Feast of Peacocks after the food served at dinner (she also cooked badger), spent much of the evening in bed wearing a corset with a whip and six men. The guests were reported to be actors, MPs and judges, and most of them were naked. Stephen Ward kept his socks on, but the party has become infamous because one of the guests was naked apart from a Masonic apron and a mask, and a sign bearing the legend, "If my services don't please – whip me". The man's identity has been the subject of much speculation ever since, with various names being put forward such as film director Anthony Asquith and Ernest Marples, the Conservative transport minister. The Marples rumour came about because Ward, annoyed at being caught in a traffic jam, said to his companion Tom Mangold, a journalist with the *Daily Express*, "Let's say it was that bloody Ernest Marples. Publish that…" Within days, most of London "knew" that Marples was a masochistic sex fiend.

1 Bryanston Mews West, London W1H 2BW

In January 1960, Keeler and a friend, Sherry Danton, moved in here briefly, having temporarily abandoned Ward, before moving back to Orme Court. Slum landlord Peter Rachman installed Rice-Davies as his mistress here where she lived for two years, Rachman refusing to let her bring anything made in West Germany into the flat. After they fell out, Keeler said of her former friend, "Mandy Rice-Davies was a true tart. There was always a shock on her face whenever she thought she might have to do more than lie on her back to make a living." The house had a two-way mirror and a tape recorder under the bed. Always savvy, Rice-Davies subsequently made a career out of the Profumo Affair, even though she had nothing to do with it and never met John Profumo. It was here on Monday 20 May 1963 that Ward and Keeler met for the last time, outside of a court room.

3 Chester Terrace, London NW1 4ND

Profumo took his young *inamorata* here, the family home, when his wife was away. Keeler was to remember: "It was late. The butler and the rest of the staff were in bed… We crept around the lovely rooms. And then we got into their bedroom…" where they had sex in the marital bed. They also had sex in his car, and, once, in Regent's Park. Profumo gave her a number of presents, a polite way of paying for her services. Keeler later summed up the liaison as "a very well-mannered screw of convenience; only in other people's minds, much later, was it 'An Affair'." At 4pm on Friday 9 August, when the "affair" was barely a month old, Sir Norman Brook , the Cabinet Secretary, told Profumo that Ward's flat was under MI5 surveillance and warned him about getting caught up in something unfortunate. The politician ended the fling in December. Profumo died aged 91 at midnight on Friday 10 March 2006 in the Chelsea and Westminster Hospital, two days after suffering a stroke. At the time of his death, he was living at **Flat 7, 20 Lowndes Square, London SW1X 9HD**. He left £3,015,102 (£4,609,245 at 2022 values) in his will.

> ### DID YOU KNOW?
> Stephen Ward and John Profumo both died in the same but different hospital – by the time death claimed Profumo forty-three years after Ward, the hospital had been demolished and a new one built on the same site.

17 Greek Street, London W1D 4DR
Telephone GERrard 8472

It was here, in Edgar Brind's studio in May 1963, that Keeler posed for Lewis Morley for the famous "nude" photograph sitting backwards on a chair. Generally regarded to be naked, she was topless but used the back of the chair to protect her modesty and pulled her white knickers up and out of sight.

Vale Court, 21 Mallord Street, London SW3 6AL

On Saturday 8 June 1963, Stephen Ward was arrested and charged with living off the immoral earnings of Keeler, Rice-Davies and other women. He was denied bail. On Wednesday 3 July, he was committed for trial and given bail. His trial began on Monday 22 July at the Old Bailey on five charges – living wholly or partly off the immoral earnings of prostitutes and procuring girls under 21 to have sex with a third party. When Rice-Davies was questioned over her claim of an affair with Lord Astor, and when told he had denied any impropriety, she said, Well he would, wouldn't he?" earning her immortality in *The Oxford Dictionary Of Quotations*. Profumo's presents to Keeler were used as evidence of her prostitution and Rice-Davies's money from Dr Savundra, "the Indian Doctor", were also used against Ward. Things looked bleak as the trial progressed and it was here, the home of advertising executive Noel Howard-Jones, that Stephen Ward took an overdose of Nembutal sleeping pills on Tuesday 30 July 1963 following the summing up by Mr Justice Marshall. Several people present in the court claimed that the judge was clearly biased against Ward. *France Soir* reported, "However impartial he tried to appear, Judge Archie Pellow Marshall was betrayed by his voice." Ward had told his defence counsel, James Burge, "One of my great perils is that at least half a dozen of the [witnesses] are lying and their motives vary from malice to cupidity and fear... In the case of both Christine Keeler and Mandy Rice-Davies there is absolutely no doubt that they are committed to stories which are already sold or could be sold to newspapers and that my conviction would free these newspapers to print stories which they would otherwise be quite unable to print [for libel reasons]." Ward left a note for Howard-Jones, "It is really more than I can stand – the horror, day after day at the court and in the streets. It is not only fear, it is a wish not to let them get me. I would rather get myself. I do hope I have not let people down too much. I tried to do my stuff but after Marshall's summing-up, I've given up all hope." Ward was taken, unconscious, to St Stephen's Hospital at 8.50am and initially doctors believed he would pull through. His trial continued in his absence and Mr Justice Marshall withdrew Ward's bail; not that it mattered much, as the accused remained comatose in hospital. At 7.09pm on 31 July, the jury found Ward guilty of the first two counts (living off the immoral earnings of Christine Keeler and Mandy Rice-Davies), but not guilty of the remaining three charges. The judge delayed sentencing until Ward could be brought to court. At 3.45pm on 3 August 1963, after seventy-nine hours in a coma, Ward died in Ward 3D of St Stephen's. He was 50. To this day, the public are forbidden from reading the transcript of the evidence and the summing up at the National Archives in Kew. It is under lock and key until 2046, unless someone who gave evidence requests a copy. In 2011, Mandy Rice-Davies's request for a copy was granted, but came with warnings she musn't pass the information on to anyone else. Ridiculously, all the names she mentioned in open court – Astor, Douglas Fairbanks Jr, even Keeler – were all redacted.

DID YOU KNOW?

The film *Scandal* about the Profumo Affair was released on Friday 3 March 1989 starring John Hurt as Stephen Ward, Ian McKellen as John Profumo, Joanne Whalley-Kilmer as Christine Keeler and Bridget Fonda as Mandy Rice-Davies. The Pet Shop Boys wrote a song for the film, "Nothing has been Proved", performed by themselves and Dusty Springfield. It contains the lyrics "Christine's fallen out with Lucky, Johnny's got a gun, 'Please Please Me's number one". In fact, "Please Please Me" only got to number two in the hit parade.

RACHMAN, PEREC
St Stephen's Gardens, London W2

The man whose surname entered *The Oxford English Dictionary* as Rachmanism, a byword for the exploitation of tenants, bought his first property for multi-occupation here for £1,000. Perec "Peter" Rachman's office was in the basement at **91-93 Westbourne Grove, Bayswater, London W2 4AB** (on the corner of Monmouth Street).

Rachman, the son of a Jewish dentist, was born in Lwów, Poland (now Lviv, Ukraine) on Saturday 16 August 1919, arriving in London after the Second World War. In the 1950s, he began buying up properties in and around the Notting Hill area. He then put pressure on the mainly white occupants to move out, through rent rises or intimidation (threats of violence, stripping the roof of its tiles, playing loud music all night, etc). Rachman then let out the rooms at exorbitant rents to West Indians, who were finding it difficult to find places to live in the capital. From his first property, he expanded into Paddington, Bayswater and North Kensington. At the height of his operations, he owned about 100 mansion blocks in west London. He also bought up nightclubs so he could meet women – one of the most famous was Le Condor nightclub at **17 Wardour Street, London W1D 6PJ (Tel GERrard 2740)**, which was renamed La Discotheque. If not for the Profumo Affair (see page 187), Peter Rachman's name would probably be a mere footnote in law textbooks. At his death on Monday 19 November 1962 in Edgware General Hospital, he was largely unknown to the public until he was mentioned in various newspaper reports regarding his mistresses, who included Rice-Davies, who plied her trade in Rachman's mews house along with Keeler. As details of his activities became public knowledge, the call for legislation to outlaw such practices became unstoppable. However, not everyone regarded Rachman as a bad man. One Notting Hill taxi driver said, "He gave us somewhere to live when most English people did not want blacks anywhere."

TURING, ALAN
Hollymeade, 43 Adlington Road, Wilmslow, Cheshire SK9 2BJ
In 1931, Alan Turing (b. at Warrington Lodge, Warrington Crescent, London W9 1EL Sunday 23 June 1912) was an undergraduate at King's College, Cambridge, but preferring rowing and running to mixing with other homosexuals. During the Second World War, he worked as a code breaker at the Government Code and Cypher School at Bletchley Park. After the war, he returned to Cambridge, where he became more open about his homosexuality (although still illegal in those days) and would loiter in the quads of King's and invite young men to his rooms for tea. Sometimes he struck lucky and, in April 1948, he began a relationship with Geordie Johnson, a

mathematics student at King's. In October that year, Turing became deputy director of the Manchester Computing Laboratory and moved north. In the summer of 1950, Turing bought Hollymeade, a five-bedroom freehold semi-detached house in Wilmslow, ten miles south of Manchester. He lived a mainly solitary life. In January 1952, Turing, 39, was walking outside the **Regal Cinema, 10 Oxford Road, Manchester M1 5QA**, when he saw Arnold Murray, a jobless 19-year-old on probation for theft. Liking what he saw, Turing invited him to lunch in the restaurant opposite; after a false start when Murray stood him up, they slept together. Turing offered the teenager money but Murray refused. The next day, however, suspecting Murray when Turing noticed some money was missing from his wallet, he broke off the relationship. A few days later, Murray turned up at Hollymeade to indignantly deny taking the money. In the end, he borrowed £10 from Turing to buy a suit for a new job at a Manchester printing works. On Wednesday 23 January, Turing's house was burgled and items worth £50 (£1,500 at 2022 values) were taken. Turing reported the matter to the police and two CID members came to dust for fingerprints. Turing suspected that his teenage catamite may have had something to do with the burglary and so he wrote to once more break off the relationship. On Saturday 2 February, Murray returned to Hollymeade; he did not know about the burglary but thought he knew the identity of the burglar. The two men slept together; the next day, while Murray waited outside, Turing went into Wilmslow police station to provide details of the possible thief, making up a tale about how he had come by the new information. The burglar was already in custody at another station and had revealed that Murray had told him he had "business" at Turing's home. When the police put two and two together, two coppers accused Turing of lying about how he had come by the information. Turing told them he was having a sexual relationship with the informant. Both men were arrested and charged with "gross indecency contrary to Section 11 of the Criminal Law Amendment Act, 1885". Murray immediately lost his new job. Both men pleaded guilty when brought to trial at the Knutsford Quarter Sessions on Monday 31 March 1952. Murray was given a conditional discharge and went to London, where he found a job at the Lyons Corner House on Strand (see page 18). Turing was offered the choice of prison or probation for a year, including hormone treatment to reduce his libido. The injections of Stilboestrol – a synthesised form of oestrogen – rendered him impotent (possibly temporarily) and he grew breasts. Turing continued his work but was kept under close surveillance by the authorities. His probation came to an end in April 1953; that summer he went on holiday to Corfu, where he spent time on the beach admiring the boys frolicking in the sea. With his probation and hormone treatment over, Turing's friends believed he was over the worst, but he committed suicide using cyanide on Whit Monday, 7 June, 1954, aged 41. At the inquest on 10 June, the coroner J.A.K. Ferns said, "In a man of his type [ie homosexual], one never knows what his mental processes are going to do next." Turing's nephew Dermot believes his uncle was having problems with a boyfriend and it became too much for him to cope with. Turing's remains were cremated at Woking Crematorium on Saturday 12 June 1954. There is no memorial. He left £4,603 5s 4d (£131,550 at 2022 values).

> **DID YOU KNOW?**
> On Wednesday 23 June 2021, Turing became the first homosexual man to appear on a Bank of England note when he was put on the £50 note.

WILLIAMS, KENNETH
8 Marlborough House, 12–20 Osnaburgh Street, London NW1 3LY

Comedy actor Williams, one of the leading lights of the *Carry On* films, was never the most physically vigorous of men, forever in and out of hospital with various complaints, many to do with his rectum. He had considered suicide a number of times before he took an overdose of sleeping pills at his London home here on Thursday 14 April 1988. He was 62, the same age his father (whom he detested) had died, and, by coincidence, the same as his radio co-star Kenneth Horne (whom he adored). Although towards the end of his life Williams worried that work was drying up and he would run short of money, he nevertheless left £538,379 (£1,538,000 at 2022 values) in his will. The coroner Dr Christopher Pease returned an open verdict, but left no doubt as to his belief that Williams had indeed committed suicide. The final entry in Williams's diary certainly left a clue: "I felt so weak I wanted to flake out. The pain got worse and worse... oh, I'm so tired these days! No energy at all. Pain came back with a vengeance! Nothing seems to allay it now... Even if the op. don't work, I can't be worse than I am at the moment... By 6.30 pain in the back was pulsating as it's never done before... so this, plus the stomach trouble continues to torture me – oh – what's the bloody point?" The building was demolished in 2007.

WYNGARDE, PETER
Men's toilets, Kennedy Gardens, Birmingham B4
Men's toilets, Gloucester bus station

Two places where the actor Peter Wyngarde was caught cottaging. In 1974, he was arrested and cautioned for indecent behaviour in the gents at Kennedy Gardens, a large traffic island at the northern end of central Birmingham, next to to Snow Hill Station and St Chad's Cathedral. The toilets were shut in the late 1980s and the traffic island was razed in 2007 for a new office, hotel and residential development. Wyngarde told the press his arrest was due to a misunderstanding. The following year, on Monday 8 September 1975, Wyngarde, then a month past what may have been his fiftieth birthday, was arrested for committing an act of gross indecency with Richard Jack Whalley, a 24-year-old lorry driver. In custody, Wyngarde told police he was a writer from Singapore where he was probably born on Friday 28 August 1925, or he may have come into the world in Marseilles. He was found guilty and fined £75 (£1,000 at 2022 values). Wyngarde blamed his behaviour on a "mental aberration". He had made his name playing Jason King in the television series *Department S* and then in his own eponymous show. The scandal cost him his career and, despite the best efforts of a Bradford housewife, Dorothy Szekely, who collected 600 signatures to "bring back Peter to our screens", he remained mostly off television until his death aged 92 on Monday 15 January 2018 at the Chelsea and Westminster Hospital. He had been living at **Flat 3, 1 Earls Terrace, London W8 6LP**. In 1982, a bankruptcy hearing found that he was living on the dole.

Chapter V
Films and Filming

ALFIE
22 St Stephen's Gardens, off Chepstow Road, London W2 5QX

This is where the seedy bedsit of Alfie Elkins (Michael Caine) was located. The film (released Thursday 24 March 1966) was written by Bill Naughton, based on his play and produced and directed by Lewis Gilbert. It made Caine a star as the Cockney wideboy. The film has no opening titles and features pictures of the cast and senior crew at the end.

AMERICAN WEREWOLF IN LONDON, AN
Princess Beatrice Maternity Hospital, Finborough Road, London SW5

In *An American Werewolf In London* (released Friday 21 August 1981), two New Yorkers David Kessler (David Naughton) and Jack Goodman (Griffin Dunne) are walking in Yorkshire and stop at a pub, the Slaughtered Lamb. After they leave the inn, they are attacked by a werewolf. Jack is killed and David seriously injured. Three weeks later, David wakes in a London hospital, filmed at The Princess Beatrice Maternity Hospital. The hospital was opened in 1887 as part of Queen Victoria's Golden Jubilee celebrations. It closed in 1978, three years before the film was released. The film was written and directed by John Landis and starred Jenny Agutter as Alex Price, the beautiful nurse who seduces David. Her flat where she continues to tend to him was filmed at **64 Coleherne Road, London SW10 9BW**. This is where David metamorphoses into a werewolf to the sounds of "Bad Moon Rising" by Creedence Clearwater Revival. The Yorkshire Moor scenes were actually filmed around the Black Mountains in Powys and Monmouthshire in South Wales.

BLUE LAMP, THE
Metropolitan Theatre Of Varieties, 267
Edgware Road, London W2 2QN

The Blue Lamp (premièred Friday 20 January 1950) was the Basil Dearden film that introduced the public to PC George Dixon (later to patrol the beat at Dock Green, 1955-1976), brought back to life after being shot dead by local thug Tom Riley (Dirk Bogarde). Riley goes to the Metropolitan Theatre of Varieties to watch Tessie O'Shea and establish an alibi. The theatre went through various iterations, beginning with The White Lion Public House in 1524. It later became Turnham's Grand Concert Hall, Turnham's Music Hall, The Metropolitan Music Hall and The Metropolitan Theatre of Varieties. The theatre opened in 1836, was reopened on Wednesday 22 December 1897) and closed on Good Friday 12 April 1963. Demolition began in September 1963.

BRIEF ENCOUNTER
Carnforth Station, Carnforth, Lancashire LA5 9TR

David Lean directed Celia Johnson and Trevor Howard in this romantic drama written by Noël Coward (see page 293) based on his play *Still Life* (1936). Married mother Laura Jesson (Johnson) conducts an affair with a married man Dr Alec Harvey (Howard) after they meet at Milford Junction, Kent. The film was actually shot at Carnforth Station, five miles north of Lancaster, because of its comparative safety from German bombs – it was shot in January 1945 and premièred in London on Tuesday 13 November 1945. The station is still in use. Lean and Johnson were both nominated for Oscars at the nineteenth Academy Awards for their roles.

BRIDGET JONES'S DIARY
Globe Tavern, 8 Bedale Street, Borough Market, London SE1 9AL

The perennial spinster lived in a flat in south London. Written anonymously by the journalist Helen Fielding, the Diary began as a weekly column in *The Independent* on Tuesday 28 February 1995 before moving to *The Daily Telegraph*. Bridget, 32, is caught between two men: playboy Daniel Cleaver and human rights barrister Mark Darcy, and the story is loosely based on Jane Austen's *Pride And Prejudice*.

In the film version, Colin Firth is cast as Mark Darcy because he played Mr D'Arcy in a 1995 BBC adaptation of Austen's novel. The column was turned into a book in 1996 and a film version directed by Sharon Maguire followed five years later, with Renée Zellweger in the title role. Although there really is a pub called the Globe Tavern in Borough Market, there is no upstairs flat.

CARRY ON LOVING
26 Queen's Road, Windsor, Berkshire SL4 3BH
This is the house where Terry Philpott (Terry Scott) went to see Jenny Grubb (Imogen Hassall, see page 173) and encountered her large family. He was not impressed when her mother (Joan Hickson) said he would be expected to look after the whole Grubb brood. He returns to the lonely hearts club headquarters, **Wedded Bliss Matrimonial Office, 15 Park Street, Windsor, Berkshire SL4 1BU**, to demand his money back, but when Jenny arrives and her image has changed from demure mouse to ravishing, busty sexpot, he changes his mind and they go on a date. The house sold for £1.31million in June 2021.

CARRY ON SERGEANT
St Mary & All Saints Church, 10-12 Wycombe End, Windsor End, Beaconsfield, Buckinghamshire HP9 2JW
The first *Carry On* film began shooting on Monday 24 March 1958. *Carry On Sergeant* was based on R.F. Delderfield's script *The Bull Boys* about ballet dancers who were conscripted for National Service. Producer Peter Rogers saw potential in the idea and gave it to Norman Hudis (1922-2016) to fashion into a workable property. The film stars Bob Monkhouse as Charlie Sage, who is called up on his wedding day to Shirley Eaton (Jill Sage). Their wedding was filmed at St Mary & All Saints Church in Beaconsfield. Topping the bill is future Doctor Who William Hartnell, who wants to retire from the Army with a top-rated platoon. He is disappointed to find Charles Hawtrey, Kenneth Connor, Kenneth Williams (see page 203), Terence Longdon and Norman Rossington among his recruits. This was the only time Charles Hawtrey's name appeared above the *Carry On* regulars on screen. *Carry On Sergeant* was the third highest grossing film of the year in Britain. Bob Monkhouse decided that he did not

want to make any more *Carry Ons* and threw in his lot with *Dentist In The Chair* (1960) instead. There were only two films in the series.

CHITTY CHITTY BANG BANG
Smock Windmill, Codmore Road, Buckinghamshire
England's oldest smock mill with wooden machinery dating from around 1650 appeared as the home of inventor Caractacus Potts (Dick Van Dyke) in the comedy film (premièred Monday 16 December 1968), co-written by Ken Hughes and Roald Dahl and based on *Chitty-Chitty-Bang-Bang: The Magical Car* (published Thursday 22 October 1964), a novel by Ian Fleming. The film stars Van Dyke, Sally Ann Howes, Lionel Jeffries, Benny Hill, James Robertson Justice, Robert Helpmann, Barbara Windsor and Gert Fröbe. Lionel Jefferies plays Dick Van Dyke's father in the film, despite being six months younger than the American.

DOCTOR IN THE HOUSE
University College, Gower Street, London WC1E 6BT
Gordon Stanley Ostlere (1921-2017) worked as a doctor on a ship and an anaesthetist. Using the name Richard Gordon, he wrote a series of comic novels about young medical students at St Swithin's Hospital in London. The first, *Doctor In The House*, was published in 1952. It was filmed in 1954 starring Dirk Bogarde as Simon Sparrow. In this film, University College played the part of St Swithin's. The "students" were rather old: Bogarde, 33, Kenneth More, 40 (Richard Grimsdyke), Donald Sinden, 31 (Tony Benskin) and Donald Houston, 31 (Taffy Evans).

DID YOU KNOW?
On Wednesday 20 February 1974, Richard Gordon was caught by Eamonn Andrews for *This is Your Life* but the author said, "Oh balls" before a live television audience, refused to appear and walked away. Andrews chased after him and said, "We've got a lot of guests waiting to see you" to which Gordon replied, "I didn't invite them." The director Malcolm Morris faded out the picture and swapped to a show on actor Sam Kydd, whose tribute was due to be aired the following week. Eamonn Andrews managed to persuade Gordon to relent and he returned to film the show. The programme was broadcast a week later at 10.15pm on Thursday 28 February.

DRACULA
King Arthur's Castle Hotel, Tintagel, Cornwall PL34 0DQ

The 1979 version of the vampire tale stars Frank Langella in the title role, Laurence Olivier as Professor Abraham Van Helsing and Donald Pleasence as Dr Jack Steward. *Dracula* was directed by John Badham and won the 1979 Saturn Award for Best Horror Film. The film is set in 1913 as Count Dracula arrives from Transylvania on a stormy night in Whitby, Yorkshire, from aboard the ship *Demeter*. Langella only took the role as long as he did not have to do any promotional work as Dracula. The asylum ran by Dr Steward was King Arthur's Castle Hotel, Tintagel, which is still in existence but is now the Camelot Castle Hotel.

FAR FROM THE MADDING CROWD
Claydon, Middle Claydon, Buckingham, Buckinghamshire MK18 2EY

Claydon was built between 1757 and 1771 by the 2nd Earl Verney (1714-1791). In November 2013, it was used as Boldwood House in Thomas Vinterberg's film version of Thomas Hardy's fourth novel (published 1874). The film, which stars Carey Mulligan (Bathsheba Everdene), Michael Sheen (William Boldwood) and Matthias Schoenaerts (Gabriel Oak), was released on Friday 1 May 2015. The ballroom scene took three days to set up. The candles were only lit when the cameras were rolling and as soon as "cut" was called, a crew member snuffed them out to prevent smoke damage to the ceiling. It also helped with continuity. An additional problem was caused by the delicacy of the staircase, now so fragile it is no longer used. The problem was resolved by the actors wearing soft-soled shoes if their feet were in shot and socks if they were not. Sound effects were added later. Bathsheba's aunt's farm was represented by **Mapperton House, Mapperton, Beaminster, Dorset DT8 3NR**.

FEVER PITCH
Arsenal Stadium, Avenell Road, London N5 1BU

It was outside the iconic home of Arsenal that the final scenes for this film were shot. Arsenal needed to beat Liverpool 2-0 away from home to win the First Division title on Friday 26 May 1989, and the houses and pubs in and around Islington were full of fans watching the game on television. Then, in the final moments, Arsenal's Michael Thomas scored at Anfield to claim the championship for the Gunners. *Fever Pitch* (released on Friday 4 April 1997) was based on Nick Hornby's autobiographical novel of the same name. The streets around Arsenal Stadium were filled with people celebrating, including the film's protagonists English teacher Paul Ashworth (Colin Firth) and Sarah Hughes (Ruth Gemmell). The film's advertising tagline was: "Life gets complicated when you love one woman and worship eleven men." In 2005, an American version of the film was made starring Drew Barrymore and Jimmy Fallon, who is in love with the Boston Red Sox. In July 2006, Arsenal (see page 273) moved to a new stadium in nearby Ashburton Grove and the old ground was converted into flats.

FOUR WEDDINGS AND A FUNERAL
22 Highbury Terrace, London N5 1UP
This Richard Curtis comedy (released Friday 13 May 1994) stars Hugh Grant (Charles) and Andie MacDowell (Carrie). This is where Charles's flat is located.
Wedding No 1: Angus (Timothy Walker) and Laura (Sara Crowe)
St Michael's Church, Church Street, Betchworth, Surrey RH3 7DN
In the film, the wedding takes place at St John's Church, Clandon, Somerset. At the reception, the place where Charles and Carrie first sleep together is **King's Arms, 30 High Street, Amersham, Buckinghamshire HP7 0DJ**.
Wedding No 2: Bernard Delaney (David Haig)
and Lydia Hibbot (Sophie Thompson)
Royal Naval College, King William Walk,
Greenwich, London SE10 9NN
This wedding, in the film at St Mary of the Fields, Cripplegate, London EC2, a Catholic church, was actually filmed at a Protestant venue. The restaurant where Carrie recounts her sexual adventures to Charles was the **Dome, 34 Wellington Street, London WC2B 7BD**. It is now a branch of Café Rouge. She says, "Well, the first one, of course, not easily forgotten – was kinda nice. Two – hairy back. Three, four, five. Six was on my birthday in my parents' room… I grew up in the country. Lots of rolling around in haystacks. Okay, seven. Mmm. Eight, unfortunately, was quite a shock. Nine, against a fence. Very uncomfortable. Don't try

it... Ten, oh, was gorgeous. Just heaven, just – oh – he was wonder-ful... Eleven, obviously after ten, disappointing. Twelve through seventeen – the university years. Sensitive, caring, intelligent boys. Sexually speaking, a real low patch. Eighteen broke my heart. Years of yearning... Twenty, oh, my God! I can't believe I've reached twenty. Twenty-one, elephant tongue. Twenty-two, kept falling asleep. That was my first year in England... Twenty-three and twenty-four together. That was something... Twenty-seven, oh that was a mistake... he kept screaming. It was very off-putting. I nearly gave up on the whole thing. But, Spencer changed my mind. That's twenty-eight. His father, twenty-nine... Thirty, eh! Thirty-one, oh, my God, Thirty-two – was lovely. And then my fiancé, that's thirty-three... You [Charles] were thirty-two. So there you go. Less than Madonna, more than Princess Di – I hope. And, how about you? How many have you slept with?"

Wedding No 3: Hamish Banks (Corin Redgrave) and Carrie
Albury Park, Guildford, Surrey GU5

Carrie married "the stiff in the skirt" in the chapel of Glenthrist Castle, Perthshire. It was, in fact, filmed in Surrey. As the groom is making his toast, Gareth (Simon Callow) drops dead from a heart attack.

Funeral: Gareth
St Clement, St Clement's Road, Grays, Essex RM20 4AL

At the burial, Gareth's boyfriend Matthew (John Hannah) reads the poem *Funeral Blues* by the gay English-American poet W.H. Auden.

Non-wedding No 4: Charles and Henrietta (Anna Chancellor)
St Bartholomew the Great, 57 West Smithfield, London EC1A 9DS

When Charles decides he cannot go through with marrying Henrietta (aka Duckface), she punches him.

HISTORY BOYS, THE
Fountains Abbey, near Ripon, North Yorkshire HG4 3DY

It is here that the sixth form boys from Cutlers' Grammar School, Sheffield go on a field trip in Alan Bennett's play *The History Boys* (premiered at the **Royal National Theatre, Upper Ground, South Bank, London SE1 9PX** on Tuesday 18 May 2004) and film (released Friday 13 October 2006). The boys are preparing for the Oxbridge entrance examination under the tutelage of three teachers (Douglas Hector, Irwin and Dorothy Lintott). The eccentric Hector, who is discovered fondling one of the boys, is based on Frank McEachran (1900-1975) who had taught Bennett and the poet W.H. Auden (1907-1973). The character of Irwin – a pushy, contrary teacher who becomes a television historian – is modelled on the Scottish author Niall Ferguson. The original cast featured Richard Griffiths as Hector, Frances de la Tour as Mrs Lintott, Dominic Cooper (Stuart Dakin), Russell Tovey (Peter Rudge) and James Corden (Tony Timms). Griffiths, de la Tour, Tovey, Cooper and Corden reprised their roles in the film, which was directed by Nicholas Hytner.

DID YOU KNOW?
In the library scene, three books can be seen – *Tudor England* (1988) by John Guy, Alan Bullock's *Hitler And Stalin: Parallel Lives* (1991) and *The Third Reich* (2001) by Michael Burleigh – none of which were published when the film was set.

MARY POPPINS
17 Cherry Tree Lane, Ealing, London W
This was the home of the Banks family whose children Jane and Michael advertised for a nanny, not expecting the magical Mary Poppins (Julie Andrews) to take the job. The film, premiered in America on Thursday 27 August 1964 and released in Britain on Monday 23 August 1965, won five Oscars, including a Best Actress statuette for Andrews. The first (of eight) Mary Poppins books by P.(amela) L.(yndon) Travers (born at Maryborough, Queensland, Australia Wednesday 9 August 1899 as Helen Lyndon Goff) was published in 1934. A second, *Mary Poppins Comes Back*, was published in 1935. Travers then took her time with the rest of the series, leaving years between books: *Mary Poppins Opens The Door* (1943); *Mary Poppins In The Park* (1952); *Mary Poppins From A To Z* (1962); *Mary Poppins In The Kitchen* (1975); *Mary Poppins In Cherry Tree Lane* (1982) and *Mary Poppins And The House Next Door* (1989). Intensely private, Travers eschewed all personal publicity. Although the film was a commercial and critical success, she disliked it. Unmarried, she died at her four-bedroom home, **29 Shawfield Street, Chelsea, London, SW3 4BA** on Tuesday 23 April 1996. She was cremated, but the resting place of her ashes is unknown as she did not want it to become a shrine for Mary Poppins admirers.

MY FAIR LADY
27a Wimpole Street, Marylebone, London W1

The home address of Professor Henry Higgins in the play *Pygmalion* by George Bernard Shaw and the film *My Fair Lady*, starring Rex Harrison and Audrey Hepburn. Higgins is a professor of phonetics who meets the Cockney flower seller Eliza Doolittle at Covent Garden flower market (now at **Nine Elms Lane, Nine Elms, London SW8 5BH**). Eliza goes to see Higgins for help with her accent so she can get a job in a florist. Higgins and his houseguest Colonel Pickering make a bet that Eliza can be taught to speak like a lady. *Pygmalion* premiered at the Hofburg Theatre in Vienna on Thursday 16 October 1913. It opened in London on Saturday 11 April 1914 at His Majesty's Theatre, starring Sir Herbert Beerbohm Tree as Henry Higgins and Mrs Patrick Campbell as Eliza Doolittle (at 49, she was a little old for the role, although Shaw had written the part with her in mind). It ran for 118 performances. A musical version of the play could not be considered until after Shaw's death on Thursday 2 November 1950. Written by Alan Jay Lerner (1918-1986) and Frederick Loewe (1901-1988), *My Fair Lady* premièred at the Mark Hellinger Theatre on Broadway on Thursday 15 March 1956 starring Rex Harrison, Julie Andrews and Stanley Holloway. The play opened at the Theatre Royal, Drury Lane on Wednesday 30 April 1958 and Harrison, Andrews and Holloway reprised their roles. It ran for five and a half years (2,281 performances). The film, which was released on Friday 25 December 1964, was directed by George Cukor, with costumes designed by Cecil Beaton and the score conducted by Andre Previn; Rex Harrison won an Oscar for his performance. Producer Jack Warner paid $5½million for the rights and wanted the box-of-fice-bankable Audrey Hepburn rather than the relatively unknown Julie Andrews. Hepburn was paid $1million. *My Fair Lady* was the only film that Harrison was determined to be in. Warners initially wanted Cary Grant and then Peter O'Toole before settling on Harrison, who was paid $200,000. The studio wanted James Cagney for the part played by Stanley Holloway, but he turned it down. As rehearsals went on, it became apparent that Hepburn's singing voice was not good enough, so she was dubbed by Marni Nixon. Filming was not withouts its problems – Harrison and Holloway did not get on, having fallen out during the Broadway run. Harrison was also suspicious of Hepburn and jealous of her large fee. In addition, Cukor and Beaton couldn't stand the sight of each other and Cukor had Beaton thrown off the set. Nevertheless, the creative tension worked and the film won eight Oscars, including Best Picture, Best Actor and Best Director.

PRINCE AND THE SHOWGIRL, THE
Parkside House, Englefield Green, Egham, Surrey TW20 0XA

On Thursday 9 February 1956 Marilyn Monroe (1926-1962) and Sir Laurence Olivier (1907-1989) held a press conference at the Plaza Hotel, 768 5th Avenue and Central Park South, New York, NY 10019 to announce the making of a new film, *The Sleeping Prince*, based on the Terence Rattigan play of the same name. It would be the only film made by Marilyn Monroe Productions. When a spaghetti strap on Marilyn's dress broke, she insisted it was an accident, but Olivier was convinced she had done it deliberately to upstage him. It set the tone for the production. Having married a fortnight earlier, on Saturday 14 July 1956, Marilyn Monroe and Arthur Miller arrived at London Airport. They stayed at Parkside House, Englefield Green, Egham, Surrey, for four months during filming. The movie was shot at Pinewood Studios. On Monday 29 October, Marilyn was present-ed to the Queen at the **Empire, 5-6 Leicester Square, London WC2H 7NA** after the Royal Command Performance presentation of *The Battle Of The River Plate*. Olivier stated that he had expected to fall in love with Marilyn during filming, but he was to be disappointed. The leading man and lady did not gel off-screen. Olivier was exasperated by Marilyn's behaviour and her reliance on Paula Strasberg, the wife of Marilyn's acting coach. However, despite their differences, Olivier was to state later, "I was as good as could be; and Marilyn! Marilyn was quite wonderful, the best of all. So, what do you know?"

REMAINS OF THE DAY, THE
Dyrham Park, near Bath, Chippenham, Gloucestershire SN14 8HY

Dyrham Park is a seventeenth-century Baroque mansion set in 264 acres of parkland with a herd of fallow deer. It was used as the exteriors of Darlington Hall in the film version (released Friday 5 November 1993) of Kazuo Ishiguro's Booker Prize-winning 1989 novel. *The*

Remains Of The Day starred Anthony Hopkins as James Stevens and Emma Thompson as Miss Kenton; it was nominated for eight Oscars but failed to win any. Stevens was a servant at Darlington Hall owned by the pre-Second World War Nazi sympathiser Lord Darlington (James Fox) who hid his feelings for the housekeeper Kenton. In 1958 she writes to him to tell him that their former employer has died. The original request to use Dyrham Hall was turned down by the National Trust, the owners of the building, but permission was granted after an appeal by Anthony Hopkins.

TASTE OF HONEY, A
The Ritz, Whitworth Street West, Manchester M1 5NQ
Telephone: 0161-236 4355

The longest continuously running club in Manchester provided a backdrop for the classic movie *A Taste Of Honey* (1961). The Ritz was immortalised in verse by punk poet John Cooper Clarke in *Salomey Maloney*. *A Taste Of Honey* was the first play by Shelagh Delaney, written when she was 19. It had its premiere at the Theatre Royal Stratford East, Gerry Raffles Square, Theatre Square, London E15 1BN on Tuesday 27 May 1958, transferring to Wyndham's Theatre in the West End on Tuesday 10 February 1959. Set in Salford, *A Taste Of Honey* is the tale of 17-year-old Jo and Helen, her sexually liberated mother. Helen begins a relationship with Peter, who is younger than her but wealthy, while Jo latches on to Jimmy, a black sailor. After getting Jo pregnant, Jimmy goes to sea and abandons her. She moves in with gay Geoff but then Helen turns up, her relationship having ended. The play became an award-winning film, released on Friday 15 September 1961 and directed by Tony Richardson. Murray Melvin as Geoff Ingham was the only actor who appeared in both stage and film versions.

WORLD IS NOT ENOUGH, THE
Stowe, Buckingham, Buckinghamshire MK18 5EQ

This was Pierce Brosnan's third outing as the iconic spy and Desmond Llewellyn's seventeenth and last as gadgetmeister Q. Multiple locations were used in the movie, which began filming on Sunday 17 January 1999, and included: Bilbao, Spain; the SIS Building (**85 Albert Embankment, Vauxhall, London SE11 5AW**); the Millennium Dome

(**Millennium Way, London SE10 0BB**); **Chatham Dockyard, Main Gate Road, Chatham, Kent ME4 4TZ**; Eilean Donan Castle in Scotland, which doubled as Castle Thane; the Bahamas; Chamonix, France; Baku, Azerbaijan; the Azerbaijan Oil Rocks; and Istanbul, Turkey. The funeral of oil tycoon Sir Robert King, supposedly on the banks of Loch Lomond, was filmed at Stowe. To give the scene verisimilitude, the film company Eon brought around twenty Highland cattle down from Scotland. Unbeknown to them, the parkland already had the same breed.

Chapter VI

Music

ABBA
The Dome, Church Street, Brighton, East Sussex BN11UG
Telephone: 01273-700747

The Eurovision Song Contest 1974 moved to Brighton after Luxembourg, the winners in 1972 and 1973, declined to host for a second consecutive year on the grounds of cost. The French entry, Dani singing "La Vie A Vingt-cinq Ans", was withdrawn because the funeral of President Georges Pompidou was held on the same day (Saturday 6 April 1974) as the contest. Katie Boyle (1926-2018), who had to have her underwear removed just before the show began because her frock was too tight, was the MC for the fourth time. Finland opened the nineteenth contest, and Olivia Newton-John (backed by The Ladybirds) representing the UK with "Long Live Love" was on second (no one performing second has ever won the Grand Prix). Greece made their Eurovision debut, represented by Marinella singing "Thalassa Ke T'Agori Mou". Swedish group Abba failed to qualify in 1972 and 1973, but were the clear winners in their country's heats in 1974. They appeared eighth with their catchy song "Waterloo", conductor Sven-Olof Walldoff dressing as Napoleon for the occasion. There were two political songs that night: the first was Portugal's "E Depois Do Adeus" by Paulo de Carvalho, which came joint last with three points. When it was played at 10.55pm on Wednesday 24 April 1974 on Emissores Associados de Lisboa Radio Station, it was one of two signals to herald the start of the Carnation Revolution, a military coup d'état that overthrew the Portuguese Government. The other was Italy's "Si" by Gigliola Cinquetti, who had won the contest in 1964. Italian broadcaster RAI did not show the contest as a referendum on divorce was held on the same night, and they did not want people to be influenced by showing a song called "Yes". When Cinquetti left the stage, Katie Boyle came on to introduce the interval act – The Wombles – who sang their first two singles on video rather than in the studio. The votes were cast as Orinoco and co sang their hearts out. The voting system was changed again, with ten jury members in every country each awarding one point to their favourite song, which meant that several juries awarded one vote to many songs. For the first time, a draw was made to decide the order in which countries would reveal their juries' results. This was the only time this method was used – from 1975 onwards, the order of the jury votes followed the order of performance. Abba won by six points from Italy, but when the writers went to receive their medals from BBC Director General and President of the European Broadcasting Union Sir Charles Curran (1921-1980), a zealous security guard did not recognise Benny and Bjorn and stopped them taking the stage. Stig Anderson, the co-writer and group manager, was left alone to take the plaudits. "Waterloo" topped the UK charts on Saturday 4 May 1974 but, perhaps surprisingly, only stayed there for a fortnight.

DID YOU KNOW?
The clothes worn by Abba were deliberately loud and garish, because if it could be proved that they could only be worn for performing and not on the street, they could claim a tax break from the Swedish government.

BAND AID
Sarm West, 8-10 Basing Street, London W11 1ET
Telephone: 020-7229 1229

The charity single "Do They Know It's Christmas?" by a celebrity "band" featuring thirty-six pop stars assembled by Bob Geldof of the Boomtown Rats and Midge Ure of Ultravox was recorded here on Sunday 25 November 1984. The Ladbroke Grove studio, originally a church, was converted by Chris Blackwell, the founder of Island Records. Geldof had seen a Michael Buerk BBC News report on the famine in Ethiopia earlier in the month and was determined to do something about it. All the stars were asked to "leave their egos at the door" and sang over a backing track laid down by Midge Ure with drums by Phil Collins. On

Saturday 15 December it went straight in at Number One, where it stayed for five weeks. The record wasn't as successful in America and failed to make the Billboard Top Ten. Ure expected the record to make about £100,000 – the final total was nearer to £10million. All the participants gave their time freely, but Geldof was not so successful with Margaret Thatcher's administration, which refused to forgo their VAT payments.

BEATLES, THE
First meeting of John Lennon and Paul McCartney
St Peter's Church, Church Road, Woolton Village, Liverpool L25 5JF

It was at the Woolton Parish Church Fête (admission 6d {£1.54 at 2022 values} for adults, 3d for children) here that Paul McCartney and John Lennon first met on Saturday 6 July 1957 at 6.40pm (so almost every source has it), introduced by their mutual friend Ivan "Ivy" Vaughan (b. at Liverpool Thursday 18 June 1942, the same day as McCartney d. at Liverpool Monday 16 August 1993). Paul remembers that John was drunk. Lennon's skiffle group the Quarrymen (Lennon, vocals and guitar; Eric Griffiths, guitar; Colin Hanton drums; Rod Davies banjo; Pete Shotton, washboard and Len Garry, tea chest bass), were hired to play at 4.15pm, 5.45pm, 8.45pm and 10pm during the day. A thunderstorm forced the band to stop for a few minutes during the first evening set. The final two performances (which Hanton missed) took place in the church hall. McCartney was invited to join the group a fortnight later. Two songs – "Puttin' On The Style" and "Baby Let's Play House" – performed that day were illegally recorded by 16-year-old Bob Molyneaux (a future policeman) on a Grundig reel-to-reel tape; the tape was sold on Thursday 15 September 1994 at a Sotherby's auction for £78,500 and was bought by EMI Records, the most expensive recording sold at auction at that time. Buried in the graveyard of St Peter's is one Eleanor Rigby (d. Tuesday 10 October 1939) but Paul, who wrote most of the song, claims that his Eleanor Rigby is entirely fictional.

DID YOU KNOW?
Only thirty seconds of "Puttin' On The Style" have ever been heard in public. Among the other songs the Quarrymen played that day were "Worried Man Blues", "Come Go With Me", "Railroad Bill", "Maggie Mae" and "Cumberland Gap".

THE CAVERN CLUB
10 Mathew Street, Liverpool L2 6RE
Telephone: 0161-236 1957

Arguably the most famous music venue in the UK, the Cavern Club played home to the Mersey Sound and was where the future singer and television presenter Cilla Black (*née* Priscilla White) worked as a cloakroom attendant. The present Cavern Club is not the one The Beatles played in. John traditionally made his first appearance at the Cavern on Wednesday 7 August 1957. The Quarry Men had impressed Cavern owner Alan Sytner when he heard them play Childwall Golf Club. The Cavern, which had opened on Wednesday 16 January 1957, was then a jazz club that occasionally hosted skiffle evenings. Colin Hanton remembered, "We did some skiffle numbers to start off with at the Cavern but we also did rock'n'roll. John Lennon was passed a note and he said to the audience, 'We've had a request.' He opened it up and it was Alan Sytner saying, 'Cut out the bloody rock'n'roll.'" Paul did not play at that gig because he was away at scout camp with his younger brother Mike. This was for many years the accepted date for the Cavern debut but, in August 2011, Rod Davies, in an interview with Spencer Leigh on Radio Merseyside's *On The Beat*, said that the date could not have been 7 August because he went on holiday with his parents to France on Monday 29 July 1957: "and I've got a passport to prove it". The Beatles made their first appearance at the Cavern on Thursday 9 February 1961 and were paid £5 (£118 at 2022 values). Their last performance here was on Saturday 3 August 1963 for which they were paid £300 (£6,700, 2022). It is not known how many times they played the Cavern, but they performed at least 155 lunchtime and 125 evening shows.

Philips Sound Recording Services
38 Kensington, Liverpool L7 8XB

This Victorian terraced house was the location of Percy Philips's private home-recording studio where, in mid-1958 (suggested dates include Saturday 12 July 1958 and Monday 14 July, although no one seems to know for certain), the Quarry Men – John, Paul, George Harrison and John "Duff" Lowe – made their first recordings: a cover of Buddy Holly's "That'll be the Day" and "In Spite of All The Danger", a Paul McCartney-George Harrison composition. Phillips

(1895-1984) charged 17s 6d (£22 at 2022 values) and continued to operate from this address until the late sixties. In 1981, Paul bought the only existing copy of the recording from John Lowe for more than £5,000 (the exact figure has never been disclosed). McCartney had fifty copies made, which he gave to family and friends.

Nems
12-14 Whitechapel, Liverpool L1 6DZ

This was the location, at the junction of Whitechapel and Church Street, of Brian Epstein's record shop – a minute's walk from Mathew Street – which was opened at noon on Tuesday 31 May 1960 by Anthony Newley. The shop – "LIVERPOOL'S NEW STORE WITH AN ACCENT ON RECORDS" – boasted "four floors of magnificent showrooms featuring televisions, records and domestic appliances". Nems claimed it could "supply ANY record that is named – and to produce it almost immediately". Brian and Clive Epstein designed the look of the interior. In 1958, Nems had opened at **50 Great Charlotte Street, Liverpool L1 1QR (Telephone ROYal 7895),** owned by I. Epstein and Sons (LV), Ltd, which had been running for sixty-five years. It became known as the North End Music Shop – Nems. The Great Charlotte Street branch held a stock of 20,000 records, while its new sibling had 30,000. On Saturday 28 October 1961, Raymond Jones, 20, from Knotty Ash, went into the shop and asked for a copy of "My Bonnie", recorded by Tony Sheridan and The Beatles. Nems did not have the record in stock and Epstein questioned Jones about the group. At lunchtime on Thursday 9 November 1961, Brian went to the Cavern to see The Beatles perform the second of their two lunchtime slots to find out personally what all the fuss was about. John and Paul tried to be the centre of attraction while George grinned at the stage and Pete Best concentrated on his drumming. On Wednesday 29 November 1961, Brian invited the group to Nems to discuss how they could help each other, but they stopped at a local pub and did not arrive until closing time. On Wednesday 24 January 1962, at the Nems Whitehall premises, Epstein became their manager. It was also here that he sacked drummer Pete Best on Thursday 16 August 1962. The Nems location has since been a Rumbelows, Ann Summers and the discount footwear shop Shu Story.

Abbey Road Studios
3 Abbey Road, London NW8 9AY
Telephone: 020-7286 1161

Built in 1831 as a nine-bedroom Georgian townhouse, the building was bought by the Gramophone Company in 1929 who began the process of turning it into flats. The studios were opened on Thursday 12 November 1931 and the event was filmed by Pathé News. The first performance took place that day when Sir Edward Elgar conducted the London Symphony Orchestra playing his own music. The Fab Four (John, Paul, George and Pete) first recorded here on Wednesday 6 June 1962 from 7pm until 10pm. In Studio Two, they recorded "Besame Mucho", "Love Me Do", "PS I Love You" and "Ask Me Why" (the latter three all Lennon–McCartney compositions). By the time the group returned on Tuesday 4 September 1962, Best had been replaced by Ringo Starr. Seven years later, Iain Macmillan (b. at Carnoustie, Angus Thursday 20 October 1938 d. at Carnoustie, Angus Monday 8 May 2006 of lung cancer) took the famous picture of The Beatles walking across the zebra crossing outside the St John's Wood studio at 11.35am on Friday 8 August 1969 which was used on the eponymous album cover. Because it was a hot day, Paul took his sandals off. Macmillan took six shots from a stepladder on Abbey Road before giving them to Paul to choose his favourite. The barefoot picture led to the "Paul is dead" rumours that plagued the Beatle and intrigued fans for years; according to the theory, he was killed in a car crash on Wednesday 9 November 1966 and a lookalike was brought in.

DID YOU KNOW?

The *Abbey Road* album cover is supposed to be a repository of clues "proving" Paul was dead. John, clad in white, is supposed to represent a heavenly figure, George in denim is the gravedigger, Ringo in black is an undertaker and Paul, out of step and bare-footed, is the corpse. The white Volkswagen Beetle in the photograph has the number plate LMW 28IF – apparently LMW stands for "Linda McCartney weeps" or "Linda McCartney widow", and 28IF the age Paul would have been if he had not "died".

The Gaumont Cinema, Princes Way, Bradford, Yorkshire BD1 1NN

Formerly The New Victoria, latterly the Odeon cinema until its closure in 2000, this was where The Beatles opened their first nationwide tour on Saturday 2 February 1963. Helen Shapiro, 16, was top of the six-act bill and The Beatles were bottom. They returned on Friday 9 October 1964 (John's 24th birthday) for the start of their only British tour in 1964.

Sunday Night At The London Palladium
8 Argyll Street, London W1F 7TF

The Beatles played five songs here for the ITV show *Sunday Night at the London Palladium* on Sunday 13 October 1963. When the audience went wild, it was decided for the band's safety that they should leave by the front door to circumvent the hordes at the stage entrance. A helpful policeman wanted to avoid a conspicuous car outside the front door so had it moved forty yards up the road. Their PR had helpfully tipped off the press about the new exit, and when the Fab Four came running out, they could not find their car. Press and fans chased them. The next day, the newspapers coined the term "Beatlemania".

Knole House, Knole Park, Sevenoaks, Kent TN15 0RP

The Beatles filmed their promo movie, the first pop video, for "Strawberry Fields Forever" at Knole Park on Monday 30 and Tuesday 31 January 1967. The film for "Penny Lane" was shot on 30 January at Knole Park and on Sunday 5 February at Angel Lane, Stratford, east London, before returning to Knole Park to wrap on Tuesday 7 February. Clips from the two films were first broadcast on BBC1 on *Top of the Pops* on Thursday 16 February 1967.

Apple Boutique, 94 Baker Street, London W1U 6FZ

The Fab Four bought the four-storey building on the corner of Baker Street and Paddington Street in 1967, intending to open it as "a beautiful place where you could buy beautiful things". The shop opened with a party at 7.46pm with a fashion show following at 8.16pm on Tuesday 5 December 1967 (the exact time John Lennon, for some reason or other, decided it should open); only apple juice was served because the shop had no liquor licence. Only John and George were present – Ringo was filming *Candy* in Italy and Paul was on his Scottish farm at Campbeltown with Jane Asher. The shop opened to the public two days later. The Beatles hired a few dozen art students to create a huge psychedelic mural on the front and side of the building between Friday 10 and Sunday 12 November, but it was painted over within a fortnight of opening after complaints from other traders. The Apple Boutique, a commercial disaster thanks to theft and poor business advice, closed on Wednesday 31 July 1968, with all the stock being given away. The night before, the group and their girlfriends had first pickings; Paul picked up "a smashing overcoat" but poor Ringo bemoaned that he "couldn't find anything that fitted me". The last customer was the actor Michael J. Pollard. A blue plaque bearing the legend "John Lennon, MBE, 1940-1980, and George Harrison, MBE, 1943-2001, worked here" was unveiled by Rod Davies on Sunday 17 March 2013. It is now home to the estate agent Marsh & Parsons.

Apple Corps, 3 Savile Row, London W1S 3PB

This five-storey Georgian house, the headquarters of The Beatles' empire, was bought on Saturday 22 June 1968 from the bandleader Jack Hylton for a reputed £500,000 (£9,300,000 at 2022 values). The group and staff moved in on Monday 15 July. It was on the roof here on Thursday 30 January 1969 that The Beatles gave their last performance. The decision to perform on the roof was only taken the night before when the previous venue, The Roundhouse, was vetoed The band wanted to include aerial shots from a helicopter, only to find out that it was illegal to fly over London. The show lasted forty-two minutes and was included in the film *Let It Be*. In 1972, Apple left the building and never returned when it was found to be structurally unsound, moving to **54 St James's Street, London SW1A 1RP.** 3 Savile Row was closed on Friday 2 May 1975 and Apple sold its interest in October 1976. As of February 2022, the building is occupied by Abercrombie & Fitch.

"Day In The Life, A"
Redcliffe Gardens (A3220), London SW10

Old Etonian the Honourable Tara Browne (b. at Portobello House, Portobello, Dublin D02 YH79, Ireland Sunday 4 March 1945), the heir to the Guinness millions, moved in the same social circles as The Beatles. Well-known on the swinging London scene of the sixties, he was the son of Dominick Browne, the fourth Baron Oranmore and Oonagh Guinness of the drinks family. He was due to inherit

£1million on his 25th birthday but never made it to that milestone. On Saturday 17 December 1966, the married but separated Browne, 21, a father of two sons, and his girlfriend, 19-year-old model Suki Potier, went to dinner in a restaurant in Abingdon Road. They left just before midnight and Browne got behind the wheel of a light blue Lotus Elan and put his foot down. He jumped a red light and drove through the junction of Redcliffe Gardens and Redcliffe Square, hitting a stationary black van in Redcliffe Gardens after swerving to miss a white car that suddenly emerged from a side road. Brown suffered a skull fracture and lacerations to his brain. His girlfriend held him for forty-five minutes as they waited for an ambulance. He was taken to St Stephen's Hospital where he died two hours later. Suki Potier later claimed that Browne had swerved his car to take the full brunt of the crash and thus saved her life. She was unhurt. He left £56,069 (£1,110,925 at 2022 values). On Tuesday 17 January 1967, John Lennon was reading the *Daily Mail* when he spotted a brief report of the coroner's hearing, which inspired him when writing "A Day In The Life". He later said, "I didn't copy the accident. Tara didn't blow his mind out. But it was in my mind when I was writing that verse." Paul McCartney disputed this: "It has been attributed to Tara Browne, the Guinness heir, which I don't believe is the case... In my head I was imagining a politician bombed out on drugs who'd stopped at some traffic lights and didn't notice that the lights had changed. The 'blew his mind' was reference, nothing to do with a car crash."

DID YOU KNOW?

Born in Surrey on Friday 14 November 1947, death followed Suki Potier. In 1969 she was Brian Jones's girlfriend (see page 244) when he drowned in his Sussex swimming pool. On Tuesday 23 June 1981, she and her husband Robert Ho were killed in a car crash while on holiday in Portugal.

Epstein, Brian
24 Chapel Street, London SW1X 7BY

Brian Epstein, the group's manager, died here. He was born in a private nursing home at 4 Rodney Street, Liverpool L1 9AT (now

Liverpool Business School) on Wednesday 19 September 1934. In November 1952, when he was 18, he was called up for National Service but was demobbed on Wednesday 27 January 1954, deemed mentally and emotionally unfit. He rejoined the family business. On his 22nd birthday, he passed an audition for the Royal Academy of Dramatic Art but left in 1957 and once more rejoined the family business. Epstein stood out in Liverpool with his refined accent, manicured nails, immaculate appearance and use of cologne at a time when almost no man in Liverpool would be smelled dead using it. Society was not especially sophisticated at the time, but those who knew recognised Epstein for what he was. He was a regular victim of blackmail and violence. On Wednesday 24 April 1957, he attended the world premiere of Jean Genet's *The Balcony* at the **Arts Theatre Club, 6-7 Great Newport Street, London WC2B 7JH**. Afterwards he caught the tube to Swiss Cottage, where he made eye contact with another man in the gents'. They began chatting and discussed where they could go for some fun, whereupon the other man revealed himself to be an undercover policeman. Epstein was arrested and charged with importuning for immoral purposes. On Tuesday 21 May at Bow Street Magistrates' Court, he was sentenced to two years' probation. On Sunday 20 December 1964, Epstein paid £60,000 for Chapel Street and hosted many parties there. On Friday 19 May 1967, journalists were invited to the house to meet The Beatles and listen to a preview of *Sgt Pepper's Lonely Hearts Club Band*. One of the photographers was a young blonde woman called Linda Eastman who would go on to marry Paul (see below). In the bathroom, Epstein had an eight feet tall picture of the face of the bullfighter El Cordobes. Epstein died, probably on Friday 25 August 1967, of an "incautious overdose" of the drug Carbrital, a month before his 33rd birthday. His body was discovered on Sunday 27 August 1967. Rumours circulated of suicide and even foul play (murder by a blackmailer because of his sexuality), but it would appear to have been a tragic accident. Six months earlier, Epstein had paid £25,000 for a large detached house, **Kingsley Hill, Warbleton, Wealden, near Heathfield, East Sussex TN21 9PT**. It had become a listed building on Tuesday 30 August 1966. Brian Epstein left £486,032 (£9,400,000 at 2022 values).

Harrison, George
Friar Park, 56 Gravel Hill,
Henley-on-Thames, Oxfordshire RG9 2EE

It was here, his home for almost thirty years, in the early hours of Thursday 30 December 1999, that George Harrison was attacked and stabbed by an intruder. The thirty-room Friar Park was bought in 1889 by the eccentric lawyer and horticulturist Sir Frank Crisp (1843-1919). It was bought by George on Wednesday 14 January 1970 for £140,000 (£2,300,000 at 2022 values) after a year of searching for a home that offered both privacy and proximity to London. George and first wife Pattie moved in on Thursday 12 March 1970. leaving their bungalow **Kinfauns, 16 Claremont Road, Fair-mile Estate, near Esher, Surrey KT10 9LU** where George had lived since Friday 17 July 1964. Kinfauns has since been demolished and another house built on the land. In 1974 George built FPSHOT (Friar Park Studio, Henley-On-Thames) on the first floor of his new home, regarded as the world's most sophisticated recording complex. After John's murder in 1980, George increased the security, but nineteen years later to the month, George and his second wife Olivia were attacked by Michael Abram, a cannabis-smoking heroin addict, who scaled the wall and walked up to the main house. At 3.30am, Abram smashed a window with a statue of George And The Dragon. Olivia Harrison was awoken by the noise, believing a chandelier had fallen. She nudged George, who put on boots and a coat over his pyjamas before going to investigate. He saw a man in the kitchen and went back to tell his wife to stay in the bedroom, but went back for another look when Olivia told him to stay there. George found the intruder with a knife in one hand and part of the spear from the statue in the other. George shouted "Hare Krishna, Hare Krishna" before Abram lunged for him, aiming the knife at his upper body. Olivia arrived and hit the intruder "about the head with a brass poker", but it made no difference. At Abram's trial in November 2000, George recalled, "I vividly remember a deliberate thrust of the knife down into my chest. I could feel blood entering my lungs. I could feel my chest deflate. I felt blood in my mouth and air exhale from my chest. I believed I had been fatally stabbed… I have no doubts that this person had the intention of killing me and my wife." Abram turned his attention to Olivia and grabbed her neck as she tried to run away. To protect his wife, George dragged himself up and jumped on the assailant's back. Olivia remembered, "This was the moment I realised we were going to be murdered, that this man was succeeding in murdering us and there was no one else there to help. I turned around and grabbed a lamp, tore the shade off and brought it down on the man's head. I struck the intruder as hard as I could, as many times as I could... I was exhausted. My husband said, 'Don't stop, hit him harder.'" Around 3.45am, the horrific incident came to an end when two unarmed policemen arrived at Friar Park. Abram was arrested and taken to Henley police station before being transferred to Oxford's John Radcliffe Hospital. Two ambulances raced to the scene and four paramedics attempted to stem the blood flow. At 5am, the Harrisons were taken to **Royal Berkshire Hospital, London Road, Reading, Berkshire RG1 5AN** and put in a side room on the Sidmouth Ward. Surgeons removed part of his partially-collapsed right lung. Once he was stable, George was moved to **Harefield Hospital, Hill End Road, Harefield, Uxbridge, Middlesex UB9 6JH** where he was kept under observation for forty-eight hours. The attack was deliberately underplayed by the Harrisons and a quote was issued in George's name: "He wasn't a burglar and he certainly wasn't auditioning for the Traveling Wilburys." Charlie Watts of the Rolling Stones said, "I spoke to Ringo about a month after it happened and he told me exactly what went on, and it was horrific. George was stabbed about forty times. It happened outside his bedroom on the landing. He would have been dead if he'd been lying in bed, he wouldn't have been able to fight." Abram went on trial on Wednesday 15 November 2000 at Oxford Crown Court and faced two charges of attempted murder. On day two of the trial Judge Michael Astill, citing the Lunatic Act 1845, ordered the jury to find Abram not guilty by reason of insanity. He was committed to **Scott Clinic, Rainhill Road, Saint Helens WA9 5BD** (since closed). George's son Dhani Harrison said, "We shall never forget he was full of hatred and violence when he came into our home. The prospect of him being released into society is abhorrent and we hope that the authorities will allow us to be consulted." On Thursday 4 July 2002, Abram was freed. George's friends believed the attack weakened him, not allowing him to fight the cancer that killed him at 1.20pm on Thursday 29 November 2001 at 9536 Heather Road, Los Angeles, California CA90210, a house owned by Paul McCartney.

Jacobs, David
2 Princes Crescent, Hove, East Sussex BN3 4GS

The Beatles' lawyer Bertram David Jacobs was a 6ft 2in flamboyant homosexual who wore thick panstick make-up in his everyday life. He had a two-tone pink Bentley, three chauffeurs and a table permanently booked at Le Caprice. In June 1959, Jacobs was hired by the American pianist Liberace (1919-1987) after the *Daily Mirror* ran a story that the musician believed implied he was homosexual. He told Liberace to hire Gilbert Beyfus, a top libel lawyer of the time. When Liberace saw Beyfus, who was 73 and suffering from terminal cancer, he was horrified. But Beyfus won the case and Liberace was awarded £8,000 plus costs. Later, when a female juror turned up at his hotel and requested an autograph, Jacobs grabbed the pianist's arm and said "Quick, run for it. If she speaks to us it could mean a new trial." In the autumn of the same year, Jacobs was hired by the entertainer Hughie Green (see page 262) to "scare the living shit out of my father and secure... a pledge that... he... will... cease and desist from ever doing anything of this nature again." Green senior had been sending hate mail to Claire Green, his daughter-in-law. At 10.30am on Friday 23 October 1959, Jacobs arrived at the mezzanine floor, five floors below where Hughie and his family lived at **186 Chiltern Court, Baker Street, London NW1 5SD** with the appropriate legal paperwork and the hate mail. Green senior aimed a kick at the solicitor, breaking his wrist before falling back onto the marble floor dead from a myocardial fibrosis and coronary thrombosis. On Sunday 15 December 1968, Jacobs, 56, who also represented Judy Garland, Diana Dors and Laurence Harvey, hanged himself with a satin cord in the garage of his home on the south coast. He had suffered a nervous breakdown and not been to his offices, **M.A. Jacobs Ltd, 55-58 Pall Mall, London SW1**, for a month. An inquest into Jacobs's death recorded a verdict of suicide while the balance of his mind was disturbed. However, rumours have since surfaced that Jacobs was murdered after he refused to help the Kray twins, who were then in custody awaiting trial. Jacobs was said to have asked for police protection in the final weeks of his life. A private detective who worked for Jacobs said, "I last heard from David two days before his death. He telephoned my secretary and told her it was urgent that I contact him. When I rang back, he burst out, 'It's no good, I'm in terrible trouble. They're all after me.'" The private eye asked who he was frightened of and Jacobs reeled off a list of six famous people in show business. The detective told him "not to worry" and rang off. At the time of his death, Jacobs was also under investigation by the police over an incident on Hampstead Heath.

Lennon, John
Mount Pleasant Register Office, Mount
Pleasant, Waterloo, Liverpool L22 5PL

On Saturday 3 December 1938, Freddie Lennon married Julia Stanley here. They adjourned to a local pub for a drink before spending their wedding night apart. On Thursday 23 August 1962, in the same room his parents had married, John got hitched to the pregnant Cynthia Powell (1939-2015), although much of the three-minute ceremony was drowned out by the noise of a pneumatic drill outside. Brian Epstein was the best man and Paul and George both wore black suits, white shirts and black ties, looking more funereal than matrimonial. Ringo, who had just joined the band, was not invited, and Lennon's beloved Aunt Mimi boycotted the event, meaning there were just seven people at the ceremony. No one remembered to bring a camera. As they left the register office, a thunderstorm began: two of the guests left and the remaining five repaired to Reece's restaurant on Clayton Square for a set menu wedding breakfast of soup, roast chicken and chips followed by trifle, paid for by Brian at fifteen shillings each. Although Reece's did have a liquor licence, the happy couple was toasted with water. On his wedding night, John performed with The Beatles at the Riverpark Ballroom in Chester. In the Seventies, the building became the headquarters of the Merseyside Racial Equality Council.

Indica Gallery
6 Mason's Yard, off Duke Street, London SW1Y 6BU
Telephone: WHItehall 1424

It was here, in the basement of the Indica bookshop, that John met avant garde artist Yoko Ono for the first time. The bookshop opened in September 1965 and was owned by John Dunbar (art critic for *The Scotsman*), the journalist Peter Asher and writer Barry Miles, and supported by Paul to the tune of £5,000 (£97,000 at 2022 values). He also helped draw the publicity flyers for the opening and the wrapping paper. Paul's girlfriend Jane Asher donated the first cash register. From Wednesday 8 to Friday 18 November 1966, the gallery hosted *Unfinished Paintings*, Yoko's first European exhibition. On Thursday 9 November 1966, John went along and was introduced to Yoko by John Dunbar. She handed him a card with one word on it, "Breathe". A few weeks before the meeting with John, Yoko had asked Paul for some original Lennon-McCartney manuscripts to give to composer John Cage for his 50th birthday. He said no.

Tittenhurst Park House, London Road, Sunninghill, Ascot, Berkshire SL5 0PN
Telephone: Ascott 23022

The seven-bedroom Georgian mansion in seventy-two acres of land was bought by John for £145,000 (£2,500,000 at 2022 values) on Sunday 4 May 1969; he and Yoko Ono moved in on Monday 11 August. John began taking heroin. He later said, "It was not too much fun. We sniffed a little when we were in real pain... We took H because of what The Beatles and others were doing to us." John and Yoko gave the drug up because they wanted to have a baby and were worried it might cause another miscarriage or the child might be born addicted. John wrote a song, "Cold Turkey", to describe coming off the drug. When the song was rejected by The Beatles it became the second release of the Plastic Ono Band (John, Yoko, Klaus Voormann and Ringo) on Friday 24 October 1969. The last Beatles publicity shots were taken at Tittenhurst on Friday 22 August 1969, two days after their last recording session together at Abbey Road. On Tuesday 25 November 1969, John sent his MBE back to Buckingham Palace, along with a note: "Your Majesty, I am returning this MBE in protest against Britain's involvement in the Nigeria-Biafra thing, against our support of America in Vietnam, and against "Cold Turkey" slipping down the charts. With love, John Lennon of Bag." John wrote "Imagine" here, inspired by Yoko's "instructional poems" and in a bid to compete with George's "My Sweet Lord" and Paul's "Let It Be". The song was recorded between Thursday 27 May and Sunday 4 July 1971 at Tittenhurst and at Record Plant East, 321 West 44th Street, New York City, NY10036. The video was filmed at Tittenhurst, with John sitting at the piano while Yoko opens curtains. On Tuesday 31 August 1971, John and

Yoko moved to America; John would never return to England. On Monday 10 September 1973, John put the house on the market and eight days later, on Tuesday 18 September 1973, sold the house to Ringo. The new owner changed the name of the recording facility to Startling Studios and opened it to other acts. T. Rex filmed "Born To Boogie" there. In 1988, Ringo sold Tittenhurst for £5million to Sheikh Zayed bin Sultan Al Nahyan, the president of the United Arab Emirates and ruler of Abu Dhabi.

McCartney, Sir Paul
57 Wimpole Street, Marylebone, London W1G 8YW

It was here – the home of the Asher family: Dr Richard, Margaret, Peter, Jane and Claire – that Paul wrote many of The Beatles' most famous songs, including "I Want To Hold Your Hand", their first US chart topper. Paul moved in during 1963, sharing a room on the top floor with girlfriend Jane's brother Peter for around three years. "I Want To Hold Your Hand" was written in the basement. Paul wrote the music for "Yesterday" in a box room at the top of the house. The story goes that he awoke from a dream with the tune in his head.

DID YOU KNOW?

Jane Asher's brother Peter was one half of the pop duo Peter and Gordon who had a Number One hit on both sides of the Atlantic in 1964 with "A World Without Love", a song written by Paul McCartney when he was 16. McCartney did not think the song was of sufficient quality for The Beatles, so the group never recorded it. It is one of two songs attributed to Lennon-McCartney to top the charts in America performed by an artiste other than The Beatles. The other was "Lucy In The Sky With Diamonds" (recorded by Elton John).

They became engaged on Christmas Day 1967 but split in the summer of the following year – Jane announced the breakup on *Simon Dee's Dee Time* on Saturday 20 July 1968. The reason for ending the relationship has never been publicly revealed.

High Park Farm, Campbeltown, Mull of Kintyre PA28

Paul has owned the three-bedroom High Park Farm since Friday 17 June 1966 when he completed the £35,000 purchase (£720,000 at 2022 values). Paul's tax advisors had suggested he buy property to protect his earnings from the Inland Revenue. The farm also had an important gastronomic effect on the McCartney family: one Sunday while having lunch and watching lambs gambolling in the field, they all decided to become vegetarians. The area inspired him to write (with Denny Laine) the chart-topper "Mull of Kintyre", which was recorded on Tuesday 9 August 1977 at Spirit of Ranachan Studio, McCartney's home-recording facility. The double-A side single (along with "Girls' School") was released on Friday 11 November 1977. It was the first single to sell more than two million copies in the UK and was the best-selling single of all time (beating "She Loves You" by The Beatles) until it was overtaken by Band Aid's "Do They Know It's Christmas?" (see page 218) in 1984. Paul bought up around 1,000 acres around the property to ensure his privacy. In 2013, he began withdrawing from the area, making his two staff redundant. It was reported in 2014 that he had not visited the farm for more than five years.

Bag O' Nails, 9 Kingly Street, London W1B 5PN
Telephone: REGent 0953/REGent 3182

On Monday 15 May 1967, Brian Epstein hosted a celebratory dinner for the finishing of *Sgt Pepper's Lonely Hearts Club Band*. Then, Paul went to the Bag O' Nails, a regular Beatles haunt where he had a private table. One writer described the club as "a hookers' hang-out... a favourite watering hole and place to 'pull birds' for the swinging set". That night Georgie Fame and the Blue Flames were performing and Paul met New Yorker Linda Eastman. Paul invited her to another club, **Speakeasy, 48 Margaret Street, London W1W 8SE**, where they heard Procol Harum's "A Whiter Shade Of Pale" for the first time. They married on Wednesday 12 March 1969 and were together until her death aged 56 from cancer on Friday 17 April 1998 in Tucson, Arizona.

DID YOU KNOW?
Bag O' Nails was also the venue where Fleetwood Mac's John and Christine McVie first met, where Justin Hayward of The Moody Blues met his future wife Ann Marie Guirron and also where, in 1966, Jimi Hendrix played his first London gig.

Starr, Sir Ringo
Hulme Hall, 23 Bolton Road, Bebington, Port Sunlight, Wirral CH62 5DH

This was the venue for Ringo's first appearance with The Beatles on Saturday 18 August 1962 following the sacking of Pete Best.

34 Montagu Square, London W1H 2LJ

This was Ringo's home after the flat, **15 Whaddon House, William Mews, London SW1X 9HG**, he shared with George was burgled on Sunday 19 April 1964. Future wife Maureen soon moved in but when the couple married they moved out to **Sunny Heights, South Road, St George's Estate, Weybridge, Surrey**, which they bought on Saturday 24 July 1965 for £37,000 (£765,000 at 2022 values). John Lennon moved in with Yoko Ono in July 1968 after his separation from Cynthia. The nude cover for their *Two Virgins* album was shot here. At 11.30am on Friday 18 October 1968, the police raided the flat and found 219 grains of cannabis resin. On Thursday 28 November, John was find £150 with 20 guineas costs for possession, after pleading guilty to save the pregnant Yoko from a court ordeal. Yoko miscarried John Ono Lennon II on Thursday 21 November in Queen Charlotte Hospital in Hammersmith. On Wednesday 19 February 1969, the landlords served Ringo with an eviction writ to prevent his "undesirable guests" from staying. Nine days later, upset by the summons, Ringo voluntarily gave up the one-bedroom ground-floor flat. In 2014, the flat went on the market for £2½million. Sunny Heights was demolished in late 2015 after being bought by a Russian oligarch.

BICKERSHAW FESTIVAL
Bickershaw, Bolton House Road, near Wigan, Lancashire WN2 4XU

It was here on Friday 5, Saturday 6 and Sunday 7 May 1972 that Woodstock came to Wigan, as the north-west town hosted the Bickershaw Festival. Organised by the future TV host Jeremy Beadle (1948-2008) and Chris Hewitt of Ozit Morpheus Records, among the acts who performed were Captain Beefheart, Country Joe McDonald, Dr John, Donovan, Flamin' Groovies, the Grateful Dead, Hawkwind, The Incredible String Band, The Kinks, Maynard Ferguson, New Riders Of The Purple Sage and

Wishbone Ash. In the crowd were Joe Strummer and Declan McManus (later to find fame as Elvis Costello), who was inspired to form a band by the five-hour Grateful Dead set. The festival was hampered by torrential rain and a lack of security, meaning many of the 60,000 crowd did not pay to get in. Beadle said that working on the festival altered his sleeping patterns for years after, and if he organised a festival again, the one thing he would remember to bring would be a pillow.

BOWIE, DAVID
Bromley Technical High School, Oakley Road, Bromley, Kent BR2 8HP

David Bowie's first live performance was here on Saturday 16 June 1962 . Earlier that month David Jones, as he then was, had joined the Konrads as their saxophone player; this was his first scheduled and publicised show. It was part of the school's parent-teacher association fête and took place on the front steps of the building. When they overran, a teacher brought their performance to an end by pulling the plug. Bowie left the group in summer 1963. The school is now called Ravens Wood School and its alumni include Pete Frampton, Hanif Kureishi, John Pienaar and Steve Severin.

COCKER, JARVIS AND THE BRITS
Earl's Court Exhibition Centre, Warwick Road, London SW5 9TA

It was here – the venue for the Brits on Monday 19 February 1996 – that Pulp singer Jarvis Cocker interrupted "Earth Song" by Michael Jackson. The American singer was given a special Artist of a Generation award. When he appeared on stage surrounded by children, Cocker ran on, lifted his shirt and wiggled his backside at Jackson before running off. Cocker was spoken to by the police but no action was taken. He said, "My actions were a form of protest at the way Michael Jackson sees himself as some kind of Christ-like figure with the power of healing. I just ran on the stage. I didn't make any contact with anyone as far as I recall." Earl's Court Exhibition Centre was opened on Wednesday 1 September 1937, closed on Saturday 13 December 2014 and subsequently demolished.

DEREK AND THE DOMINOES
Lyceum Ballroom, 21 Wellington Street, Covent Garden, London WC2E 7RQ

This was the venue for the first gig by Eric Clapton's band on Sunday 14 June 1970. The gig was originally a Clapton performance but he decided his new band needed a try-out. The band consisted of Clapton (b. 1945: vocals, guitars); Bobby Whitlock (b. 1948: vocals, keyboards); Carl Radle (1942-1980: bass guitar) and Jim Gordon (b. 1942: drums). Dave Mason (b. 1946: guitar) appeared at that girst gig. The event was a charity concert in aid of the Dr Spock Civil Liberties Legal Defence Fund (in aid of draft dodgers, GIs, "conspirators" and Black Panthers). The reaction to the new band was mixed. Four days after their debut, Derek and the Dominos with Dave Mason and George Harrison went into the Apple Studio to record their first single "Tell The Truth/Roll It Over", produced by the lunatic Phil Spector and released in September 1970. The song was withdrawn shortly after its issue. Derek and the Dominos went their separate ways in May 1971.

DID YOU KNOW?

In June 1983, Dominos drummer Jim Gordon, an undiagnosed schizophrenic, suffered a psychotic episode and murdered his mother. Osa Marie Gordon, 72, was hit with a hammer before being stabbed. Gordon claimed a voice had told him to do it. He has been incarcerated ever since.

DYLAN, BOB
Free Trade Hall, Peter Street, Manchester M2 5GP

It was here (the home of the Hallé Orchestra) on Tuesday 17 May 1966 that during a Bob Dylan concert, a member of the audience, furious that the folk legend had started using an electric guitar, yelled "Judas" at him just before a performance of "Like A Rolling Stone". Dylan replied, "I don't believe you" before telling the band to "play fucking loud". Although several people have claimed the "credit" for shouting out, it seems the most likely candidate was a Keele University student called Keith Butler, who had criticised Dylan in a documentary entitled *Eat the Document*. The entire concert – including the shout – has been issued on the double CD *The Bootleg Series Vol 4 Live 1966*. The Free Trade Hall, on the corner of Peter Street and Southmill Street (formerly South Street) closed in 1997 and was sold to a private developer. It is now the Radisson Edwardian Hotel. Keith Butler died of cancer in 2002.

The Savoy Hotel, Strand, London WC2R 0BL

The video for Bob Dylan's "Subterranean Homesick Blues" was filmed in the street at the back of the hotel after he and Donovan sat up all night writing the caption boards.

GLASTONBURY
Worthy Farm, Pilton, Shepton Mallett, Somerset BA4 4BY

The first Glastonbury music festival (then named the Pilton Pop, Blues & Folk Festival) was held here on Saturday 19 September 1970 after founder Michael Eavis saw Led Zeppelin at an open air concert in Bath. With tickets at £1 each, it attracted 1,500 people, somewhat fewer than the most recent festivals, which have been attended by 200,000 spectators. The first headliners were meant to be the Kinks and Wayne Fontana and the Mindbenders, but they were replaced at short notice by Tyrannosaurus Rex, led by Marc Bolan. The 1971 festival was the first to feature the Pyramid Stage, a one-tenth replica of the Great Pyramid of Giza in Egypt. Attendance was free and performers included David Bowie, Traffic, Joan Baez, Fairport Convention, Hawkwind and Melanie. There was a hiatus until a small unplanned festival in 1978 attended by 500 people; the main Glastonbury returned in 1979.

HAÇIENDA, THE
11-13 Whitworth Street West, Manchester M1 5DB

Factory Records opened The Haçienda on Friday 21 May 1982. Thanks to the success of New Order, the Haçienda brought "house" music to Europe and made it a worldwide phenomenon. Drugs and violence eventually caused its closure in 1991, but it reopened before the doors were finally shut on Saturday 28 June 1997. The building was demolished eighteen months later.

HENDRIX, JIMI
23 Brook Street, London W1K 4HA
Telephone: 020-7495 1685

It was here that Hendrix lived between 1968 and 1969 after Beatle Ringo Starr (see page 234) evicted him and his manager Chas

Chandler from his flat at **34 Montagu Square, London W1H 2LJ** when they painted all the rooms black. Handel once lived next door and Hendrix claimed to have seen the composer's ghost. On Sunday 14 September 1997, 23 Brook Street became the site of an English Heritage Blue Plaque commemorating Hendrix. Since November 2001, the upper floors of the house, including Hendrix's flat, have been part of the Handel House Museum, which is open from Tuesdays to Sundays. Call for admission details.

De Lane Lea Studios, 75 Dean Street, London W1D 3PU

This was the studio where "Hey Joe", the Jimi Hendrix Experience's first single, was recorded on Sunday 23 October 1966. The company is still trading from the same address.

The Astoria Theatre, 157 Charing Cross Road, London WC2

Hendrix played here – a former Crosse & Blackwell warehouse – on Tuesday 21 March 1967, the first night of a twenty-four-date tour with Engelbert Humperdink, Cat Stevens and The Walker Brothers. Hendrix set fire to his guitar – a Fender Stratocaster – live on stage for the first time. The scorched instrument sold at auction on Thursday 4 September 2008 for £280. The Astoria was demolished in October 2009 to make way for the Crossrail railway link.

22 Lansdowne Crescent, London W11 2NH

The guitar genius suffered a drugs overdose here on Friday 18 September 1970. He was 27. There are several conflicting stories about what actually happened on the night he died. According to one version, Hendrix and his girlfriend Monika Danneman (b. at Düsseldorf, Germany Sunday 24 June 1945 d. at Seaford, East Sussex Friday 5 April 1996), returned to the room they had lived in for three days at 3am and she made him a tuna sandwich. They drank wine and talked until 6am when he took two sleeping tablets. She fell asleep at 7.30am while he was still talking. At 10am, she awoke and Hendrix was fast asleep. Danneman left the room to buy some cigarettes at 10.15am. When she returned, she noticed that he had vomited. An ambulance was called at 11.18am, arriving nine minutes later. At 11.45am, it began its journey to **St Mary Abbot's Hospital, Marloes Road, Kensington, London W8 5LQ**, where, at midday, Hendrix was pronounced dead on arrival. In another version he left a message on Chas Chandler's answerphone at 1.30am: "I need help bad, man."

Chandler later went over to Hendrix's flat believing that he had or was about to commit suicide, but found it empty. He cleared away all the drug paraphernalia. An ambulance was called but Hendrix was already dead long before it reached the hospital. A third story has a much smaller role for Monika Danneman, labelling her as little more than a groupie or even a stalker. Many close to Hendrix claim she could not have made him a tuna sandwich because he did not like tuna. However the death occurred, Hendrix was dead long before his 30th birthday. Professor Donald Teare, who performed the autopsy on Monday 21 September, ascribed the rock star's death to "inhalation of vomit due to barbiturate intoxication in the form of quinalbarbitone" and an open verdict was recorded on Monday 28 September 1970. Jimi Hendrix was buried in Greenwood Cemetery, NE 4th Street and Monroe Avenue, Northeast Renton, King County, Washington 98056 on Thursday 1 October. The Notting Hill location is now the Samarkand Hotel.

HUMAN LEAGUE
Crazy Daisy, 11 High Street, Sheffield S11PU
Telephone: Sheffield 24455

This is the venue where, on a Wednesday in October 1980, Human League lead singer Phil Oakey saw the schoolgirls Joanne Catherall, 18, and Susan Sulley, 17, dancing and invited them to join the band. Members Martyn Ware and Ian Craig Marsh had recently left to form Heaven 17 with Glenn Gregory. Oakey agreed to pay Ware and Marsh 1 percent of royalties from their next LP (they reportedly earned £100,000 after the success of the Number One smash "Don't You Want Me"). Oakey also added Ian Burden as a session keyboard player for the tour. The Crazy Daisy began life as the Beer Keller (it was situated in a basement); it changed its name in 1973 before becoming the Geisha Bar and then Legends, a nightclub that closed in the mid-1990s. The venue is now used commercially. The Human League played their first live gig on Monday 12 June 1978 at Wham Bar, also known as Bar 2, in the **College of Art, Brincliffe, Psalter Lane, Sheffield S11 (Telephone 52732)**; it was later a computer suite at Sheffield Hallam University and then closed on Sunday 31 August 2008. Demolition work began in March 2010.

JONES, TOM
Treforest Non-Political Working Men's Club, 71 Wood Road,
Treforest, Pontypridd, Glamorgan CF37 1RH
Telephone: Pontypridd 2625

It was here in 1958 that Jones the Voice – 17, almost 18 – made his first professional appearance. He sang "Blue Suede Shoes" and "Sixteen Tons" during a Sunday night guest spot and was paid £1. Born Thomas John Woodward (b. at 57 Kingsland Terrace, Treforest, Pontypridd, Glamorgan CF37 1RX Friday 7 June 1940), he developed tuberculosis when he was 12. He remembered, "I spent two years in bed recovering. It was the worst time of my life." He performed for a while as Tommy Scott, leading the band the Senators, before taking his mother's maiden name and becoming Tom Jones.

DID YOU KNOW?
One of Tom Jones's biggest hits "It's Not Unusual" was originally recorded as a demo for Sandie Shaw. When she decided it was not suitable for her, she suggested Jones released it. The demo was recorded in autumn 1964 at **Regent Sound Studio, 4 Denmark Street, London WC2 (Telephone 01-836 6769)**. The full version was recorded at **Decca Studios, 165 Broadhurst Gardens, London NW6 3AX (Telephone: MAIda Vale 7711/7377)** in November 1964. Released on Friday 22 January 1965, it topped the UK charts on Thursday 11 March 1965.

MADNESS
The Hope and Anchor, 207 Upper Street, Islington, London N1 1RL
Telephone: 020-7354 1312

Formed in Camden Town, north London, in 1976 as the North London Invaders, the group was a six-piece until 1977 when Graham "Suggs" McPherson joined as lead singer. He was sacked when he preferred to spend time watching Chelsea rather than rehearse. Suggs was back behind the microphone in 1978; in 1979 the band changed their name to Madness and the sextet became a septet. Madness played their first gig here on Thursday 3 May 1979.

The Dublin Castle, 94 Parkway, London NW1 7AN

This was the venue for the filming of the video for the hit "My Girl". This pub was regarded as the spiritual home of Madness's early years.

OASIS
The Oasis, North Star Avenue, Swindon, Wiltshire SN2 1EP
Telephone: 01793-465132

Theories vary as to how Oasis derived their name. In 1991, bassist Paul McGuigan, guitarist Paul Arthurs, drummer Tony McCarroll and singer Chris Hutton formed a band called the Rain. However, Hutton did not pass muster and Arthurs auditioned acquaintance Liam Gallagher who suggested the band's name be changed to Oasis – he had seen the name of this leisure centre on an Inspiral Carpets tour poster in the bedroom he shared with brother Noel. Or, Noel was working as a roadie for the Inspiral Carpets when the band visited Swindon. Younger brother Liam came along to see the gig and was taken with the name of the local leisure centre, which had opened on Thursday 1 January 1976. Noel asked if he could join the band but only on the proviso he would be the sole songwriter. Oasis played their first gig on Wednesday 14 August 1991 at the **Boardwalk Club, 21 Little Peter Street, Manchester M15 4PS**; they were bottom of the bill below The Catchmen and Sweet Jesus.

PRESLEY, ELVIS
Prestwick Airport, 107 Glasgow Prestwick
International Airport, Ayrshire KA9 2PL

This airport, thirty-two miles from Glasgow, is the only part of the United Kingdom that the King of Rock'n'Roll ever set foot on. Having been demobbed from the US Army in Frankfurt, West Germany at 11.40am on Wednesday 2 March 1960, Sergeant Presley's plane stopped off for two hours for refuelling at the 1631 US Air Force Squadron at Prestwick, where he chatted to fans through a wire fence.

PROBY, P.J.
ABC Croydon, 225 London Road,
Thornton Heath, Croydon CR0 2SB
The Ritz, Gordon Street, Luton, Bedfordshire LU1 2QP
ABC Northampton, Abington Square, Northampton, NN1 4AE

The singer P.J. Proby was born in Houston, Texas on Sunday 6 November 1938, a great-grandson of Wild West cowboy John Wesley Hardin. After a military education, he relocated to California to be in showbusiness, taking the name Jett Powers and recording a couple of songs on minor labels. In 1960, the songwriter Sharon Sheeley persuaded him to change his name to P.J. Proby, a former high school boyfriend of hers. Proby began writing songs and moved to London, where he had Top Twenty hits in 1964 and 1965 with "Hold Me" (number three), "Together" (number eight), "Somewhere" (number six) and "Maria" (number eight), the last two from *West Side Story*. However, Proby is most remembered for the number of times he split his black velvet trousers onstage. Proby was appearing in a joint venture with Cilla Black, visiting the ABCs, Ranks and Granadas in twenty-two towns and cities up and down the country in a show promoted by Arthur Howes and Brian Epstein (see page 225), with Joe Collins (the father of novelist Jackie and actress Dame Joan) as tour manager. The tour kicked off on Friday 29 January 1965 at the ABC Croydon. Proby had a dozen velvet suits, complete with skin-tight bell bottom trousers, specially made for the tour. He began his first song "Hold Me" to audience approval. Then, as his stage movements became more energetic, something had to give: his trousers ripped from knee to crotch, exposing what one newspaper described as, "the most intimate part of Mr Proby's anatomy". He eschewed underwear. Two days later, they split again at the Ritz Cinema, Luton and again at the ABC Northampton on Monday 1 February 1965. That night, Proby was arrested by PC Bryn Harris, the father of future Radio 1 DJ "Whispering Bob" Harris. The *Daily Mirror* described him as a "morally insane degenerate" and Proby's career shuddered to a halt. He was banned from every major theatre in Britain, and from the BBC and ITV (in the days of only two channels, appearing on television was vital), replaced by Tom Jones & The Squires. Proby had a few more minor hits but nothing compared to his earlier success. He went bankrupt in 1968, owing £84,309 (£1,568,540.87 at 2022 values), with assets of 12 shillings (£11, 2022). He said that he had spent his money on "wine, women, yachts, Lear jets and a fleet of Rolls Royces". He married four times – or was it six? His third marriage ended after he shot his wife in the face with an air pistol. His fourth wife revealed he only managed one erection in their four years together, and was so happy he just sat there smiling at it for three hours. It went unused.

QUEEN
Truro Town Hall, 72 Lemon Street, Truro, Cornwall TR1 2PN

On Saturday 27 June 1970 this is where Smile (comprising Freddie Mercury (see page 180), Brian May and dental student Roger Taylor) made their first appearance. Taylor's mother had hired the venue for a fundraiser for the Red Cross. Mike Grose was on bass guitar. The venue could hold around 800 people, but fewer than a quarter of that number turned up and what they saw did not overly impress. One local newspaper reviewer called them, "Four peculiar looking young gentlemen clad in silk and too many jewels making enough row to wake half the dead in Cornwall." Mike Grose said, "We did our best to hide the gaffes but put it this way we did not expect to get invited back." It was said that Freddie sang like "a very powerful sheep". Smile were paid £50 for their efforts and played their first gig in the capital on Saturday 18 July 1970 at **Imperial College, Prince Consort Road, London SW7 2BB,** by which time they had changed their name to Queen. There were a few line-up changes: Grose left after three shows, with Barry Mitchell replacing him for thirteen gigs from August 1970 to January 1971 (including one on Saturday 31 October 1970 at the Cavern Club, see page 220); Doug Bogie played two concerts with the group before John Deacon joined in February 1971. On Friday 2 July 1971, the classic line-up of Mercury, May, Taylor and Deacon performed together for the first time.

ROLLING STONES
Hyde Park, London W2

On Saturday 5 July 1969 the Rolling Stones took over Hyde Park for a massive free concert. The Stones lived up to the hype surrounding what turned into a memorial concert in Brian Jones's name after his unexpected death two days earlier. Three thousand butterflies were released.

Jagger, Mick
48 Cheyne Walk, London SW3 5LP

It was here, Mick Jagger's Chelsea home, that drugs squad officers arrested the rocker and his girlfriend Marianne Faithfull on Wednesday 28 May 1969. Jagger appeared at Marlborough Street Magistrates' Court on Monday 26 January 1970 charged with possession of cannabis.

He was fined £200 plus 50 guineas costs but Faithfull was acquitted. Jagger accused Detective Sergeant Robin Constable and other officers of attempting to plant the cannabis during the raid and trying to force him to pay a bribe. In his statements Jagger claimed, "He said, 'How much is it worth to you?' He seemed to want me to name a figure but I did not want to. The conversation was being held in an undertone but not a whisper. He twice asked me how much it was worth. He then said, 'A thousand. You can have the money back if it doesn't work.'" An inquiry in March 1970 headed by Detective Chief Superintendent William Wilson reported, "Michael Jagger is an intelligent young man, and doubtless is on the fringe, if not embroiled, in the world of users of dangerous drugs." He added that Faithfull had a "history of mental illness", that "I would not be prepared to place any reliance on this woman," and that Old Etonian antique dealer Christopher Gibb (1938-2018), the only other person in the house during the raid, had a conviction for theft despite "coming from an excellent home". DS Constable later issued a writ for libel against Jagger, but it was discontinued when he ran out of money. Interviewed in August 2005, he again denied Jagger's allegations of dishonesty.

Jones, Brian
Cotchford Farm, Cotchford Lane, Hartfield, Sussex TN7 4DN

The Stones' former lead guitarist bought this farm – where A.A. Milne and Christopher Robin used to live – in 1968. There is a statue of Christopher Robin in the garden. On Sunday 8 June 1969 – after a number of disagreements – Mick Jagger, Keith Richards and Charlie Watts visited Jones at Cotchford Farm and sacked him from the band that he had formed. When the remaining Stones allowed Jones to make his departure public in his own way, he announced that he had decided to quit, saying that he "no longer [saw] eye to eye with the discs we [cut]". He was replaced by Mick Taylor. On Monday 23 June, schoolgirl Helen Spittal took the last-known photographs of Jones. On Thursday 3 July 1969, he died in the swimming pool after taking a midnight swim. His body was found at the bottom of the pool and he was pronounced dead at the scene, although Jones's girlfriend Anna Wohlin is convinced that he was alive when he was taken out of the pool. The coroner's report stated "Death by misadventure", noting his liver and heart were heavily enlarged by drug and alcohol abuse. In 1999, Wohlin alleged that Frank Thorogood, a builder who was renovating Cotchford Farm, had murdered Jones. Thorogood supposedly confessed on his deathbed to Tom Keylock, a driver for the Stones, although there is no substantive evidence to back up the claim. Jones's peers paid tribute to him in the way they knew best. Jimi Hendrix dedicated a song to him on American television; Jim Morrison of The Doors wrote a poem entitled *Ode To L.A. While Thinking Of Brian Jones, Deceased* and The Who's Pete Townshend published a poem – *A Normal Day For Brian, A Man Who Died Every Day* – in *The Times*. Jones was buried in a coffin sent by Bob Dylan in Cheltenham Cemetery, supposedly at a depth of twelve feet to prevent grave robbers. Bill Wyman and Charlie Watts attended the ceremony; Jagger was en route to Australia and Richards stayed away to avoid a scene.

Richards, Keith
Redlands, Redlands Lane, Itchenor, West Wittering, Chichester, West Sussex PO20 8QE

House-hunting Richards bought this Elizabethan farmhouse in 1966 after taking a wrong turning and spotting that it was for sale. He paid the £20,000 asking price (£386,000 at 2022 values) in cash on the same day. It was here on the evening of Sunday 12 February 1967 that Richards, Jagger, Marianne Faithfull and others were arrested for possession of illegal drugs. Detective Sergeant Norman Pilcher led a team of eighteen police on the raid. Rumours that an orgy was being held appear to be false, as does a story about Faithfull and a Mars bar. On Wednesday 10 May, Richards and Jagger appeared at Chichester Magistrates' Court charged with drug offences, where they both pleaded not guilty and were released on £1,000 (£19,300, 2022) bail. On the same day, Brian Jones was arrested at his London flat, also for possession of illegal drugs, and was released on £250 (£4,800, 2022) bail. On Tuesday 27 June 1967, Jagger went on trial at West Sussex Quarter Sessions at Chichester Crown Court before Judge Leslie Block, charged with the possession of four tablets of Benzedrine, which he had bought legally in Italy. The jury took six minutes to find him guilty. Two days later, Richards appeared in the same court, charged with allowing his house to be used illegally for the smoking of marijuana. He, too, was found guilty. Judge Leslie Block sentenced Richards to a year in prison and a £500 (£9,700, 2022) fine. Jagger was jailed for three months and fined £100 costs. Jagger was sent to **HMP Brixton, Jebb Avenue, Brixton Hill, London SW2 5XF** and Richards to **HMP Wormwood Scrubs, 160 Du Cane Road, London W12 0AN**. Both men were released on Friday 30 June on £7,000 (£135,000, 2022) bail and given leave to appeal. On Saturday 1 July, *The Times* ran a leader headed "Who breaks a butterfly on a wheel?" in protest against the severity of the sentences. On Monday 31 July, Richards's conviction was quashed and Jagger's reduced to a conditional discharge. Awaiting his trial on Thursday 6 July, Jones collapsed and was taken to hospital but was found guilty on Monday 30 October of illegal drug possession and allowing his home to be used for drug use; he was jailed for nine months. The next day, pending an appeal, Jones was released from Wormwood Scrubs on £750 (£14,500, 2022) bail. On Tuesday 12 December, Jones's conviction was quashed in favour of a £1,000 fine and three years' probation after three psychiatrists testified he was mentally unstable and suicidal.

SEX PISTOLS
St Martin's College, Southampton Row, London WC1B 4AP
On Thursday 6 November 1975 the Sex Pistols played their first gig here, in a venue later immortalised in Pulp's "Common People".
Lesser Free Trade Hall, Peter Street, Manchester M2 5GP
On Friday 4 June 1976 this was the venue for the Sex Pistols' first gig outside of the southeast, put on by Howard Devoto and Pete Shelley, who were so inspired by what they saw that they went on to form the Buzzcocks. Despite later claims by thousands of people to have been present, there were only forty-two people in the audience that night, but they included some of the future leading lights of the Manchester music scene such as Peter Hook and Bernard Sumner (Joy Division/ New Order), Morrissey, Tony Wilson (the founder of Factory Records) and Mick Hucknall.

SMITHS, THE
The Ritz, Whitworth Street West, Manchester M1 5NQ
Telephone: 0161-236 4355
Johnny Marr, Steve Pomfret and Steven Morrissey formed a band in May 1982. By the end of that year, Morrissey had named it The

Smiths and decided to drop his Christian name. Pomfret left the band acrimoniously, his place taken by Dale Hibbert. In August, The Smiths made their first demo at Decibel Studios in Manchester; Mike Joyce later joined the line-up. The Ritz was the venue for the band's first concert in October 1982, supporting Blue Rondo à la Turk. The Ritz is still in business and is said to have the "the bounciest dance-floor in the UK". In 1983, Morrisey banned anyone from calling him Steven. The band called it a day in 1987.

SPICE GIRLS
57 Boyn Hill Road, Maidenhead, Berkshire SL6 4HR
The five future pop stars lived in this three-bedroom semi-detached house after answering an audition in *The Stage* in February 1994 which read, "WANTED: R.U. 18–23 with the ability to sing/dance? R.U. streetwise, outgoing, ambitious, and dedicated? Heart Management Ltd are a widely successful music industry management consortium currently forming a choreographed, singing/dancing, all-female pop act for a recording deal. Open audition. Danceworks, 16 Balderton Street. Friday 4th March. 11.00am-5.30pm. Please bring sheet music or backing cassette." Around 400 young women responded and were divided into groups of ten, dancing to Eternal's "Stay" before singing a song of their own choice. The successful auditionees were Victoria Adams (b. at Princess Alexandra Hospital, Hamstel Road, Harlow, Essex CM20 1QX Wednesday 17 April 1974), Michelle Stevenson (b. Abingdon, Oxfordshire Monday 3 January 1977), Lianne Morgan (b. Sunday 15 November 1970) and Melanie Brown (b. Leeds Thursday 29 May 1975); they formed a group called Touch. Former topless model Geri Halliwell (b. Watford Sunday 6 August 1972) joined after missing the first audition. Stevenson and Morgan were replaced respectively by Emma Bunton (b. at Barnet, Hertfordshire Wednesday 21 January 1976) and Melanie Chisholm (b. at Whiston, Merseyside Saturday 12 January 1974) before the group found fame. In 1991 Raymond Taylor bought the Boyn Hill Road property as a buy-to-let investment, letting it to five young female tenants in June 1994. For months after they left, the estate agent had to clear away piles of fan mail before showing prospective buyers around. Raymond Taylor hung on to the property until 1997, when he sold it for £110,000. Each day the five

would travel to South Hill Park Recording Studios in Bracknell, and later, Trinity Studios in Knaphill, near Woking, Surrey to rehearse. In January 1995, they began working with songwriters Richard Stannard and Matt Rowe (*né* Matthew Rowbottom). Two months later, they split from Heart Management and began working with the Sheffield-based songwriter Eliot Kennedy. Everything changed almost overnight when Simon Fuller took them on in May 1995 with his 19 Management. A recording contract with Virgin Records followed in July 1995 and worldwide fame. On Sunday 7 July 1996, the Spice Girls' debut single "Wannabe" topped the charts in twenty countries. They split in 2000 and all of them – apart from Victoria – had solo Number Ones.

UB40
The Hare & Hounds Pub, 106 High Street, Kings Heath, Birmingham B14 7JZ
Telephone: 0121-444 2081
It was here that the seven-piece reggae-pop band played their first gig on Friday 9 February 1979 at a friend's birthday party. UB40 subsequently went on to chart more than fifty times, including three Number Ones, and have sold more than seventy million records.

VINCENT, GENE
Granada Cinema, 50–60 Mitcham Road, London SW17 9NA
Gene Vincent was born Vincent Eugene Craddock in Norfolk, Virginia on Monday 11 February 1935. He was given his first guitar when he was 12. Five years later, he left school and joined the US Navy. On Monday 4 July 1955, his left leg was wrecked in a car crash; he refused to allow surgeons to amputate, but had to wear a steel brace and suffered a limp and pain for the rest of his life. He was demobbed not long after. He formed a rockabilly band, Gene Vincent and His Blue Caps and, in 1956, he wrote "Be-Bop-A-Lula" and landed a contract with Capitol Records. The song reached number seven on the Billboard Hot 100. In 1957, the band toured Australia with Little Richard and Eddie Cochran, and Vincent appeared in the Jayne Mansfield film *The Girl Can't Help It*. In 1959, Vincent fell foul of the IRS and left the USA for Europe. He played his first UK

gig at this Tooting theatre on Sunday 6 December 1959 and made his first television appearance later that month on *Boy Meets Girl*. He toured France, Holland and West Germany before returning to Britain, also touring with Eddie Cochran (see page 168) and appeared with The Beatles (see page 219) in Hamburg in 1962. He moved to Britain permanently in 1963 but his career was harmed by his heavy drinking. He also had a problem with violence and at various times pointed a gun at or tried to shoot his wife Margaret Russell, Jet Harris (both in 1963) and Gary Glitter in 1968, while both were on tour in West Germany. He returned to America at the end of 1969. On his final tour of Britain, which began on Sunday 19 September 1971, he recorded tracks for Johnnie Walker's Radio 1 show. He played his last gigs at the **Wookey Hollow Club, 33 Belmont Road, Liverpool L6 4EZ (Telephone: 051-263 1475/051-263 2796)** on Sunday 3 and Monday 4 October. He flew back to America and died, aged 36, on Tuesday 12 October 1971.

WINEHOUSE, AMY
Wenn, 3 Vale Royal, London N7 9AP

Before finding fame as a singer, Winehouse worked as a journalist here with the present author in 2000. It was the headquarters of World Entertainment News Network, a showbusiness news agency founded in January 1989 by the former *Daily Mirror* gossip columnist Jonathan Ashby (b. at Norwich, Norfolk Tuesday 12 July 1949 d. at London Wednesday 6 July 2016). She rewrote showbusiness news stories for the newswire that were then sent to innumerable radio stations and newspapers around the world. Winehouse had success with two albums, *Frank* and *Back To Black*, but fell in with the wrong crowd and became an alcoholic and drug addict. She was found dead at her home, **30 Camden Square, London NW1 9XA**, on Saturday 23 July 2011. She was 27 years old.

WOMBLES
Wimbledon Common, London SW19 4UW

Elisabeth Beresford (1926-2010) created the environmental cleaners after her daughter Kate mispronounced Wimbledon ("Ma, isn't it great on Wombledon Common?"). Beresford created a family of small furry creatures who would make good use of the things that they find, things that the everyday folks leave behind. She based the characters on her family – Tobermory was her brother, Madame Cholet her mother, Orinoco her son and Great Uncle Bulgaria her father-in-law. The first Wombles book was published in 1968 by Puffin. The BBC made an animated series voiced by Bernard Cribbins. The theme – "The Wombling Song" – was written by Mike Batt and released as a single in October 1973, making number four in the charts and leading to more singles and LPs. The Wombles were the most successful music act in the UK in 1974, when they also appeared as the interval act at the Eurovision Song Contest. The group went their separate ways in 1976.

DID YOU KNOW?

In April 2011, it was announced that the Wombles would appear at Glastonbury (see page 237) in June. Festival organiser Michael Eavis said booking the group was "a bit of a mistake". Mike Batt said that Great Uncle Bulgaria was so upset by the comment that he changed his mind about offering to clean up the site afterwards.

Chapter VII

Radio Times & TV Places

BAIRD, JOHN LOGIE
22 Frith Street, London W1D 4RF

John Logie Baird (1888–1946), the inventor of television, transmitted the world's first television pictures from his workshop in the attic here on Friday 30 October 1925. Autodidact Baird borrowed £200 (£13,000 at 2022 values) to finance his experiments and began working in earnest. When Baird needed a subject, office boy William Taynton became the world's first television star – although he was scared by the bright light and had to be bribed with half a crown to participate. Baird stayed in Frith Street from 1924 until 1927, when he moved to **Motograph House, Upper St Martin's Lane, Covent Garden, London WC2** and then to Long Acre. 22 Frith Street is now the site of Bar Italia.

133 Long Acre, London WC2E 9AA

Baird moved to this location from Upper St Martin's Lane in 1927 and stayed for four years. It was here on the roof that he made his first outside broadcast on Tuesday 12 June 1928. Baird created his "televisor" from an old tea chest with a rotating cardboard disc, a spindle made from a knitting needle, lenses costing 4d each from a bicycle shop and a projection lamp in an old biscuit tin. His daily transmissions began on Monday 30 September 1929. The building, now Elme House, is home to several companies.

BAXTER, STANLEY
Madras Place, Holloway, London N7

It was here in January 1962 that the Scottish comedian was arrested for importuning. Baxter was one of the most popular television

comedians in the 1960s and 1970s until he fell out of favour because
his extravaganzas became simply too expensive to produce. Away
from television fame, Baxter had a terrible fear that the press would
out him as a homosexual. When the diaries of his close friend Kenneth
Williams (see page 203) were posthumously published, Baxter took
legal action to ensure nothing was published about his sexual orien-
tation. In 1970, he separated from his wife Moira and moved into a flat
in Highgate Village, North London, where he still lives as a recluse.
"I didn't want to be seen as someone who was once Stanley Baxter,"
he says. In August 2020, aged 94, Baxter faced his fears and publicly
admitted that he was gay. He was not happy with his decision: "There
are many gay people these days who are fairly comfortable with their
sexuality. I'm not. I never wanted to be gay. I still don't. Anyone would
be insane to choose to live such a very difficult life. The truth is, I don't
really want to be me." Baxter first came across openly gay men when
he was serving in the Combined Services Entertainment unit (CSE)
in December 1946 in Singapore, along with Kenneth Williams and the
film director John Schlesinger. Baxter did not like the effeminacy of it
all: "all chiffon hankies and make-up and flouncing about. I thought,
I really hate this. I don't want to be involved in this kind of world".
Baxter kept his homosexuality a secret for the next seventy-five years.
He married Moira Robertson in 1951, Before their wedding, when he
had told her that all his previous sexual experiences had been with
men, she threatened to throw herself out of a second-storey window,
shouting, "If I can't have you then I won't settle for anyone else."
On their wedding night, Baxter sat on the end of the bed and cried.
He later said, "I couldn't put up with very long periods of not being
with men. Thankfully Moira was very understanding. If there were
someone I were interested in, I could bring them home. And she was
very good about letting them go to bed with me. She would go off to
our bedroom and let me take the one opposite." His life as he knew it
could have ended in January 1962 when he visited a public lavatory
in Holloway, a well-known cottaging haunt, to find a man for sex
(see Joe Meek page 178 and Joe Orton page 185). Baxter was
charged with soliciting for sex and, like John Gielgud (see page 172),
considered suicide. On the advice of his agent, he hired flamboyant
gay lawyer David Jacobs (see page 229), who had helped Liberace

in his 1959 libel case against the *Daily Mirror*, which had called him a "deadly, winking, sniggering, snuggling, chromium-plated, scent impregnated, luminous, quivering, giggling, fruit-flavoured ice-covered heap of mother love". The court was told that Baxter could not have been soliciting because, apart from him and the two policemen, no one else was in the convenience. Baxter said he would not sue the police for wrongful arrest and the case was dismissed. When Moira Baxter told her husband that she wanted a baby, he refused to consider it and went on tour to Australia. On his return he went to see a doctor about his sexuality, but therapy did not help. The couple separated and Baxter began an affair with a much younger German accountant. In 1997, while he was abroad, Moira killed herself with an overdose.

BEYOND OUR KEN/ROUND THE HORNE
Paris Cinema, 12 Lower Regent Street, London SW1Y 4PE

These two iconic comedy wireless programmes were broadcast from the same location, the Paris Cinema, which opened as a cinema in April 1939. It was later converted into a radio studio. The Paris Theatre, as it later became, closed in April 1995 and is now a Pure Gym. The pilot for *Beyond Our Ken*, starring Kenneth Horne (1907-1969), was written by Eric Merriman (1924-2003) and Barry Took (1928-2002) and was recorded on Wednesday 2 October 1957. Merriman wanted to call the show *Hornerama* but Took preferred *Round The Horne*. Six names were suggested to the BBC and the corporation went with *Beyond Our Ken*. The programme was well received, but before a series could go ahead, Horne suffered a stroke in February 1958. Four months later, after Horne had recovered, the first programme was recorded on Wednesday 18 June 1958 and broadcast on Tuesday 1 July 1958 at 8pm. Apart from Horne, the show starred Kenneth Williams (1926-1988) (see page 203), Hugh Paddick (1915-2000), Betty Marsden (1919-1998), Ron Moody (1924-2015), the announcer Douglas Smith (1924-1972) and, for one programme only, Stanley Unwin (1911-2002). In the second series, Bill Pertwee (1926-2013) replaced Moody. Merriman's request for a television version of the show was denied by the controller of radio. Barry Took left after the second series and Eric Merriman continued to write alone. The seventh and final series of *Beyond Our Ken* ran from Sunday 24 November 1963 to Sunday 16 February 1964 and the show came to an end following a disagreement between Merriman and the BBC. When the corporation wanted the show to continue, Merriman refused to participate; the BBC turned to Took and his new writing partner Marty Feldman (1933-1982). The show was renamed *Round The Horne* before it took to the air on Sunday 7 March 1965, running for four series. Took and Feldman took a day and a half to write each episode in longhand, before Took's wife Lyn typed up the scripts. Horne missed the Christmas special in 1966 after suffering a heart attack on Friday 7 October 1966. When Pertwee and Feldman left after the third series, the writing reins were taken up in the fourth by Took, Johnnie Mortimer (1931-1992), Brian Cooke (b. 1937) and Donald Webster. Kenneth Williams was not impressed: "Now there are four writers on it! It is unbelievable really. Four! For half an hour of old crap with not a memorable line anywhere... of course one goes on and flogs it gutless and the rubbish gets by." Took thought the scripts were becoming rude and said to Williams, "We might as well write a series called Get Your Cock Out." The last *Round The Horne* was broadcast on Sunday 9 June 1968 and the show came to an end after Horne suffered a heart attack and died on Friday 14 February 1969 while hosting the annual Guild of Television Producers' and Directors' Awards at the Dorchester Hotel. He had just presented a gong to Took and Feldman for their TV show *Marty*. They helped carry Horne from the podium. In a 2019 *Radio Times* poll, *Round The Horne* was voted the BBC's third-best radio show of any type, and the best radio comedy series of all.

BIG BROTHER
3 Mills Studio, Three Mill Lane, London E3 3DU
020-7363 3336

The reality show *Big Brother* was created by John de Mol Jr (b. The Hague Sunday 24 April 1955) and first appeared on television in Holland on the Veronica channel on Thursday 16 September 1999 before being syndicated internationally. The show takes its name from the George Orwell novel *Nineteen Eighty-Four* (published Wednesday 8 June 1949 by Secker & Warburg). The first two series, broadcast in 2000 and 2001, were filmed in a purpose-built house on Lee Valley Park between Bromley-by-Bow and West Ham Tube stations, which was linked to 3 Mills Studio by a footbridge. Following the end of the second series, the house was demolished because Newham Council demanded it be returned to a natural habitat.

Elstree Studios, Shenley Road, Borehamwood, Hertfordshire WD6 1JG

Series three to series nineteen were all filmed on land within the confines of Elstree Studios, which are not actually in Elstree but in Borehamwood. The show, hosted by Davina McCall, ended on Channel 4 in 2010 and returned in 2011 on Channel 5, where it ran until 2018. After the completion of the seventeenth series, the house was knocked down and a new one built, playing host for two more series before it was demolished in January and February 2019.

BRIDESHEAD REVISITED
Madresfield Court, Malvern, Worcestershire WR13 5AH
TA: Madresfield
Telephone: Malvern 24

Evelyn Waugh's novel of the bright young things was published in February 1945. Brideshead Castle was inspired by his time spent at Madresfield Court. In January 1922, Waugh went up to Oxford to read Modern History at Hertford College, where he met Hugh Lygon, the alcoholic second son of the 7th Earl Beauchamp; they became firm friends. The historian A.L. Rowse believed that they were lovers. Waugh described Hugh as "'always just missing the happiness he sought, without ambition, unhappy in love, a man of great sweetness". The pair intended to share rooms on Merton Street but Waugh was sent down from Oxford for not completing his studies. He was invited to the Lygons' home, Madresfield Court, in December 1931 by Lady Dorothy Lygon, 19, one of the four girls in the family. The Lygon family has lived here for around 900 years. It has a moat; the twelfth-century oak outer doors facing the bridge leading to the inner doors have no handles or locks on the outside because the house is never left unoccupied. It has never been bought or sold and has been passed down through twenty-nine generations. Waugh fell in love with Madresfield Court and Lady Dorothy remembered him writing "slowly and reluctantly a great deal of *Black Mischief* while staying with us, groaning loudly as he shut himself away... for a few hours every day". He dedicated the book (published in 1932) to Lady

Dorothy and her sister Mary. The sisters – as unlike as they could be
– were devoted to Waugh and he delighted in them. After travelling
extensively between 1928 and 1937, Waugh returned to England but
did not feel at home in his father's house in Golders Green. Indeed, he
would walk to Hampstead to post letters, thus getting a better class of
postmark. He became a Roman Catholic and turned his back on the
hedonism that made up much of his life in the 1920s. He adopted upper
class mannerisms and pursuits with his friends at Madresfield, much
to the amusement of Lady Sibell, the one sister he did not get on with.
The property made its literary debut in the third chapter of *A Handful
Of Dust*, in the portrayal of Tony Last's ancestral home, Hetton Abbey.
Ten years later, the house is transformed into Brideshead Castle and the
Lygons feature in the book: Lord Machmain is the Earl Beauchamp and
Sebastian Flyte is a composite of Alastair Hugh Graham, Hugh Lygon
and Stephen Tennant. Anthony Blanche is based on the flamboyant
Brian Howard, another Oxford contemporary of Waugh. Rex
Mottram is said to be based on Lord Beaverbrook, Lord Birkenhead
and Brendan Bracken.

Castle Howard, York, YO60 7DA

The eighteenth-century Baroque mansion set in 100,000 acres near
York was the setting for the 1981 television adaptation of Evelyn
Waugh's novel. Castle Howard has been the home of the Howard
family since it was built in 1709. It took more than twenty years for the
roof to be repaired after a fire in 1940. The Garden Hall was rebuilt
shortly after filming began.

DOCTOR WHO
76 Totter's Lane, Shoreditch, London EC1 5EG

It was to a junkyard at this address that two teachers from Coal
Hill School in London, Barbara Wright (Jacqueline Hill) and Ian
Chesterton (William Russell), follow Susan Foreman (Carole Anne
Ford), one of their pupils, and hear her speaking from inside what
appears to be a police phone box. They push the doors open and find
themselves inside the Tardis, the Doctor's time machine, in the first
episode of the sci-fi series, *An Unearthly Child*. Susan was the granddaughter of the Doctor (William Hartnell). The Doctor would return
to the junkyard several times in future adventures.

DOWNTON ABBEY
Highclere Castle, Newbury, Berkshire RG20 9RN
Telephone: 01635-253210

After winning an Oscar for *Gosford Park* (released Wednesday 7 November 2001), Julian Fellowes decided to capitalise on its success by making a television series based around the upper classes. The result was *Downton Abbey*, which began on Sunday 26 September 2010 on ITV and ran for six series and two films. Highclere Castle was used for the outside, while the scenes featuring the servants' living quarters were filmed at Ealing Studios. **Wrotham Park, Barnet, Hertfordshire EN5 4SB**, was used as Gosford Park for exterior scenes, plus the stairs, dining room, library and living room. Wrotham Park was designed by Isaac Ware for Admiral John Byng and completed in 1754. He did not get much time to enjoy it as he was shot for treason three years later.

DUCHESS OF DUKE STREET, THE
Cavendish Hotel, 81 Jermyn Street, London SW1Y 6JF
Telephone: WHItehall 4503

On Saturday 4 September 1976, BBC1 introduced the public to *The Duchess of Duke Street*, a drama about Louisa Leyton (Gemma Jones), whose ambition is to be the best cook in London. Set between 1900 and 1925, it ran for thirty-one episodes over two series. Louisa rose from cook to owner of the posh Bentinck Hotel in Duke Street, St James's. In the show, she becomes the mistress of the Prince of Wales (later HM King Edward VII) and marries a butler to maintain public propriety; however, Edward ends the relationship when Queen Victoria dies. The programme was based on the life of Rosa Lewis (née Ovenden) who ran the Cavendish Hotel in London. Lewis was born in a cottage on Grange Road, Leyton, Essex on Thursday 26 September 1867. After leaving school at 12, she became a servant for an exiled French count. In 1887, she began hiring herself out as a cook for private dinners. Her first job was for Lady Randolph Churchill; she later cooked for the Saviles and the Asquiths and then, in 1907, for Kaiser Wilhelm II. Rosa did have a friendship with Edward VII, who was amused by her wit. Like her fictional counterpart, she married a butler: 29-year-old Excelsior Tyrel Chiney Lewis. When she bought the Cavendish Hotel in Jermyn Street in 1902, it was already very popular, but she succeeded in enhancing its reputation. Rosa, who featured in Evelyn Waugh's *Vile Bodies* (1930), spent her last years dressed as an Edwardian and quaffing vast quantities of champagne and brandy. She died at the Cavendish on Friday 28 November 1952, aged 85. She left £122,924 15s 1d (£4,317,885 at 2022 values). The Cavendish Hotel was damaged during the Blitz and was demolished in June 1962. The present Cavendish Hotel was opened in July 1966.

FAWLTY TOWERS
Hotel Gleneagles, Asheldon Road, Torquay, Devon TQ1 2QS

It was in 1971 while staying at this forty-one-bedroom hotel with the rest of the Monty Python team that John Cleese discovered the proto-types of Basil and Sybil Fawlty: Donald Sinclair and his wife Beatrice. Mr Sinclair apparently berated Terry Gilliam for using his knife and fork incorrectly, and Eric Idle returned to the hotel to find his bag had been hidden behind a distant wall in the garden. Mr Sinclair told him they thought it might be a bomb. Idle asked, "Why would anyone want to bomb your hotel?" to which the hotelier responded, "We've had a lot of staff problems lately." The other Pythons moved to the Imperial Hotel but Cleese stayed on. He once described Sinclair as "the most wonderfully rude man I have ever met". Michael Palin recalled that Donald Sinclair "seemed to view us as a colossal inconvenience", while his wife threatened them with a bill for a stay of two weeks even though they had checked out quickly. Donald Sinclair died in 1981; his wife died in a Torquay care home on Monday 13 September 2010, aged 95. The hotel closed in 2015 and the site is being developed by Churchill Retirement Living, which has been granted permission to build thirty-two retirement flats on the land.

Wooburn Grange Country Club, Grange Drive, Bourne End, Buckinghamshire HP10 0QD

The exterior shots of Fawlty Towers was actually a Buckinghamshire country club that was badly damaged by fire in 1991 and demolished. Eight homes were built on the site.

GOODNIGHT SWEETHEART
Ducketts Passage, London E1

It was through this innocuous-looking side street that TV repairman Gary Sparrow (Nicholas Lyndhurst) travelled back to 1940s London in the Laurence Marks and Maurice Gran BBC sitcom. It began on BBC1 on Thursday 18 November 1993 and ran for six series until Monday 28 June 1999. Gary gets lost on his way to Hugh Gaitskell House, where he was to pick up a television for repairs. Ducketts Passage leads to the East End, where Gary meets barmaid Phoebe Bamford (Dervla Kerwan, later Elizabeth Carling) whose father, Eric, owns the Royal Oak.

GOOD OLD DAYS, THE
City Varieties Music Hall, Swan Street, Leeds, West Yorkshire LS1 6LW
Box Office: 0845-644 1881

For thirty years from 1953 until Saturday 31 December 1983 Leonard Sachs presided verbosely over this BBC variety show for all but the first two episodes. A Grade II* listed building, the music hall was built in 1865 as an adjunct to the White Swan Inn in Swan Street and was originally named Thornton's New Music Hall and Fashionable Lounge after its founder, local publican Charles Thornton. It then became Stansfield's Varieties before becoming the City Palace of Varieties.

HANCOCK'S HALF HOUR
23 Railway Cuttings, East Cheam, Surrey SM2

It was here that Anthony Aloysius St John Hancock lived in the BBC Radio show and later TV comedy. The show ran from 1954 until 1961 and was written by Ray Galton and Alan Simpson. Anthony John Hancock (his real name) was born at **41 Southam Road, Hall Green, Small Heath, Birmingham B28 8DQ** on Monday 12 May 1924. In 1951, he joined the radio show *Educating Archie* and three years later, on Tuesday 2 November 1954, his own show, *Hancock's Half Hour, went on air* for the first time. Hancock worked with Sid James, Bill Kerr and Kenneth Williams (see page 203). In 1961, Hancock fell out with Galton and Simpson, who went on to create *Steptoe And Son* (see page 264). As his career faltered, it became obvious how reliant Hancock was on his writers. The writer and television personality Arthur Marshall said, "Seldom has such a dazzling career disintegrated so quickly." Hancock went Down Under to try again, but it was not a success. He committed suicide in the garden flat at 98 Birriga Road,

Bellevue Hill, Sydney, New South Wales 2023; his body was found there on Tuesday 25 June 1968. He left £32,559 (£602,000 at 2022 values).

I'M A CELEBRITY GET ME OUT OF HERE
Gwrych Castle, A547, Llanddulas Road, Abergele, Conwy LL22 8EU

In 2020 the Covid-19 pandemic forced the producers to move the show from Australia to Gwrych Castle, a Grade I listed country house and one of the first attempts at replicating true medieval architecture in Europe. The first show began on ITV on Sunday 15 November 2020. The castle was completed in around 1825 and has 250 acres of gardens and grounds. It housed 200 Jewish refugees during the Second World War. In the 1950s, World Middleweight boxing champion Randolph Turpin (1928-1966) used it as a training ground. The first ten celebrities were: athlete Hollie Arnold; actress Beverley Callard; journalist Victoria Derbyshire; athlete Mo Farah; podcaster Giovanna Fletcher; TV presenter Vernon Kay; DJ Jordan North; actress Jessica Plummer; dancer A.J. Pritchard and actor Shane Richie, with singers Russell Watson and Ruthie Henshall joining on the fourth day. Hollie Arnold was the first to be voted out. A second series was held in 2021 and won by Danny Miller.

LBC
Communications House, Gough Square, London EC4P 4LP
Telephone: 01-353 1010/01-353 8111 (Phone-ins)

The UK's first mainland independent radio station began broadcasting on 417m on medium wave just before 6am on Monday 8 October 1973, followed eight days later by Capital Radio. The first voice to be heard was former BBC presenter David Jessel, who was on air until 9am. This was followed by a mid-morning show *Two In The Morning* (9am to midday) hosted by Paul Callan and Janet Street-Porter, and known less respectfully as "Cut-glass and cut-froat". *The Afternoon Show* was presented by Clive Roslin, the father of *The Big Breakfast* presenter Gaby Roslin. LBC began on a budget of more than £1million (£13million at 2022 values). It moved to its more familiar location on the dial (261m) with its famous jingles "LBC – where news comes first" and "News radio for London 24 hours a day – LBC". *Blockbusters* host Bob Holness co-presented the breakfast show *AM* with Douglas Cameron from 1975 until 1985. The 10pm-1am show, later called *Nightline*, was hosted by, among others, Mike Dickin, Bryn Jones, Adrian Love, Robin Houston, Monty Modlyn, Jeremy Beadle, Jenny Lacey and Tommy Boyd. LBC's other presenters included Dickie Arbiter (later to become the Queen's press secretary from 1988 to 2000), George Gale, Brian Hayes, Alastair Burnet, Steve Allen (still with the station in 2022), Thérèse Birch, Jon Snow, Peter Allen, Bel Mooney, Colin Turner and Dominic Allan, who presented *Sportswatch* on Saturdays. In 1987, LBC was sold and moved away from Gough Square to **Crown House, 72 Hammersmith Road, Hammersmith, London, W14 8TH**.

ONLY FOOLS AND HORSES
127 Nelson Mandela House (originally Sir Walter Raleigh House), New World Estate (later Nyerere Estate), Peckham, London SE15 9LP

The Trotter family (Del Boy played by Sir David Jason; his brother Rodney, Nicholas Lyndhurst; their grandfather portrayed by Lennard Pearce; and later, Uncle Albert, played by Buster Merryfield) lived here until they became millionaires; when they lost their money, they returned to the flat. John Sullivan (1946-2011) was a scene shifter at the BBC when he approached veteran producer Dennis Main Wilson (1924-1997) in the BBC Club with an idea for a sitcom about a south London revolutionary. He recommended Sullivan hone his art, and he began writing scripts for *The Two Ronnies* before *Citizen Smith* became Sullivan's first hit. His ideas for a football-based sitcom and another about a cockney market trader were rejected. After ITV's success with *Minder*, Sullivan and producer Ray Butt (1935-2013) again pitched the market trader idea to John Howard Davies (1939-2011), the BBC's Head of Comedy, who commissioned Sullivan to write a full series. The working title was "Readies", soon changed to *Only Fools And Horses* from the saying, "Why do only fools and horses work for a living?" Filming began on Sunday 7 June 1981, and the first episode, "Big Brother", was broadcast on BBC1 at 8.30pm on Tuesday 8 September that year. The first series averaged seven million viewers (not very good in the days of only three channels, but these days most producers would give their eye teeth for those figures) and a second series fared slightly better. The show took off with the third series and regularly topped the ratings. On Saturday 15 December 1984, during the filming of the fourth series, Lennard Pearce (Grandad) died aged 69 of a heart attack and was replaced by Harry "Buster" Merryfield (1920-1999), a bank manager who turned to acting on his retirement. Greater success followed and the seventh and final series ended on Tuesday 3 December 1991 with the episode "Three Men, A Woman And A Baby". Christmas Specials continued to be broadcast until Thursday 25 December 2003. Although the Trotters live in Peckham, most of the filming took place in and around Bristol. The exterior of Nelson Mandela House was originally **Harlech Tower, Park Road East, Acton, London W3 8TZ**. The building is due for demolition in 2025 as part of a £650 million regeneration project. From 1988, it was **Whitemead House, Duckmoor Road, Ashton, Bristol BS3 2ER**; some scenes were filmed in the car park of Ashton Gate, Bristol City's home ground. *Only Fools And Horses* was voted Britain's Best Sitcom in a 2004 BBC poll.

OPEN ALL HOURS
15 Lister Avenue, Balby, Doncaster, South Yorkshire DN4 8AS
The shop owned by the tight-fisted, stuttering shopkeeper Albert E. Arkwright was actually a beauty parlour named Beautique, made up to look like a general store. The series starred Ronnie Barker and David Jason as his put-upon nephew Granville and ran from Friday 20 February 1976 until Sunday 6 October 1985. It was spawned from the 1973 Barker comedy anthology *Seven Of One*, which also gave birth to *Porridge*. A one-off 40th Anniversary special, *Still Open All Hours*, was broadcast at 7.45pm on Thursday 26 December 2013 on BBC1. It led to a full series, which began exactly a year later with Jason reprising his role as Granville.

OPPORTUNITY KNOCKS
Studio 1, Thames Television, Broom Road,
Teddington Lock, Middlesex TW11 9NW
Unctuous and litigious Hughie Green presided over the long-running talent show here for fourteen years from 1964 until 1978 on Thames TV. However, Green (1920-1997) hosted versions of the show from Friday 18 February until Thursday 29 September 1949 on BBC Radio,

but it was dropped after one series for being "too American". Green, not one to take a setback lying down, sued the BBC, entrepreneur Carroll Levis (b. at Toronto, Canada Tuesday 15 March 1910 d. at London Thursday 17 October 1968), his wife Florence (b. Monday 27 May 1918 d. 1996) and five of his family and friends for a conspiracy to stop *Opportunity Knocks* going on the air in favour of *Carroll Levis's Discoveries*, another talent show. In May 1955, the trial came to the High Court and Green was represented by Viscount Hailsham. After twenty days, the jury found for Levis et al. Although Green was declared bankrupt on Tuesday 8 May 1956, the grossly fat Levis's career suffered the most, and his last TV appearance was on Wednesday 4 November 1959. A heavy drinker, he died in obscurity of cirrhosis of the liver almost exactly nine years later. Green brought *Opportunity Knocks* back to ITV with Associated Rediffusion from Wednesday 20 June 1956 until Wednesday 29 August 1956 and then again on Thames TV from Saturday 11 July 1964 until it was dropped on Monday 20 March 1978 because of the right wing political statements Green insisted on making on the show. The show discovered a wealth of talent including Paul Daniels, Les Dawson, Berni Flint, Mary Hopkin, Paper Lace, Freddie Starr & The Delmonts, Su Pollard, Middle Of The Road, Bonnie Langford, Little & Large, Bobby Crush, Berni Flint, Tony Holland (who flexed his muscles to "Wheels Cha-Cha"), Millican & Nesbitt, Peters & Lee, Lena Zavaroni, Frank Carson, Max Boyce, Pam Ayres and Tony Monopoly. In 1958, Associated British Corporation bought the property to use as a television studio; when Thames TV took over the ITV franchise on Tuesday 30 July 1968, it became the main venue for the company's comedies, dramas, game shows and children's programmes. In 1992, Thames lost its broadcasting licence to Carlton and the studio became independent. In 2005, the company was sold for £2.7million to the Pinewood Studios Group. In late January 2016, demolition began on the site to make way for a development of 213 flats.

SAVILE, JIMMY
22 Lake View Court, Roundhay, Leeds, West Yorkshire LS8 2TX
After the UK's self-professed first DJ was found dead here from a heart attack on Saturday 29 October 2011, two days before his 85th birthday, the BBC ran tributes praising Savile's altruism, charity work and long

career. A year later, on Wednesday 3 October 2012, an ITV documentary revealed claims that Savile – on speaking terms with the great and the good including TRH the Prince and Princess of Wales (see page 41), Margaret Thatcher (see page 64) and Pope John Paul II – was a serial sex predator claiming possibly hundreds of victims over several decades. Television presenters and charity campaigners who worked with Savile claimed to have noticed nothing amiss about his behaviour. Possibly the most bizarre thing about the whole situation is that several times on television and in interviews, Savile said exactly what he was – but all the "confessions" were dismissed as merry larks. A charity fundraiser, he often used his munificence as a way to distract doubts about him: "Do you want this heart machine or not?" James Wilson Vincent Savile was born at 64 Wellclose Grove, Leeds, West Riding of Yorkshire LS7 on Sunday 31 October 1926, the youngest of seven children. After working as a miner, a scrap metal dealer and a dance hall manager (Plaza Ballroom, Oxford Road, Manchester in the mid-1950s; **Mecca Locarno ballroom, Merrion Street, Leeds L2 (Telephone Leeds 31448)** in the late 1950s and early 1960s and **Palais dance hall, 246-250 High Road, Ilford, Essex IG1 1QF (Telephone ILFord 3128)** between 1955 and 1956, it was demolished in 2007), he began working as a DJ in 1958, first for Radio Luxembourg and, from 1968, for Radio 1 where he presented *Savile's Travels* and *Jimmy Savile's Old Record Club* (1973-1987). He presented the first edition of *Top Of The Pops* (see page 267) on Wednesday 1 January 1964 and the last on Sunday 30 July 2006. In 1975, he began hosting the magic carpet show *Jim'll Fix It* that ran until 1994. He was given an OBE in the 1972 New Year's Honours List and a knighthood in the 1990 Queen's Birthday Honours. He volunteered at Stoke Mandeville Hospital in Aylesbury, Leeds General Infirmary and Broadmoor Hospital in Berkshire, where he attacked many of his victims. He was unmarried. Jimmy Savile left £4,298,160 (£5,560,000 at 2022 values).

STEPTOE AND SON
Oil Drum Lane, Shepherd's Bush, London W12

The home of totters Albert and Harold Steptoe and their horse Hercules. The show was created by scriptwriters Ray Galton (1930-2018) and Alan Simpson (1929-2017) who had met at the **Milford**

Sanatorium, Tuesley Lane, Godalming GU7 1UG Surrey, when they were both recovering from tuberculosis. Albert and Harold Steptoe first appeared as a strand in *Galton & Simpson's Comedy Playhouse*, a series of ten thirty-minute one-off comedies, after they had been dropped by Tony Hancock (see page 259). The BBC's Head of Comedy Tom Sloan (1919-1970) gave Galton and Simpson carte blanche to do what they wanted and the first episode, "Clicquot Et Fils", was broadcast on Friday 15 December 1961 and starred Eric Sykes (1923-2012) as a corrupt undertaker and Barbara Hicks (1924-2013). The fourth show, "The Offer", was about a pair who hated each other. Galton and Simpson did not hire comedy actors for the roles of the warring father and son and knew straightaway they wanted Wilfrid Brambell (see page 164) as Albert and Harry H. Corbett as Harold. The episode was first broadcast on Friday 5 January 1962 as part of *Galton & Simpson's Comedy Playhouse*, and then again on Thursday 7 June 1962 as the first episode of *Steptoe And Son*. In the first episode, it is explained that the "… And Son" is not Harold but Albert, as it was his father who created the firm and "there's no point wasting money keep changing the sign". The Steptoe name came from a photographic shop – Steptoe and Figge – opposite a flat in Richmond rented by Galton and Simpson. Genuine totters lived nearby: Arthur and Chris Arnold, on Crescent Street. They had a yard in Stebbing Street on the site of the **Edward Woods Estate, 60 Norland Road, London W11 4TX** (visited by Harold in the film *Steptoe And Son Ride Again*). Their horse Dolly appeared as Hercules in the show. Chris Arnold later revealed that they made more money for the six weeks Dolly was used than in the rest of the year put together. The show attracted around twenty-four million viewers per episode and in October 1964, with a general election on a Thursday, the Labour Party asked the BBC to delay a repeat showing for fear that the working class would stay in to watch it rather than going out to vote for Harold Wilson. The BBC ignored the request but Labour was elected anyway, albeit with only a four-seat majority. Each series of *Steptoe And Son* took four to five months to write; after the end of the third series, Brambell announced that he was going to become a star on Broadway and would be appearing in a play called *Kelly*. The BBC decided to recast the role of Albert, but Galton and Simpson had another solution – they would kill off the character. The fourth series would open at a graveside and a young man would approach Harold to reveal himself as the son that he never knew he had. As it turned out, the reworking was unnecessary as *Kelly* was a huge flop and closed on its opening night. The original run of *Steptoe And Son* lasted four series, coming to an end on Monday 15 November 1965. The outdoor scenes in the show were shot at a car-breakers' yard in **Norland Gardens, London W11**. The first four series were recorded at the **BBC Lime Grove Studios, Lime Grove, Shepherd's Bush, London W12** (demolished 1993). When the show returned on Friday 6 March 1970, it was filmed at **BBC Television Centre, Wood Lane, London W12 7RJ** (closed Sunday 31 March 2013). The last episode was broadcast on Thursday 10 October 1974. The sitcom spawned two spin-off films: *Steptoe And Son* (1972) and *Steptoe And Son Ride Again* (1973). In the early 1950s, Eric Sykes invited Spike Milligan (1918–2002) to share his office above a grocer at **130 Uxbridge Road, Shepherd's Bush, London W12 8AA**. Sykes wanted to set up a writers' agency and invited Ray Galton and Alan Simpson to join. The company became Associated London Scripts, and eventually had around thirty writers and twelve office staff. It had become too big for the premises by 1957 and moved to Kensington High Street. In 1960, Associated London Scripts bought premises at **11 Orme Court, Bayswater, London W2 4RQ**. The previous summer, 9 Orme Court was occupied by Dr Stephen Ward and his friend Christine Keeler (see page 187).

> **DID YOU KNOW?**
> *Comedy Playhouse* ran for thirteen years and 120 episodes. Apart from *Steptoe And Son*, it also spawned *The Liver Birds, Are You Being Served?, Till Death Us Do Part* and *Last Of The Summer Wine*.

TO THE MANOR BORN
West Lodge, Cricket St Thomas, Chard, Somerset TA20 4BY

West (or Westport) Lodge was used for exterior shots of The Old Lodge in Grantleigh, near Marlbury in Somerset, where Audrey fforbes-Hamilton (Penelope Keith) moves to after being forced to vacate Grantleigh Manor in the BBC sitcom (Sunday 30 September 1979-Sunday 29 November 1981) created by Peter Spence, whose father-in-law was, at the time, the owner of the real building. The show was originally envisaged as a radio programme but a full series was cancelled when it was decided to make it for television. Grantleigh Manor is bought by the arriviste millionaire businessman Richard DeVere, who owns the Cavendish Foods supermarket chain. What is worse for Audrey is that DeVere's real name is Bedřich Polouvicek, and he is half-Polish and half-Czech, having arrived in Britain with his mother in 1939. West Lodge is located on the edge of the 1,000-acre Cricket St Thomas Estate.

Cricket St Thomas Hotel, Chard, Somerset TA20 4DD

This was the exterior for Grantleigh Manor, which is about a mile from West Lodge. Horatio, Lord Nelson (1758-1805) and Lady Hamilton (1765-1815) spent many hours walking around the countryside. Its grounds were based on designs by Capability Brown, the landscape gardener. The history of the estate can be traced back to the eleventh century; the de Cricket family lived there during the twelfth and thirteenth centuries. In 1775, Captain Alexander Hood (1726-1814), later an admiral, bought the land from the politician Richard Hippisley Coxe (1742-1786). He built the present house eleven years later, although whether it is completely new or used parts of the previous build is unknown. The next owner also had a naval connection: Samuel Hood, 2nd Baron Bridport (1788-1868), who married Lord Nelson's niece Charlotte. In 1898, Alexander, 3rd Baron Bridport (1814-1904) sold Cricket House and its grounds to the chocolatier Francis Fry (1835-1918). Warner Holidays later bought the house and turned it into a hotel.

DID YOU KNOW?

As with many of our current sayings, the show's name has a Shakespearian origin, deriving from a line in *Hamlet* spoken by the lead character in Act 1 Scene 4 to Horatio: "Though I am a native here and to the manner born, it is a custom more honour'd in the breach than the observance."

TOP OF THE POPS
Studio A, BBC, Dickenson Road, Rusholme, Manchester M14 5JB

The BBC was determined to find a pop programme to rival ITV's *Ready Steady Go* and gave producer Johnnie Stewart (1917-2005) a brief to create it. He introduced two rules – only songs going up the charts would feature and the current Number One would end the show. The BBC commissioned six shows and, at 6.35pm on Wednesday 1 January 1964, Radio Luxembourg DJ Jimmy Savile (see page 263) presented the first *Top of the Pops* from the BBC's Studio A in a converted church on this road. The programme lasted twenty-five minutes and included Dusty Springfield (she performed first with "I Only Want To Be With You"), the Rolling Stones ("I Wanna Be Your Man"), the Dave Clark Five ("Glad All Over"), the Hollies ("Stay") and the Swinging Blue Jeans ("Hippy Hippy Shake"); Number One was The Beatles with "I Want to Hold Your Hand". All the artistes mimed. The show stayed on a Wednesday until September 1964, when it moved to Thursday and became a mainstay of that evening's schedule. In January 1966, the prohibitive cost of travelling to Manchester meant the show was moved to Television Centre Studio 2, and then to Lime Grove Studio G in London in mid-1966. *Top of the Pops* became exceptionally popular, in its heyday drawing in audiences of up to twenty million each week. However, the change in day release of the chart made the show less relevant and the collapse (by 40 percent) in record sales by 2003 also signalled the beginning of the end for the programe. When it was moved from Friday night on BBC1 to Sunday on BBC2, the audience fell below a million. The show was axed on Tuesday 20 June 2006 and the last edition was broadcast on Sunday 30 July 2006. Sir Jimmy Savile and the Rolling Stones appeared on both the first and last editions of *Top Of The Pops*.

DID YOU KNOW?
After Jimmy Savile (1926-2011), the second show was presented by Alan Freeman (1927-2006), the third by David Jacobs (1926-2013) and the fourth by Pete Murray (b. 1925). The quartet took it in turns to present until the end of 1966, when Jacobs left and was replaced by Simon Dee (1935-2009). With the advent of Radio 1 on Saturday 30 September 1967, its DJs began to host the programme. Freeman and Murray left at the end of 1969.

TV-AM
17-29 Hawley Crescent, London NW18TT
Telephone: 01-267 5483

The first independent breakfast station began broadcasting on Tuesday 1 February 1983 from these studios, converted from a 93,418-feet former Henleys garage dating from the 1920s. The original presenters, dubbed the Famous Five – Anna Ford, David Frost, Robert Kee, Michael Parkinson and Angela Rippon (Esther Rantzen left before the show went on air) – along with chief executive Peter Jay, promised "a mission to explain". This worthy sentiment did not last too long as viewers deserted the station. Ford and Rippon were sacked in April 1983. Parkinson stayed until 1984, hosting a Saturday show, when Kee also left. Frost ended up with his own weekend show. Nick Owen and Lynda Berry were recruited, with Anne Diamond joining in June 1983 from the BBC. The viewers returned and new boss Bruce Gyngell insisted on presenters wearing bright clothing. They included Jayne Irving, exercise guru "Mad Lizzie" Webb, Wincey Willis, Richard Keys, Commander David Philpott, Lorraine Kelly, Mike Morris, Gyles Brandreth, Kathy Tayler, Gordon Honeycombe, Timmy Mallett, Rustie Lee, Trish Williamson, a blonde weathergirl called Ulrika Jonsson plus a rat called Roland and a gerbil called Kevin. Although popular with viewers, it was not always flavour of the month with the broadcasting authorities. In October 1984 the station fell foul of the IBA when it withdrew its film crew from the Tory conference at Brighton just before the IRA bombed the hotel where Party leaders were staying. Presenter John Stapleton reported the incident over the phone. The IBA insisted that TV-am strengthen its news coverage or lose its franchise. TV-am did lose its franchise, however, when the Thatcher Government judged television companies not on quality but on how much cash they were prepared to bid to stay on air. TV-am's bid of £14.3million was not enough, as the owners of the future GMTV bid £36.4million. Margaret Thatcher (see page 64) wrote to Gyngell apologising for her Government's gaffe. TV-am went off air on Thursday 31 December 1992; the following year, the studios were sold to the music station MTV, which still occupies them.

TWO RONNIES, THE
H.E. Harrington, 1 York Street, Broadstairs, Kent CT10 1PD
Ronnie Corbett had a holiday home near this ironmonger's shop which one day was visited by Ronnie Barker. That visit inspired Ronnie B to write the "Four Candles" sketch.

UPSTAIRS DOWNSTAIRS
165 South Eaton Place, Belgravia, London SW1
In the days before the nation was gripped by the Grantham family residing at Downton Abbey (see page 257), the Bellamys of Belgravia showed us how posh people conducted themselves. The show was created by the actresses Jean Marsh and Eileen Atkins as a comedy called *Behind The Green Baize Door* which they developed with producers John Hawkesworth and John Whitney in 1969. It was turned down by Granada TV because *A Family At War* was about to begin. Stella Richman, the Controller of Programmes at London Weekend Television, commissioned the show in April 1970. *Upstairs Downstairs* began on Sunday 10 October 1971 and ran until Sunday 21 December 1975. House number 65 was used for the exterior shots of 165 Eaton Place, with a 1 painted in front. The interiors were filmed at Wembley and later at London Weekend TV.

WHITEHOUSE, MARY
Madeley Secondary Modern School, Court Street, Madeley, Telford, Shropshire TF7 5FB
It was while teaching art here that Constance Mary Whitehouse (b. at Bridge House, Croft Road, Stockingford, Nuneaton, Warwickshire Monday 13 June 1910) began her ultimately unsuccessful campaign to impose her opinions on the nation's television viewers. As well as art, Mrs Whitehouse was the senior mistress and in charge of sex education. On Sunday 8 March 1964, several of her charges were watching when premarital sex was discussed in a BBC show called *Meeting Point*. Mrs Whitehouse's complaints were rebuffed. The following year, the Government renewed the BBC's charter for another dozen years, which led to the formation of the Clean Up TV Campaign by Mrs Whitehouse, of **Postman's Piece, The Wold, Claverley, Wolverhampton WV5 7BD (Telephone: Claverley 375)** and Norah

Buckland **of Longton Rectory, Rutland Road, Longton, Stoke-on-Trent ST3 1EH (Telephone: Stoke-on-Trent 33529).** The manifesto was drawn up by Mrs Whitehouse, her husband Ernest, Norah Buckland and her husband Basil, the rector. At the first public meeting, held in Birmingham Town Hall on Tuesday 5 May 1964 which was attended by more than 2,000 people, the speakers included the Whitehouses, the Bucklands, Patricia McLaughlin MP and Patricia Duce, the niece of the explorer Sir Ernest Shackleton. *The Times* described the event as "the most extraordinary meeting ever held" there and it led to the 1965 creation of the National Viewers' and Listeners' Association. Mrs Whitehouse was not always taken seriously by her detractors and became the butt for comedians' jokes in the 1970s and 80s. She was, however, convinced that her views were correct, and attacked her enemies with a ferocity belying her schoolmarmish appearance. One of her *bêtes noirs* was BBC Director-General Sir Hugh Greene. On Thursday 9 December 1976, she sued *Gay News* and its editor Denis Lemon (b. Saturday 11 August 1945 d. 21 July 1994 from Aids) for publishing "a blasphemous libel concerning the Christian religion, namely an obscene poem and illustration vilifying Christ in His life and in His crucifixion". The case came to the Old Bailey on Monday 4 July 1977, with John Mortimer (1923-2009) QC and Geoffrey Robertson (b. 1946) representing the accused and John Smyth (1941-2018) representing Mrs Whitehouse. On Monday 11 July, the jury found both defendants guilty. Gay News Ltd was fined £1,000; Lemon was fined £500 and received a nine months suspended prison sentence. After both parties appealed the following year, the Court of Appeal quashed Lemon's sentence but upheld the convictions. Mrs Whitehouse was appointed CBE in 1980 and continued to appear on radio and television berating our permissive society, until ill health forced her retirement. She died aged 91 in Abberton Manor Nursing Home, Abberton, Colchester, Essex on Friday 23 November 2001. She left £155,990.

Chapter VIII
This Sporting Life

ANFIELD
Seaforth, Liverpool L4 0TH

Long known as the home of Liverpool, Anfield was originally the home of their deadly rivals Everton. The stadium was opened in 1884 and owned by John Orrell, a friend of the Everton president John Houlding, whose club were looking for a new home. John Orrell let Everton have the ground in return for a charitable donation to the local hospital. Everton played their first match at Anfield on Saturday 27 September 1884 against Earlestown, who were beaten 5-0. In 1885 John Houlding bought the land outright for £5,845 and the club began paying rent to its own president, although John Orrell still owned the adjacent land. The first league match staged at Anfield was on Saturday 8 September 1888 between Everton and Accrington, Everton winning 2-1 thanks to a brace from George Fleming. In 1890-1891 Everton brought their first League Championship to Anfield. When Houlding increased his annual rent to £250, the club offered only £180. John Orrell then announced that he wanted to build a road accessing his land – the only problem being that it would run straight through the newly built main stand. Everton suspected their president of involvement; fed up with their Machiavellian leader, they upped sticks and moved to Goodison Park, which was officially opened on Wednesday 24 August 1892 by Lord Kinnaird and Frederick Wall of the FA. When Houlding was left with a stadium but no club to fill it, he decided to create a new team. The Football Association refused to let him call it Everton, so, on Tuesday 15 March 1892,

Liverpool FC and Athletic Grounds Ltd was born. Their first match at Anfield was a friendly against Rotherham Town, kicking off at 5.30pm on Thursday 1 September 1892. Two hundred spectators watched Liverpool win 7-1. The first match played by the Reds in the Football League was on 2 September 1893 away to Middlesbrough Ironopolis. Liverpool won 2-0 despite the long grass, which impeded play.

ARSENAL
The Royal Oak, 27 Woolwich New Road,
Greenwich, London SE18 6EU
Telephone: 020-8317 4782

Arsenal was founded at this pub on Christmas Day 1886. Fifteen members of Dial Square FC met here and officially adopted the title of Royal Arsenal, having decided that although no one had heard of Dial Square, everyone was aware of the Royal Arsenal. The pub, near to Woolwich Arsenal station, changed its name to The Pullman. When construction began on the Docklands Light Railway extension to Woolwich Arsenal, the pub and several nearby buildings were demolished in 2007.

BANNISTER, ROGER
Christ Church Sports Ground, 58–60 Iffley Road, Oxford OX4 1EQ
Telephone: 01865-243992

It was here on Thursday 6 May 1954 that Roger Bannister became the first man to break the four-minute mile barrier during a meet between the British Amateur Athletic Association and Oxford University. Three thousand spectators packed the meet, but when winds reached 25mph, Bannister decided to save his energy and go for the record on another day. However, just before the race was due to start, the winds dropped and Bannister decided to run after all. When the announcement of Bannister's time – 3 minutes 59.4 seconds – was made, the crowd drowned out most of it. Incidentally, that announcer was Norris McWhirter (see page 298), later to become a record breaker himself. He was to comment, "There were 3,000 people at that meeting and I have subsequently met all 100,000 of them."

BECKER, BORIS
Nobu, Metropolitan Hotel, 19 Old Park Lane, London W1Y 4LB
Telephone: 020-7447 4747

It was to this restaurant in June 1999 that the former Wimbledon champion took his wife Barbara to dinner. When the couple had an argument, Barbara left. Becker stayed, continued to drink and met the model Angela Ermakova, who was working as a waitress. Nine months later, on Wednesday 22 March 2000, Ermakova gave birth to a daughter, Anna, and claimed that Becker was the father. He denied paternity and his lawyers suggested that Ermakova was part of a blackmail plot devised by the Russian Mafia. She said that they had had sex in a cupboard at Nobu, but Becker claimed she gave him oral sex, kept his sperm in her mouth and then inseminated herself. On Thursday 8 February 2001, DNA results proved that Becker was indeed Anna's father and he agreed to pay $5million that July. Father and daughter have since become very close. On Friday 29 April 2022, 6ft 3in Becker was jailed for two and a half years at Southwark Crown Court after being convicted of four charges under the Insolvency Act for failing to disclose his assets after his bankruptcy.

BEST, GEORGE
Slack Alice, 2 Bootle Street, Manchester M2 5GU
Telephone: 061 834 6470

This nightclub was bought by George Best, hairdresser Malcolm Wagner and Colin Burne in October 1973 for £10,000 (£130,000 at 2022 values). It had previously been a rundown establishment called Club Del Sol; the new name came from comedian Larry Grayson's imaginary friend. The trio spent as much again refurbishing the place. Burne remembered, "It was disgusting, a pigsty. The layout broke all the rules. Most successful nightclubs are in basements, this was two flights up. It was in the same street as a police station, which was hardly an attraction, and there was no parking." An agent for Miss World Marjorie Wallace told Best here that she would make a publicity appearance at the club for £150 (£1,665, 2022). Best refused, but Wallace turned up anyway, albeit with a large retinue. On Monday 18 February 1974, Wallace and Best ended up in bed at her mews house in Marylebone, West London. After they had made love, she spoke on the phone to the mother of her fiancé Peter Revson (1939-1975) telling her how much she was missing him – behaviour that even Best found unacceptable. When they had an argument, she stormed out, threatening to go to the press and tell them that Best was useless in the sack. Not wanting to be on his own in London, Best returned to Manchester by train but took Wallace's diary with him. On Thursday 21 February, he was arrested just before closing time at his club and taken to London, where he was charged at Marylebone Magistrates' Court with trespassing and stealing a fur coat, passport, chequebook and other items from Wallace. He was released on £6,000 bail. On Saturday 2 March, Wallace's passport and a medallion were sent to the *Sunday People*; seven days later, her tiara and some of her cash was found in a London telephone box. After Wallace twice failed to turn up to court, Best was freed on Wednesday 24 April. Seven days later, a question was tabled in the House Of Commons regarding the cost of the court case: £1,606 of public money had been spent. Wallace returned to America, never to return, while Best sold his story of the affair to the *Sunday People* for £12,000. Despite his brilliance on the football field, it was his off-field behaviour that made the headlines for the rest of his life until his death, aged 59, on Friday 25 November 2005 of multiple organ failure after years of alcohol abuse. Slack Alice is now a night-club called 42nd Street.

BUSBY BABES, LAST GAME IN ENGLAND
Arsenal Stadium, Avenell Road, Highbury, London N5 1BU

The youthful Manchester United team assembled by Matt Busby was expected to sweep all comers before them for many years, but fate was to intervene. The last match played in England by the Busby Babes before their journey to Belgrade was at Arsenal Stadium. The game was played before 63,578 spectators and was thrilling end-to-end stuff. After ten minutes, Duncan Edwards put United one in front, giving goalkeeper Jack Kelsey no chance to block his powerful shot. Bobby Charlton put the northerners two up after half an hour. Tommy Taylor made it 3-0 and the score stayed that way until the second half. Arsenal refused to lie down and David Herd pulled one back before Jimmy Bloomfield scored twice to pull the scores back to 3-3. Dennis Viollet headed home for 4-3 to United. Taylor scored in the second half to make it 5-3. Derek Tapscott scored what would be his last goal for Arsenal to take the score to 5-4. It ended that way, although Vic Groves almost equalised. Tapscott later commented, "I were the last fella to score against the Busby Babes in England. But I wish to God I wasn't."

COOPER V ALI
Arsenal Stadium, Avenell Road, Highbury, London N5 1BU

On Saturday 21 May 1966, the home of Arsenal was transformed into a boxing ring to play host to the World Heavyweight title fight between Henry Cooper and Muhammad Ali. Tickets ranged from two to twenty guineas and a crowd of 46,000 — including Hollywood stars Lee Marvin and George Raft – watched the British champion put up a brave battle before being stopped in the sixth round due to a cut over his left eye. After the fight, Cooper had twelve stitches at Guy's Hospital. Future Arsenal legend Charlie George, then an apprentice, helped build the ring for the event.

CRICKET
Test match, first
The Oval, Kennington, Surrey SE11 5SS

Monday 6 September 1880 saw the fourth Test match between England and Australia here; England fielded eight debutants including W.G. Grace and his brothers Edward Mills (who faced the first ball and opened the batting with W.G) and George Fredrick. The original intention was for Surrey to play Australia, but club secretary Charles Alcock was instrumental in arranging the first Test match in England. W.G. Grace and Bunny Lucas shared the first century partnership (120 for the second wicket) as England won by five wickets.
Wisden Cricketers' Almanack, first edition
2 New Coventry Street, Haymarket, London SW1

The bible of cricket was first published by the former English cricketer John Wisden (1826-1884) in 1864, a year after he retired, and was originally known as *The Cricketer's Almanack*. Wisden wanted the book to compete with Fred Lillywhite's *The Guide*

To Cricketers. The first edition was only 112 pages long and cost a shilling; as well as cricket, it contained the dates of battles in the English Civil War, an account of the trial of King Charles I, the winners of The Oaks, the Derby and St Leger, the lengths of British canals, the results of the Boat Race and the rules of quoiting. From 1866, it began to include full scores of the previous season's important matches; the following year it contained "Births and deaths of cricketers". In 1887, batting and bowling averages from the previous seasons and a fixture list for the forthcoming one were included. Five years later, its first obituaries appeared. From the sixth edition, it became known as *Wisden Cricketers' Almanack*, although the yellow jackets did not appear until the seventy-fifth edition in 1938. Previously, its covers had varied between yellow, buff and pink. The seventy-fifth edition was also the first to display an Eric Ravilious woodcut of two Victorian cricketers on its cover. The book has had just sixteen editors in more than 140 years of publication. Its Cricketers of the Year tradition began in 1889 with the naming of Six Great Bowlers of the Year. Usually, five players are selected annually, although there have been some surprising omissions: in particular, Abdul Qadir, Bishan Bedi, Wes Hall, Inzamam-ul-Haq and Jeff Thomson were never honoured.

ELLIS, WILLIAM WEBB
Rugby School, Lawrence Sheriff Street,
Rugby, Warwickshire CV22 5EH
Telephone: 01788-556216

It was supposedly here in 1823 that William Webb Ellis (b. at Manchester November 1807 d. at Menton, Alpes Maritimes, France, on 24 January 1872), "with a fine disregard for the rules of football as played in his time first took the ball in his arms and ran with it". A stone which was set in a wall at Rugby School in February 1900 commemorates this act. Ellis attended Rugby School from 1816 to 1825. All the indications are that, if not unpopular, he was at least an "outsider". He was a townie and a foundationer and, as such, received a free education here. Many argue that the story is in fact a myth, although Jennifer Macrory, in *Running with the Ball: Birth of Rugby Football* (1991), remained convinced it was true. Whether he did or not, the practice was not immediately adopted but gradually institutionalised over the following thirty years. Furthermore, rugby acquired such distinctive features as an oval ball, H-shaped goals, scoring above the cross bar and points for tries as well as goals in the second quarter of the nineteenth century. Thus, in focusing solely on the development of carrying, the Ellis story fails to explain all the others aspects of the emerging game. The school moved to its current site in 1750, although in 1823, it occupied the much smaller area on Lawrence Sheriff Street where the Old Quad, the old chapel and the Close are situated.

FA CUP
FA Cup, first final
The Oval, Kennington, Surrey SE11 5SS

The oldest football competition in the world began on Monday 16 October 1871 with fifteen teams entering: Barnes, Civil Service, Crystal Palace (not the current club), Clapham Rovers, Donington Grammar School (Lincolnshire), Hampstead Heathens, Harrow Chequers, Hitchin, Maidenhead, Marlow, Queen's Park (the only Scottish entrants), Reigate Priory, Royal Engineers, Upton Park and Wanderers. Donington Grammar School, Harrow Chequers and Reigate Priory withdrew from the competition before actually playing a game. Donington's headmaster entered his school because he feared the pupils were not getting enough exercise. However, they were drawn against Queens Park and could not afford the rail fare to Scotland. Wanderers reached the final having won just one game – when they played Queen's Park on Tuesday 5 March 1872 in the semi-final at The Oval, Kennington, Surrey, the match ended in a draw. However, the Scottish team withdrew when they faced the same problem as Donington School: a lack of money to travel to London again for the replay. In the final, Wanderers met Royal Engineers, who had beaten Crystal Palace 3-0 in a replay after a goalless semi-final at the Oval on Saturday 17 February 1872. Admittance to the final cost a shilling and there were no crossbars, nets, free kicks, penalties, centre circle or halfway line. Both teams had an abundance of forwards – Royal Engineers had seven and Wanderers eight. Charles Alcock, the Old Harrovian captain of Wanderers, secretary of the Football Association and creator of the FA Cup, won the toss and chose to defend the Harleyford Road end of the ground. This meant that the Royal Engineers, the favourites, had the sun and wind in their faces. With the game only ten minutes old, Lieutenant Edmund Cresswell of the Royal Engineers broke his collarbone, but with no substitutes available refused to leave the pitch. After fifteen minutes Wanderers' Morton Betts, playing under the pseudonym "A.H. Chequer", scored the only goal of the game. In those days, teams changed ends after each goal was scored. On twenty minutes, Charles Alcock scored but the goal was disallowed because Charles Wollaston had handled the ball. Wanderers continued to attack and it was only the skill of William Merriman in the Royal Engineers goal that stopped Wanderers adding to their score. *The Field* called the final "the fastest and hardest match that has ever been seen at The Oval" and Wanderers displayed "some of the best play, individually and collectively, that has ever been shown in an Association game". *The Times* reported, "Overall, the Royal Engineers appeared to possess the more skilled football team and offered much evidence they would emerge victorious; however, one has discovered anything may happen in this knockout style tournament."

DID YOU KNOW?
Wanderers did not receive the cup at the match but had to wait until April 1872 when it was presented to them at a special reception at the Pall Mall Restaurant in London by FA president Ebenezer Morley. It was not until 1882 that the tradition of presenting the winners with the trophy at the end of the match began.

FA CUP, THEFT OF
69 New Town Row, Birmingham, B6 4EH
At Crystal Palace on Saturday 20 April 1895, Aston Villa won the competition for the second time, beating West Bromwich Albion 1-0. The only goal of the twenty-fourth FA Cup Final was scored after just thirty seconds, when a shot from inside forward Bob Chatt was deflected into the goal by Villa's captain Jack Devey. The trophy went to the Midlands and the team were met at the railway station by a large group of fans who whooped their appreciation as Jack Devey

held the trophy aloft. At a party, the cup was filled with champagne and toasts made. It was then put in the safe at Villa's Perry Barr ground. William Shillcock, a a local boot and shoe manufacturer and dedicated Villa supporter, asked if he could borrow the trophy. The 73-year-old supplied boots to Aston Villa "and sixteen international players". He also offered for sale jerseys, knickerbockers and eight types of balls, including a "best cowhide" version used by Villa as well as England. Just after midnight on the morning of Thursday 12 September 1895, three men climbed onto the flat roof of the shop and pulled back the zinc cladding before smashing a hole about a foot across in the ceiling and dropping into the main premises. They took a few shillings from the till before turning their attention to the main prize – the trophy. The FA Cup stood around sixteen inches high with handles, a lid and a small, bearded figure with a ball at his feet. Towards the end of August, the trophy had attracted large crowds while sitting in the shop window. On Wednesday 11 September, Shillcock closed and locked his shop at around 9.15pm. When he arrived to open up at 8am the next day, he noticed the till was open and empty but his two safes were untouched. Then he checked the window and saw the FA Cup was missing. The police examined the scene, and looking at the small hole in the ceiling, determined the thieves were "slightly developed" youths. The club offered a £10 reward but the trophy was never recovered. Villa were fined £25 for their carelessness. There the matter rested until February 1958, when Harry Burge, an 80-year-old resident of an old people's home, told the *Sunday Pictorial*, "I stole the FA Cup". He confessed, "It was just turned midnight when the three of us forced a lock on the door at the back of the building with a jemmy. Once inside, we were able to climb through an upstairs window onto the flat roof – open to the street – over the shop's front windows. Then we all went back to my home in Hospital Street, a few minutes' walk away. That night, we broke up the cup before melting it down inside an iron pot. My pals had several moulds for making a 'snide' of half-crowns, so we used the silver to turn out a number of these coins." The trio of thieves passed the fake coins in a pub called Salutation, owned by the Villa forward Dennis Hodgetts and used by many of the players. Birmingham police did not reopen their investigation. Burge was a career criminal with forty-two convictions going back to 1897 and had spent forty-six years and eleven months behind bars. Three months after his confession, he was caught snatching three coats from an unattended van. In spite of his age, he was sentenced to seven years in prison, serving two and a half before his release. He died in Summerfield Hospital in 1964.

DID YOU KNOW?

The second trophy – almost identical to the first – was presented to FA president (and five-time FA Cup winner) Lord Kinnaird in 1911, and the third – produced by Fattorini & Sons of Bradford – was retired in 1991. The fourth, an exact replica of the third, has been used since the 1991-1992 season.)

GRAHAM, GEORGE
Park Lane Hotel, Park Lane, London W1J 7BX

It was in the lounge bar here over the course of two meetings that Arsenal manager George Graham received an "unsolicited gift" of £425,000 from Norwegian football agent Rune Hauge. The money was said to be in return for signing two of Hauge's clients for the North London footballing giants: defender Pål Lydersen (on Wednesday 20 November 1991 for £500,000) and defensive midfielder John Jensen (for around £1½million shortly after the European Championships in August 1992). Graham had previously dealt with Hauge when signing Anders Limpar, but he had turned down a number of players offered by the Norwegian, including Peter Schmeichel and Andrei Kanchelskis. The Premier League had begun to investigate the swirling rumours of cash sweeteners being offered to managers. When Graham's "unsolicited gift" came to light during an Inland Revenue investigation, he reached a secret agreement with the Arsenal board to repay the money with interest and resign at the end of the 1994-1995 season. However, when the news of the bung became public and the club was threatened with punishment, the board sacked him on Tuesday 21 February 1995 and he was banned from football for one year by the Football Association. Fifa banned Hauge for life, later reduced to a two year suspension.

> ## DID YOU KNOW?
> George Graham is one of only two men to manage both Arsenal and Tottenham Hotspur (Terry Neill being the other), and one of two to win the FA Cup as a player and manager for Arsenal, Mikel Arteta being the other.

HAMPDEN PARK
Kingsley Avenue, Glasgow, G42 8BU

The first game at Hampden Park, the home of Queen's Park and the Scotland national side, was also the first match in the Scottish FA Cup. Queen's Park won 7-0 and went on to win the trophy. Although Hampden Park has always been the home of Queen's Park, it has not been the same stadium. There have been three Hampden Parks so far, with the first being occupied between Saturday 25 October 1873 and 1884. Queen's Park spent nineteen years at the second Hampden Park before moving to the current stadium, where the first game was played on Halloween 1903: Queen's Park beat Celtic 1-0.

INTERNATIONAL, FIRST FOOTBALL
The West of Scotland Cricket Ground, Hamilton Crescent, Peel Street, Partick, Glasgow

The first football international in the world took place here at 2.20pm Saturday 30 November 1872 and was watched by around 4,000 people at a cricket ground that received £1 10s for its hire. The match, played in sunshine on a pitch that had been rained on for the previous two days, ended 0-0. Scotland's team – all of whom played for Queen's Park – clad in "dark blue shirts with a lion crest, white knickerbockers, blue and white striped stockings and red head cowls", was picked by its captain Robert W. Gardener and played in a 2-2-6 formation. The Football Association picked the England side but Charles Alcock, the Old Harrovian captain of Wanderers, secretary of the FA and creator of the FA Cup, had the most influence. He was unable to play in the inaugural match because of an injury. England, resplendent in "white shirts with three lions crest, white knickerbockers and dark blue caps", played in a 1-2-7 formation.

ROE, ERIKA
Rugby Road, Twickenham, Middlesex TW11DS

A busty bookshop assistant from Petersfield, Hampshire, Erika Roe (b. at Deben, Suffolk Monday 30 December 1957) attended the England-Australia rugby match here on Saturday 2 January 1982. Emboldened by rather too much alcohol, she and her friend Sarah Bennett took their tops off and ran across the pitch to the delight of the 60,000 fans. England mascot Ken Baily (1911-1983) covered Roe's forty-inch bust with his Union Jack and escorted her off the pitch. The tabloids offered Roe £8,000 worth of modelling jobs but Bennett, who was less naturally endowed than her friend, did not receive the same public interest. Roe recalled: "At half-time, the crowd appeared bored by a man dressed as a gorilla trying to entertain them, then someone shouted, 'Doesn't someone streak now?' For me, it was like a red rag to a bull. Totally unplanned, I removed my top and bra and streaked across the ground with a cigarette in my mouth before being chased by a policeman and hauled off to the police station." Roe now lives in Portugal with her Dutch husband and three children

TENNIS
First club: Manor House Hotel, Avenue Road,
Leamington Spa, Warwickshire, CV31 3NJ

Leamington Lawn Tennis Club, the first of its kind, was founded here in 1872 by Major Harry Gem, his Spanish friend Augurio Perera, Dr Arthur Wellesley Tomkins and Dr Frederic Haynes. Gem and Perera, enthusiastic rackets players, devised a variation called pelota in a nod to Perera's origins, which became "lawn rackets". The winner was the first player to score fifteen points. In 1872, Gem and Perera joined forces with two young doctors from the Warneford Hospital to form a club in the grounds of the Manor House Hotel, Leamington Spa. The club is no longer in existence.

Wimbledon, first: Worple Road, Wimbledon, Surrey SW

The All England Croquet Club was founded on Thursday 23 July 1868 in the offices of *The Field* magazine at **346 Strand, London WC2R 0JE**, whose editor John H. Walsh was the first chairman. On Friday 24 September 1869, the committee agreed to rent a four-acre site – in what is now Nursery Road, Wimbledon – between Worple Road and the London and South Western Railway. The rent would cost £50, rising to £75 in the second year and £100 in the third. An annual subscription for a lady or gentleman cost a guinea, while a couple would pay £1 11s 6d. A lifetime subscription would be ten guineas for an individual or fifteen guineas for a married couple. A pavilion was built in 1870 and the first croquet tournament was held in June that year. On Thursday 25 February 1875, one of the croquet lawns was set aside for tennis and badminton. On Thursday 24 June 1875, the MCC's Laws of Lawn Tennis were officially adopted, although with some modifications: the scoring would be 15, 30, 40, deuce and advantage, and only the serving player could add to his score. On Saturday 14 April 1877, the club's name was changed to the All England Croquet And Lawn Tennis Club. That June, the committee approved John Walsh's motion "that a public meeting be held on July 10th and following days to compete for The Championships in lawn tennis and that a sub-committee composed of Messrs J. Marshall, H. Jones and C.G. Heathcote be appointed to draw up rules for its management". A week later, *The Field* published a slightly amended advertisement for competition: "All England Croquet And Lawn Tennis Club, Wimbledon, propose to hold a lawn tennis meeting, open to all amateurs, on Monday, July 9th and following days. Entrance fee £1 1s 0d. Two prizes will be given – one gold champion prize to the winner and one silver to the second player." By 1877, a pony roller that Walsh had donated in return for his daughter being elected to membership of the club had broken, so he came up with the idea of the tennis tournament to raise funds to repair it. Julian Marshall, Henry Jones and Charles Gilbert Heathcote adopted the real tennis rule of sudden death at five games all, and the players changed ends after each set. The net was to be five feet high at the posts, dropping to three feet three inches at the centre. In the same year the first cricket Test match was played (see page 276), the Wimbledon Championships began, commencing on the second Monday in July with just one competition: the Gentlemen's Singles. The twenty-two participants each paid an entry fee of one guinea. Dr Henry Jones, 46, the tournament referee, even built a bathroom which he charged patrons to use. No one had figured out how to arrange a tournament with twenty-two players, so there were eleven players in the second round and three semi-finalists. To resolve the problem, William C. Marshall was given a bye into the final. Despite it being held in July, the weather for the final was poor. After the semi-finals on Thursday July 12, the tournament was postponed on Friday 13 and Saturday 14 July so that crowds could watch the Eton v Harrow cricket match at Lord's and return for the final the following Monday, 16 July. However, the Monday was a washout and the game was postponed until the following Thursday. W. Spencer Gore, a 27-year-old surveyor, an Old Harrovian and a keen cricketer, won the first championship and its prize of twelve guineas and a silver cup worth twenty-five guineas. In a match delayed an hour by rain, Gore beat Cambridge real tennis blue William C. Marshall 6-1, 6-2, 6-4 in just forty-eight minutes. The following year, Gore lost to Frank Hadow in the challenge round 5-7, 1-6, 7-9 – until 1922, the champion got a bye into the final – and never returned to Wimbledon. He was to write, "That anyone who has really played well at cricket, tennis or even rackets, will ever give his attention seriously to lawn tennis beyond showing himself to be a promising player, is extremely doubtful, for in all probability the monotony of the game as compared with others would choke him off before he had time to excel in it."

WEST HAM UNITED
Hermit Road, Canning Town, London E16

The team that now plays as West Ham United was founded here by Dave Taylor and Arnold Hills (1857-1927) on Saturday 29 June 1895 as Thames Ironworks FC, the football team of the Thames Ironworks and Shipbuilding Company. Taylor was a foreman and Hills the firm's owner. The club's first ground was described as "a cinder heap", and canvas sheets were used as fences. The team's first game was against Royal Ordnance reserves on Saturday 7 September 1895 and ended in a 1-1 draw. On Monday 16 December 1895, the club played Old St Stephen's at Hermit Road in one of the first matches under floodlights (twelve lights on poles, the equivalent of 2,000 candles). It was not a great success as the bulbs kept blowing and the ball had to be dipped in whitewash every ten minutes so that the players could see it. At the end of the season, Thames Ironworks were evicted for breaking the terms of their tenancy. They became West Ham United in 1900 before moving to the **Boleyn Ground, Green Street, London E13 9AZ** in 1904, where they stayed until a move to the Olympic (later London) Stadium in 2016. Ten thousand people watched the club's first match at the Boleyn Ground on Thursday 1 September 1904 – they beat Millwall 3-0. The Lions' goalie Tiny Joyce was so upset that he punched a hole in the dressing room door. West Ham's last match at the ground was the Premier League game against Manchester United on Tuesday 10 May 2016, with the Hammers running out 3-2 winners. The Boleyn Ground was demolished in 2016-2017.

DID YOU KNOW?

Arnold Hills, who was educated at Harrow and University College, Oxford, was a teetotal, a non-smoker and a vegetarian. One of the earliest nicknames of the club was consequently the Teetotallers. In 1888, he became the first president of the London Vegetarian Society and served on the committee with Mohandas Gandhi (1869-1948). Hills had played for Oxford University in the 1877 FA Cup Final and won a cap for England on Saturday 5 April 1879 against Scotland, winning 5-4 at the Kennington Oval.

WORLD CUP
Methodist Central Hall, Storey's Gate, London SW1H 9NH
Telephone: 020-7222 8010

The Methodist Central Hall was opened in 1912 to mark the centenary of the death of John Wesley, the founder of Methodism. The Royal Aquarium, a music hall which ran between 1876 and 1903, had previously occupied the site. The Jules Rimet Trophy was designed by Abel Lafleur and made of gold-plated sterling silver on a blue base of lapis lazuli; it stood 13.7 inches high and weighed 8.3 pounds. It had had a chequered history before arriving in England for the 1966 competition; won by Italy in 1938, it spent the war years in a shoebox under the bed of Ottorino Barassi, the Italian vice-president of Fifa, to keep it safe from the Germans. On Friday 18 March 1966, it made its first public appearance in England on display on the Stanley Gibbons stand at Stampex, Britain's national stamp exhibition at the Methodist Central Hall. The trophy was insured for £30,000, although it was only worth £3,000. At 12.10pm on Sunday 20 March, Alsa-Guard, the private security company hired to look after it, noticed that the trophy had been stolen. A nationwide hunt began and a petty crook called Edward Walter Betchley contacted the police claiming to have the trophy, and asked for £15,000 in used notes. When he was arrested, he revealed he was a mere go-between for a mystery man known only as "The Pole". At his trial on Friday 8 July 1966, Betchley was sent to prison for two years for demanding money with menaces and intent to steal, but died in 1969 shortly after his release. In case the trophy was never found, the FA and Chelsea chairman Joe Mears asked Fifa president Stanley Rous if a replica could be made. Fifa refused, but the FA secretly arranged for a gilded bronze replica to be made by George Bird of Alexander Clarke and Co. Despite the stories, Pickles, a 1-year-old black and white border collie, did not find the trophy. A 26-year-old Thames lighterman Dave Corbett of **50 Beulah Hill, Upper Norwood, London SE19 3LW**, said, "Although Pickles sort of led me in the direction of the cup, it was me who found it. There were all these stories at the time that he dug it up from under a bush. Well, it wasn't quite like that." Corbett took the trophy to Gypsy Hill police station where his statement revealed: "Just as we were about to go out of the gate, I was putting the lead on the dog, when I saw a package at the side of a bush. It was wrapped in newspaper. I stooped down to pick it up, and felt it was heavy. I had read in the papers about the World Cup, and seen pictures. Although I could not believe it possible, I went indoors for a better look. Then I felt sure it was the Cup, and I told my wife I was going to the police station at Gypsy Hill, and went there straight away." He and the cup were taken to Cannon Row station where it was identified by Harold Mayes, an FA official. Neither Corbett nor Pickles received any formal reward from the FA or even a letter of thanks, but various other monetary sums made to Corbett totalled £6,000 – six times the amount the England team earned for winning the trophy. Pickles was given a year's supply of dog food for his part in the recovery, but died in 1967 when he was strangled by his own lead while chasing a rabbit. He is buried in Corbett's back garden. Although Bobby Moore hoisted the genuine trophy on Saturday 30 July 1966 when England beat West Germany 4-2, a policeman was charged with slipping into the home side's dressing room and replacing the real trophy with the worthless copy. The Jules Rimet Trophy was taken from Nobby Stiles and the midfielder was handed the replica. It was the replica that was most often seen in public until it travelled to Mexico for the 1970 tournament, when Brazil won it outright with their third win. In Rio de Janeiro on Tuesday 20 December 1983, the Jules Rimet Trophy was again stolen and never recovered. The replica was sold at an auction in 1997 for £254,500. Fifa bought it anonymously and donated it to the English National Football Museum in Preston.

DID YOU KNOW?

Why Jules Rimet? Jules Rimet, a French lawyer, was born at Theuley-les Lavoncourt on Tuesday 14 October 1873 and died at Suresnes, Île-de-France, on Tuesday 16 October 1956. He was the president of the French Football Federation (1919-1945) and president of Fifa (1921-1954). In 2004, he was posthumously made a member of the Fifa Order of Merit.

Chapter IX
The Write Stuff

AROUND THE WORLD IN EIGHTY DAYS
Reform Club, 104 Pall Mall, London SW1Y 5EW
Telephone: 020 7930 9374

It was here that Phileas Fogg set off on his bid to go around the world in eighty days in the Jules Verne (1828-1905) novel of the same name. The book, published in serial form in French from Saturday 21 December 1872, was Verne's eleventh work. Phileas Fogg is a wealthy English gentleman living in London; he hires a new valet, Jean Passepartout, after his previous servant was sacked for not sufficently heating the shaving water. Fogg is at the Reform Club on the evening of Wednesday 2 October 1872. That day's edition of *The Daily Telegraph* features a story about a new railway in India which makes it possible to travel around the world in eighty days. Fogg has an argument with his friends and accepts a £20,000 (£2,409,000 at 2022 values) bet that it can be done. Fogg and Passepartout set off that evening at 8.45pm and must return by the same time on Saturday 21 December. The two men encounter various adventures, including avoiding a Scotland Yard detective chasing a bank robber, buying an elephant, rescuing a woman from sati, being arrested, jumping bail, visiting an opium den, working in a circus, being kidnapped by Sioux warriors, fomenting a mutiny and... does he make it back in time? You'll have to read the book to find out.

BILLY BUNTER
Greyfriars School, Friardale, Kent

William George Bunter, the Fat Owl of the Remove (the Lower Fourth), first appeared in *The Magnet* on Saturday 15 February 1908.

He was the creation of Frank Richards, the pseudonym of Charles Hamilton (1876-1961). Greyfriars School is north of Friardale and south of Courtfield Common, Kent. Bunter appeared in 1,670 of the 1,683 issues of *The Magnet* published between 1908 and its closure on Wednesday 15 May 1940. The final story was entitled *The Shadow Of The Sack*. Hamilton had no work when the comic closed; his publishers, Amalgamated Press, held the copyright to Greyfriars and its most famous pupil and refused to release it. In the end, good sense prevailed and, in 1946, Hamilton began writing the first of thirty-eight novels about the school, *Billy Bunter Of Greyfriars School*, which was published in September 1947. The last was published posthumously in 1965. It has been estimated by researchers that Hamilton wrote around 100 million words, or the equivalent of 1,200 average-length novels, making him the most prolific author in history. He was acclaimed as such in *The Guinness Book Of Records*, whose editors added that "he had the advantage of being unmarried". In addition, seven television series starring Gerald Campion (1921-2002) in the role of Bunter ran on the BBC from Tuesday 19 February 1952 until Saturday 22 July 1961.

BLYTON, ENID
Green Hedges, Penn Road, Beaconsfield, Buckinghamshire HP9
Telephone: Beaconsfield 1091

The most prolific children's author of all time wrote most of her celebrated books here, including four of the five in the *Secret* series (1938-1953; the first, *The Secret Island*, was her first full-length adventure story for children), the twenty-one books in the *Famous Five* series (1942-1963), the fifteen books about the Five Find-Outers, otherwise known as the *Mystery* series (1943-1961), the nine *Adventure* books (1944-1955), the fifteen volumes about the *Secret Seven* (1949-1963), as well as her school stories about St Clare's (1941-1945) and Malory Towers (1946-1951) and, of course, Noddy (1949-1964). Enid Blyton, her husband Hugh Pollock and their two small daughters Gillian and Imogen moved into the 30-year-old Green Hedges in the late summer of 1938, having paid £3,000. Enid Blyton lived at Green Hedges, a house with seven bedrooms, three living rooms, two bathrooms, three garages, a staff cottage and nearly three acres of garden, until just three months before her death aged 71 on Thursday 28 November 1968 from senile dementia in **Greenways Nursing Home, 11 Fellows Road, Hampstead, London NW3 3LT.** She was cremated at **Golders Green Crematorium, Hoop Lane, Golders Green, London NW11 7NL.** On Wednesday 2 June 1971, Green Hedges was sold at auction by Hetherington, Swannell and Secrett for £35,000, £5,000 above the reserve price. It was demolished in 1973 and the land on which the house stood is now a cul de sac named Blyton Close in the author's honour.

BOSWELL, JAMES
122 Great Portland Street, London W1W 6PX
It was here that Boswell finished *The Life of Samuel Johnson*, his biography of his great friend. The two men met for the first time on Monday 16 May 1763 at **8 Russell Street, London WC2B 5HZ**, a bookshop run by Thomas Davies. Boswell recalled, "I drank tea at Davies's... and about seven came in the great Mr Samuel Johnson, whom I have so long wished to see. As I knew his mortal antipathy at the Scotch, I cried to Davies, 'Don't tell him where I come from.'... However, he said, 'From Scotland.' 'Mr Johnson,' said I, 'indeed I come from Scotland, but I cannot help it.' 'Sir,' replied he, 'that, I find, is what a very great many of your countrymen cannot help.' Mr Johnson is a man of a most dreadful appearance..." Boswell moved here in January 1791, where he completed his study. The book was well received when it was published in two quarto volumes on Monday 16 May 1791, but its author was ridiculed. Boswell died here on Tuesday 19 May 1795. His house has been demolished, although a commemorative plaque is appended to a building on the site.

BROOKE, RUPERT
The Old Vicarage, 61 Mill Way, Grantchester, Cambridge CB3 9ND
Poet Rupert Brooke moved into The Old Vicarage in May 1909, paying thirty shillings a week for three rooms. The last clergyman had moved out in the 1820s. Brooke spent much of his time in the garden reading and writing, with regular visits to bathe in the river pools: often necessary because his rooms were infested with fleas and woodlice. He often slept on the lawn and was woken with dew in his hair by the birds. On Thursday 22 May 1913, he began a year of travel, starting in New York and taking in Boston, Canada, San Francisco, Hawaii, Samoa,

Fiji and New Zealand. He returned to England in June 1914 intending to settle at The Old Vicarage, but two months later the First World War interrupted his plans. On Friday 23 April 1915, he succumbed to blood poisoning and was buried on Skyros, the fabled island of Achilles in the Aegean, on St George's Day. He wrote about The Old Vicarage in his poem of the same name, that contains the lines:

> "Stands the church clock at ten to three?
> And is there honey still for tea?"

BROWNING, ELIZABETH BARRETT
50 Wimpole Street, London W1G 8SF

It was from here that Elizabeth Barrett eloped to marry Robert Browning (1812-1889) on Saturday 12 September 1846. Invalided at 15 after a horse-riding accident, Elizabeth spent much of her time indoors; her plantation-owner father Edward Barrett Moulton-Barrett (1785-1857), was overly protective. The Barretts moved to Wimpole Street in the spring of 1838 and Elizabeth had few visitors. Her father did not discourage Robert Browning, however, because he thought his daughter, then in her early thirties, was too old and unattractive to form a romantic attachment. Their correspondence began on Friday 10 January 1845 and they met for the first time on Tuesday 20 May of that year. The couple only took the drastic step of eloping when Edward Barrett refused the couple permission to go to Italy for Elizabeth's health. The Barrett house was demolished in 1936.

St Marylebone Parish Church, Marylebone Road, London NW1 5LT
Telephone: 020-7935 7315

This Anglican Church is where the couple was married. They spent much of their subsequent life in Florence where Elizabeth died on Saturday 29 June 1861 at their home, Casa Guidi.

CHRISTIE, AGATHA
Swan Hydropathic Hotel, Swan Road,
Harrogate, North Yorkshire HG1 2SR
Telephone: 01423-500055

In 1926, Agatha Christie should have been enjoying life. In June that year, Collins had published *The Murder of Roger Ackroyd* to widespread acclaim, and she was living at Styles in Surrey with her husband, Colonel Archibald Christie (1889-1962), a dashing former officer in the Royal Flying Corps. But at 9.45pm on Friday 3 December, the mystery writer got into her car and disappeared. The next day, her car was found abandoned in a chalk pit. Suspicion immediately fell on her husband, who was having an affair with Nancy Neele, his golfing partner. A tap was placed on his phone and 1,000 volunteers searched the countryside. After eleven days, Agatha was discovered at the Swan Hydro Hotel in Harrogate, where she had booked in under the name Teresa Neele. Bob Tappin, a local banjo player, recognised the author and alerted the police. When her husband came to collect her, she claimed not to know why she was there and kept him waiting before joining him for dinner. She later said that she was suffering from amnesia after a nervous breakdown following the death of her mother and her husband's adultery. She did not mention the incident in her autobiography and the real reason behind the disappearance remains unknown. Some claimed it was a publicity stunt to promote her fledgling writing career. A 1998 biography claimed that Agatha Christie disappeared to punish her unfaithful husband and throw the suspicion of murder on him. A 1979 Warner Bros film, *Agatha*, starring Vanessa Redgrave as Christie, tells a fictionalised version of the events. The hotel is now called the Old Swan; its suites are named in memory of Agatha Christie and her novels.

COWARD, NOËL
111 Ebury Street, London SW1W 9QU

It was here that Coward wrote the play that was to make his name. *The Vortex* tells the tale of drug addict Nicky Lancaster, and was initially banned by the Lord Chamberlain. When Coward presented himself to the 2nd Earl of Cromer, the Lord Chamberlain, and explained that the play was really a morality tale. Cromer relented four days before the first night and *The Vortex* opened at the Everyman Theatre, Hampstead on Tuesday 25 November 1924. Coward was to write: "*The Vortex* was an immediate success and established me both as a playwright and an actor, which was fortunate, because until then I had not proved myself to be so hot in either capacity." On the opening night, he cut his hand as he swept away some prop bottles in the last scene and had to wrap a handkerchief around it to stem the flow of blood. As he took curtain calls, the handkerchief became redder and redder. The play transferred to the **Royalty Theatre, 73 Dean Street, Soho, London W1D 3PU** on Coward's 25th birthday, Tuesday 16 December 1924. Dame Edith Evans also lived in the house (there is a blue plaque by the front door), which is now the eleven-room Lord Milner Hotel.

DAILY EXPRESS
17 Tudor Street, London EC4

The *Daily Express* was first published here on Tuesday 24 April 1900. It was founded by (Sir) C(yril). Arthur Pearson (b. at Wookey, near Wells, Somerset Saturday 24 February 1866), who was also editor-in-chief. The *Express* consisted of eight broadsheet pages and cost ½d. Pearson proclaimed that the *Express* "will be the organ of no political party nor the instrument of any social clique". It was among the first papers to cover news and photographs on its front pages instead of advertisements. The *Sunday Express* was also the first newspaper to feature a crossword. It also ran the cartoon strip *Rupert Bear*, created by Mary Tourtel, from Monday 8 November 1920, and cartoons by (Carl) Giles, which began in the *Sunday Express* on 3 October 1943. Like many newspaper proprietors, Pearson was interested in politics and in 1903 he formed the Tariff Reform League with Joseph Chamberlain. Pearson bought the morning and evening editions of *The Standard* for £700,000 in 1904, but failed in a Monday 16 March 1908 attempt to buy *The Times*. When his eyesight became bad, Pearson sold *The Standard* on Friday 22 April 1910 to Tory MP Davison Dalziel (1852-1928). Having lost his sight, Pearson became president of the National Institution for the Blind in 1914. On Friday 29 January 1915, he founded The Blinded Soldiers and Sailors Care Committee (later St Dunstan's), a charity for blind servicemen. On Wednesday 12 July 1916, he was made a baronet. On Friday 9 December 1921, while at his home, **15 Devonshire Street, Marylebone, London W1G 7AF**, he drowned in his bathtub after hitting his head on a tap. He was 55. Pearson appointed R(alph). D(avid). Blumenfeld (b. Watertown, Wisconsin Thursday 7 April 1864 d. London Saturday 17 July 1948) as editor in

1902, a position he held until 1929. Max Aitken, Lord Beaverbrook, undertook financial control of the *Express* in 1917 and launched the *Sunday Express* two years later, before taking control of the *Evening Standard* in 1923. In the late 1930s, the *Express* supported Neville Chamberlain's appeasement policies towards Hitler, running the headline "No war this year" in August 1939. Less than a month later, Britain was at war with Germany. By 1960, the *Express* circulation had risen to 4.32 million, but it began a steady decline in 1964 after Beaverbrook's death. In 1977, the papers were sold to the construction company Trafalgar House for £14.6million, and metamorphosed from broadsheet to tabloid; the company changed its name from Beaverbrook Newspapers to Express Newspapers. On Thursday 2 November 1978, the *Daily Star* was launched in Manchester, the first new national newspaper for seventy-five years; it was bought by United Newspapers in 1985. A series of cost-cutting measures reduced staff numbers from 7,000 to 1,700. The last edition of the *Daily Express* to be printed in Fleet Street (at number 120-128, a specially designed art deco building, EC4P 4JT) rolled off the presses on Friday 17 November 1989, before the company moved to **Ludgate House, 245 Blackfriars Road, London SE1 9UX**. It was eventually sold to Richard Desmond for £125million in November 2000. In 2004, Desmond moved his newspapers to a new home at **The Northern & Shell Building, 10 Lower Thames Street, London EC3R 6EN**. In February 2018, the *Daily Express* and its sister newspapers were sold to Trinity Mirror, the publisher of the *Daily Mirror*, for £126.7million; Trinity Mirror changed its name to Reach plc.

DAILY MAIL
33 Carmelite Street, London EC4 0JA
The *Mail* was first published here on Monday 4 May 1896 by 30-year-old Alfred Harmsworth (later 1st Viscount Northcliffe). It started life as an eight-page broadsheet bearing the strapline "A Penny Newspaper for a Halfpenny". The first issue sold 397,213 copies, and Prime Minister Lord Salisbury described the newcomer as "a newspaper for office boys written by office boys". By 1899, daily sales had reached 500,000 and had topped a million by 1902. From Harmsworth's original investment of £15,000, the newspaper

made a gross trading profit in its first fifty years of £18,500,000. Harmsworth told an editor, "The three things that are always news are health things, sex things and money things." Edgar Wallace was a foreign correspondent at one point, and Rudyard Kipling turned down £10,000 to work for Northcliffe. On Monday 3 May 1971, the *Daily Mail* became a tabloid and merged with the *Daily Sketch*.

DAILY MIRROR
2 Carmelite Street, London EC4

The *Daily Mirror* was first published as a newspaper for gentle-women on Monday 2 November 1903 under the editorship of Mary Howarth. Owned by Alfred Charles William Harmsworth, later Lord Northcliffe, its circulation fell from the launch figure of 276,000 to just 25,000. Mrs Howarth was sacked and Hamilton Fyfe appointed editor. The *Mirror* became the first popular newspaper to make use of news photography. Its ownership passed from Lord Northcliffe to his brother Harold Sidney, later 1st Viscount Rothermere, in 1914. In the 1930s, the *Mirror* changed from being a populist, right-wing paper to a campaigning vehicle for the working classes. By 1941, sales had risen to 1.7 million and it had become the favourite newspaper of the armed forces, with the cartoon character Jane proving particularly popular. However, a Philip Zec cartoon published on Thursday 19 March 1942 infuriated the Government. It showed a soldier clinging to a life raft, with the caption: "The price of petrol has been increased by one penny – official." In the 1950s and 1960s, the paper averaged daily sales of 4.6 million; on Coronation Day, Wednesday 3 June 1953, it sold an incredible seven million copies. On Friday 13 July 1984, Robert Maxwell, the crooked former Labour MP, bought the Mirror Group and stole its former employees' pensions. He committed suicide seven years later on Tuesday 5 November 1991 while aboard his yacht *Lady Ghislaine*. The paper then fell into the hands of Ulsterman David Montgomery, a former editor of the *News of the World*, who cut costs to the bone and earned the nickname Rommel: "because Monty was on our side". On Monday 3 July 2000, the *Daily Mirror* changed the face of gossip when it started the 3am Girls column, penned by Polly Graham, Jessica Callan and Eva Simpson.

DAILY TELEGRAPH, THE
253 Strand, London WC2R

The *Daily Telegraph and Courier*, a four-page paper, was first published on Friday 29 June 1855 and cost 2d. It was founded by Colonel Arthur Burroughes Sleigh, who took advantage of the removal of stamp duty from newspapers six weeks earlier. *The Times* then cost 7d and the *Morning Post* 5d. Sleigh had started the *Telegraph* with a definite purpose – to pursue a vendetta against the Duke of Cambridge. Despite its low price the new paper was not a success, and its first printers – Aird and Tunstall of Essex Street, off Strand – threatened closure when their bills were not paid. When Sleigh had a chance encounter with the printer Joseph Moses Levy, who had recently bought *The Sunday Times*, he agreed to take over the printing, but only on condition that if the bills remained unpaid after a certain point, the ownership of the *Telegraph* would pass to him. *And Courier* was dropped from the masthead in August 1855. In 1856, Levy sold *The Sunday Times* and concentrated his efforts on the *Telegraph*. The newspaper moved to bigger offices at **135 Fleet Street, London EC4P 4BJ** in 1860. When circulation reached 300,000, the *Telegraph* took over the adjacent buildings at 137 and 139. On Wednesday 28 June 1882, the Prince of Wales, later King Edward VII, and his younger brother, the Duke of Albany, opened 135–139 Fleet Street. In 1987, *The Daily Telegraph* moved to **Peterborough Court, 181 Marsh Wall, London E14 9SR** and, five years later, moved into floors eleven to sixteen of **1 Canada Square, Canary Wharf, London E14**. In the autumn of 2006, the company moved again, to **111 Buckingham Palace Road, London SW1**.

GUARDIAN, THE
29 Market Street, Manchester M1 1WR

The *Manchester Guardian* was first published here on Saturday 5 May 1821 by a group of non-conformist businessmen headed by John Edward Taylor, who became the first editor. Its mission statement at the time proclaimed that "it will zealously enforce the principles of civil and religious Liberty… it will warmly advocate the cause of Reform; it will endeavour to assist in the diffusion of just principles of Political Economy; and to support, without reference to the party from which they emanate, all serviceable measures". *The Manchester*

Guardian was a weekly, published on Saturdays and costing 7d (although 4d of that went to the Government). When stamp duty was cut in 1836 *The Guardian* added a Wednesday edition; when the tax was abolished completely in 1855, it became a daily at 2d. Its price was reduced to 1d in 1857. In 1872, C(harles). P(restwich). Scott became editor, staying in the chair for an incredible fifty-seven years; on the paper's centenary, he penned a celebrated editorial that included the legend, "Comment is free, but facts are sacred." When Scott retired in 1929, he was succeeded by his son Edward Taylor Scott; his turn in the chair was brief, as he drowned in a boating accident on Lake Windermere on Friday 22 April 1932. In 1952, the newspaper removed advertisements from its front page and dropped the word Manchester from its title in 1959. Since 1821, *The Guardian* has had just twelve editors. On Monday 12 September 2005, the newspaper moved to the Berliner format and changed the design of its masthead. On Monday 15 January 2018, it changed again, to a tabloid format.

GUINNESS BOOK OF RECORDS, THE
Top Floor, Ludgate House, 107 Fleet Street, London EC4A 2AB

It was here that the first edition of the world's best-selling copyright book was published on Saturday 27 August 1955. On Saturday 10 November 1951, Sir Hugh Beaver, the managing director of the brewers Guinness, missed a game bird while shooting on his estate in County Wexford, Ireland. Back at home, he wondered what the fastest game bird was and became irritated when the expensive encyclopædias on his shelves failed to settle the argument. He approached Christopher Brasher, a young executive at the brewery, with his problem, and Brasher turned to a pair of twins who ran a fact-finding company in London. Norris and Ross McWhirter were invited to lunch with Beaver; when he remarked that he enjoyed holidaying in Turkey, Norris replied, "Turkish is the language with the fewest irregular verbs, just one – imek, to be." They got the job. The McWhirters, based in two rooms in a converted gymnasium on the top floor of Ludgate House, worked for thirteen and a half ninety-hour weeks, including weekends and bank holidays, to get the book out. Their name did not appear in the book until the eighth edition, in 1960. The twins became regulars on the children's television series *Record Breakers*, hosted by Roy Castle. Ross was assassinated by the IRA at 6.50pm on Thursday 27 November 1975 (see page 177), and Norris continued to edit the book alone until his retirement in 1985 and his ousting as editorial consultant in 1995. On Monday 19 April 2004, he suffered a heart attack while playing tennis at his home in Kington Langley, Wiltshire and died later that day at the **Great Western Hospital, Marlborough Road, Swindon SN3 6BB**. (The twins were, by coincidence, educated at Marlborough College.) Norris was buried at **St Peter's Churchyard, 16 Chippenham Road, Langley Burrell, Chippenham, Wiltshire SN15 4LF**. He left £3,047,687 (£4,985,852 at 2022 values). The book that he co-created has sold more than 140 million copies.

JOHNSON, SAMUEL
17 Gough Square, London EC4A 3DE
Telephone: 020-7353 3745

In June 1746, Samuel Johnson, was commissioned to wrote his celebrated *Dictionary Of The English Language*. Having been paid an advance of £1,575 (approximately £250,000 at 2022 values), he worked on the book along with six assistants for nine years in an attic here. He used the money to rent the house, the first time that he had any real financial security. Built in 1700, Johnson lived and worked in the house from 1749 to 1759. He sat at an "old crazy deal table" and on an even older chair, which gradually disintegrated until he was left balancing on three legs and one arm. The *Dictionary Of The English Language* was published in two volumes on Tuesday 15 April 1755. The book contained humour among its definitions – Johnson described oats thus: "a grain which in England is generally given to horses, but in Scotland supports the people". Johnson was complimented by some society ladies for not including rude words, to which he replied, "Ah, so you have been looking for them?" In April 1911, the house was bought by newspaper magnate and politician Cecil Harmsworth who later said, "At the time of my purchase of the house, it presented every appearance of squalor and decay... It is doubtful whether in the whole of London there existed a more forlorn or dilapidated tenement." He restored the house and opened it to the public in 1912. It is now operated by a charitable trust.

NEWS OF THE WORLD
30 Holywell Street, London WC2

The *News of the World* was first published by John Browne Bell (1779-1855) on Sunday 1 October 1843; it cost 3d and was targeted at the newly literate working classes. The newspaper was produced from a cramped, bow-fronted, three-storey building in an area known for second-hand bookshops and purveyors of pornography. In an echo of the circulation battles that would dominate the tabloid press in the 1980s, Browne Bell was approached by London newsagents and asked to put an extra ha'penny on the cover price to guarantee their profits. He refused, believing sales would be sufficient. To ensure his success, he approached newsagents outside London and offered to supply them directly with copies. It was a shrewd move and by the time of his death aged 77 on Sunday 19 August 1855, the newspaper was selling 200,000 copies a week. This meant it outgrew its original home, and the last edition printed from Holywell Street rolled off the presses on 10 October 1852. Holywell Street was demolished in 1901 to make way for Aldwych. The *News of the World* moved to **19 Exeter Street, London WC2E 7DS**, where the new machinery could produce 4,000 copies an hour. It soon became a byword for scandal. In 1891 it was sold to the Carr family and Sir Emsley Carr was installed in the editor's chair that May, a seat he was to hold for fifty years until his death on Thursday 31 July 1941. In March 1892, the paper moved to **Whitefriars Street, London EC4** and, seven years later, to **Bouverie Street, London EC4**. George Riddell, the new owners' legal advisor, really made the newspaper, but he always tried to avoid mentioning the connection, saying that if he reached the Pearly Gates and St Peter disapproved, he would "urge in extenuation my connection with *John O'London's Weekly* and *Country Life*". Born at 2 Stanhope Place, Loughborough Road, Brixton Heath, London, on Thursday 25 May 1865, Riddell was a workaholic. When he married for the first time, he took just an hour off work for the ceremony and there was no honeymoon. He claimed that he could not afford one. He based his fortune on property and spent his weekends touring London looking for prospective purchases. Before anyone had heard of Peter Rachman (see page 200), Riddell would intimidate sitting tenants and force them to move out. "I can't afford mercy," he said. He never gave tips: when he hired hansom cabs, he refused to hand the fare to the driver but placed the exact money on a wheel, forcing the cab driver to climb down to collect it. He increased the size of the paper and installed new printing presses, often spending Saturday nights bribing printers and distribution staff to ensure the newspaper got into the hands of its readers. He became chairman in 1923. In echoes of stunts played by reporters down the years, Riddell had one young reporter travel to London with a gramophone playing in the back of a horse and wagon. He wanted the reporter to be arrested and taken to court; when he was, his £1 fine was paid for by the paper, all for publicity. Not surprisingly for someone so careful with his money, he left £2,207,702 5s 10d (£161.51million at 2022 values) when he died at his home, Walton Heath House, Walton on the Hill, Banstead, Surrey on Wednesday 5 December 1934. The newspaper's circulation reached two million by 1912, around three million by the early 1920s and four million by 1939. By 1950, the *News of the World* was selling 8.44 million copies each week. In 1960, Stafford Somerfield was appointed as editor and the newspaper merged with the *Empire*. In 1968, a battle for owner- ship began between Australian Rupert Murdoch and Czech Labour MP Robert Maxwell. On Sunday 20 October 1968, Somerfield wrote a front page leader saying that he hoped Maxwell's bid would fail: after all, the *News of the World* was "as British as roast beef and Yorkshire pudding". In January 1969, Maxwell's bid was rejected and Murdoch took over the paper, his first Fleet Street buy. He became chairman in June 1969. On Thursday 26 February 1970, Somerfield was sacked. In 1981, the colour supplement *Sunday* was introduced; three years later, the newspaper became a tabloid. It was closed by Murdoch in summer 2011 after its journalists were embroiled in a phone-hacking scandal. Its last edition was on Sunday 10 July 2011.

ORWELL, GEORGE
Keep The Aspidistra Flying
31 Willoughby Road, Hampstead, London NW3 1RT
This is where Gordon Comstock, the anti-hero of *Keep The Aspidistra Flying* (published Monday 20 April 1936 by Victor Gollancz) lives in a house that smells of cabbage and dishwater – barely disguised in the book as "dingy, depressing" Willowbed Road. Comstock is working

as a copywriter for an advertising agency when he decides to give up his job and live in a hopefully money-free world. On Saturday 28 September 1946, Orwell confessed to close friend George Woodcock that the novel "was written simply as an exercise and I oughtn't to have published it, but I was desperate for money. At that time I simply hadn't a book in me, but I was half starved and had to turn out something to bring in £100 or so." In August 1934, Orwell began working in the shop **Booklovers' Corner, 1 South End Green, Hampstead, London NW3** and lived rent-free in a flat above the premises. He moved out in February 1935, but used the shop and his experiences there as Mr McKechnie's shop in the novel. A rather unusual plaque commemorates Orwell's time there.

The Moon Under Water
**Canonbury Tavern, 21 Canonbury Place, Islington, London N1 2NS
Telephone: 020-7704 2887**

This pub in north London was the inspiration for Orwell's perfect pub, according to an article he wrote for the *Evening Standard* on Saturday 9 February 1946. Such a pub should be "uncompromisingly Victorian. It has no glass-topped tables or other modern miseries, and, on the other hand, no sham roof-beams, ingle-nooks or plastic panels masquerading as oak. The grained woodwork, the ornamental mirrors behind the bar, the cast-iron fireplaces, the florid ceiling stained dark yellow by tobacco-smoke, the stuffed bull's head over the mantelpiece — everything has the solid, comfortable ugliness of the nineteenth century. In winter there is generally a good fire burning in at least two of the bars, and the Victorian lay-out of the place gives one plenty of elbow-room. There are a public bar, a saloon bar, a ladies' bar, a bottle-and-jug for those who are too bashful to buy their supper beer publicly, and, upstairs, a dining-room... In The Moon Under Water it is always quiet enough to talk. The house possesses neither a radio nor a piano, and even on Christmas Eve and such occasions the singing that happens is of a decorous kind. The barmaids know most of their customers by name, and take a personal interest in everyone. They are all middle-aged women — two of them have their hair dyed in quite surprising shades — and they call everyone 'dear', irrespective of age or sex. ('Dear', not 'Ducky': pubs where the barmaid calls you 'ducky' always have a disagreeable raffish atmosphere.)"

1984
27B Canonbury Square, Islington, London N1 2AL

Orwell moved in here in 1945 and began work on his last novel, *1984*. He lived here until 1947, basing anti-hero Winston Smith's flat, which stank of "boiled cabbage and old rag mats", on the property. In April 2022, a first floor, two-bedroom flat in the building was on the market for more than £1.1million. **Senate House, Malet Street, London WC1E 7HU**, the University of London's main administrative building, was used by Orwell as the model for the Ministry of Truth. The ministry's canteen was based on the BBC eaterie at **200 Oxford Street, London W1D 1NU**. The police station then located at **458 Bethnal Green Road, London E2 0EA** was the inspiration for the Ministry of Love.

ROWLING, J.K.
St John's Road, London SW11 1PX

In May 2020, J.K. Rowling responded to a series of tweets about the inspiration for Harry Potter. She wrote, "This is the true birthplace of Harry Potter, if you define 'birthplace' as the spot where I put pen to paper for the first time. I was renting a room in a flat over what was then a sports shop. The first bricks of Hogwarts were laid in a flat in Clapham Junction. If you define the birthplace of Harry Potter as the moment when I had the initial idea, then it was a Manchester-London train. But I'm perennially amused by the idea that Hogwarts was directly inspired by beautiful places I saw or visited, because it's so far from the truth." In 1993, Joanne Rowling (the K is an affectation and does not stand for anything) moved to a flat at **28 Gardner's Crescent, Edinburgh** when her first marriage broke up. Unable to write at home, she spent the day at Nicolson's, a café which opened in 1991 at **6a Nicolson Street, Edinburgh EH8 9DH**. It was here, while her baby daughter Jessica slept in her buggy, that Rowling worked on the Harry Potter stories that would make her a multimillionairess. Co-owner Dougal McBride, remembers, "She would just rock the pram back and forward with one hand and write away with the other." On Thursday 21 May 2020, Rowling tweeted, "I once wrote an entire chapter in there in one sitting and barely changed a word afterwards." She would also write in other cafés, including The Elephant House at **21 George IV Bridge, Edinburgh EH1 1EN**. She completed *Harry Potter*

And The Philosopher's Stone in 1994; it was published on Monday 30 June 1997. A survey in August 2006 revealed that Rowling earned £77 a minute. Nicolson's later became a Chinese restaurant called Buffet King; it is now the Spoon Café Bistro.

SHERLOCK HOLMES
221B Baker Street, London NW1 6XE

The world's only consulting detective rented rooms here with his good friend Dr John H. Watson. William Sherlock Scott Holmes (b. Mycroft, North Riding of Yorkshire on Friday 6 January 1854; d. Sussex Sunday 6 January 1957) and Watson (b. Abingdon, Berkshire on Saturday 7 August 1852; d. Wednesday 24 July 1929) were created by doctor and author Sir Arthur Conan Doyle (1859-1930) and first appeared in *A Study In Scarlet* (originally entitled *A Tangled Skein*, which was published in *Beeton's Christmas Annual* in November 1887; Conan Doyle was paid £25 and it was published in book form in July 1888). Watson took his medical degree in 1878 at the University of London; after service in Afghanistan, he returns to London where he seeks lodgings. On Saturday 1 January 1881, he is introduced to Holmes by Stamford, their mutual friend, in St Bartholomew's laboratory. Holmes immediately says to Watson, "You have been in Afghanistan, I perceive?" He tells Watson that he has his "eye on a suite in Baker Street, which would suit us down to the ground". The two men move in to the suite, which consists of "a couple of comfortable bedrooms and a single large airy sitting-room", and have adventures detailed by Watson in four novels and fifty-six short stories. Eventually, despite his popularity with the public, Conan Doyle tired of his creation and killed Holmes off – "He is becoming such a burden to me" – by having him and his arch enemy Professor Moriarty fall to their deaths in the Reichenbach Falls on Monday 4 May 1891 in *The Final Problem* (published December 1893). Such was the public outcry that Conan Doyle was forced to bring Holmes back in *The Hound Of The Baskervilles* (published Tuesday 25 March 1902). The last collection was *The Casebook Of Sherlock Holmes* (published Thursday 16 June 1927). In later years, 221B became the home of the Abbey National Building Society; a secretary was employed to answer fan mail that arrived at the address. Correspondence were usually met with a reply that Holmes had retired to keep bees in Sussex.

DID YOU KNOW?
Holmes and Watson's original names were Sherrinford Holmes and Ormond Sacker.

SUN, THE
30 Bouverie Street, London EC4 8AX

The Sun was founded by IPC on Tuesday 15 September 1964 as a successor to the *Daily Herald*. Five years later, with the Labour-supporting newspaper losing £2million a year, the company wanted to cut its losses. Labour MP Robert Maxwell (1923-1991) offered to buy it and maintain its support for the Party, but said that he would have to make a number of redundancies. Australian newspaper tycoon Rupert Murdoch (b. Melbourne Wednesday 11 March 1931) also agreed the paper would support Labour, but promised fewer job losses. He paid £800,000 in instalments and printed *The Sun* from his Bouverie Street office from Monday 17 November 1969. On page two, the paper declared, "Today's *Sun* is a new newspaper. It has a new shape, new writers, new ideas. But it inherits all that is best from the great traditions of its predecessors. *The Sun* cares. About the quality of life. About the kind of world we live in. And about people." On its first birthday, *The Sun* introduced the first topless Page 3 girl Stefanie Marrian (b. Saturday 9 October 1948). The first editor, Sir Albert "Larry" Lamb (1929-2000), had two stints in the chair until Kelvin MacKenzie (b. Kent 1946) succeeded him in 1981. Under MacKenzie, the paper developed a brash style that alienated as many people as it attracted, but it went on to become one of Britain's biggest-selling newspapers.

WOOLF, VIRGINIA
Weymouth Bay, Dorset

HMS *Dreadnought* was launched on Saturday 10 February 1906 and showed off the might of the Royal Navy. It had cost £1,785,683 (£217,593,230 at 2022 values) to build. On Sunday 18 July 1909, *The Observer* said the Royal Navy's supremacy was "the best security for the world's peace and advancement". Seven months later, a group of friends decided to hoax the Royal Navy. Led by Boer War veteran and Neville Chamberlain's brother-in-law Horace de Vere Cole (1881-1936), the group included Adrian Stephen (1883-1948), his sister Virginia Stephen (later Woolf), lawyer Guy Ridley (1885-1947), soldier Anthony Buxton (1881-1970) and artist Duncan Grant (1885-1978), who was Adrian Stephen's lover at the time. On the morning of Monday 7 February 1910, employees of Willy Clarkson, the theatrical costumier, went to Woolf's home at **29 Fitzroy Square, London W1T 5LP** (1907-1911) and blacked Woolf, Grant, Buxton and Ridley's faces, giving them flowing robes and turbans so they could pass as members of the Abyssinian royal family. Adrian Stephen acted as the interpreter. A downside of the hoax was that the makeup meant the "Abyssinians" could not eat anything. A telegram was sent to the "C-in-C, Home Fleet" that read, "Prince Makalen of Abbysinia [sic] and suite arrive 4.20 today Weymouth. He wishes to see *Dreadnought*. Kindly arrange meet them on arrival. (Signed) Harding Foreign Office." The group made their way to Paddington station where Cole, or the deaf Herbert Cholmondeley of the Foreign Office as he called himself, demanded a VIP train to Weymouth. The Navy at Weymouth gave the "Abyssinians" a guard of honour, but the bandmaster did not know the Abyssinian national anthem so the band played *The Dover Castle March*, which had a fairly regal sound. No one seemed to notice. The "Abyssinians" spent forty-five minutes on board and used a mix of Latin and Greek to communicate, occasionally intoning "Bunga Bunga" to show their approval. Remarkably, one of the officers aboard *Dreadnought* that day was Adrian Stephen and Virginia Woolf's cousin, Commander Willie Fisher, but he failed to recognise his kin. After the incident, a music hall song became popular. Sung to the tune of *The Girl I Left Behind*, it contained the lyrics: "When I went on board a Dreadnought Ship/Though I looked just like a costermonger;/They said I was an Abyssinian prince/'Cos I shouted 'Bunga Bunga!'"

Hogarth Press
Hogarth House, 34 Paradise Road, Richmond, Surrey TW9 1SE
Virginia and Leonard Woolf lived here from Thursday 25 March 1915 until 1924. They created the Hogarth Press here in March 1917 after

buying a hand-printing machine for £19 5s 6d (£2,670 at 2022 values) from the Excelsior Printing Supply Company on Farringdon Street. On Thursday 3 May 1917, the first book published by the Hogarth Press was a thirty-two-page pamphlet entitled *Two Stories* containing Virginia's story "The Mark On The Wall" and "Three Jews", written by her husband. Among the authors published by the Hogarth Press were T.S. Eliot, Katherine Mansfield, E.M. Forster, John Maynard Keynes, Maxim Gorky, Sigmund Freud, Robert Graves and Edith Sitwell. In March 1924, the Woolfs moved to **52 Tavistock Square, Bloomsbury, London WC1H 9NA**, where they re-established their press in the basement scullery.

**Monk's House, Rodmell, Lewes,
East Sussex BN7 3HF/River Ouse, Sussex**

Virginia and Leonard Woolf moved into **37 Mecklenburgh Square, Bloomsbury, London WC1** in 1939 but had not been there long when it was bombed in September 1940 by the Luftwaffe. They relocated to their country home, Monk's House, in Rodmell, Sussex, which they had bought on Tuesday 1 July 1919. Woolf loved the local countryside, especially the opportunity it afforded her for long walks by the River Ouse. Many of her literary friends came to visit including T.S. Eliot, Lytton Strachey, E.M. Forster and Woolf's beloved, Vita Sackville-West. Virginia suffered severe mental stress, heard voices and feared her previous madness would return. Just before 11.45am on Friday 28 March 1941, she weighted her pocket with a large stone and committed suicide by drowning herself in the fast-running River Ouse near Monk's House. Her body was not found until Friday 18 April. She was cremated and her ashes buried in their garden. She left £14,051 3s. 5d (£803,735 at 2022 values).

Acknowledgements

I would like to thank the following for their help on this project: the late Jeremy Beadle, still sorely missed, who was wonderfully encouraging about the idea, so long has been its gestation; Helen Dafter, the archivist of The Postal Museum; Richard Eden, formerly the deputy editor of Mandrake on *The Sunday Telegraph* and now plying his trade on the *Daily Mail*; the late John Gibbens, with whom I worked on *The Sunday Telegraph*, was one of the world's leading authorities on the works of Bob Dylan; Paul Gill, the former general manager of The Old Swan Hotel, Harrogate; Mark Gonzales; Nina Goswami, another former colleague on *The Sunday Telegraph* and now working at the BBC; Ian Harrison; Jonathan Isaby, the Communications Private Secretary to Home Secretary Priti Patel; John Jones, another former colleague and the syndication editor of *The Daily Telegraph*; Nigel Lewis, the former property editor of the *Daily Mail* where we sat next to each other in Derry Street; Julia MacCarron of the McDonald's press office; Debbie Mason of the Imperial War Museum; Rusty McLean, the archivist of Rugby School; James Morton; Mel Sambells; Jo Sollis; James Steen, my former editor at *Punch* and now a best-selling "cook book author"; Mitchell Symons.